HERR PAULUS

HIS RISE, HIS GREATNESS, AND HIS FALL

A Novel

By WALTER BESANT

AUTHOR OF

"ALL SORTS AND CONDITIONS OF MEN" "THE WORLD WENT VERY WELL THEN"
"SELF OR BEARER" "TO CALL HER MINE" ETC.

NEW YORK

HARPER & BROTHERS, FRANKLIN SQUARE

1888

HERR PAULUS:

HIS RISE, HIS GREATNESS, AND HIS FALL.

PROLOGUE.

I.

Two young people were in a garden. Their names were not Adam and Eve, but Ziphion and Bethiah, which seem somehow to resemble the original names. It was a spacious garden, though not so spacious nor so well furnished as the Garden of Eden, which I take it covered many acres, and had gushing fountains of clear water, humming-birds, with love-birds and avadavats, beautiful, harmless flying dragons of all colors, tame leopards, tigers, hyenas, and pumas, whose eyes flamed with love and praise instead of cruelty and hunger, gold and silver fish, bright-colored and vivacious sea-snakes, and lubberly, good-natured sharks for the children to swim with, together with other delightful things which to us would be the more delightful because they would be at first so very surprising. It was, however, a beautiful garden, with some age, as they say of port. If it had been an English garden it would have been very old indeed, and would have had all round it a lovely red-brick wall covered with lichen—yellow and white and red—with wall-flowers and grasses growing tall and thick on the broad top of it. But it was in America, where I believe there are no gardens at all more than two hundred years old, and few which have seen so many as three generations of English-speaking men and women. It contained a flower-garden, a kitchen-garden, and an orchard, all in one. The orchard contained chiefly apple-trees, and the apples were now nearly ripe, for all day long they had been industriously turning their red and streaky sides to the hot sun of early September, getting every hour ruddier and streakier, as good apples should. One of the young persons was sitting on a low stool, and the other was leaning against the trunk of an old tree. This is a detail of some importance, because it shows that they were not in England, where at sunset of a day in early autumn young people are longing to run about, play lawn-tennis, go for walks, and do vigorous things. In America, where the heat is fierce, they are naturally less active. This is one reason why so many young people ask permission to be born in England. The house which belonged to the garden stood behind it, well-built and ugly; it was the house of Mr. Ruysdael, lawyer and prominent citizen of the town, which was a small town not many hundred miles from Boston.

The girl, Bethiah Ruysdael, had a box of colors and a sketching-block lying on the ground beside her. She had been engaged in making a study of trees; but now she sat with hands clasped, looking up into the face of the young man. I have elsewhere—I believe more than once—preached the doctrine that the very best kind of woman is the woman's woman, which is the same thing as the womanly woman, the woman whom other women love, of whom other women do not speak with bitterness, or with innuendo, or with eyes glancing at each other. She may be beautiful, but women do not greatly dwell upon her good looks; she may be graceful, and may possess all the accomplishments, clevernesses, dexterities, and arts which cultivated ladies desire to acquire, but other women do not greatly talk of these things; they speak of those qualities which are not taught in the schools, such as her unselfishness, her kindness, her thought for others, her sympathy, and so forth. She never studies, as some maidens use, the arts and mysteries by which man may be attracted and drawn to them as by a magnet; she does not in the least understand the strength and vehemence of the passion of love in man, nor does she inquire at all into the subject. But she knows that some women are weak, and that a pretty face does not always mean a perfectly faultless soul, whatever men may foolishly believe; and when she comes in her reading upon the pretty, passionate exaggerations of poets, dramatists, and novelists, who love to represent their hero's mistress as a beautiful goddess, full of all perfections, because she is so beautiful, she lays down the book and takes up another pitched in a lower and more sensible key. When she marries it is with calmness; she gives away her heart without illusions; she knows her own weaknesses, and is not blind to those of her husband, and she thinks that life is at best soberly happy, and that there will be no moment in it which will call for the rapture of overwhelming joy. Yet she is said to make her husband happy all his life. Very often, however, this kind of woman never marries at all.

Bethiah Ruysdael was such a girl as this. Her calm, capable face, her clear gray eyes, her firm mouth, the clear, strong curve of her cheek — all inspired confidence. Even the business-like arrangement of her dark-brown hair helped to show that she was a perfectly sensible and trustworthy person; not flighty, whimsical, or humorsome: the history of the last century presents some truly admirable studies of the whimsical or humorsome woman, but at present she is rare—not enthusiastic, emotional, or hysterical. As for beauty, being what she was, nobody spoke much of her good looks; yet she was comely and pleasant to look upon, somewhat paler in the cheek than a healthy English girl, slighter in frame and figure, and more delicate in feature. When a girl lays herself out to call attention by her dress and by her manners to her personal appearance, of course one talks about it; but Bethiah did not betray the least consciousness of beauty or the least desire for notice. Therefore such notice as she got was of another kind.

It is said that there is no place in the world where young men are so wonderfully beautiful as in New York. The ancient Greeks, it is reported, jealous of their own reputation, have sent down to know if it is really true. The young man leaning against the trunk of the old apple-tree possessed this remarkable beauty in full and brimming measure. You know the portrait of Shelley, with his girlish face and the strangely eager, passionate eyes, full of light and earnestness and fearless questioning. Well, that face has always reminded me of Ziphion's, though Ziphion was not so tall, and had a larger head in proportion to his height. By what long forgotten marriage and blending of race did this strange face break out in a small town of a New England State? Who was the ancestor or ancestress from whom the boy got that wonderful face and those wonderful eyes? His mother was certainly not an artist or a poet, nor did she in any sense belong to the imaginative race. She was a severely Christian person, and a notable housewife, whose readings as well as her imagination were, so far as one knows, as narrow as her creed. His father certainly might have been at one time a potential poet, but the general store which he conducted blamelessly had long since killed the poetic germ, if it ever existed. He was, however, a most respectable person. He sold everything, from an English pirated novel at ten cents to a string of onions, a barrel of apples, or a saucerful of treacle; he was a deacon in his church; and when he was not talking of dollars, his mouth was full of doctrine. Dollars and doctrine; the union of this world and the next; salvation and investments—the thing is not unknown on this side of the Atlantic. Both father and mother, being perfectly satisfied with themselves, ardently desired that their only son should follow in their steps and strike out a line of trade for himself ; or, failing this—because the great and glorious gift of dollar-snatching is not granted to every one—they prayed that he might become a lawyer and a politician, and so presently be elected mayor of his own city, governor of his own State, and perhaps — who knows ? — President of the United States.

Where did the boy get that face?

Perhaps—the middle classes preserve no genealogies—in some far-off generation this American youth had some Italian woman for a great-grandmother, or some passionate Andalusian, or some wild gypsy—perhaps a Provençale—from whom he derived those clear and delicate features, those black eyes which were soft and lustrous, and charged with all poetic qualities, such as tenderness, sympathy, wonder, insight, and sensitiveness. The lad's figure was slender and tall. In the mobile lips, in the pose of the head, in the long, thin fingers, one could read a temperament more nervous than that generally found even among his countrymen. Whither this nervousness will lead the American one knows not. Perhaps in the amalgam of the future, when all the nations of the world have contributed some part to the construction of the American, the nervous temperament will be modified. But how if it be intensified ? Whither, however, this highly strung organization leads the present generation one may readily observe. For of some it makes splendid orators; of some, the most eloquent preachers; of some, fiery partisans; of some, fervid martyrs; of some, the most ingenious inventors; of some, cranks, of some, the most crafty rogues; of some, impostors of the very highest order. On all it bestows qualities in the superlative.

You shall learn, presently, whither this sensitive and nervous organization brought this young man. Never since the day—too short a day—of Absalom, was there so sweet a youth. Like Absalom, but in this respect only—because in thinking of Absalom one always thinks of a *beau sabreur*—the boy wore his hair long. It was parted at the side, and rolled over his white temples with a natural curve, which in the days of the gallant D'Orsay was achieved, where it was not natural, by the aid of science, bear's-grease, and fragrant pomade. It seemed natural that he should wear long hair; if it was an affectation, it was his only one, because his dress was quite plain and even rustic, while his boots would have attracted considerable attention in the fashionable quarters of New York.

"Don't try to set me against it," he said. "Oh, Bethiah, I never wanted so much sympathy as now, and if you refuse to stand by me there will be no one. Everybody is against me."

"I am not against you, Ziph. You ought to know that."

"I met your father just now, and he stopped to read me a lecture about the safe ways and the unsafe ways. Well, there have been plenty of men who have tried this way and failed. I know that very well. But if I were to fail—I sha'n't fail, though—I should be happier than if I never had tried at all."

"You have told your father and mother?"

"Yes—it was like having a tooth out. I'd rather have two teeth out than go through it again. But I was bound to tell them. And now it's over, and—Bethiah—don't try to argue against it."

"I won't, Ziph. But oh, if you were only sure that it was the wisest and the best thing! Could you not wait a year or two?—I am sure that eighteen is full early to achieve a literary success—could you not, just for a little while, do—what your father wishes?" She added the last words with a little hesitation, from which it was clear that the paternal wishes were clearly distasteful even to herself.

"Measure calico and weigh out tea? No, no, I cannot do it."

"But he offered to make you a lawyer if you like."

"I hate law."

"Then you might be a doctor or a minister. Think of being a minister, Ziph! Why, you might put your poetry into your sermons and make us all cry."

"No, no; I must be a poet and an author. Do not try to dissuade me, Bethiah. It is my destiny." He looked grand, this young Apollo, as he rammed his hand into his waistcoat and stood upright, the breeze gently lifting his long locks. "My destiny calls me—a man must face his destiny."

Of all Biblical heroes, Ziphion, son of Gad, is one of the least remarkable. He is only mentioned twice; there is even uncertainty in the spelling of his name, and by some he is held to have been a family rather than an individual. Perhaps the name was conferred upon this young poet, while yet an infant, in a spirit of Christian humility. Ziphion B. Trinder! Neither Christian name nor surname quite consorts with a romantic face, poetical eyes, and yearning after literary fame. But what are we to do? We are born to our surnames as we are to our godfathers and godmothers, and are powerless, unless like Charles Kingsley's hero, we change both names altogether, which is a kind of forgery. By dint of very great genius, perhaps the commonest of names—even Johnny Briggs or Ziphion Trinder—might be made beautiful in the eyes of the world. Yet somehow it seems as if all great poets, novelists, painters, and artists of every other kind had names sweetly and musically resonant. How beautiful to the ear are the names of Raffaello, Tasso, Tennyson, Byron, Wordsworth, Talma, Rachel, Rossetti, Meredith, Alma Tadema! Perhaps the constant handling and daily familiar use of these names have polished them up and burnished them so that they now shine and glow and glitter in the sun, and show to the best advantage; whereas, were they merely stuck up over shops, they would attract but little admiration.

"Well, but, Ziph," the girl objected, "think a little. You may be a doctor, or a lawyer, or a minister, and yet become an author, if you like. Think of Oliver Wendell Holmes. He is a physician."

"No, no; literature is sacred. She will have no divided allegiance. I belong, heart and soul, to literature."

"You are ambitious, Ziph"—the lad blushed—"nobody except you and me knows how ambitious you are. Why not follow the regular line? Every one who wants to become a great man begins by being a lawyer. I suppose it is different in England. At least I never heard that Lord Salisbury or Mr. Gladstone began in a lawyer's office. But here—think of it, Ziph."

"I cannot think of it," he replied.

"You believe that you can make your living by your poems and stories and things." Observe that man, mere man, could never bring himself to speak thus coldly to a friend concerning that friend's dearest ambitions. Woman, who belongs to the sensible sex, who has no illusions, and tears away the veil without remorse, and disperses the golden mist, permits herself to say such things. Bethiah knew the boy's dreams, and loved to hear them; yet she knew also, or thought she knew, the trifling commercial value of those manuscripts which filled his desk, and therefore she said, "Poems and stories and things."

"Of course," the boy replied, "I know very well that at first I may not be successful. Then I must wait in patience and work. I can live on very little. I shall go to one of the cheap boarding-houses where they charge five dollars a week. One poem a week—they couldn't offer less than five dollars for a poem —an essay now and then, a short tale occasionally—one of those that you like so much —a sketch of something or other dashed off —oh, I could live very easily."

"Well, but could you persuade editors to take one poem a week? Don't think, Ziph" —for he changed color—"don't think," she repeated, earnestly, "that I do not like your poems. I am sure they are beautiful. Many poems not much better are published every week in our own paper."

"Oh, Bethiah, not much better !" Ziph choked, but repressed himself.

"And yet I fear that you may not get a poem taken every week. And if you wish to rise, you must always be learning to write better and better, and so be lifted above the first anxieties for a livelihood."

"Well, if I find any difficulties I shall become a journalist. It's a step down, but still it is literature."

"If you are going to be a journalist," the girl insisted, "why go to New York at all? Why not begin here, right away? Or there's Salem, where your father came from, and where you've got cousins. Why not begin in Salem, which isn't full of wickedness, like New York?"

"No," said the boy, "I must go to New York. In Salem I should be buried forever. It is only in New York that a man can speak so as to be heard all over the American continent and across the ocean as well. I want a world-wide fame." Here he blushed and stammered, and stopped for a moment, because he was ashamed even to speak of his own ambitions. "I want a world-wide fame," he repeated, after a gulp. "I can be satisfied with nothing short of that. I want to speak to all the ends of the earth. Nobody knows except you. Everybody would laugh at me if they knew."

"I shall never laugh at you, Ziph." This girl was younger than himself, yet the lad confided in her, asked her advice, and was to some extent guided by her. You have heard what manner of girl she was, so that you will not ask how this could be.

"Well, then, you know already what I think. How can people go on living in such a place as this? It is small and mean and ugly, and the people are ignorant and conceited and stupid. In books we read—that is, you and I read; none of the others do— about art and society, and all the splendid things that go on, but here we see none of them—we don't belong to the real world, the civilized world that has taken so many years to build."

"We read of it, Ziph. Does not that content you? To be sure we cannot go and live in London, if that is what you want. But we are quite as well off as other American citizens. We make our own culture, and everybody says it is much deeper and more real than the aristocratic varnish of Europe."

"And we read about great men, but we never see any of them. Here they are all little men. Yesterday I was in the cemetery, looking at the tombs. How many hundreds lie there! Yet not one—no, not one—who was ever known outside his native place or will be remembered when his children are dead. How can they go on contented to be so obscure?"

The lad had often talked in this way before. But his talk had more meaning in it now that he was going to cast himself upon the world.

Bethiah, who was neither an agnostic nor an atheist, hastened to administer, or at least to exhibit, the consolations of religion.

"Ye—yes," the boy replied, doubtfully, as if he would like to have, in addition to the Harp and Crown, the remembrance and the contemplation of world-wide fame. Indeed, one cannot but feel as if the great soul of Shakespeare himself must derive continually fresh gratification from the reports daily dropping in of his continued fame. A glorified person whose mortal remains lie in the Tower Hamlets Cemetery or that of East Finchley cannot have this satisfaction.

"But yet — oh, to feel that one has lived to some purpose, and has made a mark upon his generation, and is talked about wherever the English language is spoken, and will not be forgotten when the breath is out of his body, why—" He stopped and gasped.

"Always fame and distinction, Ziph," said the girl. "That is all you think about. Would it not be better to feel that your work has been good work well done, whether you have won fame or whether you have remained obscure? Then you would die with the assurance—"

"You talk as if everybody was always going to church," the boy interrupted, impatiently. "Why, to do good work and yet miss fame—one would rather—" he stopped, because on this girl's ears the sentiment in his mind would have sounded like rank blasphemy. "Besides," he went on, "do they get such an assurance, these obscure villagers? Why should they get more of it than the men who fight with all the world looking on?"

"If you talk of fighting," said the girl, "remember how many gladiators die unseen and unremembered."

"Well, they die nobly, because they die fighting. These people die ignobly, as they have lived."

Then there was silence awhile. The sun was sinking low, and the evening air was quiet, save for the bells of the cows as they were driven slowly home along the road, each one stopping at her own gate.

"Ziph," said Bethiah, whispering, "how much money have you?"

"Mother will give me a hundred dollars, father will give me nothing. When I have spent my hundred dollars, he says it will be time enough for him to send me money to carry me home again."

"I've got a hundred dollars saved, Ziph. You shall have that money too."

"Oh no, no!"

"Yes, you shall; do not say a single word. Why, Ziph, we have been school-fellows and like brother and sister always, haven't we?"

"Always," he replied.

"Two hundred dollars is not a great deal to give you a fair start, but perhaps it will do."

"It *shall* do," said the boy. "I am sure to succeed. I feel that I must succeed. And when I come back here I shall be "—his voice choked—"famous; I shall be famous."

"Famous," repeated the girl, this time careful not to wound his spirit by any prophecy in the Cassandra vein. "And then you will be happy, I hope." She had no desire for fame, and no confidence in fame as a medicine for the procuring of happiness.

"Do you remember the medium who came here last winter?" Ziph asked, suddenly.

"Yes—why? He was only a common cheat and impostor. What about him?"

"I don't know. He did strange things anyhow."

"He drank whiskey. There was no doubt about that."

I think that those Americans to whom the first outward and visible sign of wickedness is the drinking of whiskey number about twenty millions. Fortunately for the trade, the population is fifty millions.

"Perhaps he did. But suppose—I only say suppose—that by the help of spirits we could not only get a new revelation of the other world, but that we could go to them for advice and guidance, by which we could make ourselves successful. Think how it would be if we could light upon such an ad-

viser as a wise spirit who would tell one what to do."

"Well, Ziph, that is a poet's dream. Go and write a poem showing how a man was led upward by a spirit, as Dante was led by Beatrice."

"Dante—yes. He was led to Heaven and Hell and Purgatory. But I mean, if a man wanted distinction, would it not be a delightful thing to find such a spirit who would show him a way?"

He looked about the garden, as if there might possibly be one or two spirits thus benevolently disposed, wise and capable, within hearing. But there followed no sign of their presence.

"Always greatness, Ziph? Why, think of the millions who die unknown! How should you hope to escape the common lot? One or two out of every generation are remembered for their works. And yet you are dying to be one of them."

"Never mind the improbability. If there were only six men and women in all the world going to be saved, you would try to be one of the six. You know you would. Well, now, ever since I saw the medium and the wonderful things he did, I have been trying to find out if I too were a medium."

"Ziph!"

"Because, if I were, I could lift the veil, as he did, or pretended to do, for myself."

"Ziph!"

"And then I could find that spirit, and make him do whatever I pleased."

"Oh, Ziph—I am sure it is wicked. Do not—do not go on. Remember that witches were not suffered in the land."

"I have gone to my own room to try. You sit alone, and you do nothing. You look straight before you, and you keep your mind quite clear. Presently there comes a time when the room in which you are fades quite away and is lost. Then everything vanishes. You lose the sense of yourself—you are outside the body—your soul is floating—"

"Ziph, stop, I entreat you."

For, as he spoke, his voice dropped, and his eyes assumed the far-off gaze of one who looks through things and sees them not.

"Am I truly behind the veil?" he murmured, swaying gently to and fro, with hands out-stretched as in the dark. "I hear a rustling of wings and a whispering of voices. There is soft music around me; gentle hands touch me, strange lips press my lips; there is fragrance in the air; my feet are on the threshold—"

"Ziph!" The girl sprang to her feet and caught him by the coat-collar with both hands, and began to shake him vigorously. "Stop play-acting!"

He turned his eyes reproachfully.

"Play-acting!" he murmured. "She calls it play-acting!"

"You were looking exactly as the medium tried to look. He could not, because he had pig's eyes and fat cheeks. But you, Ziph, you, to descend to the level of that poor creature whose tricks have been exposed again and again. Oh, Ziph, it is worse than nonsense. No spirit will ever help you, save to your own destruction."

"Was I acting?" he repeated, dreamily. "Sometimes one doesn't know whether one is acting or whether it is reality. How do you know that you have not dragged me back from the very threshold of the next world—from knowledge and from power?"

"Stuff and rubbish!" said the girl.

II.

Six months later, a young man, shabbily dressed, whose boots were down at heel and broken in the toes, walked slowly up the Broadway of New York. His face, sharp and pinched, showed the deepest dejection. There are so many sad faces in every great city that the New-Yorkers may be pardoned for taking small notice of this one sad face.

The lad—he was no more—presently arrived at a certain door, on which was a brass plate announcing that here was the office of the *Spread-eagle Magazine*. He stopped, hesitated, and finally with a deep sigh mounted the steps and entered the office.

"I have called," he said, "about a manuscript I sent to the editor a short time ago."

"Title and name?" asked the clerk, briskly.

"It was called 'The Veiled Monk of Cordova.'"

"Name?"

"It was signed Paul."

"'Veiled Monk of Cordova,' by Paul," repeated the clerk, mechanically writing on a slip of paper. "Wait half a minute." The young man obeyed with a certain meekness.

"Not been at this business long, stranger?" said the clerk.

"What business?"

"Sending your manuscripts around."

"No, not long."

"Ah! Made it pay yet?"

"Not yet."

"Thought so;" with a look at the seedy clothes and the worn boots. "Got anything else to do?"

"No, nothing else."

"Take my advice, stranger, and give it up, give it up. Bless you, we've thousands of manuscripts. They come from all parts of the States; from Canada, even from England, with letters and without. If there are letters, they declare that the writer is starving; and if without, there is a note on the first page requesting the editor to attend to this work without the least delay, and to forward the dollars by return post. Get something else to do. Give it up, I say."

The young man trembled, but made no reply.

"Here's your manuscript. See. The editor has just looked at two pages—here's his pencil-mark — and into the basket it went. No chance for you. Give it up, I say—it's no use—and try something else."

The young man took his manuscript, and meekly retired without a word. This was his last hope. He had ventured to hope once more and for the last time that he might be accepted, and now to be told that it was no use, and that he must give it up.

The young man was none other than Ziphion Trinder. He had enjoyed six months' experience of the literary life—he called it the literary life—and he had not succeeded in selling a single one of his poems, essays, stories, or sketches—not one—not a single one.

He arrived brimful of enthusiasm and of hope; he had a portmanteau stuffed to bursting with the beautiful productions which were to take New York editors by storm, and strike the whole of the United States, not to speak of Great Britain and her colonies, with delight and amazement. He began by considering which of the magazines he should first address—whether *Harper's*, or *Scribner's*, or the *Century*, or the *Atlantic;* or whether he should try the English Journals —*Longman's*, *Temple Bar*, the *Cornhill*, the *Gentleman's*, or Tillotson, for the newspapers. Finally he resolved to be patriotic, and to send the first-fruits of his genius to the magazines of his own country. Afterwards he would cross the ocean, and make pale with envy the faces of the English writers.

Why tell the tale? Everybody will understand that the clever boy's crude productions found no favor. He pelted all the editors with his papers. He had not had a single kind word from one of them, and now it was all over. He had tried all, he had been rejected by all, and he had no money left. The situation was truly terrible. At the end of the week he would have to leave his boarding-house. It was the middle of the winter, and he would have no place to lay his head.

And only six months before he had come to the city, his head aflame, his cheek aglow, resolved to make his fortune and his name at a single bound! Here was a fulfilling of destiny! Here was a glorious outcome of ambition! Many youths of eighteen have the same dream, but few there are who believe in it so profoundly as to reduce it to actual experiment. Poor Ziphion! what is to become of him?

He was so miserable that he dared not think, but strolled along in a purposeless way, and listened to the talk of the passers-by.

First there came two girls dressed in furs, with thick veils, muffs and gloves, and protected from the cold by the solid fortification of a good luncheon. They prattled of *chiffons;* and they quickly passed him. Then followed two middle-aged men who talked of dollars; and they passed him. Then two elderly ladies who were talking of their minister; and they passed him. Then two young men who talked of dollars; and they passed him. Then other young men who talked of dollars. Then more women and more men, and they all talked of dress and dollars; and they passed him.

Then there came along a couple of men who were speaking of something else.

"I tell you, doctor," said one of them, "that you ought to take a pupil."

"I have often thought of it. The difficulty is to find a pupil."

"You are not old, but you may die, and then your incomparable powers and your knowledge will die with you; therefore, take a pupil."

"My dear friend, where am I to find one? I want a thousand qualities combined in one mind, all of which are rare, taken separately. For instance, I want youth, quick intelligence, sympathy, a highly nervous and sensitive organization, a poetic disposition, wide reading, and good education. I want a young man who is perfectly free from the trammels of relations, society, and ties of any kind. I want, besides, one who will give absolute obedience, and preserve, if I require it, inviolable secrecy. Besides this, he should be a youth unspotted ; not like these young Gothamites, up to all kinds of devilry; and he must be prepared to postpone indefinitely the acquisition of dollars. Tell me, my friend, where shall I find such a paragon, such a phœnix, for a pupil?"

They passed him and went on.

Suddenly the words fell upon Ziphion, who had been listening languidly, with a new meaning. For what purpose could this gentleman want such a pupil? He quickened his steps and followed the speakers. Presently one of the two broke off and left the other — the man who wanted to find the pupil.

Ziphion followed this man. He turned out of Broadway into one of the side streets which crossed it at right angles. Presently he stopped at the door of a house. Then — an inspiration—it was but a chance—Ziphion hurried up and addressed him.

"Sir, I beg your pardon. May I have one word with you?"

"What is it?"

"You want a pupil. Take me."

The gentleman looked at him curiously for a few moments.

"Come in," he said.

BOOK THE FIRST.

CHAPTER I.

THE VESTAL VIRGIN.

At twenty minutes past seven there came into the drawing-room, as yet empty, a girl dressed for the evening. To the general world she was Miss Brudenel, only daughter of Mr. Cyrus Brudenel, but she was known among the more frivolous of her companions, male and female, as the Vestal, or as Sibyl the Vestal, or even as Dodo, for reasons which you will immediately understand if you are patient, and place a little confidence in your narrator. She answered readily to all these names, if only for the first and most important reason that her full baptismal name was Sibyl Dodona. She would also, I make no doubt, have been baptized Manto Amalthœa Daphne Pythonissa — and then she would have had a truly beautiful name—but for the fact that her father's classical learning was rusty. It will be acknowledged, however, that her name, even without this compliment, had an oracular, mysterious, Pagan, and Vestal virgin-like ring. Such a name should properly belong to a girl of large and lustrous eyes and pale cheek and lofty brow, charged with the mysterious power of an ancient priestess, filled with the sacred fire of prophecy. But Nature loves to turn the Blanches into brunettes, and make the violets look like full-blown roses, and the pets and pansies like queens; she corrupts the sons of mathematicians so that they become poets, and the sons of poets so that they become engineers. The world, in fact, is full of people destined by their parents for the highest and most dignified offices, who have ended in occupying positions of a very different kind. I was myself destined for the archiepiscopate

—I can never gaze upon an archbishop without a mild wonder how I should look in an apron — and now you see. As for Sibyl, Dame Nature had made of her, though she was solemnly dedicated to the cause from her very cradle, a damsel less like a young Vestal—I suppose Vestals were sometimes youthful — than any young woman I have ever seen. One may be wrong. And certainly, in the day when Vestals went about reprieving criminals, adorning processions, making the sacrificial ox vainglorious with wreaths of roses, and occupying the front seats while the gladiators slaughtered each other, I seem to have been somewhere else, very likely in the ancient British city of Grimspound. Still, speaking with diffidence, one thinks of Vestals as of nuns; and again of nuns, not as the light and frivolous creatures depicted by Gresset and the author of the " Contes Drolatiques," but as beings, pale, emaciated, austere, given to mortifying the flesh till there was none left to mortify—in itself a mortifying conclusion; regardless of personal appearance ; pleased to have their beautiful hair cut off; delighted to dress up in a hideous garb; joyfully fasting; enduring hardness of all kinds ; never so happy as when they had to turn out of a warm bed— but then it was never allowed to be quite warm, so that they might enjoy the misery of cold—and to hurry along a draughty corridor into an ice-cold chapel, there to shiver and to chant a sniffling service. That, I say, is the popular conception of a Vestal virgin.

The outward appearance which this young lady presented pointed to anything rather than the life of self-inflicted torture, humiliation, or discomfort. A pair of laughing blue eyes, rosy lips always ready to laugh, light curly hair, and plenty of it, a cheek warmed with sunshine, the whole face full of possible Venus, as the Delphian prophetess of old was full of Apollo, a shapely figure and a generous stature, may be outward and visible tokens of a holy vocation, but they are not generally so read and accepted. In the same way she wore her dress of heliotrope silk, trimmed, mounted, and set off with white feathers, as if she felt a solid and substantial pleasure in merely putting on a really beautiful dress, and as if she had no craving at all for the claustral black and white. In her hand she carried a feather-fan—quite a mundane pretty thing—and on her wrist was that worldly gaud, a golden bracelet set with turquoises. And yet her name was Sibyl Dodona.

The lamps and candles — Lady Augusta had quite an eighteenth century love for wax-candles—were lit and in their places, the fire was made up; but the people had not yet arrived. Sibyl glanced first at the clock—she was in good time, twenty minutes before the guests would arrive. Then she looked in a mirror, just to see if that would confirm the general impression of her own looking-glass and the opinion of her maid. Any girl would do that, whether she was a Vestal or not: we can picture the handing round of the polished steel mirror among the real Vestals before the ladies formed themselves into procession and marched out into the open, grave and solemn and beautiful, the ugly ones, of course, stage-managed into the middle out of sight. Satisfied with the opinion of the mirror, Sibyl smiled, perhaps at the thought that she had twenty minutes start of the other people, who were asked to dinner at a quarter to eight, and would not appear until that moment. It is just possible that she smiled because she was so early, as one chuckles virtuously at getting up by six, two hours before anybody else; but perhaps there was another reason, for the door was opened and a young man came in—unannounced, because he was staying in the house — and Sibyl blushed and laughed, and blushed again when this young man, after entering with the greatest propriety, and looking about, and satisfying himself that there was nobody else in the room, ran across it with the utmost eagerness, and caught both Sibyl's hands, and kissed her on both cheeks and on the lips, with the most daring indifference to time and place, and whispered, "My dearest Dodo!" The most privileged lover could do no more.

One might have had a worse kind of lover. Many girls are obliged to put up with a very inferior brand of lover. This young man was strong, to begin with. A man ought to be strong. The length and the proportions of his limbs and the depth of his chest revealed the athlete. I do not know his record at all, nor the length or height of his jump, or anything about his performances, because these are things of which I am profoundly ignorant. But every one says that he was a good athlete, and one is glad to accept the unanimous opinion. He was, however, more than an athlete. A first class in the Natural Science Tripos, and a laboratory record already honorable, had prepared him for the post he now held as one of the demonstrators in the School of Mines. Those who hold such a post look forward to become professors in their turn, regarding even Professor Huxley himself as no more than their predecessor, considering themselves as his followers in the advance of science and in fame. They intend to be made Fellows of the Royal Society; in due course doctors of Oxford and Cambridge, members of the Athenæum Club, causâ honoris; and, to complete their scientific career, rectors of Glasgow, St. Andrews, and Aberdeen. Greater honor hath no man. Pity that they must then die. The weak point of the scientific young men is that they have a tendency to premature gravity. One loves to see a youth of five - and - twenty bubbling and boiling over with mirth, and rejoicing in the spring of his manhood. Therefore, it is pleasant to record that Tom Langston—which was this young man's name—was not yet spoiled by his profession, but laughed, and was frivolous, and joked, and was happy, just like one of those foolish prodigal young men in the old pictures, who were represented as laughing idiotically while they ran along a broad road, at the end of which was a great door, which, it could be plainly seen, led to flames, and was guarded by two horrific devils, with tails and hoofs and pitchforks. Yet it was a strong face —pleasingly ugly and charmingly rugged, though perhaps masterful. Those who knew Tom Langston would have said that Sibyl had made no mistake at all when she intrusted to him the happiness of her life.

"We only have a few minutes," she said. "It was very good of you, Tom, to dress so early. No, sir, not too close, for fear. Stand quite quietly on that side of the fireplace, and I will stand on this. So—more than an arm's - length between us, please. What if papa were to come out and find— Oh, Tom!"

"I almost wish he would," said Tom. "Then we could have it out at once. When will you let me speak to him, Sibyl?"

"Not yet—oh, it is not the least use to speak yet. There could not possibly be a more inopportune moment. Why, they have got the most wonderful person in the world coming this very night. He is going to revolutionize everything. The mediums—poor old things!—are to be quite snuffed out at last with their accordions and their tubes and rubbish. All the old spirits are to be sent to the right-about, and we are going to have an entirely new importation. Mr. Emmanuel Chick and Lavinia Medlock are invited here to - night for a last appearance, poor dears! Lady Augusta anticipates the immediate conversion of the whole world; and my education is to be neglected no longer, so that I may take up my duties as a Vestal as soon as the new man is ready for me. Of course he will only prove another humbug; but he must have his innings, I suppose. And oh, Tom, if you love me do not speak yet."

"You will be of age, Sibyl, in two months, and then not even your father—"

"Tom, do not talk like that. I must be married like other girls, with my father's consent and blessing." Her voice trembled a little, and her eyes dimmed for a moment. "You do not know how much he loves me, and what great things he expects of me. It will break his heart when he finds out that I cannot do what he expects and hopes."

"Great things, indeed! With the raps?"

"I suppose it is no use suggesting such a thing, Tom; but if you really desired to win his consent you might pretend to be a medium, and to talk with the spirits, and so work round to the subject gradually."

"It is such a sorry business, Sibyl. I could not possibly pretend to have the least hand in it."

Sibyl sighed profoundly.

"No, Tom," she said, "of course you would not practise any such deception. But it seems so sad. I feel like the agnostic daughter of a pious and earnest bishop. Like her, I do not dare to reveal my unbelief."

"Yet you do not believe in it?"

"No, I have lost every shred of belief, and I am afraid to tell them so. All my life long I have been looking on at manifestations and messages, and they have always been the same; and oh dear me, in spite of the messages, it seems to me as if we were not the least bit advanced."

"You are not," said Tom, "so that either the spirits know no more than we already know, or there are no spirits."

"And I have at last got," continued the girl, with a little laugh, "to know exactly where the things come in, and how they lead up to them—the raps and the music and the rest of it, you know—the things which may be tricks."

"I should think they were tricks!" Tom replied, contemptuously. "Why, Dodo, you are just like a girl who goes to see a melodrama every night in her life, and so gets to know all the surprises, and where they come in, and expects the startles and the jumps. To think that a reasonable man should give up his whole life to the encouragement of these miserable impostors, when there is the whole world of science before him!" This he said with all the scorn of a full - blown professor, not a mere demonstrator.

"Try to be more patient with my father," said Sibyl, "for my sake, Tom. He is not a common, curious pryer into secrets; he wants to search and find out, if he can, what is possible to be discovered of the other world—"

"And I," said her lover, "find my hands full of the world that is around us. Give me science to work for and love to live for, and when life is over I shall await without fear the life—if there is any—which lies beyond."

Every age has its formulæ. Perhaps this is one belonging to our age.

But it was twenty minutes to eight, and the people began to come.

The first-comers were two girls, who also came in unannounced, because one of them was staying in the house and the other was her companion. Cicely Langston, Tom's first cousin, and like him the ward of Mr. Cyrus Brudenel, was blind from infancy; but she walked everywhere about the house without being led, though her companion was always with her.

"You here, Tom?" she said, walking straight to the spot where he stood by the fireplace. "You are dressed early to-night. That is very unusual."

"No, Cis. Perhaps it is my anxiety to witness the fireworks we are to have to-night which made me hurry up."

Cicely smiled and sat down, her eyes closed, her hands crossed in her lap, in the patient and pathetic attitude of the blind. She said nothing in reply, because her cousin's scoffing attitude as regards the researches carried on in that house was well known to everybody. She was somewhat like him, though with that kind of likeness which vanishes when you look into details. For where his features were rugged, hers were regular; and while his face was ruddy, hers was pale; and while his expression was combative, hers was full of patience and resignation. Her features were delicate and fine; her nature, one perceived at once, was incapable of the stronger passions, but was wholly governed by the affections.

She was dressed in what seemed to be black lace and nothing else, with a bunch of freshly cut flowers at the neck. The observant person, while admiring the dress itself, which was not only costly but artistic, would have objected that it was "put on" rather than worn. This effect is produced with the best dress ever made when a shop-girl dresses a dummy, or when an artist dresses a lay-figure—no lay-figure could ever yet be made to show a pride in her "things"—or when a lady's-maid dresses a young lady who is profoundly indifferent as to what she has on. There are a few young ladies of whom this may be said, but they are all blind from birth. Cicely Langston was one of them. She resigned herself to be dressed for the evening as for a drive, but gave no thought to her raiment, except perhaps that she liked it soft and warm.

The girl who entered the room with her was her companion, Hetty Medlock. Companions, one observes, governesses and private secretaries, are all apt to fall into one of two faults. Either they go about with a sulky and discontented air, which they vainly try to dissemble, or they assume, and habit-ually wear like a grinning mask an impossibly cheerful look, as if they loved a condition of dependence, and would choose it out of all the lots and fortunes offered to mankind. Hetty was still too young for the cloud of discontent to have permanently settled upon her brow; but to-night she was clearly discontented with something—very likely with her grenadine dress, which, like a man with a gray beard, could no longer pretend to be young. This is a quite sufficient reason for any girl to be discontented. Perhaps she looked discontented because she did not like her work. Since, however, work of some kind was necessary, Hetty Medlock might have shown something of that thankful heart which one expects even in a pauper who gets a job; and, besides, many girls would have jumped at such a job as being companion to a girl who was the most unselfish creature and had the sweetest temper in the world. On the other hand, it must be confessed that to be a companion at all is to be in a way a household servant, and women especially dislike household servitude.

Hetty was the daughter of the once famous Lavinia Medlock, a medium of the first water in the day, now five-and-twenty years ago, when people still loved to turn tables, listen to raps, and receive messages of the old-fashioned kind, and when such a simple message as one from a lost child to the effect that she was happy brought inexpressible joy to a bereaved heart. No person ever was such a benefactor in this respect as Lavinia Medlock. But though she was still ready to turn on a telephonic communication with any spirit you might call for, the world no longer came to her house to inquire. Wicked people had got her into trouble by asking for messages from persons alleged to be deceased who had never existed—and yet the messages came. Distinguished spirits, such as those of Lord Byron, Shakespeare, and even Dr. Johnson, had taken a pleasure in bringing her into ridicule by rapping nonsense, insomuch that her practice had almost entirely fallen off, and she was now fain to let lodgings. Her husband had long since run away, chivied out of his own house, as he himself said, while drawing on his gloves, by bell-ringing, raps, sighs, whispers, cold breaths, and such supernatural small-ware. He bore it as long as he could, but he was not a brave man, and his nerves gave way; therefore, he went away with a small hand-bag into the night, or the shadows, or the darkness, and was no more heard of. He was by profession a clerk, and when impecunious clerks go out into the night or the shadows they generally get their feet upon those steps which go swiftly down to Sheol.

In any case Mr. Medlock had been no more heard of.

If Hetty had looked happier she would have been a very beautiful girl, much more strikingly beautiful than Sibyl. She possessed a pair of large and lustrous eyes, dark enough to be called black—an unusual thing in an English girl—and a great mass of thick black hair. It was the face of a girl in whom passion was possible — passion on a grand scale, Spanish or Italian passion, with burning jealousy and revenge. Fortunately, such girls in these days of self-restraint and repression, and the shame of showing any sign of strong feeling, are rare.

"Well," said Tom, "I hope the grand Function will come off successfully, and then there will be no room for doubt left at all; will there, Cis?"

"There is already no room left for doubt in the minds of a great many people," Cis replied, with the calm conviction of a believer.

"Oh, I only said what I believed to be the correct thing to say after every new manifestation of the spirits."

"To me," said Cicely, "life is all shadow. Whether it is a spirit of this or of the other world that speaks to me matters little, so that it is a good spirit. Sometimes we have had communications with those who are not good spirits.

"That's just it," said her cousin; "and the only way to keep out the deceiving spirits is to draw the line so as to include only the spirits of this world. From the nonsense they talk I should be inclined to believe that we never get hold of the good spirits of the other world at all. What do you think, Miss Medlock?"

"Why do you ask me, Mr. Langston?" she replied. "Has not my mother been a medium for thirty years? Am I to acknowledge that all her friends are of the baser sort?"

Then Lady Augusta came in, followed by Mr. Cyrus Brudenel; and the other guests invited to dine, and to assist at whatever might follow afterwards, began to arrive.

CHAPTER II.

THE LEADER.

MR. CYRUS BRUDENEL has been for many years, as everybody knows, the recognized leader in the spiritualistic world of London. Other people may have come to the front for a moment by virtue of peculiar powers and excellency of gifts : they have played their parts, received their applause, made their bows, and then retired; but Mr. Cyrus Brudenel remains. In every cause, move-

ment, or party there is its Mr. Brudenel, whose name is inseparably mixed up with it. He must be rich and married; he must live in a great house, and his wife must be always receiving. Further, he must be a sincere believer in the cause. In short, what Lord Shaftesbury, to take a well-known case, was to the Evangelical party in the Church, so Mr. Cyrus Brudenel was to the Spiritualists.

Mr. Brudenel was the second son of the late Mr. Abraham Brudenel, ship-owner and millionaire. His elder brother, created a baronet in 1872, in gratitude for large moneys spent in the advance of the Liberal cause, has been recently, for similar reasons, promoted to the peerage, and now enjoys the rank and title of Lord Bow and Bromley. Cyrus, for his part, passed through school and university with no incidents to speak of, and took an ordinary degree after a career marked on the one hand by no turbulence, effervescence, or hot madness of youth, and, on the other hand, by no apparent superiority of intellect or academic distinctions. In fact there was nothing at all to indicate his future greatness. On the demise of Abraham the firm was converted into the well-known Company, Limited, and the sons, who sold out their interest, bought land with the money they received. This, thirty years ago, was the recognized first step with those who wished at once to make an investment absolutely safe, and to rise higher on the social ladder. What is to take the place of land, supposing that men continue to get rich, which is doubtful, and still aspire to enter society, which is not doubtful, has not yet been determined.

I know not by what means the mind of Cyrus Brudenel was first turned in the direction of Spiritualism. Perhaps by simple curiosity, perhaps by the natural longing of mankind to inquire after the Unknown and strive to see the Invisible. For thirty years and more he had experienced convictions of the truth, and been one of those disciples whom nothing can shake from their allegiance. Yet, which is a symptom common to all Spiritualists and peculiar to them—he was not restful and settled and contented, but remained always eager after new manifestations, ravenous for further confirmations, and still unsatisfied with the messages which come in plenty to those who inquire. He has assisted in his time at numberless séances; he has been rewarded by the most stupendous miracles of undoubted and undeniable genuineness; in his presence the heaviest and most solemn tables have become frisky and frivolous; the bulkiest of mediums have lost their ponderosity and been wafted about like feathers. Yet he has never been satisfied; for in miracles, as at dinner, appetite comes to those who eat, and one is never full.

On the other hand, it cannot be denied that Mr. Brudenel has been too frequently the prey to lying spirits, and has often been imposed upon by brazen impostors pretending to supernatural powers. At one time, for instance, when he intrusted the whole conduct of his affairs to the advice of the spirits, who told him what to do by means of his then favorite medium — it was Mr. Emmanuel Chick — he was made to buy a good many shares in ventures which somehow all turned out badly. There were suspicions that the medium had been squared, but Mr. Brudenel preferred to lay the blame upon the spirits. The commercial element among those with whom we are permitted to converse is one, he says sadly, whose City record, did we know it, would probably prove shady.

His triumphs, his disappointments, his real and sincere convictions of the truth and final success of his cause; the yielding and treacherous nature of the ground on which he stood; his insatiable thirst for a fuller and a deeper revelation, with manifestations of a more startling kind, and beyond the possibility of doubt; the adulation of the mediums who lived upon his word; the consciousness of Leadership—all these things together had stamped his face with an expression as full of varied emotions as the caldron at Camacho's wedding was full of every delectable dainty. Among them might have been observed, as the reporter says, pride, dignity, importance, hope, enthusiasm, doubt, fear, suspicion, irritability, jealousy, and many other passions. He was certainly dignified in his carriage; he was certainly hesitating in his speech ; his words were brave but his manner was nervous. As for his figure, he was tall and portly; he had grown bald and gray, but had as yet no look of old age or decay. His face, handsome still at sixty, must have been far more strikingly handsome at thirty. This is not surprising when we reflect that his aristocratic features and his noble presence were inherited from a long line of ancestors who were all, to a man, porters, laborers, draymen, rustics, mechanics, and craftsmen from time immemorial until Abraham, afterwards the millionaire, left the ranks of labor to become a clerk. The enemies of Cyrus Brudenel call him names, such as Pump, Old Pump, Solemn Old Pump, and the like, which I will not repeat. To be sure, his best friends could not pretend that he was lively and sparkling; but then he was a leader in a cause on which ridicule, epigram, irony, and contempt have been freely hurled, not only by wit and by philosopher, but also by the baser sort, because there is none so vile but he can jeer at spirits and ghosts. To such a leader all laughter is like the crackling of thorns beneath a pot; and if you should be so ill-advised as to laugh in Mr. Brudenel's presence he would become that pot, and presently boil over.

As for Lady Augusta, his second wife:

There is a certain type of wife which will, I fear, with the march of woman's education and the cultivation of her critical faculty, grow rapidly rarer until it finally becomes extinct. I mean the wife who ardently adopts her husband's creed, convictions, dogmas, hobbies, and party as her own, and enters into the very inner spirit of that creed or party. Thus, there is no person in the world who more profoundly believes the doctrine of the High Church than the wife —if she be of this type—of the Ritualistic clergyman; there is no person more profoundly agitated about the future state of her own soul than the wife of the Calvinist; there is no one who more honestly believes in the connection than the wife of the minister. If the husband be a man of science, the wife will breathe the atmosphere of science, and live wholly in the scientific world; if he be an artist, she will live among the studios and talk of art; if he be a musician, she will talk and think of music all her life; if he be a shopkeeper— But here we draw the line, because there is, it must be admitted, a universal tendency to sink the shop.

Lady Augusta belonged to this type. She felt no doubts, she had no hesitations. "I have seen too much," she said, "to admit of any room for doubt. After all, my dears," she added, "one is possessed of eyes and of the reasoning faculty. Oh! we are on the verge of a new revelation. I look for it daily; I expect the prophet; he may come at any day or any moment, and then—oh, then there will begin for the world in my drawing-room a new Age of Faith which will restore happiness forever to suffering humanity."

The days passed, and the looked-for prophet came not.

Lady Augusta, a handsome woman still, and a *grande dame de par le monde*, was now thirty-five. She could therefore no longer welcome that prophet in her youth. Now, if anything wonderful is to happen to a woman in her lifetime, she would naturally prefer it to happen in the time of her youth and beauty. It would be delightful to become the friend, in pure Platonic bonds, of a prophet; to make his earthly existence smooth and happy for him; to be young with him and to grow old with him. But he came not, and Lady Augusta's youth took to itself wings and flew away.

Perhaps, however, the prophet would be a venerable sage. Meantime, five-and-thirty is not old for a queen of any cause. Lady Augusta was the undoubted queen of the Spiritualists, and she maintained her court with a graciousness and a hospitality truly admirable.

To be taken up by Lady Augusta was to secure public attention; every medium made straight for her drawing-room; her name was perfectly well known in New York, St. Petersburg, Paris, and in every spiritualistic centre. No doubt the occult plutosophers Mahatmas and Adepto of Thibet regard her with favor, though they have never yet visited her. She had her circle of courtiers as well as her continual stream of ever new and richly gifted mediums who wanted a *clientèle* and an income; round her were gathered all those thinkers who are perpetually engaged in trying to look behind the veil.

Behind the veil! We who live in this great crowded ant-hill, and struggle and toil daily with our fellow-ants, bearing our burdens and living in the present, rejoicing in the sunshine of the moment, satisfied with life, contented if we do not suffer pain, careless for the most part of what may happen when this life is done—we humble, common folk, I say, hardly know anything of the world which thinks of nothing but to pry behind the veil. To us it is a great black bank of cloud lying all round us, whichever way we look. It is as the black spaces between the stars; we cannot look long upon it without a reeling of the brain. Sometimes, to those who think of it, it seems to roll towards us, sometimes to roll back a little way; whenever we make a great physical discovery there is a feeling that now, at last, we may have rolled it away altogether and forever. But it does not roll away, and, my brothers, I think that it will never either lift or roll away, whatever we may discover, and that we know already everything that mankind will ever be permitted to know of the other world. Even if we find the secret of birth and growth and decay; even if we prolong our own lives indefinitely, the secret of the other world will never, I am sure, be found out by any efforts of human ingenuity.

But for these people life has no other interest. For them there is nothing else. Science, art, literature, philosophy are foolish and futile. Politics are unworthy the attention of a serious person. Religion, if they have any, which is not always the case, is incomplete without the supplementary revelation for which they are always looking. Reason is insufficient unless it is aided by the counsel and guidance of the spirits whom they consult every day. Even if they saw with the earthly eye the New Jerusalem itself descending from the clouds, they would go and ask the spirits by the well-known machinery if it was a real city, and a thing to be relied upon.

In every age there have always been such men. They used to consult the wise women, and to ask the future in the thousand and one ways which have been enumerated for us by the Sage of Meudon. They inquired of the oracle; they cast nativities; they sought for the Philosopher's Stone and for the Elixir of Life; they looked in the Crystal and practised palmistry; they turned tables, they listened to raps; they pretended to mysterious powers; they talked of the Rosy Cross, the Kabbala, and Hermes; they recorded the lives of necromancers and the miracles which they wrought; they looked for hidden secrets wrapped in allegory; they whispered and mumbled and made themselves into societies and sects, and in these latter days they read the secret thoughts of mankind, they put on astral bodies, they defy space and time, they boast of Charma, and they belong to the Sacred College of the Occult Philosophers.

CHAPTER III.

THE PROPHET.

BUT it was now past eight, and everybody had arrived except the guest of the evening, who always comes last. The people were sitting or standing about, with conventional smiles and hungry hearts, exchanging words which meant nothing, and boiling with indignation to think that a mere medium should presume to keep them from dinner. For although a man may boast the most undoubted supernatural powers, there exists in spiritualistic circles a widely spread feeling that a medium ought to know his place, and that it is to the last degree unbecoming for him to keep ladies and gentlemen waiting.

On such an occasion the guests belonged to the highest circle of Spiritualists—they were attended, no doubt, by their friendly spirits, but these were invisible. Among them, for instance, was the famous Athelstan Kilburn, barrister-at-law. Forty years ago Mr. Athelstan Kilburn became an original member of the first Society for Psychical Research which was founded at Cambridge, having precisely the same objects as Mr. Henry Sidgwick's later association, and was therefore probably established in imitation of it. His friends have long since gone off to practical questions, and some have gone up the ladder and become bishops, judges, Q. C's., archdeacons, deans, physicians, Quarterly Reviewers, editors, professors, head-masters, leader-writers, and even novelists. But Athelstan Kilburn went on researching, and for the sake of the spirits has sacrificed his ambition and his career.

There was again the equally well-known Rev. Amelius Horton, Senior Fellow of King Henry's College, Cambridge, who heals the sick by touch, and cures the halt and lame, and makes the rheumatic go upright. At least he says he does. He also foretold the earthquake which happened in Egypt on the occasion of the transit of Venus ten years ago or so. At least he says it happened in accordance with his prediction, and that he distinctly felt the shock, though the papers agreed to pass it over. Lastly, he keeps up direct communication with a great quantity of spirits, some of whom make drawings for him consisting of curves of quite wonderful design and of previously unheard-of color. As might be expected, these pretensions and powers make him an immense favorite with his brother Dons, who are greatly puffed up with pride in him, and talk about him as much as ever they possibly can.

The professional medium was represented by Mr. Emmanuel Chick. He is now advanced in years, and has dropped out of fashion, like his former rival, Lavinia Medlock. But in the old days he appeared at the Tuileries before the Emperor, and at St. Petersburg before the Czar; he has been made the subject of papers and leaders in the *Saturday*, the *Spectator*, and the dailies; he has also submitted his "claims" to the investigation of Professors Huxley and Tyndall. He has therefore a glorious past to remember, even if the present be a time of tightness. In appearance Mr. Chick resembled a waiter in a third-rate City dining-room. One looked for the napkin.

While they waited and talked, the voice of Lady Augusta was raised a little louder than usual, as if she wished all to hear.

"Yes," she said, "Herr Paulus is actually in the house. He arrived an hour ago."

"Oh! and you have seen him?" The speaker was Mrs. Tracy Hanley, whose Sunday Evenings are well known.

"Not yet. He went straight to his room. But I can tell you something about him, if we have time. I have here a letter from our friend Anna Petrovna, the well-known adept of St. Petersburg, you know. She says"—Lady Augusta opened the letter and read—"'Our brother Paulus, who is on his way to England, is one of those rare and precious human creatures who acquire early in life powers which the more dull can only attain to after years of work and struggle. He proposes, if he meets with a sympathetic circle'"

"He will—he will," sighed Mrs. Tracy Hanley.

"'To preach the Higher Philosophy in a way which will be entirely new to you. I declare that until conversing with Herr Paulus, and seeing with my own eyes the exercise of a power which I had before only heard and read of, I had no true conception of his philosophy. My dear sister, in those ties which are more sacred than the ties of blood begin by dismissing from your mind all preconceived ideas of Spiritualism, as well as all prejudice and suspicion. He makes a new departure. His soul is candor itself; he is as pure as the white leaf of a lily; he is as incapable of deception as one of the lofty spirits with whom he holds habitual communion; he trusts, and expects to be trusted. In a word, my dear Augusta, take him to your heart.'"

Perhaps it was a pang of hunger which made Mr. Emmanuel Chick snort at this point.

"'It is only by sympathy, by confidence, and by affection that he can be won, step by step, to unfold his soul. He is entirely beyond and above any considerations of money; his wants, which are simple, are supplied by his friends; take care not to offer him any money.'"

It was no doubt hunger again which caused Mr. Emmanuel Chick to breathe loud at this point.

"'I do not know that there is anything more to say by way of introduction. My dear sister, we are on the eve of the most stupendous revolution of thought that the world has ever seen. It will begin in England—Christian, bigoted, prejudiced, conservative England.'"

"Oh"—Mrs. Tracy Hanley clasped her hands to her bosom—"how delightful! how wonderful! And his name—Paulus—Paulus—German for Paul. Why do they always have such strange names?"

"I believe the people who possess the largest portions of these gifts have generally—I know not why—been sons of the soil." Here Lady Augusta dropped her voice, because Mr. Emmanuel Chick undoubtedly looked like a gentleman who had made himself, after an imperfect training in the art of sculpture. "They have got an astounding collection of names—down there. This man, however, seems in some essentials quite different from others whom we have received here."

"From his name he must be a German," said Mrs. Tracy Hanley. "He is probably middle-aged. He will be too careless to think of his dress; he will trample a good deal on our little social *convenances*—that matters nothing; he will have spectacles and blue eyes and a big beard, and he will talk about nothing but the spirits."

"That we must expect of such a man, and in this house. As for me," said Lady Augusta, looking round the room and through the bodies of her friends, "I live among them—they whisper to me continually, and I hear their wings at every moment."

Her friend shuddered. But it was a strange house.

"Well, then, dear Lady Augusta, I am only afraid that he will smell of tobacco and say 'Zo.' But oh, what matters the smell of tobacco if a man has such gifts!"

Lady Augusta smiled with superiority of knowledge.

"Dr. Paulus may be the exact opposite of all that you imagine. I think, from another passage in Anna's letter, that he will be a great success, not only in the way pointed out by Anna Petrovna"—here she lowered her voice again—"but also a social success. How much more I dare not think. We want a new departure. Everything has grown stale. All the answers to all the questions have failed. All the old systems are breaking down. We are on the eve of a universal collapse of systems and of faiths, and nothing really new has been proposed. In fact, my dear, we want—we must have—a new gospel. I pray that this stranger may preach it to the world—in my drawing-room."

At this moment Herr Paulus himself appeared. I believe that everybody had expected just such a person as that described by Mrs. Tracy Hanley. That is the only way in which we can account for the fact that everybody with one consent gasped. Because the man who stood before them was not in the least like the middle-aged, spectacled German imagined by that lady. There was nothing Teutonic about him at all but his name; nor was he middle-aged, nor did he wear spectacles, nor did he carry a big pipe in his hand. Instead of all this they saw before them a young gentleman, apparently much too young to have achieved anything worthy of remark. As a rule it is only senior wranglers who ever get the chance of being famous before five-and-twenty, except a poet or two, a lucky officer or two, and a Prime-minister or two. This young man—could he really be Herr Paulus?—was certainly not more than four-and-twenty. He was not bearded, bald, or grizzled, but smooth-faced, save for a light mustache; he was not attired in the stage dress, so to speak, of the German philosopher, but in that of a private gentleman who knows the power and value of personal appearance, and is attentive to every detail, so that he was not only well dressed, but simply dressed, with no more jewellery than a gold chain across his waistcoat, and a single *pearl* stud in his shirt,

and no other ornament than a small white flower.

Could this man be the great luminary of occult science spoken of in such glowing terms by the theosophic sister of St. Petersburg? In height he was reasonably tall, or tall as a young man need desire to be—namely, about five feet ten; his figure was slight, and not in the least athletic, but active and full of spring—more like the figure of a Frenchman than an Englishman; his features were curiously delicate and regular. "Dodo," Tom murmured, "I believe he's a young New-Yorker. I've seen them made that way." His black eyes, though somewhat deep-set, were keen and swift and full of light; his forehead was white and high; his cheek was pale; never, certainly, since Spiritualism, clairvoyance, telepathy, and occult philosophy first began, was there seen such a medium. Always the medium was uncouth, and unused to the ways of polite society, and always he was ill-dressed as well as ill-mannered; generally he was middle-aged. Surely, if this man was a medium, he was the pearl of his profession! Again, his hair, so dark as to seem almost black, was worn rather longer than is the fashion with most young men; he wore it parted on the left, and it rose over his forehead in a natural arch that is unusual and most effective.

"I'm sure he's a New-Yorker, Dodo," Tom whispered again. "He's one of the sort they call dudes."

In one detail only he differed from the ordinary young man of society. It was that he wore kid gloves. To be sure he had only just come from St. Petersburg, where the white kid glove is *de rigueur*, and perhaps, though this I do not know, it is always customary in New York.

It was, in fact, none other than the Doctor Mirabilis, Herr Paulus himself. He stood at the door for a moment, and surveyed the assembly with a rapid glance; then, without the least embarrassment, and with a manner perfectly easy and assured, and yet entirely devoid of slide and swagger, he quietly stepped across the room to his hostess. Perhaps he knew her by the single step she made to meet him. Anyhow, there was no hesitation.

"Lady Augusta." He bowed low, putting his heels together. Therefore he was not an Englishman, because no Englishman knows how to make a bow. But he raised his head and took her hand. "I have seen you already," he murmured, "while I was in St. Petersburg. I came here in the spirit. And I am assured already that our souls will be in sympathy."

His voice was extremely soft and musical; his eyes met Lady Augusta's with a steady glow of affection and friendship which moved her strangely. And he held her hand in the warm long grasp of one who greets a long absent friend.

Could he—oh, could he be the long-looked-for prophet?

Then he turned to Mr. Brudenel, whom also he seemed to know.

"Mr. Cyrus Brudenel," he said, "I have brought many messages for you and some gifts from my friends, who have long recognized your true worth."

Mr. Brudenel generally gave his mediums two fingers to shake, after the manner of the late Lord Shaftesbury with the inferior clergy, but in this case he surrendered his whole hand. Herr Paulus took it with less warmth than he had taken Lady Augusta's, and he looked curiously into Mr. Brudenel's face, as if trying to read something there.

"Very glad, Herr Paulus," said his host, trying to put on the air of patronage with which he generally received his mediums, "very glad to make your acquaintance."

"I was with you—in the spirit. Yesterday morning it was, Mr. Brudenel, in your library. You were reading."

"I was," said Mr. Brudenel.

Everybody knew that Herr Paulus had only that day arrived from St. Petersburg. But nobody expressed the least surprise. In this house anything might happen.

"You were reading a novel by Ouida, called 'Moths.'"

Mr. Brudenel changed color, and some of the people smiled.

"Ah! yes—in fact—yes—I was looking into one of her books."

"You turned the page down at 144," Herr Paulus continued, "and you resumed your reading this morning until you arrived at page 280."

"Yes—yes," said Mr. Brudenel, much confused at being found out in reading Ouida. "Ah, in this house, Herr Paulus, we are never surprised even at being reminded of trivial actions in the—ah—privacy of a study. We are never surprised, and we expect a great deal—ah—a great deal."

He meant, I suppose, to indicate, first, that they were all quite used to people going about without their bodies, and being able to see things; secondly, that his study ought to be considered private and confidential; and thirdly, that after this nasty one he intended to be critical and exacting.

"Ouida's novels," said Herr Paulus, severely, "are not the best preparation for spiritual study. Your attitude of mind prevented my communicating with you, Mr. Brudenel."

Everybody lowered their eyes at this rebuke, and no one ventured to look at their chief. Had any one ever before seen or heard the like? To Mr. Cyrus Brudenel, from a medium!

Then Herr Paulus turned again to Lady Augusta.

"I must apologize for being late," he said, in softer tones. "After I was shown to my room, a message was brought to me—rather an important message—from my friends."

"A message, Herr Paulus?" You see he had only been in the house for three-quarters of an hour, and had come straight from St. Petersburg. "A telegram?"

"No"—he smiled—"not a telegram. My friends do not use the wire. The message came from the heart of Abyssinia. I had to attend to it at once, though I kept you waiting."

He spoke without the least appearance of boastfulness — though a man who receives messages from Abyssinia more swiftly than would be possible for mortals, even if the Palace of the Negus and St. Martin's were united by a wire, might reasonably stick out his chin. But no; he spoke as if such a thing were common.

"Dodo," whispered Tom once more, "this Johnnie is going to be far better fun than poor old Chick. Here's a splendid cracker to begin with."

Then dinner was announced, and the sigh of relief from Mr. Emmanuel Chick was heard through the whole room. And Herr Paulus, instead of meekly waiting to be put in his place, and to follow last without any lady, as had always happened to Mr. Emmanuel Chick and the other mediums, calmly offered his arm to Lady Augusta.

"It is my first evening in England," he said, "and my first dinner with you. May I exercise the privilege of my rank, Lady Augusta? Here we are all Spiritualists—in name at least"—did he mean anything by looking at Mr. Chick?—"and in spiritual rank I am the first and the chief."

Then they all marched out to dinner in pairs—male and female went they.

CHAPTER IV.

AT DINNER.

EVERY well-ordered and old-established house has certain usages, traditions, manners, and customs of its own. It is only the New Rich who are exactly like each other, and have machine-made manners. Why not, if they are copies of good-manners? The leading tradition of this house was the silence which always reigned in it. There was never any trampling heard in it, nor any banging of gongs, ringing of bells, knocking at doors, striking of clocks, or chatter of servants. The only bells were the electric contrivances, which are not heard beyond the room for which they are intended. The servants went about their work without so much as a whisper. It was said that even snoring was forbidden, and Lady Augusta certainly once dismissed a butler, otherwise virtuous, for trumpeting with his nose. The phenomenal silence of the house was supposed to be rendered necessary by the presence of the spirits.

The silence of the service was most marked at dinner. Only those who have lived in countries where the servants go barefoot know the value and beauty of perfectly silent service. Lady Augusta could not, unfortunately, make her people go barefoot, but she made them wear noiseless shoes, constrained them in their serving not to whisper instructions to each other, not to chink glasses, rattle plates, or knock bottles together. In the last century, when the Regent of France and his friends held those suppers of theirs which were assuredly the most delightful and the most wicked of all suppers, they were fain to turn out all the people and to wait upon themselves, because they had not yet been able to train their servants — whom they were always admonishing with whacks, kicks, cuffs, and canings — to silence and order. Even in the present day the loud and noisy zeal of the waiters at a restaurant, their jostling of each other, and their clatter and rattle of plates and knives, inflict anguish upon every sensitive soul, while in many private houses King Scrimmage reigns absolute. Another tradition imposed upon the house by the peculiar conditions under which its occupants lived was that the conversation at dinner should be always pitched in a highly intellectual key. This made the meal a function greatly beloved by the younger members of the family.

Once, to be sure — alas! the conspiracy failed—goaded to desperation by the dulness of the talk, Tom and Sibyl resolved on the introduction of something comic. Had the thing come off, I am convinced, in spite of their apprehensions, that it would have produced no greater effect upon the company than a word or two of Hebrew or Zulu. They resolved that the something comic should take the form of a pun, as being a weapon easier to handle and more suitable for a dinner-table than a comic song or a practical joke. Then they set to work to make a good pun. This seems easy, but to the unpractised hand there is nothing more difficult. It is, in fact, as hard for a beginner as a Ballade or a Villanelle. One does not like to say how long this pair worked at

their miserable pun, but when, after superhuman efforts, it was completed, they arranged to lead up the conversation artfully to the point where Tom was to be intrusted with the production of the calembourg. Sibyl felt that a pun is somehow unfitted for the lips of a maiden; when one comes to think of it, no woman was ever yet known to make a pun, though a few here and there —only a few — have been known to tell a good story.

Very well. At the last moment, when the conversation had been led up to the point, and Sybil was looking round the table, expecting the bewilderment which would immediately fall upon this profoundly solemn circle, Tom broke down. He said afterwards that he felt a qualm of pity for his uncle, who was more solemn than all the rest of mankind put together. But I doubt this explanation. I believe he was afraid. He says further that he felt himself unable to inflict so heavy a blow upon the finest part of man, his dignity. But I doubt this statement. I am sure he was afraid. As for the loss of the pun, that is nothing; no pun is ever really lost, because it is always being made over and over again. I have no doubt that Messrs. Hook, Hood, Lamb, Burnand, and Byron have made Tom's unlucky pun on many occasions, and that in many a screaming burlesque it has caused the faces to broaden from pit to gallery hundreds of times. But the loss of the proposed experiment seems a pity.

Mr. Cyrus Brudenel himself was certainly by no means the kind of person with whom one would like to take a personal liberty. I have often wondered what would happen if a man should venture to slap a really great and correspondingly solemn man upon the back. Suppose, for instance, that a curate— one of the inferior clergy—had ventured to slap the late Lord Shaftesbury on the back. What would that venerable nobleman have said or done? To cuff and kick the presumptuous curate would be undignified; to swear at him would be impossible; to splutter and get red would only make him laugh; to find a fitting rebuke in short but eloquent words, which would leave an indelible scar on his soul, would be difficult. Merely to look at him might do no good. Yet something, one feels certain, would have been said or done, so that the miserable curate would have crept, pale and trembling, with fearful remorse, and foreboding of dreadful punishment to come, into some dark and secret recess of the earth—say the cavern at Buxton.

Conversation was long in beginning at this dinner, partly because everybody wanted to hear what the newly arrived young great man was going to talk about, partly because everybody was hungry, and cross at having been kept waiting, and partly because some of the guests regarded each other with the jealousy and suspicion not uncommon among specialists, actors, conjurors, and those who are rivals for the public applause.

"Our sister, Anna Petrovna," said Herr Paulus, presently, "has already written to you from St. Petersburg announcing me."

"Yes. Did she tell you that she was going to do so?"

"I knew that I should have no need of a letter of introduction. I had hoped that you and Anna were both able to converse without the vulgar necessity for letters. In that respect the Russians are far in advance of the Westerns. Nothing is more common among our friends in Russia than conversation at any distance. That, however, will doubtless come in due course."

"I hope that it may," said Lady Augusta. "We hear from time to time of this wonderful power of annihilating space, but we have not yet been able to witness any manifestations of the kind. And you, Herr Paulus—"

"Space and time do not exist for my friends. Do not speak of me, Lady Augusta; speak rather of my friends, who will be yours."

"Oh, if they would become my friends! We are weary, Herr Paulus, of the dull round of our English and American Spiritualism. We have been greatly harassed by frivolous, lying, and wicked spirits. We ask for a more real and a deeper communion with spirits whom we can trust—those who will not deceive us, those who will give us messages able to lift up our hearts and to carry us out of ourselves."

"You shall, before long, commune with my friends," he replied, softly.

Lady Augusta sighed deeply. "Our sister, Anna Petrovna, told me so many wonderful things about you, Herr Paulus, that we have been thinking of nothing else since we had her letter."

"I know the contents of that letter. They were communicated to me in the train between St. Petersburg and Berlin."

"Communicated! Oh, I understand."

"By my friends. They also communicated to me many things which are necessary to me here. For instance, they told me much concerning yourself."

"Concerning me!" She blushed and looked startled. It is disquieting for a strange man to tell a lady that he knows all about her.

"Do not imagine that I know everything. I know only what I have been told. Thus, I was told the history of Mr. Brudenel, of *this house,* of your step-daughter, and so

forth—more things than I can tell you in an hour or two—yet if you were to examine me, you would find that in some points I am still quite ignorant."

"It seems strange that your friends should wish you to know such trifling matters as the private concerns of this household."

"How do we know what are trifles and what are things of importance? For instance, I am here your guest, for how long I do not know. I am here with a definite mission. Surely it is well that I should begin, not as a complete stranger, but with some knowledge of your difficulties, and the nature and disposition of those among whom I am to work. It saves time, and the trouble of explanation."

"Yes. But should not the confidence be extended, Herr Paulus?"

"You mean, should you not know as much concerning me? Certainly. But as yet my friends are not in communication with you. And, pardon me, Lady Augusta, I think there are no spirits with whom you do confer who are strong enough to do you so simple a service as to tell you who and what I am."

"It is, unfortunately, too true. There is not a single spirit who has ever done anything for me of a practical kind."

"You have here, I perceive, one medium at least." Herr Paulus looked down the table.

"We have several. There is Mr. Emmanuel Chick. Have you heard of him?"

"No. Yes—I have this moment heard of him." Herr Paulus shuddered as if in pain. "Lady Augusta," he whispered, "mistrust that man's communications. His spirits are lying spirits."

"There is the Rev. Amelius Horton."

Herr Paulus looked curiously and doubtfully at the clergyman. Then he smiled.

"He is the sport and plaything of the spirits. Oh! I understand now how it is that I could not communicate with you when I was here yesterday. This house is haunted with inferior spirits. It is full of them. I shall send them all away immediately."

"And will nobler spirits take their place?"

"You shall see. But you have a much better medium present—a young lady."

"Who is that?"

"I told you that I was ignorant of many things. I mean the young lady next the blind girl—Miss Langston—who, too, might in good hands—"

"Oh! It is Hetty Medlock, Cicely Langston's companion. You think that—"

"I do not think only. I am sure that she is gifted with the temperament of the medium."

"Look at my step-daughter. How rejoiced would be her father if you could discern in her the signs of power!"

Herr Paulus shook his head. "No," he said, firmly, "I discern no such signs in her. Meantime, to return to myself, you shall in due course learn anything you want to know about me. I must have no secrets from you, Lady Augusta, if our relations are to be—what I hope and trust they will become." Again he lowered his voice, and their eyes met, his limpid, and filled with that expression which she had observed before.

"I expected, I confess, a very different person. But yes"— she answered his eyes— "we will be friends, and you shall do for me what you can."

It was almost with the smile of a happy lover that he received these gracious words. Neither spoke for a while.

"Herr Paulus," she said, presently, "I confess that, thinking you were so very different, I have asked a good many people to meet you this evening, and"—here she blushed— "I fear I have held out hopes. But do not mind them. Forgive me, and do not show them anything."

He laughed.

"You want the signs and the miracles. Very well; it is natural. But, Lady Augusta, you at least will very soon pass beyond the region where signs and wonders are necessary. My mission is not to do these things, but to teach. Yet I dare to think that I shall be able to satisfy your friends' expectations even in this direction."

"Oh, will you, really?"

The young man's manner, assured and easy, yet not presuming, impressed her with a sense of sincerity. She believed in him from that moment implicitly, and without the least doubt.

"The Ancient Wisdom does not consist in making people open their eyes and stare; but it confers powers on those who deserve them, which they may use for their advancement in true knowledge. You would like to see some illustration of those powers?"

"Yes, yes; we who live and move on the lower planes always ask for some sign. Is it not natural?"

"It is the old story," he said, somewhat sadly. "Lady Augusta, your friends shall have their sign—from my friends."

Then there was silence for a space with the commonplace business of eating, and Lady Augusta made the useful discovery that even the highest flights of philosophy and the Ancient Wisdom do not deprive a young man of his appetite. On the other hand, they seemed to take from him the power or the desire to drink wine. Herr Paulus drank a bottle of Apollinaris.

"Do not think me curious," said Lady Augusta, presently, "but may I ask, is it often that the secrets of your philosophy are intrusted to men so young as you—so very young—while they are withheld from men as old and as eager to acquire them as my husband?"

"What is my age, Lady Augusta?"

"I suppose about three-and-twenty."

"I do not pretend to be the Wandering Jew. But I will tell you a strange thing. It happened the other day, only a few months ago. Perhaps you will not believe it."

"I will believe it if you tell me that it is true."

He raised his voice a little. Then there was silence at the table, and all listened.

"It was in Abyssinia. Some natives were digging for the treasure which is everywhere believed to be hidden underground. They found instead of treasure a great stone vault, into which they broke an opening, for it had neither door nor window. Around it the earth lay apparently undisturbed for ages, and above it grew a tree hundreds of years old. They found within the vault not indeed the treasure they looked for, but an old man. He was thin and worn — say rather wasted; his beard was white and his head was bald. How had he lived in that stone vault? How long had he been there? I repeat, there was neither door nor window, no means of getting fresh air, no visible means of communicating with the world, no way of passing food into the vault. And the roots of the tree, hundreds of years old, were lying over and around the vault. We who know more than the world generally knows immediately recognized in that old man a famous philosopher once celebrated by his disciples, long, long since lost sight of, and forgotten many, many generations ago—and all these years, with animation suspended, he had been meditating in the highest rapture—that state which few, indeed, can possibly attain."

"Well? Finish the story," said Lady Augusta.

"They brought him out into the open air, and as he breathed again he opened his eyes and looked around him. Then a wonderful change came over him; for his wrinkled skin filled out, and his flesh came back to his bones, and his eyes became bright, and his hair became black. He was once more a young man, strong and comely."

"Oh!" they all murmured together. But Mr. Emmanuel Chick drank off a whole glass of champagne, and pretended not to listen. And Tom grinned.

"Then he looked about him, and saw the city close by, and the shepherds with their flocks. And suddenly he vanished, and was no more seen."

"That young man—it was you yourself, Herr Paulus."

"No, Lady Augusta," he replied, sadly. "I wish it had been; for that young man has now attained the highest felicity possible for man. I tell you the story that you may understand that among my friends there is no such thing as age or youth or death, unless it be willed and chosen. In other words, if my friends please they may look young; and if they please they may look old."

This was a strange kind of talk to hear in a London house, at a London dinner. But then this was no ordinary house.

"Oh!" Lady Augusta heaved a profound sigh—about the twentieth at that dinner. "I had always longed, but never ventured to expect, that one of the wise men of whom we have read would actually come to my house."

"There are Englishmen among us," Herr Paulus added. "Not many, but a few who break away from the shallow creeds of the present, and seek to conquer for themselves the powers and the secrets of the past. But they refuse to leave the place where they reside, even to preach among their own countrymen. Therefore I am sent."

"No better ambassador could be sent," said Lady Augusta, graciously.

On the other side of Herr Paulus sat Lady Augusta's old friend, Mrs. Tracy Hanley. She had been privileged to read some of Sister Anna Petrovna's letters. She was thinking all the time that if the young man talked in this beautiful and bewildering way, what an effect he would produce at her Sunday Evenings, especially if he would "do" things. This was a selfish view to take of the highest philosophy and the Ancient Wisdom, but ladies who have Sunday Evenings are often inclined to that form of selfishness. She looked at him and listened. The longer she looked the more she was impressed—wholly from the Sunday Evening point of view—with the strange beauty of his face and his lovely dark eyes. The more she listened the more she fell in love—always from the Sunday Evening point of view—with his soft and musical voice. If he would only "do" things. At this house, where manifestations of all kinds were common, whatever he might do would be received in a coldly critical spirit, like the jugglery of a conjurer among his professional brethren. But at hers, where nothing better than the common medium of commerce had ever been introduced, he would be received with delightful surprise. A young man, mysterious in name and of *unknown origin; a young man* who might

be of fabulous age; a young man romantic in appearance, possessed of good-manners, and endowed with miraculous powers; a veritable prophet of old, but in evening dress, not a sheepskin; a youth sent from the Lord knows where by the Lord knows who, to preach a new and mysterious doctrine—but it all depended on what he could "do." Why, such a man as this, if he could really do things, would make her Sunday Evenings celebrated. He would cause them to become the talk of the town. It would be a privilege to have the entrée at those Sunday Evenings. The world would rush to her rooms. This pleasing vision floated through her brain while the young man talked. Why should it not be realized?

She began to recall all the successive prophets and lions who had passed through her house in the last ten years. There was the Baboo, for instance, clever and fluent, who had come over to England all the way from Bengal on purpose to teach us Theistic doctrines which we knew before. He could talk, certainly, but when he had been talking for an hour or so the men stole away and the women yawned. For his discourse was charged with the deadly flavor of the commonplace, while his conceit was profound, and his new gospel was certainly a poor thing compared with the old one. But even the Baboo was better than him of the sorrowful visage, that Agnostic who felt so profoundly the presence of the Abysmal Unknown, and yet was compelled by his enormous intellect to acknowledge only the Phenomenal. Both Baboo and Agnostic were played out. Then there was the languorous Æsthete, now also played out, though in his day he could satisfy the deepest yearnings of the soul with art, blue china, peacocks' feathers, and a dado. As for the Anarchist, the Nihilist, and the Socialist, they were only uncomfortable creatures who terrified people. No one would come twice to talk with a wild and spectacled Anarchist, who desired to destroy everything first, whatever was to be done next. No one who wished to keep the good things which the gods had given him would care to meet a Socialist more than once. Should he prevail, there would be no more drawing-rooms, and no more evenings anywhere, except upon the cold curb, and no more social gatherings except outside the street door. Again, there was the medium who might be hired at half a guinea, and who brought mysterious rolls and an accordion, and had the lights out, and played tricks too thin to delude the most credulous. Time was when he was seen at many houses; but he, too, was a thing of the past. What were such clumsy things as rappings, levitations, writing on the ceiling, and the rest, compared with such things as were told and hinted at by this beautiful and wonderful young man?

Here Lady Augusta looked round and rose.

CHAPTER V.

THE FIRST FUNCTION.

"No miracles yet, Dodo," Tom whispered, when, a quarter of an hour later, the gentlemen came into the drawing-room.

"This is not a common medium, remember, Tom," said Sibyl. "I suppose he must not be asked to sit down and show off, like Mr. Chick."

"We must have something, though," Tom replied, "if it's only to back up that awful cracker of his about the red man of Abyssinia."

The general impression in the room, which was now crowded with a large company invited to meet Herr Paulus, was that something very startling, indeed, was expected. The people looked at each other and at the guest of the evening with eyes that plainly spoke of general expectation. What did they expect? Most of them were old hands in research, who looked for nothing but some modification of the usual business to which they were thoroughly well accustomed. There might be music in a darkened room, but there was no accordion; there might be messages and raps, but there were none of the tubes, rolls of paper, and other accessaries of the common séance. There might be spirit photographs, an incarnated spirit or two, or perhaps some message a little out of the common. More than this was not expected by the experienced. Of course there was a sprinkling of young people, beginners in the mystic science, to whom every creak of furniture is a message from the dead, and every note on an accordion out of tune is the music of the heavenly spheres. And there were some, like Cicely Langston, who fervently believed in and ardently prayed for the coming of a new prophet with a new revelation. But the greater number consisted of the old hands. Among the latter was the well-known Lavinia Medlock, parent of Hetty, once the most fashionable of all the mediums, but now, like others, fallen into neglect and obscurity. She looked on with an anxious and wistful air, as if longing for a wrinkle which might start her afresh. Just so, if the comparison be allowed, the professor of legerdemain, when he is out of an engagement, frequents the exhibitions of those who are on the platform, in hopes of picking up something new. But Lavinia's day was passed. The Rev. Benjamin Rudge, too, historiographer in ordinary to the cause, await-

ed the events of the evening with more than common interest. It was long since there had been a sensation in Spiritualism, and he scented materials for "copy." He was hungry for new things, because there are lines of literature, one need hardly explain, which are more lucrative than that of chronicler to the Spiritualists.

"Again, Herr Paulus," Lady Augusta whispered, "will you forgive me? I have asked all these people to meet you, as if you were a common medium, such as come over to us every year from America, and want to get money from us."

"Your friends shall go away satisfied," he said, smiling.

In fact, a blank dulness was already falling upon the party, because it seemed as if the expected programme was not to be carried out. No arrangements had been made for a séance. Now, if one is asked to a party to meet a ventriloquist, ventriloquism is expected; if to meet a conjurer, we look for tricks; if to meet a pianist, we expect to hear him play; if to meet a most eminent professor of Spiritualism, we expect to have quite a conversation with the other world, and to get some new lights, at least, on the way that things are managed there.

"Will you have the room arranged?" Lady Augusta asked him. "My people are very quick in moving and arranging furniture."

"Not at all," Herr Paulus replied. "I want no special arrangements."

"The room can be darkened in a minute by removing the lamps. Shall I have a screen before the fire? and shall the people sit down?"

"No darkness, if you please. Oh, Lady Augusta!"—his eyes spoke pity, not reproach. "Darkness? And with the spirits of light? My friends, I assure you, have no need of darkness."

Lavinia Medlock heard and hung her head. All her manifestations had been produced in a darkened room. She had never known a single spirit who would work for her in the light.

Mr. Chick heard and sniffed, incredulous.

Everybody sat down who could find chairs, leaving a space in the middle of the room. Tom Langston remarked with some interest that Mr. Emmanuel Chick took up a position beside the piano-forte. This gave him a back view of the performer, and suggested a watchful, even a suspicious, attitude. Mr. Rudge and Lavinia Medlock were not slow to observe the movement, and nodded to each other, meaning that the evening might possibly end with a row—such a row as happens when a treacherous person strikes a match, and the medium is discovered capering about the room as the incarnated spirit, and playing the music of heaven upon an accordion.

Herr Paulus stepped quietly forward. He looked slowly round the room, and then, raising himself to his full height, he lifted his right hand suddenly and unexpectedly. Everybody jumped. No manifestation, however, followed this action.

Then he spoke.

"I have come to this country," he said, "with a message. Do not think, pray, that I am here as a professional interpreter and a medium by which spirits can convey messages to you. My friends, and those who are the accepted, have intercourse so free and unrestrained with the souls of the living and the dead, and with the spirits of the other world, that the poor and feeble utterances which have reached your ears are worthless to them. Look, if you please, into the record of the communications, and ask yourselves how far the world has been advanced by them. My mission is to teach—to those who are worthy the old wisdom — the Ancient Way. You see in me a servant, a messenger, one who simply carries out his orders. But as it is well to prove in some way that I am what I profess to be—a messenger—I have asked for and obtained certain powers. Do not, I pray you, think that these powers constitute my message. They do no more than illustrate it. Such powers as have been conferred upon me are within the reach—not of all"—he looked, perhaps unconsciously, at Lavinia Medlock — "but of some in this room"—his eyes fell upon Hetty Medlock, who sat in the front beside Cicely. "Those who desire the Ancient Way for the sake of getting the powers will never go far along that way, which is only to be trodden by the pure and unselfish. Listen!"

He threw up both hands, and seemed listening expectantly. In a few moments there were heard faint sounds of music far off. The sounds grew nearer and louder, though the strain was still soft, and the music seemed to be hovering over the operator's head—then it slowly receded, and died away in the distance.

"This," Tom whispered, "is a very good beginning. It beats the dark room and the concertina."

The habitués of the house — those who were accustomed to manifestations—nodded their heads approvingly. This was certainly, so far, better than the ordinary business. Still, they looked on calmly critical. Music at a séance is not an original feature. Mr. Emmanuel Chick scowled, perhaps because he did not understand how it was done, perhaps because he felt himself ill-used by his own spirits, who had never consented to

vouchsafe music except in a darkened room.

When the music died away it was followed by a most melodious tinkling of silver bells, which behaved exactly like the music, drawing nearer, tinkling immediately above Herr Paulus's head, and then receding.

"Good business again, Dodo," Tom whispered, "but old. We've heard the bells before. To be sure the room was always dark. Wonder how the beggar does it."

Then lo! a miracle! Herr Paulus suddenly threw up both his arms, and there were seen fluttering into his hands two light and thin packets of silver paper. Where did they come from? Observe that the room was quite full of people; that they were all looking on; that there was a blaze of light; and that the testimony of all—all but one—would have been exactly the same. "I saw," they would have said, "the papers fall from the ceiling into Herr Paulus's hands." The one exception was the young man of science. Tom, more prudent, would have said, "The papers seemed to fall into the man's hands." This, it will be observed, involves great reservations.

Herr Paulus gave the packets into the hands of Lady Augusta.

"Do not open them yet," he said. "You are going to witness a really remarkable illustration of the powers possessed by my friends. Take it as a special mark of their favor."

Then he turned and surveyed his audience without the least touch of triumph in his eyes; and he did not, as Mr. Emmanuel Chick would have done, proceed to call attention to the wonderful manifestation of the spirits. He looked round the faces slowly, as if searching for something. They represented all the stages of bewilderment, from the cataleptic condition of those who believe everything they see, to the irritated and puzzled condition of those who see, and yet preserve something of the critical faculty. Mr. Emmanuel Chick from his position in the rear watched the operator jealously, Lavinia Medlock enviously, Tom suspiciously.

"The fellow conjures," said Tom, "as well as Maskelyne and Cook."

"Hush!" said Sibyl. "Perhaps he is going to do something much finer. See."

Did you ever see the mild Hindoo perform his feats? When you have done so, you will go about for the rest of your life declaring that the impossible became possible; that miracles were performed before your eyes compared with which the saintly records are poor and tame. Men are decapitated before the eyes of the audience and then restored to their heads; boys are stabbed and gashed all over without consequent injury; deadly snakes are handled with impunity; dry sticks blossom like Aaron's rod. Why, a great Indian emperor has set down in writing, so that all may read, how some jugglers came to him, and performed before him and all his court twenty-eight distinct miracles, each one more wonderful than its predecessor. Do you think they actually do the tricks? Not so; and yet those who tell of them do not lie. What happens then? If one could answer that question one could produce exactly the same effects as those for which these same jugglers got the Imperial gift of fifty thousand rupees, many years before the depreciation of that coin.

"Some of you," said Herr Paulus, "have heard of certain Orientals who possess powers which are now unknown to the West. I say now, because there is evidence that in the Middle Ages, and even later, there have been many who had attained in some measure to these powers. There have been monks who could converse with the spirits. There was a nun named Hildegardis who in moments of rapture could compel the other nuns to think exactly as she pleased. There were also the brothers and sisters of the Free Spirit, who arrived at great powers; and the so-called friends of God, who were also Spiritualists of a high order. It is, therefore, no new thing that you are invited to observe. Among the powers are those of conversing with each other without respect to distance; of joining each other instantaneously; of knowing what their friends are saying and thinking; of telling what is in the minds of those who are not their friends; of making people see what they order, say what they wish, think what they choose. These powers are not born with us; they are conferred or acquired as one advances in true wisdom. You know that as you climb higher the air grows clearer and the vision sharper. It is so with the Ancient Way. Or, to take another illustration, if you dig wells in the ground they will naturally fill with water. You do not pour water into them. The waters fill them by the laws of nature. I do not pretend to these powers in their highest form. But I will try to show you what some of them mean."

He looked again about the room. All faces were turned towards him; all eyes looked into his, and to some it seemed as if his eyes saw through them into the hidden soul. But perhaps that was due to the excitement of the nerves.

The blind girl, Cicely Langston, sat immediately before him. Beside her sat her companion, Hetty Medlock. Cicely was sitting in her customary impassive attitude, her

hands in her lap, but her cheek was flushed, and she was excited by the strange music and the bells, and the wondrous talk about supernatural powers of the young man with the soft and musical voice. Her fingers nervously opened and closed, her lips trembled, half parted.

"Hetty," she whispered, "why is he stopping? Tell me—tell me—what is he doing?"

"He is asking Mrs. Tracy Hanley to play something. It is she who is playing."

"Oh, it is coarse and common after the other music," said Cicely. "Go on, Hetty, what next?"

"Oh, is it true? Is it true? Can it be true after all?" A strange question for the daughter of a medium. Hetty had turned pale and her eyes were fixed upon Herr Paulus. "Now he is standing quite still; he is looking slowly round the room, he is looking at Sibyl and at lady Augusta. He is looking—oh, he is looking—at me!"

She said no more. The magician's eyes met hers, and she rose and walked across the room before them all and stood before him.

"Oh, my daughter! Oh, my child!" cried Lavinia Medlock. But the accents were those of joy and surprise, and not of terror. Never before had she seen that look in her daughter's face; and it betokened—she recognized it with delight—a higher gift than ever had been hers—the strange and wonderful gift of clairvoyance.

"Sit down," said Herr Paulus.

There were some who said afterwards that before Hetty left her seat there was no chair in the middle of the room; but this lacks confirmation.

Hetty obeyed. Then with a single motion of his hand he seemed to close her eyes. The girl was now leaning back in the chair, pale, with set lips and closed eyes. Her hands were lying in her lap, tightly clasped. She did not look as if she slept, but as if she was waiting to do something—one knew not what.

Herr Paulus bent over her, and it seemed as if he breathed gently upon her head.

"We inhale oxygen and hydrogen into the natural lungs," he explained. "With the spiritual lungs we breathe what for want of another name has been called aura. My aura has fallen upon this young lady's head and has entered into her soul. She will now, as you will see, think only as I shall direct her."

"It ought not to be allowed," Tom murmured.

"Why not?" said Sibyl, the experienced. "I have seen them like this dozens of times, and it never does anybody any harm."

She spoke as one who has been watching

these phenomena all her life, and thought little of them and expected nothing from them.

"This," cried Mr. Emmanuel Chick, loudly, "is nothing in the world but pure mesmerism."

"I beg," said Mr. Cyrus Brudenel, firmly, "that there may be no interruption at all! After the séance any one who wishes shall have the opportunity of speaking or of producing, if he can, by his own powers, similar manifestations."

Mr. Emmanuel Chick subsided, but with an effort. Herr Paulus, for his part, behaved like a practised speaker at a public meeting when some one unexpectedly gets up in the middle of his speech to propose an amendment; that is to say, he stopped speaking, but took no other notice of the interruption, treating the thing as if it had no kind of connection with himself. Meantime Mrs. Tracy Hanley went on playing mechanically, but wondering if the music and the bells and the leaves fluttering from the ceiling could be secured for her Sunday evenings. Like many sensible women, Mrs. Tracy Hanley considered the wisdom and the genius of man; his science, art, and letters; his inventions and his discoveries; his skill and dexterity; his genius and his ingenuity, as shadows and unsubstantial things compared with the solid realities of life as represented by herself and her Sunday evenings.

"I will now ask Lady Augusta," said Herr Paulus, " to give me one of the papers in her hand — any one. Thank you. There is a drawing on the paper. I command this young lady to see, in her vision, the subject of this drawing."

There was silence for a space. Hetty Medlock made no movement nor any sign of life. Herr Paulus gave back the paper to Lady Augusta, and made another single pass with his right hand. Hetty Medlock opened her eyes and looked about her.

"Where am I?" she asked.

"You are safe — with friends. Do not fear. You have had a vision in your sleep. Can you recall it? Can you tell us of what you dreamed?"

She hesitated.

"Nay, tell us the whole. There is nothing to fear."

"I was in a country—I know not where—I was happy, much happier than I am in this world." She spoke with a kind of constraint, as if reluctantly. "I was free to do what I pleased and to go where I pleased. I could have what I wished—pictures and music, and a beautiful house and gardens, and money to give away. I was not only rich, but able to write the most wonderful

things. The people sang my songs and I was powerful. Then they brought me out and crowned me Queen!"

"Do you remember the place and manner of your coronation?"

"Yes, perfectly."

"Lady Augusta, will you kindly give me the paper I have just been holding in my hands? Yes—thank you. Will you tell me, Miss Medlock, if you recognize this picture?"

Hetty took the paper. There was a watercolor drawing upon it, though the paper was thin. The girl looked at it, and cried out in amazement,

"Oh, it is the very scene! And this is I myself whom they are crowning. Oh, give me the picture!"

"You shall have it when everybody has seen it. Let me pass it round."

There was no doubt possible that the girl had seen the crowning of herself. The dream itself was such as a girl, poor, young, not too clever, might easily dream—a vision of the unattainable. Yes, here was drawn in pale tints, Hetty herself, large-eyed, unmistakable, clad in a wonderful dress, going forth in grandeur, the people shouting around her.

And the drawing was good. Mr. Cyrus Brudenel held the paper up to the light.

"The water-mark," he said, "is Petersburg."

"I dare say it was painted there," said Herr Paulus, carelessly. "It must have been painted somewhere. Lady Augusta, I have done what I promised. Let me make one more experiment. May I ask Miss Cicely Langston to take Miss Medlock's place?"

"Oh, I say!" cried Tom. "Not my cousin."

"No harm—not the least harm shall be done to Miss Langston," said Herr Paulus. "I pledge my word as a—not as a gentleman —but as the messenger of my friends."

"I doubt the security," Tom murmured; and, satisfied with the repartee, which seemed rather sharp, he made no further opposition.

But the blind girl had risen at the first invitation, and walked without guidance straight to the spot where the chair was placed. Then she sat down as if she had neither the power nor the inclination to resist.

"The deepest wish of the blind is to see," said Herr Paulus. "I restore to you, for a few moments, Cicely Langston, the power of sight. Tell me what you see."

"I can see," she replied, but in a strange voice, and without the least movement of hands or head; and her eyes remained closed. "I can see. The room is full of people.

You are before me. You have dark hair and black eyes; there is a white flower in your button-hole, and you have a gold chain with a thing like a beetle hanging from it. You are looking at me. Yes. I will look round the room "—but he had not spoken. "I can see the others, but not so well as I can see you. Their faces are blurred. Why is that? I see Sibyl and Hetty and Tom, and many others; but they are not so clear and distinct as you are. And now they have all faded away and it is dark again."

"I cannot restore her sight permanently," said the young magician. "The time may come when this and many other things which now seem impossible will be in our power."

"Oh, I saw the room. I saw all of you. Oh, it was wonderful—wonderful," said the blind girl, reaching out her helpless hands.

Sibyl stepped forward and took her hands and led her back to her place.

"You have been persuaded, dear," she said. "You are among us—with your friends. Nothing has really happened. Nothing of the least importance."

"Nothing of the least importance," repeated Herr Paulus, gravely.

Then the people wondered what would come next.

"Since the séance has concluded," said Mr. Emmanuel Chick, "at least I suppose it has concluded—I think I may offer, as an older man, our congratulations to our younger brother on his progress in the mesmeric art. The display of mesmeric power is very creditable—very creditable indeed. So far we have seen nothing that could not be done by pure mesmerism. But I understood that we came here to receive communications from the spirits. In this house we are accustomed to converse freely with the spirits. We have been offered a mesmeric performance. That's all I wanted to say. A very good performance indeed; but it is not conversing with the spirits." He tossed his head and sat down with a sniff.

"It is not for me," Herr Paulus replied, with dignity, "to discuss the things that have happened. Perhaps the mesmeric force may explain the whole of the phenomena you have witnessed to this gentleman's entire satisfaction. If so, I have nothing to object. As for conversing with spirits, we converse daily and hourly with those whom I am allowed to call my friends. These are the wise spirits of humanity, living and dead, around us, here and everywhere. They converse with me without the intervention of knocks and raps. They tell me more in a quarter of an hour than you in England have learned from the raps in forty years. They have spoken to you twice already. They will

speak, if you wish it, once more. Is there any here who would like a message of consolation or of hope? Do not mock my friends, or it may be bad for us. Let no one speak who is not deeply and earnestly desirous of such a message."

The party sat perfectly still and silent. Then Cicely Langston spoke again.

"Tell me," she said, "about my brother."

"Your brother? Who is your brother? Oh, do not tell me. Yes—now I know—now I know. He has been gone for five years and has sent no letter, and you fear that he is dead. Yes. . . . I understand." He spoke quickly and without connection, as if he was listening to some one at his ear. "I understand. He has been at sea. His name is Percival—Sir Percival Langston. He is a baronet. He is not dead—he lives—he is well."

"Oh"—Cicely burst into tears—"is this true? Do you really know?"

"I know nothing," said Herr Paulus. "I have been told, just now, since you stood up, Miss Langston."

"Can it be true?"

"My friends are always true. But you shall see more. Sit down and raise your eyes to me. Think that you can see me."

Again he breathed upon her head.

"Lady Augusta," he said, "you have a second packet. I was wondering why the second packet came. Please give it to me."

He held it, still wrapped in the tissue paper, flat between both his hands.

"Tell me," he said, "what you see."

She replied, just as Hetty had done, as if she had no choice.

"I see a ship rolling about in the night on a rough sea, under a black sky. It is a sailing-ship. The decks are wet and the waves are breaking over her bows as she plunges. At the wheel I see my brother. He is dressed in big boots and a water-proof. He is a common sailor by his dress, and he is steering the ship. He does not think of me at all; his mind is full of religion; he cannot see me as I see him. Oh, I see his face and I know it is my brother, but I cannot tell why. Percival," she cried, holding out her arms—" Percival, speak to me—look at me."

Some of the ladies began to cry, and Sibyl again stepped forward to support the girl.

"You have played with her enough," she said. "Impostor or honest man—I know not which—you have played with her enough."

"Your brother will return," said Herr Paulus. "Sleep in peace to-night. Is it playing with her to calm her heart with the assurance that her brother is safe?"

He opened the packet in his hand and showed Sibyl the picture within.

The picture was what Cicely had described. There was the stern of a ship and there was the man at the wheel ; in the blackness of the night one could see little but the shrouds and the dim outline of the ship's bulwarks. "Who is that man?" he asked Sibyl.

"He is Sir Percival Langston," she replied.

Herr Paulus gave the picture to Lady Augusta, and it was handed round. Then a great awe fell upon the multitude. They were in the presence of one who could compel the truth. He had proved his power. Even Tom Langston scoffed no longer, though he would not give in.

Herr Paulus returned again to the middle of the room and spoke to the people, now silent and terrified. He spoke slowly, gravely, and with the utmost dignity.

"I have done what I was commanded to do this evening. You have seen something of the powers possessed by my friends—alive or dead. It is not some lower and baser spirit of the other world who may show himself, as you have proved, over and over again, untrustworthy, fickle, and even frivolous "— Lavinia Medlock groaned and hung her head as one who is the victim of misplaced confidence—"it is a man—whether alive or dead —whether in the flesh or out of it, matters nothing—who is wise and benevolent, who has acquired powers of which you cannot even dream—who has spoken to you this evening. Nay, there are many men whom I call my friends, but their action is as one. The manifestation has been made—the teaching will follow—to those who are accepted."

And then he retired into the throng and became only a simple guest like the rest. The séance, if that can be called a séance where there was not so much as a single rap, was concluded. But it had ended in a function which gave a solemnity to the evening. Out of the Unknown had come a manifestation of a kind never before experienced. The sightless saw; the absent became visible; the blind sister recognized the brother whom she had never seen before; she asked for news of him, and she received an answer in this strange and mysterious manner.

I cannot omit to add a concluding incident in the history of the evening.

Both pictures vanished.

They had been handed round and they vanished. Perhaps some one stole them and now keeps them secretly as precious spirit-paintings; perhaps they were drawn away as they came. The most diligent inquiry failed to trace them, and they have never since been seen.

Mr. Emmanuel Chick stepped briskly forward and held out his hand with fine effusion.

"Herr Paulus," he said, heartily, but with a gulp, "I congratulate you. Don't mind what I said about the mesmerism. Lor! I recognized a brother from the very first. We are fellow-workers, and we've got lots to teach each other."

The poor old professor looked deplorably common and shabby beside this handsome young man. His nose was red; his cheeks were puffed; he had taken at dinner as much wine as he could lay hands upon, and his voice was thick.

"Pardon me," Herr Paulus replied, coldly, and without seeing the proffered hand, "I think that you have nothing to teach me. I am certain that I have nothing which I shall teach you. We are not, I assure you, either brothers or fellow-workers."

Emmanuel Chick fell back snubbed and disgusted. He has never since quite recovered the effects of that public snub. Indeed, he still spends long hours at times in trying to think what would have been the proper retort; and he can find none. There are cases in which the proper retort, which should be at once dignified and epigrammatic, is extremely difficult to find. For instance, there were once two men, both members of the Utter Bar, who met in the courts of the Temple — the one in wig and gown, hastening to court, the other in a pot hat, lounging to his chambers. Quoth the former to the latter, "That's a pretty kind of hat to wear in the Temple." The other waited till his friend was gone a little distance and well within hearing of a circle of men. Then he replied loudly,

"Not 'at, my friend; not 'at. Hat—hat. H A T."

The retort to this remark has never yet been discovered, any more than the retort to Herr Paulus.

Mr. Emmanuel Chick speaks of this evening still, with contempt, as one thrown away upon a bit of mesmerism and something artful done with the ceiling and some bits of paper. "As for the music," he says, "a confederate on the stairs with an accordion did the trick. Probably a footman. I've known spirits — real disembodied spirits— who would have done more than that for me. The picture business I call contemptible. It looked new at the moment, but it was contemptible. I'm old, I suppose, though, and out of fashion. But to think of the things I've actually done myself in that very room! Why, sir, when I was twenty years younger I have set every table spinning like a whipping-top. I've been carried up into the air by the spirits. I've been taken out of one window and brought into another; they've written on the ceiling for me;

they've sent messages by hundreds—comic messages, some of them, because they will have their joke—and why not? Why not, I ask you? Bless you, the room has been crammed with spirits—Peter, Katey, Joseph, Alexander—ay, dozens of 'em, and all willing and wishful to talk and be comfortable. And all he's got to show is a bit of fluttering paper and a mesmeric trick and a brazen, impudent, arrogant, supercilious cheek. It makes a man sick, sir, sick, to see the women 'umbugged and only wanting more."

That, in fact, is what people always do want—more. The smallest, briefest glimpse behind the veil, the least glimmer of light in the blackness around us, makes us only long for more. To-night afforded the clearest vision of supernatural powers which had yet been vouchsafed to seekers in any age. Things had been done which could not be explained by any theory of mesmeric force—strange, weird, and unexpected things; none of the ordinary machinery of raps, no darkness of the room, no sitting round tables, no singing of hymns, no uncomfortable suspicion of tricks, no vulgar medium, uneducated and coarse, holding out his hand to be paid beforehand, but a gentleman, refined in manners, language, and appearance, who would take no money.

They came—these friends of Lady Augusta—prepared to witness the common feats of Spiritualism. Some of them expected to go away and declare that the spirits had written on the ceiling in the dark; others looked for another example of the well-known frauds: people banged on the head with paper rolled up in long cylinders, writing on the ceiling by means of a piece of charcoal in a pair of lazy tongs, the medium capering about the room in a white shawl, and so forth.

But there were none of these things. The believers went away with awe, and yet with their hearts aglow. And the incredulous felt that here was something which could not be accounted for by any of the previously discovered tricks and machinery. Mesmerism? But mesmerism will not cause pictures to descend from the ceiling, nor will it bring music into the air, nor will it cause blind girls to see and to know their long-lost brothers.

Alas! there was no more. And presently the people began to break up.

CHAPTER VI.

GOOD-NIGHT.

WHILE they were slowly dispersing there was a little opportunity for whispered confidences.

Lavinia Medlock, for instance—she had once been so truly great that nobody called her Mrs. Medlock, but Lavinia Medlock, just as one says George Eliot—succeeded in getting Lady Augusta to herself. She was one of those who always want to whisper confidentially, and, whatever she had to say, always led the conversation round to herself and her own wants.

"Oh, dear Lady Augusta!"—she sighed and clasped her hands—"Oh, it was too delightful. Nobody but you would have found and secured such a man. Oh, how fortunate we have been! Such powers! Such a fulness! Such an abundance; and what an outpouring upon my poor Hetty! Oh, he makes us poor common mediums feel so cheap and small. Oh, I should think he is too great to be ever taken in by a lying spirit, as happens sometimes to the best of us. Think of what I am and what I used to be. Oh dear—dear—and I so trusted Peter!"

"Yes, Mrs. Medlock, we are now on a different plane altogether."

"We are, indeed; and yet one feels, after all, that one has been a worker in the same field. Lady Augusta, it is already whispered in the room"—here she became very confidential—"that you are going to found a college—actually a college—for the pursuit of the Ancient Way."

"Really, it is the first I have heard of it."

"Oh yes, it is confidently whispered, and I would so gladly hellup."

"Well, Mrs. Medlock, I assure you that I know nothing of it. Any developments that may follow do not depend upon me."

"Not altogether. But everybody knows that you are our real leader, and I would so gladly hellup. And oh, Lady Augusta, you saw my Hetty—poor Hetty! I could never teach her anything—and to-night she has come out so beautifully. There is clairvoyance in her of the highest order. If she would only be guided by me!"

"You must not teach her to think of money, Mrs. Medlock, or you will spoil her."

"Well—perhaps—not yet. However, I hope she will keep better company among the spirits than her poor mother could contrive. And oh, Lady Augusta, a college wants secretaries and clerks, and how gladly would we hellup. Hetty could do the spirit-work and I could receive the fees, you know."

"All this is really premature."

"It is exactly the work for which I was fitted; I have been looking for it all my life. I could give you so much hellup. And oh, if you did but know how badly I want the work. The last society is broken up, and—and—here is that Mr. Rudge. Do you know why he was turned out of his last situation?"

Lavinia retired and the Rev. Benjamin Rudge advanced, smiling and unctuous. "A rich treat, Lady Augusta. A rich treat, indeed. Before retiring to rest this evening I shall commit a full account of the evening to paper. It has been an evening full of surprises and of instruction; an evening at once intellectual, spiritual, and religious—especially religious. The future will see magnificent developments of what we must now call, I suppose, the Ancient Way. As the movement grows and spreads—as it spreads and r-r-r-ramifies"—he swept space circularly with his hands—"you will want an organizer, a lecturer, a secretary. You may command me, Lady Augusta. My services are at your disposal. Poor Lavinia Medlock, it was kind to ask her here. You know why she lost her place the other day? The usual trouble," he whispered.

The worst of Spiritualism is that there is so broad a fringe. Every cause has its fringe, broad and narrow. Spiritualism has so very broad a fringe. Lavinia Medlock, for instance, now that people no longer ran after her, was fain to lecture for anybody who would employ her: she would act as secretary to any society; she would collect moneys to be applied to good objects; and her enemies said that there was always, sooner or later, trouble about those moneys. The Rev. Benjamin Rudge, on the other hand, the historiographer of the cause, had enemies too. They were constantly raking up old passages in his life—for he was no longer young—which he himself would willingly have forgotten. It is unmanly to rake up things which their authors would fain bury in oblivion. He had no cure of souls, and he darkly whispered that the bishops were in league to keep him out of any. He had been connected with societies, and terminated his connection in consequence of what he himself called the bad business habits which are always found among scholars and gentlemen; but his enemies called them by a different name. Whenever he stepped to the front in the public gaze, somebody always wrote nasty letters asking if this was the same reverend gentleman who ten years ago did so and so. He had written a book or two on subjects not commercially valuable, he occasionally got some hack literary work, and was generally attached to some unsuccessful journal. But concerning this evening's work he saw his way, by the exercise of a rather limited imagination, to write a paper or two which would be worth a month's dinners.

Then Sibyl advanced to the young prophet. *She intended to speak* her mind to him

boldly; but she was stricken with awe like the rest.

"Herr Paulus," she said, earnestly, "do you, in very truth, possess these powers? Are you only mocking a poor girl who lives in constant anxiety about her brother? Are you only mocking a poor girl who lives in constant anxiety about her brother?"

"Indeed, Miss Brudenel," he replied, earnestly, "you do me an injustice by the mere suspicion."

"Other mediums have been asked, but they told us nothing. Yet it is easy to deceive a girl through her affections."

"Miss Brudenel, I assure you on my honor—on my word—I swear to you that I have not deceived you."

"It was the likeness of my cousin, but in a common sailor's dress."

"I do not understand that any more than you do. My friends permit me to tell you more. Your cousin is, in fact, a common sailor at this moment. He is in mid-Atlantic, on board the *Willing Bride*, of Quebec, sailing-vessel, laden with timber, and bound for the port of London."

"Is it possible? And he will come safe to shore?"

"I do not know. Believe me, I have told you all that I know—all that I have learned —from my friends."

"I thank you, Herr Paulus."

Sibyl retreated, and a gentleman slipped forward who held out his hand.

"To our better acquaintance, Herr Paulus." He had a commanding presence and a remarkably deep voice. "My name is Kilburn — Athelstan Kilburn — not quite unknown in the spiritual world here, though perhaps in Abyssinia—"

"My friends know everybody, Mr. Kilburn. I confess, however, that they have not instructed me as to your history."

"Never mind, that will follow. My history, sir, is the history of the cause in this country from the very beginning. I identified myself with it even before my friend Brudenel came into it. We are coarse and common operators compared with you, Herr Paulus. But such as we are I shall be glad to tell you all about us. There have been rogues among us—plenty of rogues among us; and lying spirits have vexed us. But you shall hear. And you have come to instruct us—me among the number, I hope. Good-night, Herr Paulus." His voice sank deep as if he was going to sink into the earth.

His place was taken by the Rev. Amelius Horton, the Senior Fellow of King Henry's College, Cambridge. Mr. Horton's friends were perhaps right in considering his manner as flighty, but there was confidence in his assertions,

"Pray, sir," he asked, "have you ever turned your thoughts in the direction of healing?"

"Sometimes."

"I possess, myself, the gift of healing in a somewhat remarkable degree. Only last Sunday, in the Gray's Inn Road, I made a cripple throw away his crutches and walk upright."

"Does this power remain always with you?"

"N—no. I confess that it does not. It is fitful. If it were steady I should establish myself as a healer, and close all the hospitals."

"I have been enabled myself, on occasions, to exercise this power. The last time was a year ago, when I healed a whole village in Abyssinia, where every inhabitant was stricken with the cholera."

Mr. Horton gazed at him with admiration, mixed, perhaps, with a little incredulity.

"My dear sir," he said, "if you have that power, why not rid the whole world of disease?"

"It would be a truly useful work, if it were permitted; but I will answer your question by another, Mr. Horton. In your ordination as priest, I believe the bishop gave you power to absolve sin?"

"Certainly."

"There was no condition attached?"

"Certainly not."

"You possess, then, a much more precious gift than I, and since you have this power, Mr. Horton, why do you allow the sins of humanity to weigh upon us for an instant? Absolve us all, dear sir. Let us all start from this moment with a clean slate. As soon as the sins of mankind are taken away, I will rid them of their diseases."

Mr. Horton made no reply.

Then other guests came and murmured words of applause and congratulations, and of hope that this evening would be followed by many others equal in interest and in wonder. Very pretty things they said, and the young man replied to each with an admirable grace and ease. And to the ladies the wonderful charm of his eyes brought conviction as to his truth and sincerity. As Lady Augusta prophesied, he was already a success. The last was Mrs. Tracy Hanley.

"I want to ask you to my Sunday evenings, Herr Paulus. We are quiet people; there is no crush with us; you will find in my rooms rest and sympathy. I feel that after those manifestations you will need repose and sympathy. You will not be asked to exhibit your truly marvellous powers, and you will find only friends, true friends, who have learned to trust and love each other."

"You are really most kind," the young man replied, astonished at this unexpected proffer of friendship from a complete stranger. "I am, however, in Lady Augusta's hands."

"That will not prevent you from coming. Then I shall expect you, Herr Paulus, next Sunday evening?"

"Perhaps not next Sunday. I never make appointments, because I may be called away by my friends, or ordered upon some special service. Will you kindly let me come on any Sunday evening when I am free?"

"Certainly, we shall always be happy to see you. Not as a lion, understand. I never have any lions." This was quite true, but oh, how devoutly she wished that she could have one or two in the season! "Only a very quiet circle of friends, with music and talk. Where the people are anxious to make each other happy the talk is always pleasant. Mere wit, mere epigram, is apt to wound. Sometimes my friends do what they can to amuse each other. If you feel disposed—but no; you shall feel yourself perfectly at liberty; you shall not come hampered by any feelings of obligations. We shall lay ourselves out to amuse you, Herr Paulus, and you shall repose and be happy."

Was there ever a kinder or more gracious lady? She pressed his hand, smiled most sweetly, and retired.

"All the same," she observed to her husband—he was something in the City, where he toiled every day from ten till five, going out with his wife in the evening, and taking a back seat from eleven till one, two, and three in the morning, so that he really was a happy man—"all the same, if he does come I will have something out of him, if it is only a thought-reading."

And now the people were all gone, and only the house party remained. When the door shut upon the last of them, Mr. Cyrus Brudenel spoke. Hitherto he had said nothing; now he spoke. When a leader speaks, the broad earth trembles. He spoke with a certain tremor in his voice which showed that he was deeply moved, and he spoke with that earnestness of conviction which always made Sibyl feel so guilty, and he began by grasping Herr Paulus by the hand.

"This night," he said, "marks a new departure in spiritual research. Herr Paulus, I thank you in the name of all those who, like myself, have believed, through cruel disappointments and most unworthy deceptions, in the future of our cause. We have been like blind men—I see it now—waiting for a guide, or like ignorant men in a labyrinth trying all ways but the true way. What use to us have been our Chicks and our Medlocks?

What power had they? What control over the spirits? None. You have been sent by those you call your friends to show us the way. It is no longer by the fitful light shown by deceitful and vicious spirits that we shall try to advance, but by the steady glow of the lantern held up to us by your friends. We thank your friends through you. We have tried to maintain the constancy of our faith, but there have been times, I confess it, when our feet have seemed to be placed on the shaky and uncertain turf of a hidden quagmire. Now, thanks to your friends, we stand at last on *solid rock*. At last, I say, on *solid rock!*"

"You stand, indeed, upon the *solid rock*," repeated Herr Paulus, gently.

" Long ago, before I half understood whither our steps would lead us, I resolved that this house and all in it should be dedicated to the sublime research of spiritual truth. I have adhered to this resolution. I have given up my ambitions, my time, and my friends. My wife has given up her whole life cheerfully to the work. I have dedicated and set apart my daughter to be the Vestal Virgin of this great cause. If there is aught else that I can give, command me in that as well."

" My friends will take what is useful," Herr Paulus replied, with a quick glance at Sibyl, the Vestal, in whose eyes and in the quick flush of her cheek he saw rebellion. " Perhaps they will ask of you less than what you are willing to give. But your reward will be tenfold what you can give."

"And what — oh, what can we give you yourself?" asked Lady Augusta.

" Nothing, except your friendship, and— perhaps—your love. I want no money. My friends keep me supplied with all that I need. See. This is my purse." He drew it out and opened it. There were three or four small foreign copper coins in it. " That is my slender store. Food you can give me, and shelter."

" All the house shall be at your service," said Mr. Brudenel.

" Let me come and go unquestioned?"

" You shall have perfect liberty."

" There are times when I may have to keep my room for days or even weeks together, if my friends desire my presence, and I have to be absent in the spirit."

" You shall do in all things as you wish," said Lady Augusta.

" Do you always take meals like other people?" Sibyl asked, coldly. " Do people absent in the spirit eat?"

" The earthly body takes food."

" In that case, Herr Paulus, let us descend *once* more to earth. Please remember that *breakfast is served at half-past nine* and lunch-

eon at half-past one. There are no gongs in this house. Tea goes on here at five, if you care for tea. Good-night, Herr Paulus." She bent her head slightly and without the least enthusiasm. She had had time to recover from her surprise, and reflected that, after all, he was but a medium. " Come, Cicely dear. Good-night, mamma."

CHAPTER VII

THE SMOKING-ROOM.

IN Tom Langston's study, or workshop, the two young men, the prophet of the Ancient Way and the student of the Modern Way, sat on opposite sides of the fire. No two young men, apart from their professions, could be more unlike in appearance. The one ruddy, healthy, athletic, tall of stature, long of limb, and broad of shoulder, toughened and hardened by a thousand athletic sports—cricket matches, foot-ball matches, lawn-tennis matches, and boat-races, brave and comely and tenacious; the other thin and slight of figure, yet not fragile, as active and as springy as a young Frenchman, his tread as alert as a leopard, his eyes as quick as a hawk's, his features as delicate as those of any girl, his long, nervous fingers never for a moment in repose.

They both had cigarettes. Hermes, thrice greatest, would himself take tobacco if he lived in these days, and so would the two Bacons, Roger and Francis. Before each stood a glass of effervescent water innocent of whiskey.

They sat in silence and looked at each other furtively, for one was suspicious and the other was conscious of the suspicion, and, besides, was now for the first time in his life alone with a young English gentleman, a creature he had never before encountered. Apart from a natural irritation at feeling himself the object of suspicion—a thing which every prophet has to face — he was asking himself whether, with all the trouble he had taken to overcome certain early - contracted manners and customs, he had really acquired the tone which this young man possessed, of belonging naturally and, by birth to polite society.

" You are thinking of me," he said, presently.

"That is not a difficult piece of thought-reading," Tom replied. " I was."

" You were wondering who I am."

" More than that. I was wondering how you do it, first; and why you do it next."

" And you mistrust me."

" That also is not so difficult to perceive. I mistrust every man who pretends to super-natural powers, whether he calls himself Medium or Mumbo Jumbo."

"And you cannot clear your mind of the suspicion that I am come to plunder your guardian, and that I live by the exhibition of certain—may I say—powers—or shall I say—arts?"

"Well," said Tom, "let me ask the question once for all, why the devil do you go about the world masquerading and pretending?"

"What do I pretend?"

"You assume a name which does not belong to you. It is a German name and you are an American."

The young man reddened slightly. There is always a weak point in every man's armor, and he wished that his nationality should not be discovered by his speech.

"I have not pretended to be a German. I pretend to no country. Believe it or not—my name was imposed upon me by my friends. It is not, of course, the name of my birth. If I were to tell you my whole history you would regard me as a greater humbug than you do at present."

"Why?"

"Because I should have to tell you so much that you could not possibly, with your prejudices and ignorances, even pretend to believe. How else, pray, do I pretend?"

"You pretend that your performances of this evening were the work of spirits."

"Let me remind you that I did not say so. I said they were the work of my friends."

"You spoke of a message."

"True. I have a message. From my friends. I am here to deliver it. My message is for all who will hear it—to those of this house just because I have come here first—to you if you please."

"Well, then, take another cigarette. If it was the work of your friends you will not mind, I dare say, getting them to repeat it in this room. Let us have a flight of papers from my ceiling, or a little music in the air; or you may, if you please, try to make me think what you please."

Herr Paulus shrugged his shoulders.

"My message," he said, "is not for the incredulous. Let me look in your eyes. Steady. Look me straight in the eyes. So. Why, I might spend a lifetime upon you without any result. You would never be able to understand that there was anything in the world beyond what you see. You have not the first and most elementary sense required of those who try the Ancient Way. You believe in nothing but phenomena."

"Thank you; yet I do not believe all that I see."

"You saw that I compelled two ladies to think as I chose."

"That was pure mesmerism. Old Chick saw through that at once."

"You mean the spirit-rapper. Yes, I know his kind. It was by something of the nature of that force which you call mesmerism that these ladies were moved to think and act as they did. Many people of the lowest kind have this force, but cannot use it aright. In the hands of a person like your friend Chick it is like the electricity of a machine exhibited at a fair to make the rustics gape. In the hands of my friends it is a force far subtler, far more potent than you can even conceive. This force is the basis of all spiritualistic influence."

"It sounds pretty, but isn't it rather a waste?"

"Without this force," Herr Paulus went on, regardless of this rude interruption, "the communion of minds is impossible, and the understanding of speech would be impossible: living men could not influence and advise and lead each other; the power of oratory would be gone; the poet's words would have no meaning; the writer would write in vain; spirits living would no longer be able to converse with spirits dead; distant friends could not converse—"

"Come, I say!"

"You believe nothing. You think that all is answered when you explain a thing by saying that it is mesmerism. Scientific men thought that all was explained when they discovered the law of gravity. But the discovery of the law does not explain the force which is governed by the law. So the explanations of phenomena by referring them to mesmerism do not really explain them. Not at all. Mesmerism of the higher kind is the machinery by which we work. Ask your friend Chick to do what I did to-night. He can, I suppose, mesmerize in the old-fashioned clumsy method, and on patients who are easily moved. But when he has got them into the mesmeric trance what can he do more? Nothing. Why? Because he has got to the end of his power."

"Do something with me now; let me prove your powers."

"No; I can do nothing with you or for you. Why should I try to convert you? It is not my business. If all the world refuse to believe, it will not harm me."

"Then why did you come here?"

"To speak to those whom it may concern. To give my message."

"Did you make any inquiries about us before you came?"

"Of course. On my way from St. Petersburg I was informed by my friends of many particulars concerning this family. I will tell you some of them. I do not pretend

3

to know more than I am told. Mr. Cyrus
Brudenel, your guardian, is a man who ardently desires to be a Spiritualist and to acquire power. He is not, however, a medium,
and he never will be. He has been greatly
imposed upon, and yet he has done excellent
service in preparing the minds of men and
women, against all kinds of ridicule, for the
reception of higher truth. Lady Augusta,
again, is a fervent believer, and yet is not a
medium. But she too has done good service
by her unwavering faith; and she has social
position, which has also proved and will continue to prove useful. Miss Brudenel is not
a believer, though as yet she has not ventured to confess her infidelity. The *rôle* of
Vestal imposed upon her by her father will
never be played by her, nor will she ever become an oracle. Your cousin, Miss Cicely
Langston, deplores continually the loss of
her brother, who is not dead. He went away
from home, giving up his title and his fortune, five or six years ago, intending to take
up his lot with the common people; and he
has never made any sign of life. You are
the heir of his property and of the baronetcy
if he is dead. But I think you will never
succeed, because he will return. I shall take
his sister to him unless he comes to her."
"Where is he, then? And when will he
return?"
"He is on board a sailing-ship bound from
London to Quebec. I shall be told in good
time when he returns. Why should I trouble to find out things when my friends tell
me what is wanted? As for you, your fortune will be given to you by your guardian,
Mr. Brudenel, in about a month's time, when
you arrive at your twenty-fourth birthday—
exactly on the same day your cousin will be
twenty - one and will receive her fortune.
You have a mechanical turn, and you oc-
cupy your time when you are not in the
physical laboratory in making those pretty
little ingenuities in brass which I see on the
table there. I confess that I know nothing
about them. Have I told you enough?"
"You undoubtedly know a great deal.
But you might have learned all that by inquiry. My people are not quite unknown."
"Then I will tell you more about yourself. You have been touched by the preva-
lent socialist ideas, like your cousin, Sir
Percival; you think that every man ought
to live by the work of his own hands."
"Yes," said Tom, now really surprised.
"I think it is for most men the greatest misfortune in the world to be born rich."
"You would not think so, perhaps, if you
had been born poor. You think, besides,
and you have constantly asserted your belief,
that we are on the eve of the greatest revolu-

tion—a universal revolution—that the world
has ever seen."
"I do. How do you know that?"
"You are right, and yet the revolution
will not be what you think. Yes "—his eyes
lit up and his whole face smiled—" it will be
the greatest revolution that the world has
ever seen. A revolution in everything; the
rich will become poor, yet not as you think,
and the prizes will once more fall to the
strongest hand, yet not as you think. You
believe this, and you have said it more than
once among your friends."
"I have. How do you know it?"
"Certainly I have never talked with any
of your friends. How did I know it? By
mesmerism? How did I learn the facts
about your family? By mesmerism? How
did I learn the existence of your cousin?
Was it all by mesmerism?"
He threw away the end of his cigarette
and walked over to the table, where lay cogs
and wheels all in shiny brass of some curious and beautiful machine which Tom was
making.
"I understand nothing, for my part, about
machinery. Wheels and mechanical contrivances of all kinds bewilder me. I cannot
even try to understand how cogs and springs
produce effects so marvellous. Yet I give
you credit when you tell me there is use in
machinery, and that you understand its laws
and can make it your servant."
Tom laughed.
"You have me there. You mean that I
should give you credit for understanding
something that I cannot."
The philosopher looked him straight and
full with the eyes of an honest man.
"That is precisely what I mean."
"It's half-past twelve," said Tom, looking
at his watch. "See now—are you going to
stay long in this house?"
"I think a month or two. Perhaps more.
There is talk of a great conference.'
"And will there be much hanky-panky?"
"Perhaps a great deal."
"Old Chick, before he took to drinking,
used to fill the place with spirits. They were
the very worst kind of spirits you ever saw.
And they talked the very worst kind of drivel. They did, upon my honor. If you knew
what a lot of humbugs and impostors my
uncle has been harboring and encouraging—
if he found one out it was only to welcome
another—you would not be surprised at my
distrust."
"I am not in the least surprised. When
I meet with persons like Mr. Emmanuel
Chick I am surprised at the strength of the
cause, since it survives even him."
"That's all right, then. Don't play more

than you can upon the women's feelings. But if you really bring back my cousin— poor old Percy—I'll forgive you everything. And—and"—Tom said this very unwillingly —"you are not like the ordinary run of 'em. Your voice rings true; and—well—look here now, we'll be friends, unless I find you out. Mind, I shall always be on the lookout for you."

The messenger laughed pleasantly.

"I tell you how I work, but you do not believe me. It is through my friends beyond the seas. We shall be friends, then, until you find me out. Give me your hand. Now, since you will never find me out, we are friends for life."

Ten minutes later Tom laid himself between the sheets in the room adjoining his study. He was a young man absolutely without the least sense of the supernatural; he never felt the air around him grow still and his heart tremble with the vague terrors which assail some men even in places and at times when they least expect to feel that phantoms of the outer world are round them. He would have slept in a charnel-house, surrounded by skulls and skeletons, without a tremor; all the associations possible of murder, cruelty, and guilt and remorse would have failed to move him. Therefore, when just as he was dropping off to sleep he heard strange music over his head, seemingly in the room, he was not terrified at all, but only startled. He sprang out of bed swiftly, locked the door and took out the key. Then he struck a light. There was no one in the room, and the music ceased. He blew out the candle and got into bed again. Then the music began once more.

"It's deuced clever," said Tom. "For a trick, it's as good as anything I ever saw, and it seems a pretty kind of tune—soft and melting—twice as good as old Chick's accordion. Well, if his friends mean to be polite they haven't been long in making up their minds. Very pretty indeed it is. Very pretty. I take it kind of them."

Then he fell asleep, and I have never heard how much longer the supernatural music was continued.

CHAPTER VIII.

THE SUBMISSION OF THE LEADER.

AFTER breakfast—always, in this house, a hushed and solemn function—Mr. Brudenel led the way to his study. He was more than commonly ponderous this morning, and more than commonly nervous. The events of the preceding night would have filled him with delight but for the unfortunate revelation about the novel. It has been often proved that the gravest and most reverend of men have been, in their lifetime, devourers of novels, but it is disconcerting when a reverend leader is charged with spending the time supposed sacred to the study of magic and mystery in reading Ouida. Moreover, it was a true charge, and since Herr Paulus could only have known its truth by supernatural powers, the charge must have been brought forward either as a rebuke or as a threat. If a rebuke, it was presumptuous to the last degree in so young a man, and if a threat— how much did the young man know?

"This is — ah — my small library, Herr Paulus," he said, pointing with proud humility to the shelves filled from top to bottom with works on the subject to which his life had been given. "You will—ah—have my full permission to make any use you please of this small collection. Here you will find, I think, all the masters in the art—Cornelius Agrippa, Barrett's "Celestial Intelligence," the "Romance of the Rose," Eliphaz, Lilly and Dee, Manetho's "Fragments," Salverte's "Science Occulte," Naude's "Apologie," the recent works of Blavatzky, Olcott, and Sinnott." He stopped short in his communication because he perceived that the young man was looking at him and not at the books. "Perhaps," he said, coldly, "you already know the contents of these books."

"On the contrary," said Herr Paulus. "Outside certain lines I am a most ignorant person. I have, it is true, studied Solomon's Book of Wisdom, but these works of mediæval and Oriental pretenders I have not taken the trouble even to look into. Only it amuses me that you, the leader of Spiritualism in the country, should seriously invite an inspection of these writers."

"Yet the results of mediæval research—"

"There were no results." The young man spoke with a dogmatism which would have been offensive but for the calm assurance of his manner. "There never were any results. The books are absolutely without value."

Mr. Brudenel put up his eye-glasses and looked at the books on which he had spent so many hundred pounds. Would no spirit issue forth to contradict this arrogant young man?

"No—no results? No value?"

"Well, there is the value of history. These men, provided with a fragment of truth, groped about in the dark and found nothing. The books preserve the history of their researches. If that is valuable the books are valuable. If not—" He shrugged his shoulders.

"Have you read them?"

"Not one."

"How, then, do you know?"

"I know because I know. It is part of the wisdom of the Ancient Way to distinguish between truth and falsehood. How many of them have you read yourself, Mr. Brudenel? You do not reply. I will tell you. Not one. You have turned over pages which you could not understand. You have not read one. Burn your library, Mr. Brudenel. Burn it all."

"Burn my unrivalled collection? Sir, you presume too far. I would have you to know—"

"You have not read one single book, Mr. Brudenel. You know nothing of the subject. Here is a book which professes to show you how to raise spirits." He took a volume from the shelves. "Do you know the method? Have you ever tried to raise a spirit? Here is another book which teaches you how to find the Philosopher's Stone. Have you found it? Here are the secrets of Astrology. Can you cast a nativity?"

"But—but—do you pretend that the claims of all the mediæval philosophers have been baseless?"

"Not quite baseless. In the same way the modern so-called occult philosophers and esoteric Buddhists are not baseless. Their pretensions rest on the fragments which were brought to the East from Syria. So the pretensions of the mediæval seekers rest upon the fragments preserved by the learned Jews of Spain and Morocco, and handed down from father to son. But in Abyssinia we have the perfect book, the King's own book, brought to us by Prince Menelek."

"It is something to be told that we have fragments," said Mr. Brudenel, coldly.

"Yes, you have fragments. They have enabled you to get a little way, but you can get no farther. Consider! You have been a seeker for thirty years, and what do you know now more than you knew when first you began?"

"There are some who think we have made great advances."

"You have made no advance at all," said Herr Paulus, firmly; "and if you continue in your present line you will make no further advance."

"After all," the leader objected, but without much force, "one cannot overthrow the fabric of thirty years on the dictum of a strange youth."

"Fabric!" Herr Paulus drew himself up and assumed the aspect of one who teaches and admonishes. "Fabric! What fabric? You have none. You have not even the dream, the simulacrum, the deceptive image of a fabric. In your thoughts at this moment I read the secret consciousness of failure. Confess! Failure! Your whole life has been

a failure. You have been buoyed up by false hopes; you have trusted in one impostor after the other. Deceptions have met you at every turn. Confess! Your whole life has been a failure. You have nothing solid—nothing—nothing. Confess!"

His dark eyes flashed, his accent was stern, his forefinger was menacing. Heard one ever before of a leader thus rebuked? His aspect was severe. Mr. Brudenel turned away as if afraid to meet those eyes, and hung his head and stammered something about the joy of research. But it was very feeble.

"Your life has been a failure, and you know it and feel it. Confess! Look in my face—look at me. So." Mr. Brudenel obeyed slowly and unwillingly, as if he was compelled. He raised his eyes and met the steady, fervent gaze of the masterful young man. "Confess all that is in your mind!"

Mr. Brudenel sunk into a chair. All his dignity was gone, and his stiffening. He collapsed. And still his eyes were fixed and held by those of his guest.

"I do confess," he said. "My life has been a failure. For long years I have known it, but I was ashamed to acknowledge it. And I was surrounded by believers who looked up to me. Had I confessed the truth, it would have been a dreadful blow to my wife and to everybody. Every year I have felt it more and more. I have lost my self-respect. I have been a wretched humbug, pretending to believe. I have come here, every morning, pretending to study, but in reality to read novels and to forget the cant of the Spiritualists."

"It is enough. Say no more. Own, however, that I read your thoughts rightly."

Mr. Brudenel, the power of those eyes removed, began to recover a little. He sat up in his chair and put up his glasses.

"I have told you, Herr Paulus," he said, "what I never thought to tell any man. You have the secret of my life. Respect it, sir."

"Indeed, Mr. Brudenel, I had the secret of your life before. Do not doubt that I shall respect it."

"I am glad to have told you. Now you know all, and there is no longer any occasion for us two to talk about the phenomena. Perhaps some day you will tell me how you did the things last night. I seem to know how most of them do their tricks, but yours, I confess—"

"You are terribly wrong—most terribly wrong, Mr. Brudenel. If I have been sent to you in your hour of deepest dejection, it was not only to tell you that your efforts have been unavailing, nor was it to perform tricks."

"The time was," the leader continued, without listening to this interruption, "when I rejoiced in my researches, and looked joyfully forward to the fuller light which was certain to come. Alas! that time has now gone, and I have nothing but regrets that I have thrown away my life among enthusiasts and common cheats. I confessed to you, Herr Paulus, because — you are young, but you seem honest — because you compelled me. That is done. Go on and frighten the women, and come here when you please to laugh at the whole business with me."

"Again, it is not my object to frighten the women and to laugh with you. Your past life is done with. But a new life begins if you wish for some splendid—"

"Oh, how am I to trust any one?" cried Mr. Brudenel, helplessly. "I want no new life, man. Henceforth I will go on like the rest of mankind. I shall cease to inquire into the other world. I shall go to church with my wife and the girls. No new splendors for me, thank you. I have done with it all." He threw out his arms with an expressive gesture. "Done with it, Herr Paulus. Done with it, I say."

"Permit me, Mr. Brudenel. I read in your looks—nay, in your mind—I read your dejection last night. You expected nothing but to be bored. Then you were surprised out of yourself. Then you expressed what you felt at the moment; but this morning another cold wave of doubt has fallen upon your soul. You no longer trust your eyes."

"That is so."

"The credentials which I exhibited have satisfied the rest of those who saw them—except your ward and—and perhaps one other. But you, rendered suspicious by frequent disappointments, recall them with doubt and questioning. The music in the air; the silver bells — you have heard something like them before in the darkened séance—they were produced by your Chicks and your Medlocks, with their concertinas; girls in a trance have been seen before; clairvoyance is no new thing; perhaps the picture of the very scenes which had passed through the girl's mind—which they actually saw—is an old trick too."

"No, no; I do not say so. The things were new and striking."

"Very good. Now, Mr. Brudenel, I am sent to you especially. It is to you that my message is given. If you are not convinced I will show you more credentials. What do you ask? Do not be afraid. Ask boldly."

"Do for me," said Mr. Brudenel, "what the occult philosophers have not done. Put in my hands an Indian newspaper of this very day."

"That is very easy," replied Herr Paulus. He put his hand in his coat-pocket and produced a paper stamped by an Indian postmark, addressed to Cyril Brudenel. "Here it is. Here is the *Friend of India* of this morning. Before you open it I must make a condition. There are in the paper all kinds of news—political, social, deaths, marriages, share markets — things not thought worthy of the telegraph—which *must* not be read before the day when in the ordinary course the paper would arrive. Open this paper. Satisfy yourself that it is the paper of this very day, which will arrive in London this day four weeks; then lock it up in some place accessible only to yourself, and do not look at it again until the day when all the world can see it. Do you promise this?"

"I would rather have its contents published to all the world."

"Consider. There may be things in it which it will be best to be learned at their proper time. To publish the paper may cause the ruin of merchants. Do you promise?"

"I promise."

"Then open the paper."

Mr. Brudenel tore open the cover, which Herr Paulus tossed into the fire. He looked at the date. Saturday, March 26, 1887. The date was printed on the front and on every page. He folded it up again with a deep sigh.

"You have actually done this wonderful thing," he said.

"Lock up the paper in the safe. So. That drawer will do. Lock the drawer and put the key on your ring. No one has access to the safe but yourself, of course. You will get the paper out and read it on the day when it is due by the mail, and not before. No one but yourself will know until then of its existence. Remember, you are not to look at the paper or to open the drawer until the time comes."

Mr. Brudenel did as he was told.

"And now sit down and let us talk."

It was then eleven o'clock.

At half-past one Herr Paulus and Mr. Brudenel came to luncheon.

The ladies became instantly aware that something had happened. I mean, of course, something important. Mr. Brudenel plainly showed that something had happened to him. In that house they were always expecting something out of the common, and last night's events had shown that they were on the eve of something very great indeed. Therefore Lady Augusta's heart beat faster when she saw that her husband had things to communicate.

"My dear," he whispered, just before they

sat down, "the most wonderful, the most stupendous manifestations have occurred. I will tell you about them after luncheon."

"Were they—were they—of the nature of last night's appearance?"

"No, no; quite different. Herr Paulus has done for me alone what the occult philosophers have never been able to do; and I have been translated in the spirit to Abyssinia. I have spent two hours—it seemed to me to be five-and-twenty—on a hill-side with the sole living possessor of the Wisdom which Herr Paulus calls the Ancient Way. Augusta, we shall not only be the happiest people in the world, but we shall also be the most powerful and the most celebrated. Be very, very kind to him, Augusta. We are on *solid rock* at last—at last—on *solid rock!*"

At luncheon Mr. Brudenel could eat nothing, being still under the influence of the morning's mystery. His cheek was flushed, his eyes were humid; the eager, nervous look was changed for one of satisfied assurance; his voice was soft. Some great change had passed over his spirits.

As for Herr Paulus, he attacked the luncheon with the appetite of four-and-twenty, and as if there were no dinner ahead. But the girls, Cicely and Hetty, waited for further information; and Sibyl looked suspicious.

In the afternoon Mr. Brudenel, worn out, perhaps, by the exertions of the morning, fell fast asleep in his study.

He slept from two o'clock until half-past four, in the deep and comfortable chair by the fireside in which he was wont to read Ouida while they thought he was pursuing cabalistic or other research. At half-past four he awoke with a violent start, springing to his feet.

"Good heavens!" he said, "was it only a dream?"

He rushed to his safe, unlocked it, and opened the drawer where he had laid the paper—the *Friend of India* of that morning, brought all the way to England in an hour or two by Herr Paulus's friends.

He had laid the paper in the drawer. He was certain he had; there could be no doubt in his mind about it.

But the paper was gone! There was not a trace of the paper left. Stay, at his feet was a scrap of the paper which had wrapped it, with a piece of his name, "—el, Esq.," and a corner of the Indian stamp. It was no dream, and then he remembered his promise that he would not open the drawer until the time came. He had broken the promise and lost the paper. Good heavens! he had practically fooled away the most stupendous of modern miracles by curiosity unworthy of a school-girl! The paper was gone. He

had held in his hands that very morning a paper brought all the way from India since daybreak. And it was gone! What a miracle! What a misfortune!

CHAPTER IX.

THE CONQUEST OF THE HAREM.

"WE spoke yesterday of the Ancient Way," said Herr Paulus. "Perhaps you would like to hear something more definite."

It was the afternoon of the same day, about half-past five. Tea was going on, and there were present only the ladies of the house, with Hetty Medlock. The twilight was falling, but the lamps were not yet lit nor the curtains drawn.

"The son of King Solomon and Queen Sheba," he began—

"What?" Lady Augusta was not often surprised, but this beginning startled her.

"The son of King Solomon and Queen Sheba," Herr Paulus repeated, "was, as every Abyssinian knows, the Prince Menelek. He was born in the Queen's capital, and was brought up in his native country. It is said that it was his mother's sole delight and solace, as soon as the boy could understand anything, to fill his mind with stories of the greatness and glory of his father, the wise King of Syria. When he grew to manhood he resolved to visit the city where his father had been king, and with a great retinue he set off. His route has been preserved, with many details, which are curious, but you would not care for them. He went down the Nile as far as the site of the modern Cairo, and then journeyed through the desert by the Serbonian Lake and the River of Egypt to El Avish, Gaza, and Joppa, whence he journeyed to the Holy City.

"He entered the gates of Jerusalem at break of day. He had not gone far when the people began flocking round him, the old men weeping, the women crying for joy, and the young men shouting; for his resemblance to Solomon was so great that they thought the old King had come back again to them with renewed youth."

"No part of this story," Sibyl interposed, severely, "is in the—"

"My dear!" said Lady Augusta, "we have here, perhaps, a contemporary chronicle."

"The tumult," Herr Paulus continued, "was heard in the Palace, where the King was sitting with his council. They heard the people cry, 'King Solomon has come back again! May the King live forever!' and sent a messenger to learn the cause. At first it was proposed to send soldiers to kill the man who presumed to be so much like the dead King; but it was finally agreed to bring him before the King, and to question him. Now, when he stood before the King, those who were old cried aloud, like the people in the streets, for astonishment, because it seemed to them that it was Solomon himself in the beauty and strength of his youth who stood before them. But the young man bore himself modestly, and made obeisance to the King, and when he had caused presents to be brought, he asked leave to speak, and said, 'O King, I am Menelek, the son of Solomon the Great and Queen Sheba of Abyssinia, from which country have I come, bringing gifts to thee, and desirous of seeing the great and glorious Temple which the King my father caused to be built, and his palace and all his glory, and then to return in peace into mine own country, if it please the King to suffer me to depart.'

"And it was done as he asked, and the King entertained him courteously, and all his following, for thirty days. And at the end of that time Prince Menelek would depart. Therefore, the King ordered all manner of precious things to be given to him, in order to show his friendship and good-will towards his brothers, and among the gifts thus prepared was a copy, so exact that you could not tell that it was not the original, of the Ark which is in the Temple, and it contained exact copies of all that was in the Ark. And here, the Abyssinians say, a strange thing happened, for there was in the Temple a priest named Isaac, a man stricken in years but full of learning, one who knew the hidden things. The priest, by much conversation with Menelek, fell into so great an affection for the young man that nothing would do but he must go back to Abyssinia with him, he and all his house. Nay, so greatly did he love him, partly because he was the son of Solomon, his master, and partly because he was a goodly youth, and one who loved to talk of things hidden from the multitude, that he did a strange and wonderful thing, of which the Jews to this day are ignorant. For, by the power of the Hidden Way, he threw a charm over the watchers and guardians of the Temple, so that they slept, or rather so that they saw, but saw not, and in the morning had forgotten, for they walked to and fro in their watch as if they were awake, and challenged each other and called the dawn, and sang the morning Psalms, while with his sons this old priest brought into the Temple the imitation of the Sacred Ark and exchanged it, taking away with him the real Ark and leaving in its place that which had been made for Menelek. And this, they say, would have been impossible in the lifetime of the King, partly because his servants, the Jinns, who day and night worked for him in and about the Temple, would have prevented it, and partly because the Shechinah above the Ark, which left it when Solomon died, would have blinded those who touched it. They brought away the Ark, therefore, with the tables of stone, and laid it on a camel, covered with a carpet, and led it away with Menelek and his train when he left Jerusalem. And the old priest took with him secretly the Book of the Wisdom of the Great King, the loss of which was never suffered to be known unto the people unto this day; and many of the Jews went with him because they would rather serve Menelek than Rehoboam; and their descendants, who are now called Falashas, remain in the land of Abyssinia to this day, worshipping after the manner of their ancestors. And to this day the Ark itself is in the hands of the Abyssinian King. And the Book of Wisdom, by some called the Book of the Hidden Way, and by others the Book of the Ancient Way, is in the hands of that priest's descendants to this day. This book is our book; this wisdom is our wisdom; the descendant of the priest Isaac is my master, Isák the Falasha, called Isák Ibn Menelek; and the Ancient Way is the Wisdom of King Solomon himself."

There were four women listening to this story. Three of them, like Queen Dido, listened with eager eyes and beating hearts. To them already this young man was an infallible prophet, before whom they were contented to surrender whatever of judgment, reason, and critical faculty they possessed. Is it wicked—I mean in the modern sense— to advance the doctrine that most women are entirely devoid of the critical faculty? Less than four-and-twenty hours had sufficed to make this young man the master of these three women. That he had not also become the master of the fourth was solely due to the extraordinary dislike with which this girl regarded all pretenders to supernatural powers, so that at the very aspect and first appearance of one she hardened her heart and stiffened her soul. But with regard to the others Herr Paulus came and conquered. His victory was due to his appearance and his manners almost as much as to the exhibition of his powers. If he had been the tobacco-reeking German they expected, badly dressed and badly mannered, uncouth and vulgar, his powers would have been acknowledged, but there would have been no enthusiasm for him.

"It was from Isák," Herr Paulus continued, "that I learned all I know. It is he who continues to teach me. I am in conversation with him every moment; even now, while I am speaking, I am receiving messages of instruction and support."

"Oh, it is wonderful!" Cicely murmured. "And I have seen my brother!"

Sibyl looked furtively at the man who dared to talk like this. Many men had come to that house and talked. Many pretentious assertions had been made; in every one she had recognized some old familiar stroke, some familiar stage business, and in every one there was at bottom the commercial element. Here the language and the pretensions were equally new to her, and the commercial element was, so far, wholly wanting. She hardened her heart with resolution, and looked at him again. His eyes met hers with a strangely searching and commanding look. Then a sensation fell upon her—one quite new and terrifying; she felt her brain overshadowed as by a cloud; she was drawn towards this man as by a rope; it was by a desperate effort that she seemed to snap that rope and to drive away the cloud from her brain. Again she met his eyes, and this time he turned away.

"There are many women," he said, "as there are many men, who cannot, if they would, tread this path. There are others— a few—who have the gifts but refuse to use them."

"They know, while they are free," said Sibyl, "what they are and what they do. They know not what may happen to them when they have surrendered their freedom and their will."

"Oh," murmured Lady Augusta, setting the worst possible example, "when a prophet leads, who would not follow and surrender all?"

Cicely and Hetty sighed, and the latter blushed a rosy red, as if there were too much happiness only in the thought of perfect slavery and submission.

Only four and twenty hours since he arrived. To be sure he had lost no time, nor did he fool around; but by methods known only to himself he dominated those three women and made them all his slaves. What he had said to each separately I know not. But now they were his.

"It is wonderful," said Cicely again, to whom new worlds were opening. "It is truly wonderful."

"I was selected—I know not why nor where—for the work by Isák himself."

"Were you taken in infancy?" asked Lady Augusta.

"No," he laughed, gently. "I am going to tax your credulity to the utmost."

"Oh, after last night is there anything which we would not believe?"

"Thank you, Lady Augusta. It was for you and for this house that the manifestations of last night were granted. In them-

selves they were trifles light as air; but they served for credentials. You will believe me, therefore, when I tell you that the earliest thing I remember is when I was seventeen years old. As for my previous life, where it was spent, what was my name, who were my parents, what was my country, I cannot tell you. Isák called me Paul. I could not speak a word of the language at first."

"What is their language?"

"The Falashes preserve the knowledge of Hebrew; but among themselves they speak Amharic. My education was in that language. But to us all languages are alike. When we find ourselves in a foreign country we speak its language."

"Anna Petrovna says that you speak Russian like a native."

"While in Russia I did, no doubt. If you asked me for a Russian sentence now I suppose I could not give you one. But there is one thing which makes me think that English is my native language—it is that I am sometimes taken for an American. This seems to me to show that my childhood may have been passed in the United States, and that when I speak English I return to the tongue of my forgotten years."

"It is possible," said Lady Augusta, thoughtfully, as if she had heard of many similar cases. "But how long ago is it since you found yourself in Abyssinia?"

"Again, I do not know. There are cases in which a man may spend his whole life upon the study and never advance beyond the gates of the Ancient Way. There are cases in which a man may develop the highest powers in a year or two. There are other cases in which a man can never acquire anything, however long he may study. It is with mankind, as regards the Ancient Way, just as in the heaven revealed to the Swede, in which the spirits find their levels, and some are contented to remain forever in the lower levels, while others are continually rising to higher plains. I do not know how long I have studied, but I think I am still a young man. There is no reason why we should interfere with the course of nature, in which age and decay of the body are but incidents in the long eternal life. The men lose for a while their strength of body and of mind, the women their beauty. It is but an incident; strength and beauty will return again, and the onward march to wisdom will be renewed with greater joy."

"Do women walk alone upon that road?"

Herr Paulus hesitated.

"It is the modern fashion," he said, "for women to claim independence and equality. But in the Ancient Way they do not walk alone. We will talk of this further; at present you will perhaps be content to walk with me."

Lady Augusta looked as if she would have liked to inquire further into this interesting topic, but she reserved it for a more fitting time—when the three girls would not be with them.

"I will lead you," he went on, "until you are so far advanced as to choose another leader. You will then know all who are on the Ancient Way, whether living or dead. As for myself, it will not be long, perhaps, before I shall be recalled to the quiet joys of study and meditation among the Abyssinian mountains."

"But there is the glory of the missionary," said Lady Augusta. "You must not forget that."

Herr Paulus turned his sad but not reproachful eyes upon her.

"You speak out of your ignorance," he said, "else you would know that with us there are no such words as glory or honor. What is it to be well or ill spoken of by men? We are taught to despise all earthly shows ; titles, rank, honor, wealth, have no meaning for us. These things do not advance upon the Way. I came reluctantly because I was enjoined to come. I shall stay with less reluctance, because I have met with a reception so warm and hearts so sympathetic."

"Yes, yes," Lady Augusta murmured, giving him her hand, "you must stay with us a long while. We have so much to learn; we are so ignorant; we are as yet hardly on the threshold. Oh, you must stay with us a long while, Herr Paulus."

"Make my name English," he said. "Call me Paul. And you, my sisters, I will call by your own names too "

Sibyl shook her head.

"You will except me, if you please," she said.

"Sibyl!" It was Cicely who expostulated.

"Be it so," said Paul, with a sigh. "In everything human there is the touch of discord—one wonders why."

"Promise to stay with us," Lady Augusta urged. "Stay with us, Paul—Paul, our master!"

"Stay with us!" said Cicely.

"Stay with us!" murmured Hetty.

"Yes, I will stay until—" his eyes met the gaze of Hetty, whose eyes were fixed upon him as those of a nymph of Delos might have been fixed on Apollo, had that god vouchsafed to appear to her, with as much awe, respect, and submission.

"I will stay," he corrected himself, "a long while. I will stay—until you yourselves order me to depart."

"Paul," said Lady Augusta, clasping her hands, "do you know—do you understand what you have promised?"

"Yes," he repeated, firmly, but looking at Hetty. "I will stay until you yourselves order me to depart."

BOOK THE SECOND.

CHAPTER I.

IN THE STUDIO.

Two girls were talking together in a studio. It was not a very magnificent studio, such as one may visit in Fitz John's Avenue or in St. John's Wood on Roving Sunday. There were no pieces of tapestry, no bits of armor, no mediæval weapons, no galleries and stairs of carved wood; not at all; it was a simple room built out at the side of the house; not originally intended for a studio, but yet serving very well for one. The house to which it belonged was an old-fashioned square red-brick house, still surrounded by a bit of its old garden, which had been extensive, and could still show apple and pear trees; and still had some of the old red-brick wall standing at the end of it, moss and lichen covered, crowned with wall-flowers. The studio served at the same time for a keeping-room. But it was a studio first. There was an easel at which one of the girls was standing; on a table beside it were the usual implements of the craft; a quantity of drawings and sketches and half-finished things were pinned against the wall and lay piled upon the chairs and even stacked upon the floor. A lay-figure—nothing so horribly human as a lay-figure, or so piteous and ghostly in its silence and the horror of its helplessness—stood in a corner, its head serving as a peg for a bonnet, while its arms carried stiffly, as under protest, a jacket and a silk handkerchief and a veil. On the residential side, so to speak, of the furniture, there were a few chairs, a shabby, worn carpet, a small round table, and a hard black sofa.

But the hardness of the sofa was mitigated by soft and pretty wraps, shawls, and woollen things which made it look Oriental and splendid, and the shabby carpet was hidden by rugs, while the general poverty of the room, whose paper and paint had not been renewed for many years, was redeemed by the pretty things hanging from the wall or standing on the mantle-shelf. And there was everywhere such a heavenly litter as proved that the occupant could never have belonged to a large family of girls, all living in the same room, and therefore taught, as girls in a large family must be taught, that real religion is always proved by tidiness. The occupant was clearly a girl, apart from the evidence of the young lady at the easel; gloves and a veil lay on the table, and there was a feminine atmosphere in the room. She was also a girl, one could perceive, who read a good deal, for the sofa was piled with books, and there were hanging shelves also filled with books and magazines. Most of the books belonged to the dear, delightful, much-abused tribe of novels.

The room, in fact, made a comfortable keeping-room, large enough to walk about in and to hold plenty of things and to contain quite an extensive litter; it did very well also for a studio, with a strong light in the proper quarter, but it had been built for a very different purpose. In the house adjoining, Mrs. Lavinia Medlock, in the old days when she was more than illustrious — everybody can be illustrious, but not everybody can be fashionable—held every day her now historical séances. Those days are gone—this is not wonderful, because all old days are gone —and with them is gone Lavinia's greatness. She then wore the finest and newest of satin dresses and received the best of company. Her friends came all day long; they came in omnibuses, in cabs, in broughams, and in stately chariots; they had all kinds of titles to their names, from plain miss or mistress to gracious duchess and even serene highness; they came by appointment and without; they would not be denied, and because the drawing-room was not large enough—it had been formerly the front parlor—Lavinia built a salon at the side of the house for the reception of her friends, those in the flesh and those out of it. The former, who concealed as much of the flesh as they could in furs, jackets, cloaks, and other things, so as not to make the spirits jealous by the show of what they themselves lacked, were not attracted to the house by Lavinia's appearance, which was homely, nor by her conversation, which was plain, nor by her manners, which spoke of certain omissions in early training, but by the reputation she possessed of being the finest interpreter in the world of things said and done out of it, and the most favorite medium known to the spirits. Certain it is that you could, by Lavinia's help, converse with any spirit you chose to call. So affable and condescending were they, or so powerful was

the influence of Lavinia, that the most illustrious spirit possible to name would come if invited, and converse with the most obscure, and answer any question, even the most impertinent, as to their own happiness or the happiness of their friends. The immortal Homer, the equally immortal Bard of Avon, Sir Walter Scott, Lord Byron, Milton himself, or Charles the First, would not disdain to rap out a message, dictate a poem, or show personal acquaintance with the inquirer's great-aunt.

Oh, these are old stories, but I am talking of old days; yet they are but as the day before yesterday. Do we not remember how scoffers used to call attention to the fact that our knowledge of the other world was never advanced an inch, and that the messages were idle trash? Do we not remember how the spirits were proved to have told the most barefaced lies, and to have perpetrated the most astounding blunders? Do we not remember how Lavinia herself was shown up in scientific journals for having caused to speak one spirit of a living person and another of a person who had never lived? Nay, we may remember more than this. For it is on record that none of these exposures and attacks seemed to injure Lavinia until a fatal thing happened to her. She ceased to be the fashion. She drew no longer; she excited no more curiosity. As for the credulity of people, that can never be exhausted, and any man among you, my brothers, who desires to get notoriety and to live in clover, has only to pretend to do what he cannot do, and to be what he is not, in order to gain his desire for a while. Lavinia ceased to be talked about. Then the people all went off to the next show, and deserted her, and she began to fall into poverty. All that she had in the world was this house, which she had fortunately bought during the time of fatness, and a small and yearly diminishing clientèle of those who still believed in her, just as they would have believed in Joanna Southcote, and employed her as they would have employed a wise woman, and inquired of the oracle, after the fashion of the ancients, in the conduct of their affairs.

She now received this scanty remnant in the old "front parlor," and let the studio and a bedroom to an artist when she could find a lodger. Her present lodger was an American girl, who lived alone and travelled alone, with more than the average independence of her country. She had lived thus alone in Rome and in Florence, and was now working at her profession alone in London. But she was a girl who made many friends, and was never really alone.

The clause in the creed of women which says, "We believe that it is impossible for a girl to live alone," has been of late years so much questioned and attacked that some think it will have to be struck out of the creed altogether; in which case, asks the Conservative, what will become of the rest of that sacred and ark-like monument? In fact, women who work for their living have long since discovered that it is a clause which has no foundation in the Eternal Verities, because in every town there are girls who must live alone. In London there are thousands; they live with each other, sharing rooms; they live in the places where they work; they live in boarding-houses. When they are rich enough they live, as this young lady lived, in their own lodgings, with a sitting-room as well as a bedroom, and in a solitude which is pleasing after the work of the day; thousands and thousands of girls in this city, not work-girls, like certain poor friends of ours, but girls of respectable parents and responsible brothers, whose self-respect is as great as that of any young lady who lives at home. They are artists of all kinds — musicians, singers, governesses of every degree, writers, chiefly of small fiction, reviewers and journalists, shop-girls, saleswomen, copyists, translators, type-writers—I say nothing about actresses, because they have long since flung the women's creed to the winds—women of all professions and trades. They live alone: they have the latch-key; they go where they will; they ask for and they need no protection; they are not in the least afraid.

As for one of these girls, the slighter of the two, the girl with the light-brown hair and the hazel eyes, you have seen her before, when she was painting in an American garden and talking to a poetic youth. This is Bethiah Ruysdael, who is now known to her friends as Kitty, I believe, because she thinks Kitty prettier than Bethiah; as it is, perhaps, though not so uncommon. The other girl, the girl with the great, black, limpid eyes and the pale cheek and full figure, is the daughter of Lavinia the Great — Hetty Medlock. She had been standing for a model, a kerchief tied about her head, and the early spring sunshine fell through the window and painted her face through the crimson silk, and made her cheeks glow and her eyes burn like coals. She was standing for a Neapolitan, I believe; or perhaps it was a Bohemian, or an Irish peasant, or indeed an Andalusian or a Catalonian. But in reality the picture came out a very fine likeness of Hetty, and a very beautiful portrait it was, though the painting had faults of color. The carnations, some said, were brutal. The light, some said —but what matter what they said?

"Now, Hetty dear," said the American girl, "you must be tired. Take a rest."

Hetty threw off the handkerchief and came round to the easel to look at the picture.

"Kitty," she said, "it is beautiful."

"You like it, really? Yes. I do think it is pretty good. How glad I am that I painted out the first hideous thing!"

"Yes. But it was like, too."

"Oh, like—" the artist repeated, impatiently. "I dare say it was like— But you were dull and downcast, Hetty. And now you have changed. It seems to me as if another look altogether had come into your face since I began to paint you a month ago. You are ten times as lovely, Hetty."

Hetty blushed. Another look, she knew, had come into her face.

"I suppose," she said, still blushing, "it is because we have all become so much happier."

"Oh, you mean the German person who pretends."

"Don't, Kitty. Oh, you don't know what he has done."

"Why, dear, he is only a—"

"No, Kitty, he is more — far more than that. It is no common Spiritualism. The most wonderful things happen every day. He takes Mr. Brudenel into far-off countries—"

"Hetty!"

"And he teaches Lady Augusta the most wonderful things, and he talks to Cicely and to me as nobody, I am sure, ever talked before."

"Oh, but Hetty—"

"He is not at all a solemn person, with airs and pretences, but just a young man full of life and spirits. Even Tom and Sibyl, who will not confess that they believe in him, like him. The house is so lively that you would not know it again. We talk and laugh at dinner. Mr. Brudenel is no longer pompous, and Lady Augusta laughs with us. And there is no more question at all about conversing with spirits. Paul says that we may converse with as many as we like, but that on the lower plane they will only mock at us and deceive us. When we reach the higher plane we are to be brought face to face with the spirits who cannot lie."

"Hetty, do you believe all this?"

"Kitty"—the girl dropped her voice to a whisper—"I declare that if there is anybody in the world who ought to hate Spiritualism it is myself. Oh, I cannot tell you all. It has ruined my mother and driven away my father, and made my name a by-word. Oh, one day last winter somebody read aloud in my presence Browning's 'Sludge, the Medium,' and I prayed that the earth would open and swallow me. But even I cannot doubt any longer the power that Herr Paulus possesses."

"What does he do with his powers? Why does he come here? If a man really had such powers he would employ them, surely, to make some fresh discovery for the welfare of the human race. Consider, my dear, if he would only destroy one single disease."

"I can only believe in what he says. He has been sent by his friends to teach philosophy in the West."

"Why has he been sent?"

"I do not know."

"All the things you have told me about him are wonderful. But so is conjuring. It is wonderful when a plum-pudding is made in a hat."

Hetty shook her head.

"You do not understand. Oh, we have been all our lives living close to the other world, within reach of conversation, but we have never been told anything worth hearing, and this man comes and tells us the most beautiful things, and does the most wonderful things." Hetty paused. "When I think of the things he tells us my brain will not work. I cannot tell you what they are; but while he is speaking your heart glows and you are full of the most lovely thoughts. Cicely says that he opens the gates of heaven — but we forget when we come back to earth what we have seen there. Oh, it is wonderful!"

"Hetty, take care."

"Every day he makes Cicely see her brother at sea. Sometimes he reads our thoughts, sometimes he makes me—but only in our own room—say and do all kinds of things; sometimes he—yes, Kitty—he works miracles for us. Reading, he says, is too slow for us, and he makes us feel in a moment, and ten times as strongly, all that one feels when one reads a beautiful poem. And he is so handsome. There is not a man in the world so handsome as Paul. Not broad-shouldered and jolly-looking like Tom Langston, but delicate and pale, with eyes which go right into your very soul."

"Hetty," Kitty repeated, "take care; this is dangerous."

Hetty blushed, but she laughed.

"Dangerous! Oh, no; there is no danger. I dare say any girl might fall in love with him, but he—oh, he is far, far above any girl; she might as well fall in love with the moon."

"Fortunately, Miss Langston cannot see those eyes of his."

"She can feel them, and in a moment she becomes his servant."

"Does Mr. Brudenel know of all this?"

"Why, of course; he does not lay his will upon us before people—since the first evening. But Mr. Brudenel is as much under him as we are. He has conquered the whole house. He cures the servants of toothaches and things. Yesterday he overpowered the butler and made him confess his whole past life and his rogueries; he is the master of the house."

"Strange," said Kitty. "I wonder how it will end?"

"He will go away soon and leave us all miserable for life," said Hetty. "Well, one will remember. And oh, how stupid and dull all other men seem beside him. I think, Kitty I am quite sure, that he has lived for thousands of years, and that his name is Apollo."

"Well, dear, I hope he will go away soon. It seems to me that the atmosphere of the house must be unwholesome."

"Yes, he will go away soon. And then—" Hetty broke off with a sigh. "Don't let us talk about him any more," she said.

She began idly to turn over some sketches in a portfolio. Suddenly she started and snatched up a drawing in chalk. It was a study of a head, showing the back and giving a little outline of the cheek.

"Who is this?" she asked.

"That is the head of a very old friend of mine—a school-fellow. Poor dear Ziph!"

"It is exactly like the head of Herr Paulus."

"Is it? I drew it in the garden one day before Ziph went away to New York."

"What did he go there for?" She still kept looking at the picture.

"He was a poet. He went there to sell his poetry."

"Oh" (Hetty put down the picture), "only a poet!"

"And I fear he came to grief, because after three or four months nothing more was heard of him. And his parents could never get the least clew to what became of him. They think that he failed, and took to drink, and died. He was always delicate, and drink kills very rapidly in America. Poor dear Ziph! He was going to do such splendid things. He had a portmanteau full of poems, and he was going to become famous, and he promised he would write to me and tell me of his grand successes. But he never told me of any, and that portrait is all I have of my school-fellow."

"Were you in love with him?"

"No, Hetty, I think not; but I was fond of him. He wanted sympathy and some one to talk with and confide in, and I was handy for him. I was very proud of him, but not in love; at least, I suppose I was not. Poor Ziph!"

"What was his name?"

"Ziphion B. Trinder. I called him Ziph. His father kept a store—what you would call a general shop—in the little town where my father was a lawyer. But Ziph would not weigh out tea and sugar, and measure yards of calico; nor would he study law, which in our country is the only way to become President. "Ziphion Trinder. It is a funny name. Oh, how like the head is to Paul!" "In New England some of us still have funny names. They christened me Bethiah, for instance, though you call me Kitty. I changed my Christian name, you see, because Bethiah is, somehow, impossible out of New England. Poor Ziph! He is a genius, and the least fit person in the world to struggle for himself. He must be dead, or I should have heard something about him long since. Poor Ziph!"

A tear stood in her eye as she laid down the picture.

"It is so like Paul," said Hetty. "It is wonderful."

CHAPTER II.

IN THE OTHER ROOM.

A HOUSE is a theatre with many stages, on which many plays may be going on all at the same time, with no "front," unless M. le Diable Boiteux takes out a side of each room. Thus, while two girls full of their future talked in the studio, two old people with little but their past talked in the front parlor, which no longer pretended to be a drawing-room. Here Lavinia Medlock carried on, but in a small way, the business of wise woman, adviser, and interpreter for the Intelligences. In this country, if a woman lives in a back street and tells fortunes by cards, the police run her in, and the magistrate gives her two months, and her house is broken up, and her children are ruined for life, and she goes to the workhouse, and foretells misfortunes to the other collegians, for even in the workhouse there are still fresh misfortunes to encounter in the shape of aches and pains, and twists and tortures, before the chaplain finally puts on his surplice to do them honor by walking before them in a short procession —which shows how determined we are to suffer no witch to live in the land. But if a woman lives in a respectable house, and calls herself a medium or the chosen confidante of the spirits who dwell in the other world, she may do whatever she pleases without fear of police or magistrate — which shows that we know how to distinguish.

Spirits are well known to choose for their favorite resorts places and chambers which appear little desirable to cultivated man. It is no business of ours. This room, for instance, was very shabby and humble. Yet to think of all that had gone on in it—the séances, manifestations, levitations, table-turnings, rappings, messages, counsels, oracles, letters, verses, incarnations, spirit photographs, spirit songs, spirit humors, spirit hands, spirit kisses, spirit pinches, spirit tweakings—wonderful to think of. And the room was just the same as it was before the spirits came at all, while her husband was still a clerk on a hundred and twenty pounds a year. And they let the first and second floor to pay the rent and taxes, and anything else they could get. The same chairs with black horse-hair seats, the old black sofa, the same old red paper, now faded and patched with other colors laid on by Time, who is a painter as well as a destroyer, and the same cupboard beside the fireplace—Hetty's heart sank every morning at sight of it—the same great cupboard filled with stores of groceries and food. People who live in one room generally keep their tea, sugar, coffee, jam, cakes, pies, bacon, ham, butter, bread, and wine — only there never is any wine—in the big cupboard beside the fireplace. Last year I paid a visit to the Marshalsea Prison and saw how Mr. Dorrit and his companions lived. In every room there was a great cupboard beside the fireplace for the reception of household stores, a fact which throws a flood of light upon the imprisonment of debtors. And as it was in the Marshalsea Prison, so it was in Mrs. Medlock's ground floor front, except that there was no bed in it.

Mrs. Medlock sat in her professional chair at her professional table. She was exercising her profession. She was answering questions, solving difficulties, and consulting the spirits for her clients. Even in consulting the spirits there is a fashion. Many of them who once came to consult them regularly had gone off in other directions. They are now faith healers, captains in the Salvation Army, believers in the ten tribes, astrologers, votaries of palmistry, not to speak of Esoteric Buddhists. Somehow or other they get the same excitement, though in different ways. But they consult the spirits no longer. It is only in New York that the spirits are still consulted in the practical conduct of life.

This morning, however, Lavinia Medlock had two visitors.

The first was an elderly lady, richly dressed, who came in her carriage. She came once a week regularly, and used the spirits as a way of getting secret tips as to stocks. She came in her own carriage; she was quick and imperious in her manner, and her eyes were exactly like small bright beads.

"Well, Lavinia," she said, sitting down, "I'm very well satisfied on the whole with the last week's work. The spirits were right for once."

"You know them too well," replied the medium, humbly, "to expect them to be always right."

"After the awful losses they've caused me, I certainly do, Lavinia. Not that I blame you for it, you poor thing. You can't help it, though sometimes I think there must be something wrong about your life, or your thoughts, or something. More holiness, Lavinia, more personal holiness, now, might attract a better class of spirits. Can't you try for more holiness—early celebration, say —or a hair shirt—or something? Your usefulness and your income might be trebled."

Lavinia shook her head.

"Well, never mind; now listen." She took a pocket-book out of her bag and extracted a paper.

"Now get an answer to all these questions."

This lady, in fact, spent her whole life and gave her whole thoughts to speculations on the Stock Exchange. She was a suspicious person, and mistrusted her broker; and as she had no knowledge of her own, she turned for help to the spirits.

Presently, after the usual business, and having got her answers, she gathered up her bag and pocket-book and muff, and rose to go.

"Lavinia," she said, "think of what I said. More personal holiness, my dear."

Half an hour later she had a second visitor. This time it was her old friend, Mr. James Berry. He was a little spare old man, one of those who dry up as they grow older, and shrink. His head was ornamented with a thick crop of gray hair, and a couple of white and shaggy eyebrows. When Mr. James Berry began to consult Lavinia, thirty years before, that gray hair was black. Otherwise there was no change in him at all, either in dress or manner. As for the latter, it was slow and precise. He was certainly a methodical man, probably something in the city. Lavinia did not know what his profession might be. His convictions, based on certain startling replies to questions proposed, were now unallowable in spite of many rubs, and although the spirits sometimes treated him with mortifying neglect and even mendacity. In all times of difficulty and doubt, when most men find out the wisest course by examination, weighty argument, reason, and wakeful thought, Mr. James Berry cast himself upon the spirits. That he was now, at sixty-five years of age, retired from active work, his savings all invested in shares of the company in whose service he had been employed for fifty years, these shares producing fifteen per cent. on their first price, was acknowledged by himself as due solely

to the prudent counsels bestowed upon him by the spirits. That prudence caution, good conduct, and thought had also something to do with it may also be conceded. "The spirits," he said, "may sometimes, when waggishly disposed, deceive and lead astray—and a wise man will look out for jokes—but in the long-run they truly serve and advance the interests of those who trust them."

When Mrs. Medlock's popularity began to wane, this excellent disciple remained faithful; when actual poverty fell upon her, he gave her money, and now, though his affairs seemed concluded, he still came to consult the oracle, because this method of guiding your life is like the practice of auricular confession, or the taking of opium or chloral. It relieves a man of personal responsibility, and drugs the conscience and deadens the will.

"Mam," he said—not madame or madam, the variety of speech which we spell ma'am, but plain short mam—"I have come here to-day to consult you upon very petic'lar business—very petic'lar indeed."

"Well, Mr. Berry, you know that I am always ready and willing, though the spirits do sometimes, I allow—"

"They certainly do take liberties; but not, I hope, this morning. Katie's last mistakes I am willing to put down to skittishness; and young folks will be young, whether spirits or flesh. But not this morning, mam. If Kitty is in the room"—he looked about, and then came three sharp raps from behind the fireplace—"then I beg of her to be serious or to go; because this is a serious matter."

Again three raps were heard.

"I think, Mr. Berry," said Lavinia, "that you may trust Katie this morning."

"I hope I may, mam." He put his hat on the floor and took off his overcoat and comforter. "I hope I may; for this is a very serious morning with me, mam, the most serious, I may say, in my life."

"Good gracious, Mr. Berry"—Lavinia was startled at the haggard look in his face, which was generally comfortable and contented—"what has happened?"

"Nothing, mam, yet. But a great deal may happen."

"Well, sit down, Mr. Berry, and tell me all that's in your mind."

Mr. Berry looked round the room.

"Ha!" he said, "I've been very uneasy; I've been awake two long nights thinking of it. But there's a holy calm in this room. It soothes my mind only to be here, mam; I feel better already."

The shabbiness of the furniture did not appeal to him, nor the poverty-stricken aspect of the place; he knew all about poverty, and shabbiness of furniture had been with him, so to speak, from childhood; and the artistic side of his character, if he had any, was wholly undeveloped. This was the room where he had conversed with the spirits; it was sanctified to him by the awe with which even the most frivolous messages struck his soul; it was to him as sacred and as holy a place as any Baptist chapel to a fervent believer.

"It is my own business that I am come about, Mrs. Medlock. Mam"—he leaned forward, breathing hard—"it may be ruin and the workhouse. Listen carefully. Don't let the spirits make so much as a single rap till you have heard the case right through. Do you know what my profession has been?"

"No, sir, I do not. That is a question which I never put to any spirits."

"I have been all my life, mam, a clerk in the service of a great company." He paused to let his words produce their full effect. "Never mind the name of that company. It was formerly a big house of business, owned by a single man, who made a great fortune and died. Then his sons turned it into a limited company. I've been in that house, under the father and the sons and the board of directors, for fifty years."

"Well, Mr. Berry?"

"I was always a careful man, and had no wife to spend and squander. I saved money. When I retired from the company's service last year they gave me a small pension; and one of the directors offered me, very kindly, as I thought, as many shares in the company as my savings would buy. They give fifteen per cent. on the issue price, and I get, at the price I bought them—for they've gone up since—six and a half per cent.; so that I thought I was doing pretty well."

"You certainly did very well, Mr. Berry."

"Yes, so I thought. But yesterday I got news which knocked me over. It came from an old friend in the house. He says he has found out the truth. He says that the house —it's a ship-owning company—has been shaky for years, and now it may go any minute. On the other hand, it may keep afloat and even weather the storm."

"Well, Mr. Berry?"

"That is one man's statement. But another man, an older friend who is in the confidence of the directors, tells me that the company never was so safe and the shares never so high, and never so certain to go higher."

"Well?"

"Well, what am I to do? If I believe the second man, I may be ruined if he is wrong. If I believe the first man, I shall have to sell at once, and I shall have to put up with three

and a half or four per cent. instead of six and a half; and if he is wrong I shall have shown that I had no confidence in the old house where I have made my living. Advise me, Mrs. Medlock. It's life or death to me to do the right thing now. I never asked you before on anything half so serious. Life and death it is. Tell me if the company is safe. Put it fair and square to them. Oh, it is life or death or the workhouse to me. All my savings—all—are in the company."

Mrs. Medlock put the question. But she trembled and turned pale, because this, she saw, was a juncture beyond her powers to control. And if she misdirected her old friend—one may be a medium and yet have affections and passions—she would consign him to a workhouse. And she could not rely upon her spirits; therefore she awaited the result with terror.

The answer began with a hail-storm of raps, apparently from all parts of the room at the same time. Presently they all ceased except from under the table, and the message began.

It is slow work receiving messages by raps, and it is greatly to be desired that the spirits would adopt the tape system, which is rapidly and easily read.

Presently, after many futile messages, and seeing Mrs. Medlock's face growing paler and more dejected, Mr. Berry sprang to his feet. "It's too much," he said. "There is ruin before me, and she tells me nothing but that she is happy, and so is her grandmother. Damn her grandmother, Mrs. Medlock!"

Lavinia burst into tears.

"I am so sorry," she said. "Of late I seem to have lost my power. I am the sport of the spirits. Oh, my poor old friend, what shall I do for you? what can I do for you? Oh, and after all these years! and when I ought to guide you in your difficulty! Oh, it's no use to go on—not a bit of use." She wrung her hands, while Mr. Berry sat down and gazed at her blankly. Then an idea struck her.

"Mr. Berry," she said, "there's a wonderful young man staying with Lady Augusta Brudenel."

"With whom?" he asked, sharply.

"With Lady Augusta and Mr. Cyrus Brudenel. Let me ask him."

"No, no; not the Brudenels—not the Brudenels."

"I don't want to ask them. I will not mention any names. I will only say—'Herr Paulus, here is a case,' and I will tell him your case. 'Advise me on it for this gentleman'—and perhaps he will advise—' and say nothing to anybody about it,' and he will keep the secret. Oh, Mr. Berry, it's our only chance. Let me ask him. Let me. Oh, my poor old friend, you have done so much for me, let me try to do something for you. Let me ask him!"

"But hide the name," said Mr. Berry.

"I will ask him this very day. I will go to him this afternoon, and unless he is in Abyssinia—sometimes he spends his afternoons in Abyssinia—he will give me an answer. I am sure he will."

"It's the workhouse, Mrs. Medlock. Think of that! Ruin and the workhouse, unless you get a true reply."

CHAPTER III.

IN ABYSSINIA AND ELSEWHERE.

Mr. Cyrus Brudenel, engaged with his new instructor in the study, was greatly changed in one short month from the Cyrus Brudenel who had proudly introduced Herr Paulus to his priceless collection of books on Spiritualism, magic, sorcery, astrology, alchemy, and the great world of jargon and pretended power. The brain reels only to think of the colossal lies which are bound up in their volumes; and of all the mendacious literature, and of the multitudes who have been dragged into the paths which lead inevitably to more lies and more pretence. Mr. Brudenel's own chief lie had been comparatively harmless; it was merely the pretence of reading and studying these books, truly terrible in their stupidity, weariness and falsehood. Now, even that pretence was abandoned; the books stood untouched upon the shelves, the papers and journals relating to the old Spiritualism were unopened. Mr. Brudenel no longer caught at some miserable platitude as a message from a glorified spirit; the whole current of his thoughts was deranged.

As for the study, it was a large and noble room, built out at the back of the house, where was a broad and generous garden, as generous in its proportions as if the house had been miles away from London instead of in St. John's Wood, and flanked with great trees, as well as with lawns and flower-beds. There were two windows, one at the end of the room and one at the side; they were fitted with double sashes, to keep out the noise of the outer world.

The silence of the study was almost as perfect as if it had been placed in the middle of Dartmoor, save that there was no distant tinkling of a deep bell and no song of the lark in the sky. If any sound reached this retreat it was nothing louder than the low rumbling caused by a coal-cart, or a parcel post-cart from the road outside. The books were arranged in mahogany bookcases, built *out as in great* libraries, but low, except at the back, where the shelves went up to the ceiling. There were busts of great magicians placed about, and before the fire there was a large table, with one or two chairs. The silence of the room, the air of mystery which its use imparted to it—you may feel the same thing in an empty freemasons' lodge; the books, which looked as learned as if they contained the works of Plato and his disciples, instead of the pretenders and the liars, all fitted the room for the message which was being delivered in it.

Mr. Cyrus Brudenel sat in one of the chairs to receive the message. On the table at his right hand was a little pile of unopened letters. His face was troubled by something, but a great and remarkable change had fallen upon it. All the pomposity had gone—that was immediately apparent. His eyes were no longer irritable and suspicious; it was a face which betokened submission.

The leader had wholly submitted himself. He was now led. He was a disciple, he had no longer any authority. The young man who stood before him was his master.

"So," said Paul, "it still troubles you, does it? I thought we talked it over yesterday."

"It is so extremely mysterious. Every day, with your help, I go away and receive instruction. Every day, when I come back, it is with the most glowing heart and with a mind full of happiness and gratitude. I cannot describe to you the infinite joy I experience at that moment."

"I know it myself," said Paul.

"And then, immediately, while I seek to recall what I have been taught, it vanishes away, and I cannot recall it. Nothing could possibly be more baffling and disappointing."

"It must be purposely done. You advance without knowing it in those hours when you are not with the master. There goes on in your brain a process of unconscious growth. Unfelt by yourself, the things you have learned are gradually taking root while the soil is being prepared for their growth."

Mr. Brudenel shook his head doubtfully.

"I cannot understand it," he said.

"Some day you will remember suddenly and fully. Then you will have enough to think about. But as to the manner and the time—leave it to the master."

Mr. Brudenel shook his head doubtfully.

"It is not for me," he said, "to question any methods that may be adopted. I looked, when the instruction began, for slow progress, because I am not naturally quick of apprehension. But I am tenacious. When I was a boy they all owned that I was tenacious, and yet I have retained nothing."

"You must have patience."

"I am no longer young, and the time is flying."

"Mr. Brudenel"—Paul, who was standing, shook an admonitory forefinger—"all this comes of an unwillingness to put away the old ideas. Time! youth! What are these among our people? What does it matter if months or even years pass away before you acquire the perfect knowledge? Do you suppose that Isák, the master, does not know what happens? Do you think that he would suffer it to go on if he did not approve of it? Remember that you are in new hands, receiving new ideas. Why, your mind is not cleared of the old ones even yet."

"Why, truly, it may be so."

"May be so?" repeated Paul, impetuously. "Why, of course it is. It must be so."

"You always bring me hope, my friend."

"What else have I come for except to bring you hope as well as wisdom? Patience, patience. Presently all will be at your feet. Truth, which is power ; knowledge, which you can use for the benefit of your fellowmen. You will heal and prevent disease. You will lengthen life. You will solve the difficulties of social life. Why, sometimes I, who belong to the School of Meditation, think that yours is the happiest lot of all."

Mr. Brudenel's cheek flushed and his eyes brightened.

"If I could always believe this. But there are times, Paul, I confess, when I crave just as I used to crave for a fuller manifestation —even fuller than this."

"Glutton, what more can you have?"— Paul showed a smiling face, full of reassuring cheerfulness. "Yet a fuller shall be shown to you, and that before long. As for me, I could never use the power as you will use it, because to me the acquisition of knowledge is sufficient, while to you the exercise of power is everything. So in science, there are men who spend their lives in following pure mathematics for the sake of the things continually revealed to them; while others must stop at every step to make a practical application to the uses of the world of what they have discovered. I am the pure mathematician; you, Mr. Brudenel, are the practical applier. Now—silence; it is the time. Listen. When you hear the voice of the master, fix your eyes upon mine intently; separate your thoughts from all earthly things; speak not, move not." He raised his hand and looked up as one who waits to hear a signal. "Master!" he cried. "Isák Ibn Menelek!"

Then, far, far away, yet distinct and clear and audible, there followed the reply, "My children, I am ready."

"He is waiting. Now. Oh, move not, speak not, think not ; a moment more, and you will be gone, swifter than thought, swifter than electricity, to the hills of Abyssinia."

As he spoke he leaned over and met his pupil's eyes with his own, black and lustrous, commanding and compelling. In less than a minute Mr. Brudenel's head bent forward, his face grew rigid, his eyes dilated, and his frame stiffened. Paul stood up and breathed deeply ; then he pushed up an eyelid and looked at the glazed eye, as one who administers chloroform and wishes to ascertain if it has yet taken full effect.

"You are now, my friend," he murmured, "on the high-road to Abyssinia. Isák Ibn Menelek has much to say to you. Stay there a while."

Thirty years of physical research had perhaps made Mr. Brudenel a ready as well as a willing subject to certain influences which some call by one name and some by another. They may all be reduced to one and the same force. He was now, as Paul had promised him, in Abyssinia, or somewhere else far away from his own study, apparently lifeless and unconscious.

Paul stood looking at him for a few moments. It is not every one who can assist his friends to go in an instant to Abyssinia, and he might fairly have shown some pride in the achievement. But he did not. The smile had left his lips and his face was grave and full of business, and he proceeded to behave in a very strange and remarkable manner. First, he went to the door of the study and locked it, though no one in the house would have dared to disturb Mr. Brudenel in his study. Then he drew the heavy curtains across the door so that no one should be able to see through the key-hole, though not even a house-maid would have dared to do such a thing.

Paul next took up the handful of letters which had arrived that morning, opened them all, read them, and laid them in the basket which received the day's correspondence until it was answered. Apparently the letters yielded him no information.

Mr. Brudenel's bundle of keys lay on the table beside the letters. Paul took it up and opened the safe, which stood against the wall in the far corner. It was full of papers, legal documents, and such things. Paul laid everything upon the table and leisurely examined all the papers. This took him half an hour, during which the unconscious man moved not so much as an eyelash.

"There isn't," he said, "a single scrap of paper to help. Yet I am perfectly certain, from what Lavinia said, that the old man meant Brudenel & Co., the ship-owning com-

4

pany, the man who made his fortune by the business, the same who retired and made it into a limited concern—it *must* be Brudenel & Co." He considered a little. "I just hate to do it," he said. "If there was any other way—but it does him no harm —and knowledge is power. Come, old boy. He made a gesture, and Mr. Brudenel moved and half opened his eyes. "No, not yet; you can come back from Abyssinia, but you have got to do some work for me before you wake up. Turn your chair round to the table." Mr. Brudenel sat in one of those chairs which revolve upon their seats without altering the position of the legs. "So, that will do ; take up your pen, now the note-paper. Write at my dictation in your own handwriting." Mr. Brudenel, still with closed eyes, obeyed. That is to say, he took certain sheets of note-paper and wrote, one after the other, at Paul's dictation, a few short letters in his usual handwriting, signing in the usual way. Paul read the letters and laid them in the basket.

"There," he said, "you will never know how these letters came to be written. Now you must answer a few questions, if you please."

The sleeping man sat bolt-upright in his chair, with eyes closed and pale cheeks. There was not the least sign of life in him, or of attention, or of hearing what was said to him.

"Tell me," said Paul, "What fortune does your daughter possess in her own right, and apart from anything you may leave her."

"Sibyl has ten thousand pounds," Mr. Brudenel replied. One unaccustomed to these things would have shuddered and trembled ; for his voice sounded weak and far away. He spoke with no more movement than the mere opening and shutting of his lips ; when he finished his answer his lips closed with a snap. It was like insulting Roger Bacon's famous head; it was like questioning a corpse. The answer came—a true answer—but one felt that the will was held captive, and the brain was unconscious.

"Are you her sole guardian?"

"I am."

"Where is her money invested?"

"It is all in Brudenel & Co."

"Are you also sole guardian and executor for the two Langstons, Cicely and her cousin Tom?"

"I am."

"What fortunes have they?"

"Tom has fifteen thousand pounds. Cicely has twelve thousand pounds. If Tom's cousin, Sir Percival, should prove to be dead, he will succeed to the property and the title."

"When do they receive their fortunes?"

"Tom is to have his at the age of five-and-twenty ; Cicely at one-and-twenty. Their birthdays fall on the same day. Consequently, they will both come into possession of their property on April 23d."

"And it is now March 23d. Where is their money?"

"It is all invested in shares of Brudenel & Co."

"As for your own money, now. Have you any shares in the company?"

"No. I sold out to buy land."

"And Lady Augusta's fortune?"

"It is in the hands of trustees."

"Brudenel & Co. has been a great house, has it not?"

"Yes, a very great house."

"You have trusted it entirely, have you not?"

"Entirely."

"Do you know the present secretary?"

"Yes."

"Go to his office. Is he engaged?"

"The chairman of the company is with him. The books are open on the table. They are talking."

"Tell me what they are saying."

"The secretary says, 'I do not see how the smash can be averted another month. It must come then—it may come before.'"

Then the narrator changed his voice and became the chairman, and from the agitation of his voice you would have inferred the mental anxiety of the chairman.

"Not another month. It is a terrible situation. And the shares keep up. Not a breath outside."

"That breath may blow any moment. You had better think of the position of the directors when the smash does come! If we do not declare the truth before long, you may all be put in the dock. As for me, I suppose I am only a servant."

"Yet—yet—for God's sake let us keep the position of the company secret as long as we can. While there is life there is hope."

"That will do," said Paul. He considered for a few minutes. "There is a great deal more here," he said, "than the interests of poor old James Berry. There is a thing to do here which may be a grander feat than any I have ever dreamed of. Tell me "—he addressed the inanimate Cyrus Brudenel— "tell me where you have put your share certificates."

"They are at the bank."

"Oh! I wonder if they are necessary. Hang it! a man ought to know everything. I wonder how long an operation of this sort takes, and how it can be done. Tell me "— again he addressed Mr. Brudenel—"who are your brokers?"

"I have none. The bank would do any business for me if I wanted it done."

"Oh, turn your chair round, and write one or two letters now in your own handwriting."

He dictated two or three letters. Then he took the check-book out of the safe and made his patient sign three blank checks.

"So," he said, "that is accomplished. I wonder if anything will happen to prevent the thing from coming off? Why should anything happen?"

"One question more," he asked. "Do you know anything of one James Berry?"

"There was a James Berry in my father's service. He went into the company's service afterwards. He was in the accountant's department."

"Has James Berry any shares in the company?"

"Yes. He has invested all his savings in the company."

"Humph! My conjecture was right, then, and Brudenel & Co. are going to smash. Fifteen thousand for Tom, twelve thousand for Cicely, and ten thousand for Sibyl; and all the old man has got is an estate which can't be sold. That's bad for Tom and Cicely and Sibyl. On the other hand, if the thing comes off—oh, it's wonderful. Lavinia, I owe you a good turn for this; and somehow I'll pay you back, though at present I don't see any way. And now," he said, putting the three checks and the letters very carefully into his pocket-book, "unless I am very greatly mistaken, here will be a bigger *coup* than anything ever before attempted or accomplished by medium, clairvoyant, or occult philosopher. Paul, my boy, when this thing is noised abroad your head shall touch the skies. And then, when all the world is talking about you, in the very nick of time, when everybody is expecting something even greater, and they are prepared for any miracle, you will suddenly vanish, go back to Abyssinia, or else to the old place—they can't think of looking for so great a man in the old place—and live forever in the memory of men. How to support the rest of life? Well, I don't know. That's a problem which must wait. Meanwhile—" He shook his head as if there was a side of the question which he did not care to look at.

Then he sat down and pondered for a whole quarter of an hour. Beside him sat the figure of a man who might have been a corpse, so still and white and silent was he, so rigid and so regardless.

"Is it worth the trouble?" he asked himself. "A month or so of glory and success, with all the people wondering and staring, and all the scientific-men angry and discon-certed, and a thousand pens set agoing, and the Spiritualists triumphant at last. Then they will look for more, and there will be no more; because I cannot expect any more coincidences, and the worker of miracles must retire, if possible, without being seen to go. He must vanish like a goblin in a story, And he must never come back again. To be seen again would be fatal. He must never more be heard of. Well, I think I know a place which is obscure enough and forgotten enough for any one to live unknown and concealed. It will be miserable enough after all I have seen and done; but after all it will not be half so miserable as if I had stayed there all the time, no better off than the obscure folk who live out their dull and monotonous lives there, and are buried at last in the cemetery. I shall at least have the memory of the great stir that I have made in the world.

"Chatterton," he went on, walking backward and forward, "had his gift and he used it. Nobody blames him now for the deceit which he employed. He had his gift. I have mine. There is not a man in the world who can do what I can. Not one. They can all mesmerize, but they cannot make the patient see things far off, report secrets long since hidden away, hear conversations and repeat them, and think as I choose them to think. I use my gift in my own way, and for the same purposes as those of Chatterton. I want honor, not money.

"No one shall ever say I wanted money. I came here without asking for any, and I shall go away with clean hands. Money? Why, what money could repay the services I shall render this household if the *coup* comes off? And I suppose that unless I tell them, no one will ever know why I came, or why I did it, or how I did it. And now for Mr. James Berry."

He sat down at the table and wrote a short letter:

"DEAR MRS. MEDLOCK,—I have thought over the difficulties of your friend, and have been enabled to help him. Tell him to lose no time in selling out—but to do so secretly. Let him tell none of his friends what he has done. As you have not told me the name of this company, it is not possible for me to advise you more exactly in this matter. Tell him, however, that he *must sell*, and that immediately. Yours very sincerely,
"PAULUS."

"That," he said, "is the first step in the history of the great *coup*."

He looked round the room. The table was covered with papers which he had taken from the safe. These he replaced carefully.

"The drawer of the safe," he said, "reminds me that the day after to-morrow the Indian paper is to be discovered there. I thought that was rather clever, but the new surprise beats it hollow." He locked up the safe, put the keys into Mr. Brudenel's pocket, and arranged the table exactly as it had been before unconsciousness fell upon him.

When he was quite satisfied, he bent over Mr. Brudenel as he had bent over the heads of the two girls.

"You have been in Abyssinia," he said. "You have been conversing with an aged philosopher, standing under a palm-tree beside a fountain; on every side arise mighty mountains; there were no signs of human life; the sun was hot and the skies cloudless. No one was with you but the philosopher. As he talked with you your heart leaped up and your eyes glowed, for he spake of things which filled you with awe and wonder and a trembling joy; and he promised that you, too, in the future— Awake."

Mr. Brudenel opened his eyes and looked about him. Suddenly he understood where he was, and he seized Paul's hand and clasped it warmly.

"Oh, my friend—my friend," he cried. "I have come back too soon. I have been—I have been—in a heaven of joy and happiness." It is rare, indeed, that an elderly man is forced to exhibit the outward and visible signs of joy. We know them in youth. Many causes may make the cheek burn, the pulse to beat faster, the heart to glow, the breath to come and go, the eyes to be dimmed and dewy. Dear me! I have known a young man taken in this way just because a girl has allowed him to kiss her. But I have never seen any old man except Mr. Brudenel exhibit these signs of youthful joy and happiness. "Paul!" he cried out in an ecstasy. "I have never, never enjoyed such a memory."

"Tell me about it."

"I was received by the master in the bottom of a valley beside a spring of water; there was a palm-tree or two; on all sides ran great mountains. He taught me all the morning. He filled me with a joy unspeakable. He promised that, before long, I too—" Here he stopped.

"You too?"

"It is the same thing always," Mr. Brudenel cried, the joy going out of his face. "When I return I forget all that I have been told."

"Again, you forget. It is as I told you. Your mind is not yet saturated. You have not yet shaken off the old prejudices and traditions. My friend, you have spent two hours"—he looked at his watch—"two

hours and a half in Abyssinia. You have meantime sat in this chair, to all appearance dead. Now remember. You came here after breakfast; you read your letters; you appear to have answered some of them; you then received me."

"I remember that. But I have forgotten the letters."

Paul handed him the basket. Yes, there were the letters in his own handwriting. "You then detached your thoughts from things earthly and were transported to Abyssinia. I went with you and stood with you, invisible to yourself, and returned with you. I would repeat the whole conversation, but I must not. It is not allowed. Patience, however. A few more days and you shall be master of the whole. And oh, I had nearly forgotten! It is the day after to-morrow that you are to present the Indian newspaper to your friends."

Mr. Brudenel colored, and became confused. "Paul, I must confess. What will you think?"

"There is no need to confess anything. You have been to the drawer, tempted by curiosity to break your promise; what did you find?"

"Nothing."

"You see what comes of trying to deceive your friends."

"I deserve everything. I have fooled away the most wonderful manifestation."

"Certainly, you deserve everything. Perhaps it is on account of your brother's promise that you are stricken with forgetfulness every day. But do not despair. The master is not implacable. You may invite your friends just the same as if you had not looked in the drawer. By-the-way, you are quite, quite certain"—Paul's eyes were of searching severity—"that no one could possibly have had access to the safe?"

"No one could possibly open the safe except myself."

"Then, Mr. Brudenel, invite whom you please, and enjoy a triumph which has yet been achieved by no Spiritualist or so-called occult philosopher. It is a mark of signal favor; and, believe me, my dear friend"— Paul clasped his hand warmly—"not the last—not the last—that you will receive."

CHAPTER IV.
SHOULD THIS HAPPEN?

ONCE more the two young men were sitting at midnight in Tom's workshop, but their bearing towards each other was now changed. There was no diffidence on the one hand nor suspicion on the other. Diffidence had changed to confidence, and in place of suspicion was avowed enmity on public grounds with allowed friendship on private grounds.

"People are clamoring for more of your confounded miracles, old man," said Tom, presently.

"So I gather. They will not be satisfied. At least—well, there is one thing I promised. If you are at all interested in what you call miracles, you may be present to-morrow evening."

"You mean the great Indian trick? Yes; my guardian has invited his friends to witness it. He says you gave him the paper a month ago."

"He asked for a copy of that day's *Friend of India;* so it came. That is very simple."

"Perfectly simple. Quite simple; what happens every day, in fact. Nothing miraculous about that, is there?"

"He then placed it in a safe, of which he alone keeps the key, and he undertook not to show it to any one until the day when the mail should bring that day's paper to London. It will arrive to-morrow, and his copy can be compared with that received in the usual way."

"I see. But it seems rather a pity, doesn't it, that he waited a whole month?"

"You mean—" Paul knew perfectly well what Tom meant, but yet he asked this question.

"A miracle, my dear boy, in order to be perfectly conclusive, should leave no loophole at all for doubt as to the fact. That is the whole essence of a miracle, and it is here that your friends go bungling. Now, if you produced to-day's *Friend of India* in open court, so to speak, before a body of scientific men, who might photograph it, so as to multiply copies, and if you on the same day had the whole contents of that day's paper telegraphed from Delhi, the question would then be, not whether the thing had been done, about which there could be no doubt, but whether there was any way of explaining it other than miraculous. For instance, the old slate trick—"

"Oh, but everybody knows how that is done."

"True, but the fact is that it was done. We recognized that, and had only to find out how it was done. How about your miracle of to-morrow?"

"I did not say it was mine."

"Your friends' miracle, then. You see they haven't complied with the first conditions of a miracle, that the fact itself must be beyond doubt. My guardian says that four weeks ago he received a copy of that very day's *Friend of India.* Very well, it rests on his word, not on yours as well, does

it?" Tom looked up curiously as if he was trying to get some admission.

"If necessary, my word would perhaps not be wanting." There was the least possible absence of heartiness in the answer.

"Quite so, if necessary. Very well, then. He says he put it in the safe. Why did he not instantly produce the sheet and confound the infidel? Can't you see that a more miraculous thing than the transportation of a newspaper ten thousand miles in an hour was never attempted even in the palmiest days of witchcraft and magic? Don't you know that the occult philosophers have been asked over and over again to do this, and that they have always refused to do it?"

"You forget one thing, that if such a thing was done it might be made subservient to commercial purposes and an object of self-interest."

"That is what the occult philosophers say. It is only worth considering on the supposition that everybody could perform the miracle. If your friends have the secret in their own hands, they can keep it and make the performance a rare and interesting event. Come, now, put it to them frankly. Let us have, for once, a miracle that cannot be attacked anyhow. My guardian deposits this precious paper in his safe and keeps it there for a month. He says that nobody can get at that safe except himself. Rather than believe in this miracle I am prepared to disbelieve his assertion. Come, now, old man, I don't mind being frank with you. I think you are up to some game which may be anything, but isn't, I am sure it isn't, the old vulgar game of plunder. I rather believe you are trying by the exercise of certain gifts and clever dodges to make yourself a great man. Very well, I have a similar ambition about myself only in another direction altogether. You are going in for miracles. It isn't worth while carrying on the stale old spiritualistic humbug. You know that, and you are trying to strike out a new line. Give us a real, genuine, indisputable miracle, the fact of which cannot be denied."

"I am pleased to have your good opinion, Tom," Paul laughed, cheerfully. "Whatever my ambitions may be, they do not work in the direction of plunder. You shall never be able to say that of me. And as to what you think—" He paused. "Tom," he said, earnestly, "you were so very frank with me at the outset as to tell me you thought I was a humbug like the rest of them. You know now that I have no intercourse with their world of lying spirits. I do not send round the hat for a little collection. Yet, believe me, Tom, there is far more in the world than you have yet understood. There are powers of which you know nothing."

"That," said Tom, "I do not deny."

"Would you believe in those powers if I were to give you what you call an undeniable miracle?"

"I should accept the fact and try to find out how it was done."

"Very good," Paul laughed again. "I think I may hope. I do not promise to work such a miracle as will satisfy even you. That is to say, you will not be able to deny the fact, and you will not be able, the least bit in the world, to find out how it was accomplished. No natural force with which you are acquainted will be able to account for it. No explanation will occur to you, or to any of your scientific friends, that will in the least satisfy you. I say that I don't actually engage myself to do this thing, but there seems a chance that I may do it."

"I should be very much obliged to you if you will. I shall take it as a personal compliment, and a great kindness to myself. A genuine miracle, I confess, would be received by the whole world, scientific and otherwise, with considerable satisfaction. Nothing in the way of mesmerism, though."

"Very well. Mesmerism, however, must not be despised. It is a natural force entirely outside the investigations of scientific men, and neglected by them. It would be well if you were to consider the subject. I could teach you a good deal in it, for instance, which might astonish you and lead you to follow it up."

"I will be your pupil, perhaps, but not now."

"As for my miracle, now. Conceive of some event happening which would seem at first absolutely destructive of your dearest wish."

"What is my dearest wish?" Tom replied, quietly, with a flush in his cheek.

"I will tell you. I believe that there is no one in this house or outside it who knows or suspects that you are engaged to Miss Brudenel."

Tom started. "How do you know that?"

"How do I know a great many things? I know, you see, the dearest wish of your heart."

"Well, you have found out somehow what we thought was unknown to anybody but ourselves. It is true we are engaged. And now, I hope, you can keep the secret you have discovered."

"I can. Miss Brudenel will never be the Vestal virgin of the cause. Suppose, however, that something — I know not what — interfered between you. I talk at random, perhaps — say, something which would pre-

vent your marriage for years—perhaps altogether. Suppose it required nothing short of a miracle to remove that obstacle."

"Well?"

"Well, suppose that miracle performed, would you still disbelieve?"

"I should. No doubt I should accept the miracle in such an event with profound gratitude, but I should then want to know how it was done; because, you see, everything in the world is worked by laws, and your miracle could only be worked by some law unknown to myself."

"Lady Augusta and her friends," said Paul, smiling, "would follow the unscientific method. They would accept the miracle just as you would, and they would then ask for more."

CHAPTER V.

THE SECOND FUNCTION.

THE second great manifestation, though more brief in its duration and simpler in character than the first, was universally acknowledged to be of far greater importance. Nothing, in fact, not even the events which followed—to be sure, these were chiefly of a private nature, and could only be whispered —did more to raise Herr Paulus to that eminence which for a brief season he enjoyed, and might have been still enjoying but for circumstances which will be duly narrated. The First Function was undoubtedly sweet and pleasant, both to behold and to describe afterwards. It thrilled, but the emotions excited were on familiar lines; it awed and impressed those who assisted, but it did not actually take one unexpectedly. Things like unto it had been seen before. Invisible bells had been rung, invisible music had been played—indeed, mediums always bring along a concertina or an accordion for fear the spirits—who cannot play anything else, not even a harp—should forget to bring an instrument; invisible hands have often done very astonishing things; papers have before now fluttered about the room, descending like the rain from a clear sky; there has been the exhibition of spirit photographs and pictures; there has been telegraphing; there has been clairvoyance; all such feats have an historical character. Stories of a like nature could be adduced, narrated, and compared. In point of picturesqueness and beauty and fitness, however, the First Function left nothing to be desired; while its operator appeared to be of a much higher character than any of those who accomplish their results in the dark. One could not imagine Herr Paulus stooping to impose upon his audience by the common and well-known methods; even those who were least credulous acknowledged his immense superiority.

But as regards the function of this evening, as Mr. Brudenel truly said at its close—it is only the anticipation of a few pages—"The thing"—he modestly called it a thing—"which we have this day been privileged to witness is an achievement beyond a parallel in the history of Spiritualism." You will acknowledge as much when you hear what it was. "It marks an epoch. It announces our arrival upon a higher plane; it shows that we have left behind us forever the days of lying and mocking spirits; our labors have not been in vain; it is the first visible step of our new departure; it shows us clearly that our feet are standing at last upon the solid rock; it teaches us without a doubt that our faces are turned towards the way of truth."

Truly, as you will see, Mr. Brudenel exaggerated not a whit. Those who witnessed this stupendous conquest over time and space went home awed and humbled. The longer they dwelt upon it, the more it impressed their imagination; the more they pondered over the possibility of deception, the more they were bewildered. Even the sceptics were for the moment confounded. Nothing, however, really confounds the sceptic. He is like those little figures made of painted pith resting on little globes of lead which spring to their feet with only the greater elasticity and resolution the harder you knock them down. The best miracle in the world is wasted on a sceptic. You might as well tell ghost stories to a lawyer.

The company invited to witness this manifestation was less numerous than that which gathered together for the first, but it included all the important people. There was no dinner-party, and they were invited for nine. When they arrived, they were shown into Mr. Brudenel's study, where Sibyl received them. It was understood that Lady Augusta and Mr. Brudenel would appear at the right moment with the hero of the evening.

All the well-known leaders of the Spiritualists were there, including Mr. Athelstan Kilburn and the Rev. Amelius Horton. The Society of Psychical Research was represented by a deputation, specially invited, from Cambridge. It consisted of a Junior Fellow of Trinity and a certificated graduate in honors from Newnham. On the way—it has nothing to do with the story—the deputation fell in love with each other, and got engaged on the way back, but fell out over the report which they had to draw up, and so the marriage never came off. Science, always suspicious, was represented by a professor of the highest distinction. He was known to be hostile to everything which he could not reduce to the realm of known physics, and always went about to such manifestations with the avowed intention of exposing the trick—he always called it a trick—and he never did expose anything, because he knew nothing of legerdemain, although he was learned in electricity. The profession was represented by Mr. Emmanuel Chick and Mrs. Lavinia Medlock, as usual—there are few recent additions to the old school of Spiritualists. The Rev. Benjamin Rudge was also present, prepared to chronicle whatever took place. There were also present a large number of the ladies who "take interest;" among them the ardent believer, who has always something to whisper, some new mysterious utterance or promise; the woman who only half believes, but trembles and thinks it is wicked; the woman who loves to be startled and prefers a séance to a melodrama; the woman in search of a new gospel—she is very common in these days; the woman who talks the language of the Esoteric Buddhist; the woman of unsatisfied soul who yearns for a fuller life—with others. I suppose that the purely incredulous world was represented by Tom Langston, who changed his mind and came—to meet the professor, he said, but I think he was anxious to see what would be done. Cicely Langston sat retired, with Hetty beside her.

"I understand, Miss Brudenel," said Mr. Rudge, in a loud and masterful voice, "that we are summoned here to-night in order to witness what will be—if we are rightly informed—a truly stupendous event, and the most remarkable manifestation of spiritual power ever witnessed."

"Pray, Mr. Rudge," Sibyl interrupted, shortly, "ask me nothing. I know nothing. I can promise nothing."

"It is rumored, then"—Mr. Rudge smiled with amicable forgiveness, because he was used to be snubbed by Miss Brudenel—"we will only say, then, that it is rumored that we are this evening to behold a document which has been transported from some part of India to this house with the swiftness of an electric message. If this be so—"

Mr. Emmanuel Chick sniffed loudly. He looked not only shabby this evening, but hungry. In fact he was hungering for Paul's blood. It was the first note of hostile incredulity.

"Oh," cried Lavinia, clasping her hands, "it will be the exercise of a power far beyond anything ever vouchsafed to me. And yet there was a time—"

"Before we all go off into ecstasies," said Mr. Emmanuel Chick, "we had better see what happens. On the last occasion there were fireworks—I call them fireworks—with mesmerism. Perhaps we shall only have, after all, more fireworks with mesmerism."

"It cannot be said," said Mr. Athelstan Kilburn, "that our young friend receives either sympathy or encouragement from his professional brethren. Surely they are above the petty feeling of jealousy."

"He will get no encouragement from me," Mr. Chick replied. "I pretend to nothing but the good old lines. I am a medium—only a medium. No fireworks for me, sir. You know what to expect from me. If the spirits wish to speak through me, they can. That's all. I believe some people have received messages which spoke for themselves, and were a little more important than a lady in a mesmeric trance. We shall see."

"Hetty," Cicely whispered, "it is that odious man who always makes me feel as if he carried evil spirits about with him. Do you think that his presence will affect Paul's powers?"

"No, I am sure it will not. But, oh, I wish it was over! And oh, I wish he would not show off to a great roomful of people."

"Perhaps he must."

"His powers should be kept sacred, and shown to none but—but the people he loves," Hetty murmured. "Oh, to make a trade and a show and a means of gain out of such a power as his! It would be too dreadful."

"Whisper me everything, Hetty dear, just as he does it. Oh, if he would only make me able to see it! He could if he chose. Perhaps this evening—but tell me all, Hetty."

"I suppose," said the Professor of Science to Tom Langston, quietly, "that there will be an opportunity afforded one of submitting any experiment we may be privileged to witness to the ordinary tests."

"Oh yes," Tom replied; "why not? Herr Paulus's performances are unexpected, but they are all done in the light. I don't quite see how anything he has done as yet could be tested. You see things, and you wonder how they are done; that is all."

"Tell me about him."

"He is a young man. He has been staying here a month now. In this house, you know, we are always up to our necks in magic and mystery, but since he came we have learned to despise the old things. We do not care about rapping; we no longer ask if our grandmothers are happy; we do not look for incarnated spirits; we have no dark séances."

"All this seems distinct gain," said the professor.

"Yes; in their place we have acquired a beautiful freedom of transport. We converse with anybody all over the world. We find out what is going on everywhere. Mr.

Brudenel, my guardian, goes off to Abyssinia every morning for instruction, and arrives home in time for luncheon. Lady Augusta is going through a course of King Solomon's Wisdom; the girls are always more or less mesmeric; the house-maids no longer go to the dentist when they have got a toothache. Herr Paulus leaves his earthly body on his bed while he goes off to have a crack with his friends in Russia, in Thibet, in Africa."

The professor laughed.

"You cannot test any of these things," he said. "If people choose to believe in common cheats and impostors—"

"Pardon me, professor. Herr Paulus is not a common cheat and impostor. I do not quite know what he is, but he wants no money, to begin with."

"That is unusual."

"It is, in this house, at least."

"But they talk of a newspaper, or something interesting, brought here in a single moment from an enormous distance."

"Ten miles would be as good as three thousand, but it wants a big distance to strike the imagination. In fact, professor, I have reason to know that the claim set up this evening will be the power to convey things —not only messages, or by the wire—but actual things—parcels—what you please, at any moment to any distance by unseen agency."

"In that case," said the professor, "I am come on a fool's-errand indeed."

"At Simla, only last year"—it was the Rev. Benjamin Rudge, in his loud, coarse voice, which irritated some people beyond endurance—"some of the so-called occult philosophers were invited to bring over a copy of that day's Times. They refused to do so, on the ground that every request for a miracle could not be complied with, and that to ask such a thing showed mere curiosity. The refusal and the excuse made scoffers laugh. If a man claims to have great powers, he must prove them. Our young prophet, if I may call him so, has claimed very great powers on behalf of his friends. He has shown us certain things which we should have called manifestations of a very high order. If he actually does the thing of which we have heard, he will establish himself and his friends on the highest pinnacle which science and philosophy have yet realized. Time and space will be annihilated, and even the power of electricity will be surpassed."

He had spent the afternoon rounding off this and a few other sentences, with a view to a letter announcing the miracle, if it should come off. That letter was duly sent, and being signed by himself, and backed by another from that well-known, sober, and well-balanced intellect, the Rev. Amelius Horton, it met with universal incredulity, and smiles and snorts and jeers. But when the professor himself gravely and soberly described what had taken place, so far as his senses enabled him to see and to hear, a sensation was produced as of a new revelation; and everybody asked who was Herr Paulus, and nobody knew, and all the world waited eagerly for more.

"When is he coming, Hetty?" asked Cicely.

"Very soon, I believe. Oh, how can he do things in the presence of people who want to make him out an impostor?"

"Tell me all; whisper everything, dear."

"The explanation," said Mr. Amelius Horton, "will, of course, be found in the development of will energy. The unknown force is will energy. It is to be the force of the future. It will be cultivated like strength of body, and we shall take rank in the future according to the strength of the will energy."

"Who is that person?" the professor asked Tom.

"It is the Rev. Amelius Horton, Senior Fellow of King Henry's, Cambridge."

"Oh! Is that the result of classical study or of mathematical research? Well, let us begin and let us keep our eyes wide open. Of course it is all nonsense about time and space. There will, I suppose, be a good deal of talk to wrap up the real thing."

"Yes; the only thing I have yet found out about our man," said Tom, "is that he has a curious power of mesmerism. That awakens suspicion, but it does not explain anything."

"Mesmerism," repeated the professor. "Yes, it is a strange power, and ought to be taken out of the hands of quacks and impostors. It is an undoubted power. Everybody who can persuade other people that he says or does things impossible must have something of that power. But I think he will not mesmerize me. Perhaps thought-reading is only a form of mesmerism, so that the patient is forced to think what the operator compels him and forces upon him. Has he mesmerized you?"

"No; he has tried. But he can't."

"I remember," the professor continued, in his quiet and reflective way, "going to see a performance by a certain Dr. Slade about ten years ago. He did all sorts of foolish things first—quite insulting to common understanding—and then he did the famous slate trick."

"I know. Showed it to you clean; put it on the table, presently turned it over, and showed it covered with writing."

"Quite so. That is exactly what I saw, and precisely as I described it. The writing itself was pure drivel. It seemed to me a most mysterious thing, only to be explained by some hypothesis about writing which should be invisible until after a certain time. And this was on the face of it absurd. But the man I had brought with me was a professional conjurer, one Hellis by name, who is now dead, and he enlightened me. Dr. Slade caught my eye and held it. He thought he had caught my companion's as well, but there he was mistaken. And Hellis saw him actually changing the slate for another, and shoving the first one into a receptacle under the table. He did it quite coolly, being confident that he held the eyes of both. Well, the audacity of the announcement of what we are going to see this evening reminds me of Dr. Slade's slate. It is so beautifully simple, and at the same time so impossible."

Tom laughed. "We must not, however, rank Herr Paulus with Dr. Slade. He has not converted me, and I am convinced that he is playing some game. But I cannot find him out. Meantime, we are very good friends, and he knows that I am watching him. Hush; here they come."

At that moment Lady Augusta entered on Herr Paulus's arm. The ancient philosopher looked like nothing more than an extremely handsome young gentleman of the modern time. Mr. Brudenel, who followed, looked assured and easy, without any of his customary nervousness.

The guests divided right and left, and they advanced, taking up a position in the middle of the room. Mr. Brudenel's table, in the drawer of which lay that novel by Ouida, which he had not found time to finish since the Abyssinian tour had commenced, was pushed back, and a clear space was formed.

Lady Augusta greeted her guests and sat down; some of the ladies did the same. Others, too much excited by the expectation of what was to come, preferred to stand.

Mr. Brudenel, his face glowing with triumph — after thirty years of psychical research it is indeed a triumph, and was never before vouchsafed to man, to stand on the living rock — his eyes full of joy and his voice full of confidence, raised his left hand, and spoke:

"My friends," he said, with a quiet dignity, new to him, "some of us have worked together in the pursuit of spiritual truth for many years; we have grown gray in our researches; we have been continually baffled; we have been deceived and disappointed; we have been dejected; there have been times when it was difficult to maintain a cheerful front in presence of so much disappointment and so much ridicule."

"We have known many such times, Brudenel," said Mr. Athelstan Kilburn.

"At one of the moments of deepest humiliation I was found by Herr Paulus; you remember how, on the very first night, he filled our hearts with new faith, and kindled new enthusiasm within us."

"We remember that night very well," Mr. Kilburn again interrupted.

"Perhaps it happened to some of you as to me, that in the morning a cold wave of doubt followed the hope and enthusiasm of the evening."

"It did," said Mr. Kilburn. "It always does."

"What we had seen we thought nothing but the effect of mesmeric power, with the exhibition of certain phenomena by no means new."

"By no means new," said Emmanuel Chick.

"Though brilliantly executed, and in the full light for all to see. I say, my friends, that some of you felt as I did."

There was a general and sympathetic murmur at the recollection of these unpleasant symptoms. They were perhaps a common experience among Spiritualists.

"In the morning, therefore," Mr. Brudenel went on, "I repaired to this study, oppressed and dejected. Herr Paulus followed me. He began by reading my thoughts accurately and exactly, a thing which should of itself have reassured me. He then voluntarily proposed to give me a private proof of his credentials, and begged me to ask him something—anything apparently impossible. I asked him to place in my hands an Indian paper—the *Friend of India*—for that very day. He reminded me that the difference of time between London and Delhi is about six hours, so that at ten o'clock in the morning with us it is already four in the afternoon with them. If, he said, I had asked for a copy of the paper at midnight, I might have had one just hot from the press of the next morning. As it was—I know not how the paper came into his hands—he handed me the *Friend of India* of that very morning."

"This is an interesting statement," said the professor.

"I opened the paper and read it from beginning to end;" here Mr. Brudenel's memory played him false, because in fact he had really read no more than the title and the date. "It had already been cut, and, I presume, had been read six hours before. In one corner was a brown stain as of spilled coffee. I then, at the request of Herr Paulus, folded the paper, placed it in an envelope, tied it round with ribbon, to which he affixed his own seal, and deposited it in a drawer of my safe. No one, remember," he added, solemnly, "has a key to that safe but myself. That key never leaves my possession."

"And now," said the professor, "you are going to open the drawer and to show us the paper. But first, how are we sure that no one has got at the safe?"

"You have my word."

"Precisely. But how do you yourself know it?"

"I repeat that no one has a key except myself, and that no one knew of the deposit of this paper except myself."

"You are now going to show it to us. Permit me to say, Mr. Brudenel, that it would have been more satisfactory had we seen it on the day that you received it."

"Much more satisfactory," said Emmanuel Chick.

"Permit me one more question," this heckling professor continued. "Have the copies of this paper been sent round by the post already?"

"I believe not," Mr. Brudenel replied; "they will be received by London subscribers to-morrow morning."

"That is highly important, and will have to be ascertained. Now, sir, we will, if you please, proceed to the verification of the document."

Mr. Brudenel drew forth his bunch of keys. Then he turned pale suddenly, and whispered a word in the ear of Herr Paulus.

"The friends have forgotten and forgiven," said this oracular young man. "Have neither doubt nor fear."

Mr. Brudenel gave his daughter his bunch of keys.

"Sibyl, my dear," he said, "go and open the safe. Get me the packet in the left-hand drawer."

Sibyl obeyed. In the left-hand drawer there lay a packet of brown paper tied up with ribbon, and sealed.

"It was sealed in my presence," said Mr. Brudenel, "by Herr Paulus. He will examine the seal before it is broken."

The professor looked at the seal.

"There is a pentagon with some Hebrew letters on it," he said.

"Here is the seal." Paul drew a ring from his finger. "It is my own—the seal of Prince Menelek."

Then the professor opened the packet. Within it was the *Friend of India*, four weeks old, the paper which would be delivered in the morning.

The professor looked at the paper suspiciously; he marked the brown coffee-stain, he read the telegrams—they were dated four weeks ago—the date at the top of the page was four weeks old. Everything seemed genuine. Yet he doubted.

"It seems to be—I suppose it is," he said, "the paper of the date named." He gave it

to Tom Langston, who examined it with
equal care.

"It is very odd," he said, glancing quickly at Herr Paulus, who received the look and
the remark without apparent emotion. "It
is extremely odd—it is, in fact, wonderful.
The paper has been lying in the drawer of
the safe for a month; it came over sky, so to
speak, all the way; yet it smells of the ship
or of the letter-bag just as Indian papers do
always smell. Foreign letters have all got a
double smell, in fact." He smelled the paper
curiously. "One of the place where they
come from. There's a Calcutta smell, and a
Bombay smell, and a Delhi smell that I can
detect; of course every city has its own peculiar smell. And there's the smell of the
voyage as well. Now this paper has never
been on a ship at all, and yet it has the smell
of the voyage. How are we to explain that?"

"As for me," Paul replied, cheerfully, "I
explain nothing. I am not responsible for
the paper, or for the way in which it came."

"Why try to explain?" asked Mr. Brudenel. "The fact is before us. Every one
here can testify to that. And now"—he
looked round with an air of assurance and
triumph—"I presume that no one will doubt
my statement of the case. And I hope, I
trust, that this miracle—I can account it as
nothing less—will remove the last shreds of
doubt if any remain as to the mission of my
young friend here."

All those who had any right to be considered persons of authority here stepped forward and shook hands, first with Mr. Brudenel and then with Herr Paulus.

It was at this point that Mr. Brudenel
delivered himself of the speech which has already been mentioned. It was a purely spontaneous and unpremeditated speech, springing straight from the joy and triumph of his
heart. And everybody felt that he had the
right to make that speech.

Sibyl, who preserved her presence of mind
and remained unmoved, looked inquiringly
at Tom, who only shook his head incredulous-
ly. The case was beyond him. It seemed
for the moment as if the scoffers were silenced. Certainly his laboratory contained
no such secret as would enable him to annihilate time and space, except by means of the
electric spark, which does not convey a book
and parcels. The professor, however, rallied.
He was beaten down but not conquered.

"I admit," he said, "that you have a very
strong case, particularly if it could be shown
that no one could receive a copy of the paper
by post in time to place it in the safe. Until that is proved I cannot acknowledge the
genuineness of this miracle. We must not
accept the impossible as accomplished until

there remains no room for doubt. Have you
anything to add, sir?" He turned to Herr
Paulus.

"I? Nothing." The young philosopher
was standing carelessly, as if he was not at
all interested in the case. "Nothing at all.
If you cannot accept Mr. Brudenel's statement, it is waste of time adding mine by way
of corroboration. Perhaps, as you say, the
safe has been tampered with. Yet the tam-
pering must have been effected between the
earliest possible time when the paper would
be received and nine o'clock, the time when
everybody here arrived. Let us get our limits of time exact. I ought to add, however,
that it is not my business to perform conjuring tricks, even of this kind; but it was
thought necessary to impress upon people by
some such manifestations the reality of certain messages. I am not a medium in the
ordinary sense of the word."

"You are not," said Emmanuel Chick.

"My friends converse with each other
freely, whether they are dead or alive; whether they are together or apart."

"Are we not mixing things?" asked the
professor.

"No — if I succeed in showing you exactly what I claim to be and to do. If you
come here expecting the ordinary raps and
things, you are mistaken. The arrival of
this paper is not due to any spirit, but to a
living person."

"Humph!" said the professor.

"The original intention of that living person has been carried out. Mr. Cyrus Brudenel has no longer any doubt at all."

"None," said that gentleman; "none
whatever. We stand upon the solid rock—
upon the solid rock."

The repetition of this assertion unfortunately weakened its strength. It seemed as
if the incredulity of the professor had taken
something from the solidity of the rock.

"There are some," said Herr Paulus,
"who are so prejudiced that they will never
believe. Come, sir," he turned sharply to
the professor, "what is it you would like
to have?"

"Give me this day's paper."

"Well, I gave it Mr. Brudenel, but you
won't believe me. Still, if you are not contented, and if my friends are willing to grat-
ify a sceptical mind—not that you will believe a bit the more—but still—" He said
this very slowly, and with meaning, insomuch
that there was once more a hush of expectation, and all eyes were turned upon him.
"See!" he cried, throwing forward his right
arm with the same gesture that he had employed on the first evening. Then he raised
his left hand and caught something folded—

how it came or whence, no one saw. It was a folded paper, and he handed it to the professor.

"What is it?" he asked.

The professor opened the paper, looked at the title and at the date.

"Good heavens!" he cried, "it is *to-day's paper!*"

"Oh!" Everybody said that.

"To-day's paper," he repeated, again looking at the title and the date. "The *Friend of India* published at Delhi this very day. Is it possible?"

Herr Paulus took the paper from his unresisting hand and gave it to Lady Augusta, who gave it to Hetty, who passed it on to another, and so it passed from hand to hand, for everybody wanted to see for themselves this most wonderful thing.

"Tom," Sibyl whispered, "I feel as if my head was going round. What does it all mean? Can there be any reality in it?"

"I believe," Tom replied, "that we are all mesmerized, and that he makes us see and say and testify exactly what he likes. Keep your head steady, Dodo. The professor looks like the proverbial stuck pig. Put a pin into me if I begin to look like that."

"I should like," said the professor, recovering a little, "to see the paper again. May I take it away and keep it?"

"Certainly," Herr Paulus replied. "Where is it? Who has got the paper?"

Wonderful to relate, nobody had it. The paper had vanished. Some there were who thought that the Rev. Benjamin Rudge had taken it for literary purposes, but he declared that he had done no more than read the title and the date, like the rest. Others, again, thought that Mr. Emmanuel Chick might have slipped it into his pocket in order to hide the evidence of superior skill; but he denied the charge. Everybody had seen it; everybody had passed it on; and no one could find out who had it last. It was gone—lost —and it has never been seen since.

"Shall we offer our pockets to be searched?" asked Herr Paulus.

"Oh, nonsense," said the professor.

"My dear sir," said Herr Paulus, "those who sent the paper here could take it away again. Understand, sir"—for the first time this evening he abandoned the easy, half-careless manner, and became grave and admonitory—"understand that my friends do not suffer dictation. They have chosen to show you this wonder. Believe it or not, as you please. Put any construction upon it that you please. And now there will be no further manifestations."

"Herr Paulus," the professor replied, "I have no reply to make and no explanation now to suggest. But I always remember Dr. Slade's slate," he added in a whisper.

"Herr Paulus"—it was Mrs. Hanley Tracy—"remember, you promised to seek us out on Sunday evenings. Come next Sunday."

"Dear Lady Augusta"—it was Mrs. Medlock—"you *must* keep him here. Oh, that college of which we spoke. How gladly would I hellup! I have been asked to lecture for the new Society for the Extension of Psychical Learning. It is a most interesting and attractive subject, full of ghosts. But oh, how much rather would I hellup your college!"

"Old man"—it was Tom who laid his hand on Paul's arm, and whispered—"it was wonderful—truly wonderful! It was beautifully done. How the devil did you do it? And what became of the paper?"

CHAPTER VI.
BEAUMONT STREET, MARYLEBONE.

IF you walk up that street, now wellnigh forgotten by the fashionable world, called the Marylebone High Street, just after you pass the old parish church, and before you come to the stately new church of St. Marylebone, you will come upon a small row of little houses running eastward. A street called Beaumont Street begins here, but long before there was any Beaumont Street these houses were erected. They are two-storied houses, and painted drab, and always look as if they had been "done up" last summer, and their shutters—they still have shutters—are green. If you keep one eye upon the old parish church and another upon these houses, they are quite in place, and harmonize perfectly. If you think of the great new church, and of the opposite houses, they are incongruous. The little old parish church is just exactly now as it was when Hogarth painted the service in it, save that they have cruelly removed the old three-decker; indeed, I know not where to look for the three-decker now, nearer than Whitby. There used to be one at Lyme-Regis, but I hear that it has been removed. If you go to this church on a Sunday morning, and shut your eyes to the congregation, which somehow seems to consist chiefly of gentlemen's gentlemen and of ladies' ladies, you may fancy yourself back in the days of wigs and commodes, of purple satin coats and hoops. Moreover, if you contemplate this little row of houses steadily, you are presently enabled to remove all the houses and streets opposite to them, and to restore in their place the dear old Marylebone Gardens, beloved of Pepys, frequented by Captain MacHeath, by the roistering blades of London Town, by the sparks from the Temple and Gray's Inn, by grave citizens who brought their wives and daughters for an evening of innocent amusement, and by riotous young noblemen who came with Cynthia and Chloe. At the back of the church was the workhouse, whither in due course Cynthia and Chloe retreated, a good deal battered by the Joyous Life; and south of the workhouse lay the great burying-ground, oldest of the London cemeteries, which is now a garden. Cynthia and Chloe both lie buried here without any tombstones. Oh, the tales that these houses could tell — the nights they remember when the horns resounded in the gardens, and when the men sang at their suppers, and Kitty and Jenny and Polly pranced around with their gallants, and the highwaymen swaggered within and the footpad lurked without, and the gamester and the pluck-pigeon prowled about in search of their prey! But their *historiettes* would be more amusing than edifying.

The gardens are long since shut up and and built over, like Cupid's Gardens and Ranelagh and Vauxhall and Cremorne; for there is to be no more innocent happiness allowed to anybody on account of the serpent who gets into all the gardens and tempts the young folks with that apple. Streets cover up these gardens as they cover up the great Queen Anne Square which lay beyond; the turnpike at the end of High Street is gone, and there is not a single remnant of fashion left from end to end. Yet if a man wanted a quiet corner, unfrequented and unknown, there is no more likely spot for him in all London than this little bit of Beaumont Street, Marylebone High Street.

One afternoon there walked slowly across the church-yard from the Euston Road to the High Street a young gentleman dressed in a most beautiful and expensive fur-lined coat. His hat was new and glossy, his gloves and boots were good, and he carried a new and very slim umbrella; a young gentleman clearly of fashion and fortune, if outward seeming be worth anything.

The old woman opened the door for him in one of the little old houses, let him in without question, and he entered the front room on the ground-floor without being announced. Clearly, therefore, *ami de famille*, or perhaps a son of the family. There was sitting by the fire in a low chair, his feet upon a cushion, a man well stricken in years. He was asleep when the door opened, but woke with a start and sat upright, clutching the arms of the chair. "Paul!" he cried, "I thought you would come to-day. I felt you coming."

He was certainly enjoying a green old age;

his shoulders were rounded, his beard and his abundant hair were both long and white and venerable; his limbs were thin, and looked as if they would tremble under him if he stood upright, but his eyes were strong and clear. There was no senility in those eyes; and his face, once awake, was full of life and interest in life. Some of us, the happiest among us, die upward, slowly; others, more unhappy, die downward, from the top to the trunk. This old man was dying upward.

"Paul, it is a month since you left us. How have you fared? Sit down; you have much to tell. Sit down and begin."

There was something in his voice and way of speaking which resembled the manner of the younger man; a winning smile, a soft voice, a gentle tone, a sympathetic and earnest look in the eyes. Had the younger man caught his manner from the older and improved it after capture?

Paul removed his coat and sat down.

"First, then," he said, "I found it easier to succeed than I thought. My success has been wonderful. Now I will tell you all about it."

We know how he had succeeded, and can therefore omit his narrative, though there were many points in it omitted in our own. History is nothing but careful selection, and were all the truth told there would be nothing dramatic and nothing interesting.

"For a beginning, Paul," said the old man, "you have done well. Nay, my boy, you have shown genius. But how will you keep it up?"

"By genius again. At present I have only just begun. Oh, it will be the most splendid thing out. And it is all so simple, so simple, so wonderfully simple."

"Simple, indeed — to you. But there is no one in the whole world who has your powers, Paul."

"The idiots! the clumsy idiots! Why, more miracles have been performed in that one house during the last month than by the whole of the Spiritualists since the rappings first begun, with the Esoteric Buddhists thrown in! The idiots! And they go on practising their tricks and little crafty cheats, and people go on believing in them."

"Good, lad, good." The old man gently rubbed his hands. "This is the right spirit — contempt for the inferior practitioner. You have your powers, he has his tricks. You have your secrets, he has his machinery. Yes, you can drive him out of the field. And after that—"

"I shall found a new system of philosophy," Paul went on, with enthusiasm. "I shall become the leader of a great school. I call it the Ancient Way. I have a Sacred Book—I am writing it now—it is the Book of the Secret Wisdom of King Solomon, taken to Abyssinia by his son Menelek."

"Very good. Abyssinia is good. Thibet is played out. Abyssinia is very good."

"We shall have a college and chosen disciples. Only there will be the Illuminati, who have powers corresponding to my own. There will be degrees—from the Initiate to the Adept. Oh, I see it before me clearly. And when this college is established, and my name is made forever, and I am in the midst of my power, I shall vanish suddenly and be no more heard of, and so be a problem for all ages."

"Ye—yes." The old man received the conclusion of this programme somewhat doubtfully. "Ye—yes, Paul. The college and this school of philosophers are very good ideas, because you would be the head of the college, and they must pay their head. But it would be hard work—very hard work—keeping it up. And if you were to vanish, my dear boy, how about the dollars?"

The young man's face, which had been glowing, fell, and he changed color.

"The dollars — oh, the dollars! it is the curse of being an American, that one is never permitted to think of anything but dollars."

"You are young, lad ; you are young. When you are old you will think as I think. There is nothing but dollars worth considering. Where is your independence if you have got no dollars? What is your glory worth? What will you do in your old age if you have no dollars? I have got few enough, because, like you when I was young and foolish, I wasted myself in idle display of powers to make the world open its mouth and gape. It is glorious, my son. Your scheme is splendid; and the secret history, if it were ever revealed, would be more glorious to you than the belief of your disciples and the foundation of a sect. But you are young. A few years—perhaps a single year—will do all that you wish to do here; and then—you have a long life before you. There is nothing that you can do to make your living. How will you live?"

"Like the sparrows."

"On crumbs and worms. Will you like it?"

"Well, then, I will keep on the college. I will attract students by hundreds. I will take all their fees to myself and build up a great fortune."

"Now you talk sense, Paul. Better still —go over to America and found a sister college. If you want to make a very large fortune, give out that the younger sister is going to surpass the elder, by reason of the enormously superior intellect of the Americans. There are plenty of credulous people in both countries, my boy—here they call them mugs or jugginses. But there are more mugs in the States than in England."

"I do not like the use of slang," said Paul, coldly.

"No? Let us not speak of mugs, then. There are more inquirers in the States than in Great Britain. Will that do?"

"Besides, there is another reason why I think I could make money—only sometimes," he said, apologetically, "one gets carried away. There is a girl—"

"Paul, Paul!" the old man sat upright, holding tightly to the arms of his chair and speaking earnestly; "I have warned you again and again. Your power depends upon your keeping brain clear and heart cold. If you suffer your brain to be filled with the thoughts of a woman, if your heart beats at the sight of a woman, if you fall in love, you are lost. You can only work that power so long as you remain unmoved by any woman. It was a woman who destroyed Samson. A woman will destroy you. Let all the women love you, pretend to love them in return, but never, never let your imagination dwell upon one of them. Take care, take care!"

"This is not a common girl. And I am not talking of love at all "—yet he blushed. "This is a girl whom I have discovered—one girl of a thousand. She is to other girls what I am to other men. She *has the power*, daddy. Yes, she has the power; she does not know it, though she knows that I can at any moment take her out of herself. She has the power in a wonderful measure. Oh, if you had had the luck, the special luck, to have fallen in with such a girl a long time ago, you would not have been contented with advising New York merchants and consulting spirits about the price of stocks. You would have gone for higher game. There is no better clairvoyant in the world, I am certain, although she suspects nothing of her powers. She is the daughter of a low-class medium, three - fourths humbug, one - fourth sensitive, and she hates the thing because she has long since found out her mother's tricks. But in my hands—" He paused and sighed.

"Is she young, Paul? Is she young and beautiful?"

"She is young and beautiful. In better dress she would be—yes—she would be the most beautiful girl you ever saw. She believes in me, too. Perhaps, perhaps "—he blushed again—" perhaps she loves me. I do not know. You never had such a woman in your hands, I guess,"

"Perhaps not. Perhaps I have. Well, and how is the girl to help in the college?"

"You ask me such a question! What are the things which would most attract the people? The manifestations. Only a sensitive like you—and your pupil and my pupil—could manage these—to call it management. Then think of clairvoyance—I know what that girl can do. I have experimented upon her with nobody looking on. And there is thought-reading. I could teach her how to read thought—I am certain I could—better than I can do it myself. And there is prophecy. There is a clear field for you. I don't mean spotting the winner, but high-class prophecy, which has never yet been attempted. I am quite sure that any one who knows all the facts—that is, more than the inquirer knows—can predict what is going to happen. There is telepathy. That is a new subject which requires to be developed. There is plain and simple mesmerism, with mesmeric healing and mesmeric anæsthetics. Can you ask what such a girl could do for the college? Why, her example alone would create a crowd of clairvoyants."

"Paul, you are indeed a genius."

"There are plenty of girls like her, though not so wonderful. There is Cicely Langston, for instance."

"Who is she?"

"She is the blind girl. I have as much influence over her as I have over Hetty."

His voice dropped a little as he pronounced the name of the girl. This was a bad symptom, properly understood.

"Does she, too, believe in you? Is she, too, in love with you, Paul?"

"Love? No, I think not. She believes in me, and she trusts me. Now, daddy, be sympathetic. You used to be sympathetic enough in the old New York days."

"Yes, because I had a pupil who promised wonderfully well, and only wanted encouragement. I gave him that, and all the help I could. And now, I am happy to say, there's not a man in the world can show a candle to him; not a man in the world who's got a greater influence over people, or who's more highly sensitized."

"There isn't, daddy," said Paul. "Thanks to you, there isn't one." He laid his hand affectionately on the old man's arm.

"But don't forget the dollars, Paul. Remember, the people are longing to pay over their dollars to some one—any one who can make them laugh or cry or frighten them."

"I believe that is so," said Paul, thoughtfully.

"Of course it is. They make their money only to give it away in exchange for pictures or statues, or to buy laughter, tears, terror, comfort, and hope. We find these things for them, Paul, my boy. I have taught you how to do it. Catch their eyes and their minds, and hold them tight. Hold them with a grip. The man who has got the quality of grip is the successful man, whether he is actor, or novelist, or dramatist, or conjurer, or whether he knows the secrets of the occult philosophy. Grip is the thing—grip!"

"You are always right, daddy."

"Hold them with a grip, and don't let go till the dollars are all raked in."

"Well, daddy, but let me have my little play first."

"No, boy, no. Don't waste time."

"Think of the splendid position, the College of the Ancient Way, the Book of Wisdom, the troops of illuminati, and the adepts, and the clairvoyants."

"If you will only stick to it, Paul; but you won't. I am afraid you will want to play a deeper game."

"And then think, only think, of disappearing suddenly, leaving not a trace behind except, perhaps, a postal address to Abyssinia!"

"Yes, Paul, if you could afford it—but you can't. Besides, there is another danger."

"Oh, I know; have no fear, daddy."

"It is a terrible danger for so young a man. Your power, I tell you again, is like the strength of Samson, and when you fall in love with a woman you will lose it. Samson's is a very instructive history for you, Paul. Keep your heart free and cold, and your brain clear; else you will lose your power as Samson lost his strength."

"Never fear, daddy. I love my power too well; whether I disappear or whether I stay on, I shall keep that, even if I have to turn my thoughts and my eyes from the contemplation of beauty. Anyway, my college would be better than telling New York operators when to buy and sell. Fancy wasting such a beautiful gift on bulls and bears."

* * * * * * *

They talked all the afternoon—the master and the scholar, who had long gone beyond anything the master could teach him—and soared upward in flights far beyond the old man's powers of imagination. Yet the master had his points.

They talked of many things; but one thing they avoided. Two of a trade always agree to avoid one subject: it is that side of their business which they do not present to the world. Outsiders may talk generally, and with an affectation of knowing them, of the secrets of the trade; those who are actually engaged in any trade avoid the subject. They know that secrets may be called by another and a much more ugly word. So many trades, so many secrets. So many secrets—so many —no—let them remain secrets. Thus shall every craft have the power of reforming itself, and of becoming honest to the smallest detail. Those who are in the line of Spiritualism, Theosophy, Occult Philosophy, and the like, have, like drapers, grocers, and the whole tribe of trade, their trade secrets. Even those who dwell upon the highest planes and possess powers to which the general practitioners only pretend, avoid speaking with another of the machinery, so to speak, by which those powers are illustrated. A certain amount of stage management, in fact, is absolutely necessary before the higher flights of creative genius can be attempted. In all art, of any kind, there must be grouping.

At last Paul got up. "I must go, daddy," he said. "I shall come to see you again before long, now that things are going on so well."

"Do, Paul, do. By-the-way, I've a letter here from a man called Medlock. He says you know him."

"There was a man of that name went about with Kate Flight, the medium. He was her secretary or clerk. What does he want?"

"Business. He is over here. Says he could run you—he doesn't know where you are—on advantageous terms next winter."

"We'll see. Medlock—Haynes Medlock it was. I wonder if he is Hetty's father, who ran away. Medlock!" Paul started. "Daddy, find out all you can about the man, and tell me when he comes."

"I will, Paul."

"Don't forget, daddy. It may be most useful to me to know all about the man. Do you think you will be able to walk soon?"

"I could walk now, but this cursed east wind keeps me at home."

"Do you think you could make just one little expedition for my sake?"

"What is it?"

"I have often thought that if the learned Abyssinian, the Falasha, Isák Ibn Menelek— he who possesses Solomon's Book of Wisdom, and is the chief prophet of the Ancient Way—would come to the study some morning and present the book in person, it might have a good effect."

The old gentleman laughed merrily.

"Your hair and beard are beautiful. Your eyes are as keen and bright as any philosopher could desire. I would provide a robe, and as for the book, it is nearly ready. It is in parchment—a roll, you know—venerable with age, but written in modern English, because all languages are alike to us."

"I will come, Paul, if you will arrange for me to come and go unseen."

"That will be very easy. You can keep the cab waiting close to the house, and—oh yes, it can be easily arranged."

"Then it shall be done. Have your fling, my dear boy, and found your college. But for making the dollars we shall have to establish that other institution which is to surpass and outstrip her English sister, because of the enormous intellectual superiority of the American people. Next to grip, Paul, comes the spread eagle."

CHAPTER VII.

THE INSTRUCTION OF THE VESTAL.

"HERR PAULUS."

Sibyl stood at the open door of the study. It was after lunch. Paul was sitting beside the fire in the easiest of chairs, one especially made for Mr. Cyrus Brudenel when that student should come here in order to read his great books on the supernatural. On the floor there lay an open novel which had fallen from his hands. The youthful sage was asleep. Thus slept Endymion. I do not know whether this comparison occurred to Sibyl's mind, but I think that even she—the scornful and the hostile—must have been moved to admiration at the wonderful beauty of this young man as he lay back, the long hair rolling off his forehead and his eyes closed.

"Herr Paulus," she repeated.

"Miss Brudenel!" He woke with a start and sprang to his feet. "You here? I was—"

"Please do not take the trouble to explain that your astral body was in Abyssinia or Thibet, Herr Paulus."

"I will not," he replied, now fully awake. "I was only going to explain that the fire was warm, and the atmosphere of this collection of venerable rubbish was drowsy, and the novel I was reading was dull, and so I fell asleep."

"I have come in obedience to my father, Herr Paulus. He is continually urging me to receive instruction from you in something wonderful. I believe you are teaching it to him, but at present nothing seems to have settled in his mind. Would it be convenient for you to begin this afternoon?"

"All my time is at your disposal," he replied. "Pray take a chair. I can only teach, however, those who are willing to learn."

"Did I not explain that I come in obedience to my father? That shows, I suppose, willingness."

"Not at all. You are not only unwilling, but you are hostile."

Sibyl was more than unconquered. She

was unconquerable. The others had all, as we know, been subdued. Even Tom had so far yielded to Paul's influence as to laugh and talk with him while he professed to be watching him, and to call him by the Anglican form of his name. Sibyl alone never relaxed from her attitude of open enmity.

"Miss Brudenel," Paul went on, "there is nothing, I assure you, that I can teach you. It is perfectly useless for you to take the trouble of staying here."

"Of course I know that. But, just to please my father, let me pretend that you are trying to teach me things. You may tell me about your friends, and all the wonderful things they pretend to do. Pray go on, I am listening."

"No," said Paul, "it is impossible. I can only talk in that way with those who are in sympathy with me and with them. You are not. You openly deride them, and you do not attempt to hide the hatred you nourish towards myself. Do you not understand that your proposition is insulting? But you do not mind that, perhaps. Your whole attitude since I have been here proves so much."

"I do not wish to insult any one, Herr Paulus; I am here in obedience to my father. I cannot help it if I am out of sympathy with you."

"You might have become one of us. There was a moment, about a month ago, when I fancied that your heart was softening, but it passed away, and now I shall make no further attempt to dispel your prejudice. I must endure it."

"That will cost you very little trouble. Meantime, if you refuse to instruct me, what am I to do? I have promised my father to sit at your feet and listen. I must do that, even if you teach me nothing."

"We might talk about other things, perhaps."

"I do not know any other things which I wish to discuss with you," Sibyl replied, sharply.

"Shall we, then, sit in silence?"

"Yes; that will be much better. Don't speak to me at all."

Paul sat down again in his easy-chair, while Sibyl sat opposite, her hands folded in her lap; and for a space neither spoke.

So far Sibyl had certainly the worst of the conversation; for her opponent showed not the least sign of ruffled temper, and even looked as if he thoroughly enjoyed the conditions of the lesson, and was quite happy and at his ease. Nothing is more irritating than to be cross with a person who keeps his temper.

Naturally, it was the woman who first broke the silence.

"How long," she asked, looking at the clock, "should the first lesson last?"

"As long as you please."

"Then let it finish now. Herr Paulus"—she changed her manner instantly—"never mind me and my—my distrust; but tell me what it is you have done to my father."

"You have observed a change?"

"It is so great a change that I want you to tell me what you have said or done. I have asked him, but he does not seem able to speak coherently about it. He is much happier; he has lost his restless manner; he seems, for the first time, satisfied and contented. What have you done to him?"

"We talk here of things which you do not understand. They are foolishness and pretence to you, but they lift up the soul for us."

Sibyl made no direct reply. Always this man's explanations put her in the wrong, and made her feel humble for the moment and angry afterwards—else angry first and then humble.

"Is it all, then, to end in vague talk which lifts the soul?" she asked.

"I do not say so."

"You came with a message. You said so. You have done all kinds of wonderful things to show that you were a properly accredited person. You talked of conversing with people far off, and with the dead; of making youth and age, life and death, only phrases."

"It is true; I said all this and more."

"But everything is as far off as ever. You are only like the medium who brings messages from the dead which tell nobody anything."

"What does your father say?"

"He says—" Sibyl hesitated, because she saw another trap. "He says that he spends his mornings in Abyssinia or somewhere."

"I suppose you can trust your father's word? So you see things are not, after all, so far off as they were, except to yourself."

"I can trust my father's word, and yet—yet—oh, it is nonsense. How can he go to Abyssinia?"

"Why does he say that he goes there, then?"

"Herr Paulus"—Sibyl looked him straight in the face, with a spot of crimson in either cheek—"Herr Paulus, I think you deceive him in some way."

Paul smiled gravely and compassionately, as one smiles at an outburst from a wayward child.

"It is as well to say a thing as to think it. Of course I have known all along what you think. So be it. Let it be. I deceive your father; yet I make him happier, lest restless, and more confident. He has abandoned his old gods, he has destroyed his idols, and will consult the spirits no more."

5

"Yes, that is true; we shall have no more séances here. And oh, Herr Paulus, if it is quite true that you want nothing for yourself, be content with what you have done, and go away. I implore you to go away while my father's mind is relieved of one superstition."

"You would add—'before he falls into another.' Miss Brudenel, you have spoken too late. That is, it is impossible for me to obey you. Things must develop—nothing ever stops still—he must follow in the path we have entered. But do not be afraid. For your father and for this house all will be pure again, as you will find and acknowledge —even you."

"Never!"

"Meantime, is there anything that I can do for you?"

"You may cease to fill Cicely's head with hopes of her brother's return."

"That, too, is impossible. Her brother may return any day. His ship is not far from port. Sir Percival thinks that he has cut himself off from his family altogether, and we must go to find him if he will not come here. You may, if you please, come with us."

"Oh! Still mystery and pretence. Then, will you leave off mesmerizing Hetty?"

"No, I will not." Paul put his foot down firmly. "Hetty has a gift that must be most carefully developed. Do not ask me, Miss Brudenel, to interfere with what concerns my teaching."

"You will stay here, then?"

"Until Lady Augusta orders me to go."

"Then you will stay here forever."

"Perhaps. I know not."

Sibyl looked round the room filled with the books of her father's priceless collection. "Oh," she said, "when shall we get out of this hateful atmosphere of mystery? If you knew"—she pointed to the shelves—"how I hate the awful rubbish that is here!"

"It is pretty bad," Paul replied, blandly. "In fact, there is nowhere a better collection of venerable rubbish than your father's."

"And yet you encourage him with your Solomon's Book of Wisdom and your story about Prince Menelek, and Izâk the Falasha. How can you talk such stuff?"

"It is sad stuff to you, is it not? I am sorry. On the day when it ceases to seem sad stuff you will become sympathetic. But that day will never come."

"No, never."

"As for us, we find it full of comfort and wisdom and knowledge and power."

"I cannot believe it. No, Herr Paulus, you are either a person of wonderful credulity, or you are—"

"Let me finish your sentence."

"No; let it remain unfinished. As for me, I am persuaded that nothing can ever come of looking beyond the veil. There will be no new revelation. The gulf between the living and the dead will never be bridged except by death. No voices will ever again come to us from the other side. Until we die ourselves we shall never know more than we know already."

"That is your creed. Let us possess our own. I shall not try to convert you by any arguments. I leave you to the care of— Science."

Sibyl colored. Yet his eyes seemed to have no second meaning.

"Of Science?" she asked.

"Yours is the creed of Science. She is constantly discovering the most wonderful things, and will not allow us to discover anything. Science holds conversation thousands of miles apart by means of the little wire. We do the same thing in a simpler manner without a wire."

"So you say, Herr Paulus."

"And you do not believe me. Very good. You think that nothing will change your attitude?"

"Nothing."

"Nothing will change your hostility to myself?"

"Nothing, unless it might be your departure."

"Miss Brudenel, sometimes, when I know all the circumstances of a case, I permit myself to prophesy. Let me be a prophet in your case."

"If you please."

"The time will come—it will come very soon—when your hostility will cease altogether, and be changed into gratitude and friendship."

"Oh!"

"Yes, gratitude, certainly; because you will associate my name with the removal of certain obstacles of which you know."

"What do you mean?" Again Sibyl blushed.

"And the adjustment of certain coming troubles of which as yet you know nothing."

"Such a prophecy means nothing."

"You shall see. Even then you will not believe. Now, Miss Brudenel, your first lesson has come to an end. I have taught you nothing, but I have ventured on a little prophecy which I beg of you most earnestly to remember when the time comes. You will then acknowledge that I must have known, when I uttered that prophecy, what had already happened and what was going to happen."

When Sibyl left him, Paul sat down again

by the fire and continued to read his novel till five o'clock. Then he went in search of tea and the accompaniment of feminine talk, which he loved, with warmth and ease, and the flattery of his disciples. How little do we want to make us happy!

CHAPTER VIII.

A TRIFLING INCIDENT.

EVERYBODY remembers that fateful morning when the news of the Great Smash brought dismay upon thousands, and opened the doors of the workhouse to hundreds ; when the weeping of women and the curses of men were borne upon the wings of the wind, and flew abroad into all lands, and hung over the great city of London like a fog ; when the guilty directors would have called upon the rocks to cover them—if there had been any rocks—from the wrath of the share-holders; and from one end of the land to the other one event alone occupied all minds, though the Czar might imagine vain things, and though the dynamiter was abroad.

On that morning Paul came down-stairs a little later than usual, and appeared in the breakfast-room with his customary cheerful mien, ready with an affectionate smile for Lady Augusta, a cold greeting for Sibyl, and a warm pressure of the hand for Cicely. At the aspect of the assembled party, however, his flow of spirits experienced a most disagreeable check. It was just as if a sparkling and vivacious mountain - stream, prepared to run gayly down the valley babbling over the stones, with here and there a trout, and here and there a grayling, were to meet a big insurmountable and ugly dam, behind which it would be compelled to accumulate —mountain-stream language for labor—until a lake should be formed.

There was not on any face, not even on that of Lady Augusta, the least response to Paul's smile of greeting. They all turned and saw him, and then looked blankly at each other.

Something had happened.

When one says "something," one understands the word disastrous. On the faces of all present, in their attitude, in their eyes, that fact was apparent. Confusion, consternation, amazement, dismay—this beloved goddess has all these names and more—reigned in that breakfast-room. She manifested her dread sway in various ways, according to the disposition and the age of each. Mr. Brudenel sat upright; his pale cheeks, his terror-stricken eyes, his open lips, his trembling hands, would have caused him in the last century, which was a time of great tenderness and deep feeling, to be likened unto a stuck pig

—pity and sympathy could not be more fittingly illustrated than by this simile. Whatever had happened, it affected him most painfully. Lady Augusta was standing over him, her hands clasped, and a prolonged "oh!" still visible upon her lips, though the sound of it was only faintly heard echoed among the cups and saucers. Sibyl, in charge of the teapot, as usual, had risen in her place, and was now looking—not at her father, but at Tom—with eyes full of pain and amazement. Cicely held out her hands helplessly, as if feeling for support. Tom, who was also standing, had the paper in his hands—he had caught it as it fell from his guardian's hands and fluttered towards the floor—and he was reading something which appeared to interest him greatly, but did not cause his eyes to dance with mirth and joy. That is not, somehow, the function of the daily paper. When I establish that morning journal which will trample the life out of all the rest, I shall call it the *Daily Saddener.*

"Something has happened?" Paul asked.

Considering how great a thing had happened, how extraordinary were his own powers, and how peculiar were his facilities for obtaining information, how ready of access for him was the Universal Intelligence Department, this question was weak. He felt immediately how weak it was, and wished that he had taken his place in silence.

"Oh, Paul !" said Lady Augusta. Was there reproach in her voice?

He suspected nothing ; in spite of the knowledge he had obtained, and the advice he had given to Mr. James Berry, he had at this moment no suspicion at all of what had happened.

Tom looked up from the paper.

"Something *has* happened," he said.

"Is it in the paper?"

Tom laughed, but not mirthfully.

"You don't mean to say you have been left in ignorance of it?"

"I have been told nothing."

"I wonder you were not told last night. I wonder you were not permitted to prophesy the event. It would have been something to have learned what was coming—even a fortnight ago. Come to think of it, Paul, your friends have behaved in a most unhandsome way not to have warned you of it."

"Meantime, I know nothing."

"What's the use of friends who won't tell a man beforehand, and prevent people from coming to grief?" Tom continued.

"Oh!" Mr. Brudenel groaned. "All this time wasted in discussion about philosophy, when a single word of caution might have saved us. I remember when one of Chick's spirits warned an inquirer against a voyage in which the ship was cast away. One of Emmanuel Chick's spirits did this! And your great and powerful friends could do nothing!"

"Paul," said Lady Augusta, solemnly, "a great and most unexpected blow has fallen upon us. Nothing could be more unexpected. Hardly any disaster could be heavier. It is so terrible a calamity that I cannot refrain from asking, like my husband, why your friends should have permitted it?"

"I know now," said Paul—"Brudenel & Co. have failed."

"You have seen the paper, then?"

"No, I have just been told. The company has failed. It is a complete collapse. Three fortunes — Sibyl's, Cicely's, and your own, Tom—were invested in it and are lost, I dare say hopelessly, because the share-holders will get nothing. That is the news in to-day's paper, is it not?"

"That is the blow, Paul."

"It is only money, then, after all," he said, astonished. "Why do you look so distressed?"

"Only money!" said Tom. "Only our little all that has vanished!"

"What of that? Let us have breakfast."

He sat down, and without paying any more attention to the distress of his friends, he looked round the table and considered what he would take for his breakfast. He began with a little fish, keeping an eye on some sausages, remembering that the ham on the sideboard was excellent, and thinking that a boiled egg, followed by a little confiture, would fitly conclude the meal. He had as yet—but then he was under five-and-twenty—a most excellent appetite, and he tackled breakfast with regularity, punctuality, and zeal.

"Let us all take breakfast; and after breakfast we will discuss the real importance of this trifling incident."

Tom laughed.

"Trifling, sir? Trifling?" cried Mr. Brudenel, looking upon him wrathfully. "Let me tell you, sir, it is you who are trifling. The fortunes of my daughter and my ward are gone. The concern which bears my name is ruined, and you call it a trifling incident!"

"Trifling, indeed. An episode not to be heeded by the wise man."

Mr. Brudenel gasped, but said nothing in reply. The sight of that calm and undisturbed face, master of itself, though all his friends' fortunes were lost, and the authoritative repetition of the adjective, subdued him.

"There is a short leading article on it," said Tom. "I will read it:

"'The presentation, yesterday, of a wind-ing-up petition for the great trading company known as Brudenels'—after the name of the founder—together with the fact that it was unopposed, have struck with consternation others besides the unfortunate share-holders themselves ; for if this house, apparently so prospering, thus suddenly collapses, who knows if others may not be in the same rotten condition? It has long been certain that the carrying trade has been bad, not owing so much to the depression of trade as to the multiplication of ships. But no one, it is safe to say, except, perhaps, those who were acute observers in the City, predicted the downfall of Brudenels'. The secrets of the Board have been well kept. Meantime, many rumors are afloat. It is confidently asserted that the high dividends hitherto declared must have been paid out of capital. It is said that the bankruptcy of the company is complete. A meeting of share-holders has been already hastily summoned to consider what steps should be taken as regards the conduct of the directors. The firm whose business was taken over by this company was founded by the late Mr. Abraham Brudenel, one of those successful, enterprising, and keen-sighted merchants who have made the English name. He was succeeded by his sons, the present Sir Abraham and Mr. Cyrus Brudenel, who formed it into a company while it was still in a perfectly solvent and flourishing condition. For thirty years the company has seemed to be advancing; its capital has been greatly increased; it has always paid large and steady dividends. The shares have gone up, until only two days ago they were quoted at 327, and business at that figure was actually done on the Exchange. So sudden and unexpected a collapse is almost without a parallel. We trust that a searching inquiry will be made into the causes of the failure, and that some explanation will be demanded as to the high dividends. It is pitiful to think of the unhappy share-holders, many of whom are widows, ladies, and orphans, whose shares in Brudenels' were regarded as perfectly safe and trustworthy, and who find themselves now in helpless and hopeless poverty. It is understood that one of the brothers, Mr. Cyrus Brudenel, has retained a large stake in the business, though he has taken no part in the direction since the formation of the company.'"

"This is your trifle, Paul," said Tom, concluding.

"Is it?" Paul replied, carelessly. "Let us go on with breakfast. People have lost money. Some who intended to do nothing all their lives will have to work ; some who thought they were going to wear silk will wear stuff; some who thought they were going to die in their own houses will die in the workhouse; some—"

"Paul," said Lady Augusta, "do not be too high for us. Consider—consider ; we have not all reached that level. Be patient with us."

But Paul shook his head impatiently. "This fuss," he said, "about money!"

"My company!" Mr. Brudenel answered. "My father's concern — bankrupt—ruined. The children's money all gone! Cicely, you are a pauper, my dear! Tom, your guardian has thrown away your fortune; you've got nothing but your brains and your hands."

"Lucky for Tom," said Paul.

"Why did they not help us?" asked Mr. Brudenel. "They *ought* to have helped us. What have they done for us? Nothing! What are they going to do for us? Nothing!"

Paul went to the sideboard and helped himself.

"This is an excellent ham," he said. "The English ham at its best is really superior to any other, though I have tasted very good hams in Russia."

Nobody replied. One or two, however, thought this conduct and these words an exhibition of heartlessness.

"When it comes to something practical," said Tom, "your friends, Paul, are not so good as poor old Chick's spirits."

"Practical ! You call money practical ? But I forgot, Tom, you believe nothing. To you money is, doubtless, a very practical thing."

He continued to eat his breakfast with undiminished appetite and vigor amid the stricken family. Sibyl poured out his tea for him with set lips and red cheeks ; Cicely hung her head; Lady Augusta drooped; but Paul ate and drank, and was as cheerful as if nothing at all had happened.

Then Mr. Cyrus Brudenel, after the manner of the ancients, and quite forgetful of divine prophecy and the precepts of Izák Ibn Menelek, just as if the Abyssinian sage had not taken him in hand at all, began a monologue or lament over the lost company. It was almost an epic. It opened with a narrative of the circumstances which led his father to leave his native village and repair to London with twopence in his pocket. Nobody ever really succeeds in London if he is so unfortunate as to have more than twopence to begin with. The paternal Brudenel, the original Abraham, became a shopboy, a clerk—Heaven knows what—and in the fulness of time founded the great concern which bears his name. At first it was not a great concern, but only a small venture, which was nursed, followed, and developed

with as much care as Abraham had been wont to lavish upon the turkeys in his native county of Norfolk, until it grew into a concern. Then, Mr. Cyrus Brudenel related, the time came when his father had to die. He did this with the utmost reluctance, not because he was afraid to die, but because it seemed so great a pity to leave the concern until it was fully developed, and there were still some shores and ports in the world that knew not yet the name of Brudenel. The death-bed scene was truly touching. Then changing his key, like a minstrel who knows how to touch the hearts of his hearers, Mr. Cyrus Brudenel went on to relate how he and his brother carried on the concern for a while, but resolved at length to make it into a company, and did so, taking a large sum of money and so many fully paid-up shares, which they immediately sold at a large premium, and bought land in the days when land was still valuable; and how his brother got a baronetcy, and how he himself devoted his life to the science of spiritualistic philosophy, and how he invested, unfortunately, as trustee and executor, the whole of his ward's fortune, and that of his daughter, in the company. "And now," he concluded, "I have made them paupers, because the company is bankrupt. My father's business is ruined ; our name has become a by-word; thousands of innocent people who are wrecked with the company will curse us forever. I am an executor and guardian who has thrown away the property of his wards. You, Tom, will have to work for your bread. You, Cicely, have no longer anything. You, Sibyl, have lost all that your mother left you. Children, I will try to make it up to you; but oh," he said, "it is a disgrace to the family name from which we shall never recover—never!"

While he wailed and lamented, his wife leaned over him. Paul, who had eyes in the back of his head and ears all over, observed that Tom was holding Sibyl's hand under the table, and he heard them whispering.

"Sibyl, will you wait for me ? Do you know what this means for us? Do you see what a barrier it raises? Will you wait till I have regained by work what we have lost?"

And she replied,

"For a hundred years, Tom, if it must be, I will wait!"

The observer and listener made as if he saw and heard nothing. Presently, however, when Mr. Cyrus Brudenel had run down, and stopped exhausted, rather than satiated, with lament, Paul said, quietly,

"No, Mr. Brudenel, disgrace cannot be brought upon one man by the *laches* of any others. I perceive, however, that it will be useless for me to join you in the study this morning. Your mind seems utterly over-whelmed for the moment by one of the com-monest of human reverses. Izák Ibn Menelek will not want you in your present temper." Then Mr. Cyrus Brudenel sprang to his feet and broke out in revolt. "Izák Ibn Menelek!" he cried, in con-tempt. "What has he taught me? Noth-ing! Not so much as Chick's spirits. How has he helped me? In no way. What will he do for me? Nothing. Do not speak to me any more of Izák Ibn Menelek. Let us have done with this pretender of Abyssinia. The spirit-rappers and the ancient philoso-phers are all impostors together. There is no help in and of them. Give me back my daughter's fortune—you—with your pre-tence and your sneers about the trifling in-cident. Give it back or never speak to me again! If you can help us, let that be your way of help. If you have no help for us, go! Go—you and all your tribe! Depart, and leave us to be ruined by ourselves!"

He rushed from the room. They heard his footsteps making in the direction of the study, and they all looked at each other in consternation first, and at Paul next.

"I will take a little marmalade," he said.

Sibyl's eyes ought to have withered and consumed him as she followed her father.

"This insensibility does you great credit," said Tom. "I can't quite reach it myself; but I do wish that you had, say, a couple of millions, and that I could imitate your ex-ample and look on unmoved while you lost it all."

"Ask yourself what you have lost, Tom," Paul replied. "You have been lazily ques-tioning Science. You will now persecute her. The law of existence is that a man shall develop himself under the goad of ne-cessity. You will now become a great pro-fessor instead of an amateur. You ought to rejoice."

"Every man who works for money is a slave," said Tom. "I have become a slave."

"That is because men are such fools that they do not combine. When they have learned to combine there will be no slaves."

"Wise philosopher! Nevertheless, I will betake myself to the family solicitor, and see what can be saved out of the wreck. And so far from rejoicing, if I can discover any engine or contrivance of law which can be used for clapping those directors in quod, I shall set that engine in motion."

"I do not object. It will be a legitimate exercise for your brain."

"Now that we are left alone—we three," Paul continued, rising from the table where he had displayed so remarkable a callous-ness, "we can talk. We understand one another. First, Lady Augusta, tell me what you think."

She hesitated.

"It is beautiful," she said at length, "to hear and to talk about voluntary poverty and renunciation. Your friends, who are superior to fortune, are lovely to contem-plate. But when it comes home to one—frankly, Paul, I am not—we are none of us so far advanced in philosophy as to bear with patience such a blow."

"My friend," said Paul, "it is not a blow, believe me. That alone is a blow which can deprive you of any portion of the wisdom you have learned, or could make it impossi-ble for you to advance. If, for instance, you had lost all, and had to work for your living, it would have been a blow, because your whole nature would have become degraded by work for which you have not been trained. But this will not, I apprehend, affect your present style of living."

"No. My husband has his land, and Sibyl is his heiress. She has lost only her mother's fortune of ten thousand pounds. It is Cicely who is most affected, because she has lost her all. Yesterday this poor child was possessed of an ample dot, and she now has nothing. Yesterday she was indepen-dent, and to-day she is dependent."

"I cannot," said Paul, reflectively, "con-sider that my friends would think it worth while to pay the least attention to this in-cident I have never known them interfere in matters of money. To them, as to all wise men, social conditions which require money are foolishness, and those who suffer by these conditions—that is, those who have to work in order that others may save money, and those who fall into despair when they lose it—ought to combine for the purpose of changing their social conditions. At the same time, so great is the interest felt for this household— which is destined, I believe, to be the centre of a light which shall radiate everywhere and fill the whole world—that I cannot, I really cannot, believe that my friends are ignorant of this accident, nor can I believe that it will prove to be a disaster. I would rather believe that it was permitted by them for your own help and instruction."

"If he could only think so!" said Lady Augusta. "If you could show us that!"

Nothing endeared Paul to these ladies so much as his passage from the light and cheerful air which he wore in society, or the apparent callousness with which he regarded certain mundane things, to the grave and serious discourse which he held with them en petit comité. Women like men to be grave and serious. No one except Lady Augusta, Cicely, and Hetty saw him when he became, not a prophet or a teacher, dogmatic and authoritative, but a humble seeker after truth, sympathetic and full of pity.

"As regards Tom, for instance," he said, "can anything better be desired for a clever man than that he should be compelled to develop himself to the utmost? What is the history of the world's greatest men? They have all been poor; most of them have sprung from the soil; it is when men are young that they acquire the habit of work. Tom, as I told him, will no longer read and lazily question Nature. He will persecute her; he will no longer look on while others dig into her sides; he will take a spade and dig among them. As for Sibyl—" He paused.

"As for Sibyl?" Lady Augusta asked.

"I do not know Sibyl's heart. It is a closed book to me. Yours, Lady Augusta, I can read, and yours, Cicely." Strange! There was the least little touch of jealousy in both of these ladies as he named them. Would each of them, then, have preferred that hers should be the only heart open to his inspection? "I cannot tell how the loss of this money will affect Sibyl. Then let us remember you, Cicely."

"Yes. Tell me, Paul," she replied, "how I am to bear the loss of my fortune. I am so helpless in my blindness that I have always thought it my chief blessing that I should always be able to command attendance. Tell me. Teach me, Paul, and I will resign myself."

"Let me try, Cicely." The simple faith of the girls who cling to the knees of father confessors, directors, vicars, curates, pastors, ministers, shepherds, and prophets sometimes touches their hearts and dims their eyes. It is a truly beautiful thing, but are they infallible? And that ecclesiastical edifice of theirs which seems so sublime, is its history quite what they have taught their women? "Let me try, Cicely," Paul repeated, with a touch of humility. "Consider. You have looked forward to a lifetime in which you could buy whatever you wanted; you were to be independent of others' help; you would pay people to amuse you, to find food for thought, to teach you. Very well. That is all changed. You will now be entirely dependent on the services that are given for love; you are not abandoned to strangers; you are among those who love you, and will never let you suffer or want; your very dependence upon them will endear you to them. Their constant care of you will make you feel how real and deep and unselfish is their love—"

"My child," Lady Augusta murmured, laying her arm round Cicely's neck.

"You will learn the difference between what is paid for and what is given; you will

no longer seek to be amused all day; your character will grow; you will become what you were intended to be; you will meditate and climb upward. When you pass out of this life, your eyes will be opened upon a plane far higher, among spirits far loftier."

The Good Young Man of the Good Novel could not possibly speak more beautifully.

"Oh, Paul!" The girl's heart glowed within her and her eyes filled with tears. The words may seem inadequate to produce their effect, but consider the soft, musical voice, the tones of one who is earnestly feeling after the truth, and the strange, magnetic power of the speaker.

"Let us, dear ladies," Paul continued in another voice, less sympathetic, less tender— "let us consider the remaining case, that of Mr. Brudenel."

"Be very gentle, Paul," said Lady Augusta.

"I will be very gentle. I confess, however, that I have been grievously disappointed. You know that he has been under direct instruction for some weeks past—daily instruction."

"Yes, we know. He has told me all."

"The strange thing about this instruction is that he forgets when he returns from Abyssinia all that he has learned. I confess that I was under the impression that his mind was being gradually cleared for the reception of the Hidden Wisdom, just as one clears away the jungle and weeds before planting. I thought that a day would come when his mind would be quite rid of prejudices, and he would become receptive. The Ancient Way is impossible to a mind clogged with prejudice."

"Well, Paul?"

"You saw that terrible exhibition of prejudice. How far has his mind been cleared? I am ready to make allowance. Cicero, who was a philosopher, gave way to inordinate grief when his daughter died, not remembering that death is but a narrow gate-way between the two lives. Can we tell how many such gate-ways we have passed, and how many lie before us? Yet, with all allowance made, after he has been taught—after the lesson has been so earnestly impressed upon him that wealth is nothing, that this house, with his pictures, furniture, his grand library, full of useless and lying literature, his broad lands, and his income, are all nothing — absolutely nothing — except that they afford him shelter, food, clothes, and time to meditate — I say, after this has been impressed upon him with all the earnestness and authority possible, to witness such an exhibition of prejudice is more than disappointing. It makes one despair."

"Bear with him, Paul. You who are so sympathetic must feel with him and for him. It is not his own money that he laments. He has been guardian and executor for these three young people, and he has been the innocent means of losing the fortunes intrusted to him. Is this nothing? And then the company was his own; it was the movement of his father; it represented the life-work of the man whom most my husband venerates —his father. That this company should break is no common affliction for my husband."

"It is possible," said Paul, "that it may be permitted by the friends in order to show how little real progress he has made. He has been rudely startled out of his complacency. Yes, yes, and he will feel it; and —and—oh!" Paul started. "I see it, I see it all clearly, clearly — oh, so clearly." He stretched out his hands and threw up his head, and there appeared upon his face the glorified look of one who beholds a vision. "Yes, my master; yes, my friends; I see—I see—"

"Paul!"

He dropped his hands and lowered his head, and looked around him as one who awakes from sleep and wonders what has befallen him.

"Paul, what is it? Oh, what have you seen?"

"Lady Augusta," he said, solemnly, "do you believe in my truth and honesty? Do you always, always—answer me truly—always believe in me?"

"Oh, Paul!" she bowed her face in her hands. "There are times, I confess, when I have a dreadful doubt; for instance, when this blow fell upon us an hour ago. Forgive me; it is a grievous, a terrible thing, to doubt you. If you were false, nothing would be true—nothing could be true."

"Dear lady, look into my eyes, take both my hands; tell me, do you doubt me now?" Never were eyes more clear and limpid, more straightforward and honest.

"No," she replied, low and murmurous. "No, I cannot doubt you, Paul."

She withdrew her eyes and sank into a chair. Upon her, too, as upon the girls, his influence was as a gas that one breathes, and presently loses the consciousness of self. Besides, he was her prophet, and she loved him like a son of whom his mother is proud. The desire of her life seemed to have come to her at last, after many failures and many disappointments. The reign of the Chicks, and the raps and the table-turnings was gone; it was a bad dream. She no longer believed —Paul taught her not to believe — in their *pretentions.* She was Paul's disciple. She

was to him almost what Khadijah was to another prophet. Never, surely, had there been prophet younger, more comely, more winning, more worthy of motherly love.

"Paul," she said, lifting her head, "you made me confess, against my will, a momentary weakness. Forgive me."

"Dear lady, there is nothing to forgive. But to continue thus to doubt would be to estrange yourself from me. Could I stay in this house an hour longer if your affection were to cease?"

"No, Paul; I am sure you could not."

"In the Ancient Way, you know that the woman rules through love—not the earthly but the spiritual love—in which there is not one man for one woman, nor one woman for one man, but all for all, and yet each for each."

He pressed her hand.

"When next you doubt me," he said, "ask yourself what I gain by staying here. If all my story were false, why should I stay here? Sibyl does not like me. Tom does not believe in me. My work in the study is harder than you think. What is my reward? I know not, unless it is your faith and your affection."

"I cannot see Paul's eyes," said Cicely, "but I hear his voice. It is the only voice I have ever heard which could fill my soul with happiness. If that voice were false, all the world would be false."

"Strange things have happened in this house," Paul went on, "stranger things still will happen. Meantime, about this incident which I have called trifling."

"No." Lady Augusta betrayed herself; the incident was not by any means trifling in her eyes.

"In this matter my friends will interfere. I can promise you the strangest thing possible, but in what follows have faith, and do exactly what is ordered."

"Oh yes, yes, we will have faith."

"I think it must be for your sake," Paul said, softly, "not for that of Mr. Brudenel. Do not ask me any question, but have faith," he repeated, solemnly, "and do exactly what is ordered."

"Yes, you may trust us, Paul. Only tell us what we are to do."

He paused, as if thinking what stupendous task should be imposed on them. They expected—what? Anything might be ordered. That women should be ordered to do anything was in itself strange and exciting. Knights are instantly ordered to do things— kill dragons, ride through enchanted lands; all kinds of things. But who ever heard of a middle-aged lady and a young lady being told to do things?

"Lady Augusta," Paul said at length, "go tell your husband to send immediately for—for his bank-book."

Her countenance fell. "Is that all, Paul?"

"That is all. It is enough, is it not? A light task is laid upon you. But he will be angry, and will use hard words about me and my—your—friends. Bid him from me, in the name of Izák Ibn Menelek, to send instantly for his bank-book." It seemed a small thing, indeed, after all the preamble. How could the Ancient Philosophy help by the medium of a bank-book? But Lady Augusta obeyed.

"Cicely," said Paul, laying his hand, as soft as her own, upon hers, "Cicely—" His voice was sweet and musical. She raised her sightless face, which looked as if it belonged already to another world—that world where women are permitted to sing in the choir. "Cicely, whatever happens, never doubt that you shall be guarded from evil."

"Paul," she said, "you bring help and comfort to us all. Oh, how could we have lived all these years without you?"

CHAPTER IX.

THE MESSAGE OF THE BANK-BOOK.

MR. BRUDENEL retired to his study. But this retreat, sacred to learning and meditation, was now transformed, in the manner peculiar to the operations of Fate, into a chamber or cave of despair, peopled by monstrous fiends, who accused him of wasting and throwing away the property intrusted to his charge. For a man of honor and integrity to lose trust-money, the fortunes of wards and children, is a very dreadful thing. By crippling himself and living in poverty, he might, in course of years, replace the money. But he was now old; he would certainly reach the allotted term long before the money could be replaced. He would bequeath his lands to make up the amount for Tom and Cicely, and then Sibyl would have nothing. And to think that the great and honorable and prosperous company, which he himself founded, and endowed with the magnificent business created by his father and christened with the name of his father, should break! Is it a light thing to hear one's name associated with failures and bankruptcy and the curses of thousands?

Sibyl came to console him by all the endearing acts and the soothing words at her command.

"Go, child," he replied—"go, Sibyl, and leave me alone. The family is disgraced. We can never hold up our heads again. I have lost the fortunes placed in my charge. I am a defaulter. Yours is lost, child, as well as Tom's and Cicely's. Leave me alone to face the disaster."

Then Lady Augusta came to him, bringing, in token of peace, the message concerning the bank-book.

Mr. Brudenel scoffed at that message; and indeed a bank-book seems a futile thing in itself with which to retrieve a loss of five-and-thirty thousand pounds. One might as well retrieve a lost battle by collecting the spent cartridges. Lady Augusta conjured him to obey in the name of the great and wise Izák Ibn Menelek. He derided that sacred name. She implored him for the sake of Paul, their guest, their guide, their friend, to obey. He blasphemed the name of Paul.

"He shall go," cried Mr. Brudenel; "Paul shall go this very day. Since his friends are unwilling or unable to avert disaster, let him go. I want not their kind of friendship any longer, Augusta; we have been tormented all our lives by the apathy, the ingratitude, and the mockery of those whom we have striven to help. What did Emmanuel Chick's spirits —or Lavinia's either—ever do for us? Nothing. We sacrificed our lives for them; we tolerated all kinds of self-seeking people. They did nothing for us in return. What have Paul's friends done for us?" In spite of his disappointments, Mr. Brudenel still believed fervently in the spirits and their messages, as well as in the Seer of Abyssinia. "Tell him, Augusta, that I am bitterly disappointed in him. He had better pack up and leave us. I want to see him no more. His friends must have known what was wrong. They can annihilate space, they can transport things and people two thousand miles in a moment; yet they could not interpose to save these innocent children from losing their all. And he calls it a trifling matter! Tell him he may go, my dear. When he is gone we will have nothing more to do with the other world, or with those in communion with it, or with those who have acquired powers over the spirits. I will sell my library; we will sell this house and go and live in some country cottage, so as to save for the children some of their fortune back again. And we will go to church, Augusta, like other folk, satisfied with what they know. That shall be enough for us, my dear. Tell Paul he may go this very day. As for sending for the bank-book, I might as well take and draw a check for the whole five-and-thirty thousand pounds. Go, my dear, and leave me alone, since I am deserted by those who ought to help; leave me to think, if I can, what may still be done."

Lady Augusta withdrew in tears and reported this contumacy; and presently they all retired in various directions. Sibyl was somewhere apart, and the sound of the piano and her singing was not heard. Cicely went to her room, where Hetty was waiting for her, but there was little reading done; mostly the two girls talked over what had happened, and Cicely considered the subject of poverty, as applied to herself, partly in the light of Hetty's experience, which was certainly wide and deep, and also most discouraging, and partly from a speculative point of view, deducing its lessons and finding its consolations, on which the girl who had never known its pains discoursed movingly in the manner of Paul to the other, who had known those pains and pinches. As for Tom, he was consulting the family solicitors.

Paul himself was out. He went, in fact, to spend the morning with his amiable friend in Beaumont Street, about whom, for his own reasons, he did not tell anybody.

On his return at one o'clock he met Sibyl crossing the hall.

"Herr Paulus," she said, regarding him with the utmost severity, "I wish to tell you that nothing in the whole history of the impostors who have been the curse of this house has ever inspired me with more disgust than your conduct this morning."

Paul bowed gravely, putting his heels together in the foreign fashion. He was clad in his magnificent fur-lined great-coat, and, with his hat in his hand, looked like some young foreign prince or potentate. But Sibyl regarded not his looks.

"Had you really possessed those powers which you claim"—Paul raised his eyebrows slightly—"you would have prevented this calamity. Otherwise you would deserve to be turned out-of-doors with ignominy for your treachery. That you have not done so proclaims aloud that you are an impostor." Sibyl was really astonished at her own freedom of speech, and went on encouraged: "Your affectation of superiority to money considerations also proves your trickery. It was overdone, sir. It was brutal. It was underbred." Paul reddened at the last word, which perhaps touched him in a tender place. "No gentleman could have behaved in that manner. I have always strongly suspected and disliked you; now I despise you. That is all, Herr Paulus, that I have to say. Except," she added, "that I trust my father's eyes may be opened by this incident, and that we shall very soon indeed bid you farewell."

Again Paul bowed.

"There is something written somewhere," he said, "about heaping coals of fire upon your enemy's head. Perhaps—" He bowed again, and, leaving the sentence unfinished, he went up-stairs to his own room.

The luncheon, which had become, since Paul's arrival, an animated and cheerful meal, enlivened with many a youthful jest and merry tale, began most gloomily. Only the ladies were present, and they were all dejected. Sibyl, in addition, had great wrath, and was also, perhaps, a little ashamed of herself for her attack on Paul. He, however, preserved a cheerful air, and worked his way through the dishes with a steady appetite and continued display of that callousness which Sibyl called brutal and underbred.

On such occasions as that of a family calamity, the cook ought to make the table itself glow with sympathy. A bereavement requires cold meat; if it be a bereavement which brings a legacy or a succession, it should be cold chicken; if it possesses no such consolation, cold boiled mutton. Loving memory should be marked by the disappearance of the lighter and more festive dishes; there should be no *purée*, no fillet of sole, no cutlet *à la Soubise*, and no *ris de veau;* no jolly little birds, such as plover, snipe, partridges, pheasants, or blackcock. No *gelées*, aspics, omelets, ices, creams, or pretty cakes. A sombre array of chops and steaks, plainly cooked, suggestive of solid plebeian work-a-day comfort, cold boiled beef, tongue, with at most a half-pay pudding, should alone be served up. Perhaps the reason why Sibyl ate nothing at the meal was because this rule had not been carried out, and the table smiled and sparkled with artistic plenty and festive variety as if nothing had happened. Had the cook no feelings ? Yet all the household knew by this time that the fortunes had been lost.

"Where is your father, dear ?" asked Lady Augusta, with a sigh.

"He is still in his study. I do not think we shall see him at luncheon," said Sibyl, with a profound sigh and a glance at Paul. "The trifling incident of this morning has been too much for him."

Then Tom came in, cheerful, but with that cheerfulness which the brave young man preserves and exhibits on all occasions, say, after losing a boat-race, or having his play damned, or after being beaten at the hundred yards, or after losing his first class, or on getting his manuscript returned by the editor, or on getting the sack; or after proving to himself how easily and swiftly and unexpectedly a fortune of fifteen thousand pounds may take wings and fly away without saying farewell and be no more seen, leaving not a trace behind, nor anything to prove who has got it all. That is the most wonderful thing to understand; who does get all the money that is lost?

"Well, good people," he said, "let me have

luncheon. One may be a pauper and yet get hungry. Paupers are always getting hungry, and it is a great nuisance for the ratepayers. Eating ought to be a luxury for the rich. Cicely, you and I are paupers. Yes, Sibyl," his voice dropped a little, because this meant so much more to her than to Cicely," I have now got to work in earnest."

"That is, indeed, a great misfortune," Paul observed. "Your friends ought to go into mourning for you, Tom."

"My dear philosopher, you bear up so well and so nobly that I hope you will yourself shortly meet with a similar affliction. I should rejoice to keep up my own pecker while you lost your money, and I would follow your example in not being depressed more than I could help with other people's misfortunes. I will take a cutlet. Well, I have been since breakfast to Lincoln's Inn Fields, where I have conversed, but without getting any comfort, with the man of law. I have been likewise into the city. So far as can be learned, there is no chance of anything being saved. There is but one opinion: total wreck; cargo lost; crew—that is, the shareholders—cast away. Many are already, I hear, inquiring into the *menu* of the workhouse dinner, and whether the nature of the sleeping accommodation has been maligned, and what is the uniform. The liabilities are anything you please, and the assets are as low as they make 'em. Beer for me. We shall be lucky, all of us, if we continue to get beer."

"If everything is gone," said Paul, with a sweet smile of patience, "can we not agree to say no more about it? We talked about nothing else at breakfast, and Mr. Brudenel actually lost his temper over it."

"We can, Paul, and we will," Tom replied. "I am going to whistle fortune down the wind. I don't quite understand how to do it, but you shall show me. It is part of the Ancient Way, I am sure. If Fortune is not kind to me, what care I how fair she be? You are quite right, Paul; it is best to talk about it no more."

"More is lost than money, Tom," said Sibyl, shaking her head solemnly and mournfully; "the family name is disgraced. We can never look people in the face any more; we can never get over it; we can never go into society any more; we can never lift up our heads again; we can never, never recover from the dishonor of—"

At this point Mr. Brudenel himself appeared, and so transformed was he, so miraculously changed, that Sibyl could not, in common decency, finish the sentence, though she had been quoting her father word for word. If the family name had been really disgraced by the event of the morning, he must have found some wonderful soap capable of instantaneously removing any stains, because joy and satisfaction shone upon his face like the sun upon a field of golden grain. Yes, joy, satisfaction, content, and happiness were all shown on that happy face, wreathed with smiles. He walked as if he wanted to break out into a dance; he spoke as if he wanted to laugh and sing.

"Paul," he cried, "forgive me! I ought never to have doubted. How could I doubt? Forgive me! I was hasty and of little faith. Oh, my dear friend, they have not forgotten me after all! They have not forgotten me! They remember that whatever my own views might be as to the worthlessness of money, I had wards, and a daughter—and a daughter."

He offered his hand, which Paul grasped with effusion.

"There is nothing to forgive," he said. "I know what has happened. But you will tell us, will you not? Your doubts were natural. Tell everybody what has happened. You have the bank-book, I see." It was in Mr. Brudenel's hand.

"It was only five minutes ago that it was brought to the door. Who sent for the bank-book? Did you, Augusta?"

"Have you forgotten, my dear Cyrus," she replied, somewhat coldly, "what passed in the study when I suggested the sending for the bank-book? It was not likely that I should take upon myself after that to send for the book."

"Then it was you, Paul, was it?"

"Certainly not. You can easily ask the clerk at the bank who sent for it. Go on. You have got your bank-book. Let us start with that."

"Well, Augusta, girls, Tom, we are saved after all; we are saved. That is what I have to tell you—we are saved."

"This morning," said Tom, "we were lost. Are we the shuttlecocks of fortune? Perhaps to-morrow we shall be lost again. I beg your pardon, sir, for interrupting. How were we saved? Some swam ashore; some clung to—"

"Well"—Mr. Brudenel's face showed bewilderment. It was always an expressive and a candid face, which revealed every emotion, and there was no doubt now that he felt the extremity of bewilderment—"by some extraordinary accident I had forgotten —clean forgotten—I cannot understand how I should have forgotten—but as a matter of fact—I—I—I—I—sold out, it seems—yes I sold out all the shares in the company standing to my name three weeks ago."

"Sold out!" cried Tom. "Is it possible? How could you forget such a thing as that?"

"I sold the shares. The bankruptcy of the company, I rejoice to say, has passed over our heads like a harmless thunder-storm. It cannot hurt us in any way."

"But the disgrace to the family name," said Sibyl.

"My dear"—Mr. Brudenel hastened to impress a distinction of so much importance upon his daughter—"a thing which seems disgraceful when it is coupled with such a loss of money loses its terror when there is no loss of money. We have been separated so long from the direction of the company that no stain, I now perceive, can attach to us."

"And we are not paupers after all?" said Cicely. "Then I know whom we have to thank."

"No doubt," said Sibyl. "Herr Paulus will explain it all to us presently."

"Why did you sell the shares?" asked Tom.

"I—I—I cannot remember." Never anywhere had one seen more bewilderment in the face of human creatures. "It is a most wonderful thing. I cannot remember anything at all about it."

"Not remember making so great a change in your investments?"

"No; it is a most remarkable thing. I see that it is; I confess that it is. Yet I cannot remember why I sold the shares, or how I gave instructions, or anything at all about them. It is most remarkable."

"It is, indeed," said Tom, gravely. He remembered his guardian's complaint about forgetting every day what passed in his excursions to and from Abyssinia. He didn't believe in those excursions, but he began to suspect some sort of softening. Only a man whose brain was going could forget such a thing as the transfer of thirty-five thousand pounds.

"I did sell them, that is certain, and I have not yet invested the money in anything else," Mr. Brudenel went on. "It is all in my current account. Most wonderful. Paul, do you know anything? Can you throw any light? Can you help us to understand this?"

"Ask me anything," Paul replied, "except about business. I know no more of shares and money than I know of Tom, cogwheels, and springs."

"Here is the bank-book, with a note from the manager, which I found in the drawer of my table."

Paul took both. On the left-hand side of the bank-book was an entry—

"By sale of shares, £35,456 13s. 6d."

The manager's letter, dated on the same day as the entry in the book, was short:

"DEAR SIR,—In accordance with your in-structions I have sold all your shares in Brudenel & Co. The stock was at 357¼. I have placed the amount realized, viz., £35,456 13s. 6d., to your credit until further instructions."

That was all.

"You see," said Paul, "he says, 'in accordance with your instructions.' To be sure, he could not sell them without your instructions. At least, I suppose not."

"And you do not remember giving those instructions?" Tom asked. "To begin with, you must have had reasons for selling them."

"Well, Tom, I must have had reasons. I suppose I had reasons. What do you think my reasons were, now? If anybody could remind me of those reasons I might remember."

"Somebody must have warned you, told you something, aroused your suspicions. In such a matter as the solvency of this company—your own company—it must have been something very serious indeed that could make you resolve to take such a step as to sell out all your shares. You must have gone through a considerable period of doubt and hesitation; you must have argued with yourself; perhaps with some one else—"

"Never with me," said Paul, on whom Tom's eye rested first.

"Nor with me," said Lady Augusta, for the same reason.

"You must, one would think, have passed days of consideration and doubt; you must have felt most anxious about the safety of the company. The resolution must have caused you the greatest pain. And yet you forget—you forget."

"Of course," said Cicely, "Paul's friends helped. He asked them this morning to help, and they did. They told us to send for the bank-book."

"Unfortunately for that theory, Cicely," said Tom, "the transfer of the shares took place three weeks ago. Even Paul's friends, I presume, without wishing in any way to limit their powers, cannot actually put Time back for three weeks. To annihilate space is one thing; to bring back and alter the past is another."

"Perhaps," said Mr. Brudenel, "my daily visits to Abyssinia absorbed my attention altogether and made me forget everything."

"Possibly," Tom replied. "If I went to Abyssinia and back every day, I should think the journey would account for everything."

"It is most wonderful," Mr. Brudenel said, for the tenth time.

"If I might offer a suggestion," said Paul, gently, "it would be this: On the 23d of this month Mr. Brudenel's guardianship ceases. He may have intended to hand to each of his wards their portion entire, to be reinvested as they might think best, and therefore he sold out, without any doubts at all in his mind as to the solidity of the company. He had invested theirs to the best advantage; he would now, in surrendering his trust, give them not an investment, but the whole portion in a check."

"That was it — that was it!" cried Mr. Brudenel, eagerly jumping at the suggestion. "I remember now. That was the reason why I sold out; that was my intention; that was in my mind; that accounts for it. In fact, I remember everything now. You see, Tom, don't you, why I sold out? Thank you, Paul. You always come to our help in everything."

"But," said Tom, who had now looked at the other side of the bank-book, "there is something else here. How do you account for paying away the whole of the money a week after to other people?"

"What paying away—to other people?"

"In three checks. Tom read the following entries: "To Izák Ibn Menelek, £20,000; to Rupert P. Zeigler, £10,000; to Surabjee Kamsitjee, £5000."

"What!" This was more unexpected even than the entry on the left-hand side.

"Look for yourself. Do you remember those checks?"

Mr. Brudenel read the entries. Yes; the whole of the money so wonderfully rescued from the failing company had been paid away in those three checks.

He looked about him helplessly. "What does it mean?" he asked. "I remember nothing at all," he said — "nothing at all about any of these checks."

Then all, with one consent, turned to Paul. Even Thomas the doubter and Sibyl the infidel turned to Paul for explanations.

"Come," said Tom. "The first of these gentlemen, Mr. Izák Ibn Menelek, the illustrious Sage of Abyssinia, who gets a check for £20,000, is, I believe, a personal friend of yours, Paul. The least you can do for us in the matter is to ask him for an explanation how and why he got the money."

"Certainly, I will ask him to explain the whole business. But they are all three friends of mine. I will ask them all."

"Put it to the wise man," said Tom, "from a modern point of view. Let him understand that money is in these days only paid to people in return for services rendered or promised; explain to him what getting money under false pretences means. Perhaps he is only posted in the Ancient Law and the Hidden Way. Tell him how awkward things are made nowadays for people who persuade other people out of their money."

"I will ask them all why they took the money; but perhaps they will not tell me."

"That is very likely," said Sibyl.

"Perhaps we may make them. Let us understand each other, Paul. It is Sibyl's money and Cicely's and mine that is concerned. I want no fooling around in this matter."

"My friends never fool around. If they will not tell me I cannot make them. And, frankly, I believe they will not tell me."

"I shall hold you responsible for this money," said Tom.

"If you please. Let me, however, point out to you that you will find it difficult to connect me with the checks. One of them has been presented by a friend of mine now in Abyssinia; another by a friend in Philadelphia; and the third by a friend now in Bombay. That is all I can tell you. Why the checks were drawn by Mr. Brudenel, for what consideration, or the thought of what promise, I cannot tell you. Ask Mr. Brudenel."

Very good. This was reasonable. Mr. Brudenel had not connected Paul with the checks; he remembered nothing at all about them.

"Let us," said Tom, "see the checks."

They were in the pocket of the bank-book. They were drawn in Mr. Brudenel's own handwriting — firm, clear, straight up and down—a handwriting which was difficult to imitate. There could be no doubt at all that they were all drawn and signed by himself. They were made payable to order, and were crossed. They were also endorsed. They were therefore paid into some bank, not across the counter. Tom replaced the checks in the pocket, and put book and all into his own pocket, saying nothing.

"Am I," said Mr. Brudenel, dropping into a chair, "the sport of the spirits? Is it their revenge upon me for deserting their cause?"

"Oh"—Cicely clasped her hands—"why do we make such a fuss? Why do we doubt? Why do we fear? Paul told us that we must send for the bank-book. Only let us have a little faith!"

But Tom laid his hand upon the breast-pocket of his coat, in which lay the bank-book and the checks, and he tapped that pocket, as much as to intimate that faith, even when taken in large quantities, would not render inquiry unnecessary.

CHAPTER X.

THE FIRST INVESTIGATION.

IT was the morning after.

On the morning after a storm, as everybody knows who has been wrecked at sea, the sun always breaks gloriously; the sky is clear, the air is soft and balmy, though the sea may heave and still be unquiet.

The shares were sold. That was the first thing. It was like escaping in an open boat from a sinking ship. But all the money was mysteriously conveyed away into the hands of three unknown persons, one of them certainly the instructor, but hitherto the unseen instructor, of Mr. Brudenel, and all three stated by Paul to be his own personal friends. This was like the dangerous heaving of the boat. No one knew what might happen with those uncertain factors in the problem. That was like having no port within a thousand miles, yet to be lying in the track of vessels.

After breakfast, Sibyl followed Tom to his workshop.

"No one comes here, Dodo," he said; "we can talk as much as we please, undisturbed. My dear Dodo, what shall we do if the money is all gone?"

"You will make yourself a great name, Tom; and I will wait—oh, and perhaps you will get tired of waiting."

"My dearest Dodo, if you look so sweet I shall get tired of waiting immediately."

* * * * * * *

These are the marks which show that what followed is irrelevant, and beneath the dignity of the historian. They are also symbols which silly lovers in the humbler walks, where they are less eloquent in words than the better-educated, use as tokens to show the depth and intensity of their passion, their fidelity, and their constancy. Like all symbols, they fall very far short of the reality.

"And now, Tom, let us talk soberly. You said you had 'quantities of things to tell me.'"

"Quantities, Dodo? None of them half so important as the things I have just told you; as that I lo—"

"No, Tom; not again. Let us proceed to business."

"Well, then, if one must. We are persuaded, are we not, that this fellow Paul—I wish I didn't like the beast—is at the bottom of the whole business?"

"Perfectly certain."

"For some purpose of his own we are assured that he has decided the whole thing—how, we are not yet certain."

"We are agreed so far, Tom; I am also perfectly certain that he means to carry off the whole of this money."

"There we differ. I am convinced that his was the hand that executed, and his the head that planned, the whole plot. But I am not so sure that he means to stick to this money. It would be a *coup* too audacious even for a man who sends another to Abyssinia and back, all in a single morning."

"Then what does he do it for?"

"I don't quite know. I've watched Paul ever since he came here, and I've talked with him nearly every night in this room, Dodo. I like him, and I believe in him. That is, I believe that he has not come here after money."

"Dear Tom, they all come after money."

"He knows that I am watching him and trying to find out how he does it. We always talk on that assumption. It is understood."

"Who is this man, Tom, that he should be different from the Emmanuel Chicks and the rest of them?"

"He is an American. Of that I have not the least doubt. Not that such a fact necessarily lifts him above old Chick. Do you know, however, that there is a certain kind of American who craves for notoriety above all things? There are plenty over here who would give a good deal for notoriety, but with this American kind it is a craze. Paul is one of them. He has betrayed himself to me a hundred times. He cannot bear the thought of being one of the common herd, to live unnoticed, and to be forgotten as soon as he is dead. He wants distinction."

"Oh, what distinction! One of the tribe of impostors who pretend to supernatural powers?"

"Perhaps Nature did not give him the qualities which go to make a man successful on the ordinary lines. But then, on the other hand, she gave him more than his share of nervous quickness, so that he sees at once while ordinary people are only feeling their way."

"Well?"

"Then I have been reading up the subject lately. I used to laugh at it. There is the power called mesmerism, about which so much nonsense has been written. It is a real power, though so little under control that physicians refuse to use it. Paul has that power, and he has developed it. You saw, Sibyl, how he acted upon Cicely and Hetty."

"Yes; he mesmerized them."

"He made them think as he pleased, and he made them see what he willed. It is an uncommon phase of this force, but there are instances of it."

"Well, Tom. But all this does not remove him from the tribe of impostors. How about Prince Menelek and the Abyssinian sage?"

"They are the patter of the profession. Did you ever hear a conjurer talk while he does his tricks? The faster he talks the more he diverts your attention, the more astonishing are the things he does."

"But the papers from India?"

"They are also part of the patter. The great trick in this case is, I am persuaded, the exercise of mesmeric influence."

"Oh!"

"You see that an immense reputation may be established by the performing of miracles. Paul aims at the reputation of supernatural powers; hence his miracles. The blind girl sees her brother; the photograph of the brother floats down from the ceiling; the paper comes all the way from India."

"And all this money takes wings and flies away, Tom."

"You persist in believing the man to be dishonest, Sibyl. Let me go on. Paul is locked up every morning with your father. Every day he spends an hour with Lady Augusta. Most days, I have ascertained, he has an hour or so as well in Cicely's room. He has acquired influence almost absolute over your father, and over the two girls, while Lady Augusta firmly believes in him; but he does not move her to the same extent as the others."

"Yes, I suppose that is so."

"We hear of daily visits to Abyssinia. But mark! Your father forgets every day what he has said and done there. Cicely sees her brother as often as she wishes, by Paul's help. Hetty obeys if he lifts his little finger. This is a dangerous state of things, Sibyl. In the hands of an unscrupulous person it would be very dangerous. The man has opportunities which no one should be allowed to have."

"Yes; and how has he used them?"

"He has taken all our money, Sibyl. Of that I am certain. And yet I do not believe he has stolen it."

"I do, Tom."

"Now, I have made one discovery which may help us. I have found out that he knew a month ago that Brudenel & Co. were shaky."

"Oh, and he pretends to know nothing at all about business."

"We must be tolerant, my dear. When a man goes in for this line of life he must be prepared with a good many crackers and a brazen brow. He is like a novelist."

"Everybody knows that a novelist makes up."

"Yes, but if you stop to think that it is made up you are lost. Now listen: I have found out one of the crackers, which is something. Four weeks ago Lavinia Medlock had a visit from an old gentleman, all of whose money was in the company. He had received a private and confidential warning from somebody who had access to the books or could put things together. He had also received an assurance from somebody else in the office that the company was most

flourishing. Then this old gentleman, bewildered and uncertain, went to Lavinia for counsel. He might as well have asked the town pump. Lavinia's spirits behaved in the usual ridiculous manner, and she finally gave it up, and made out a case for counsel and sent it to Paul, who ordered the old gentleman to sell out instantly."

"But how did he know the private affairs of the firm?"

"My dear child, I told you that Paul possesses extraordinary faculties. He found out, I suppose, just as I have found out, only much more quickly, that in the present condition of trade, and considering what the company have done of late years, the concern could not possibly keep up the high dividends which it has been paying. If I had given my attention six months ago to the subject, I would have convinced your father as well as myself. Very good; that is my discovery. As for the letter of introduction to the manager, it was written—I have seen it—by your father. Nothing could be clearer. The checks were also signed by him. Moreover, the three persons to whom the checks were payable—the Right Honorable Izák Ibn Menelek, the Falasha, Mr.—probably General—Rupert P. Zeigler, of Philadelphia, and the respectable Surabjee Kamsitjee, of Bombay—have all opened accounts in their different banks, each giving the name of your father as a reference of respectability. In each case he has written a letter attesting the respectability of the person. No hesitation was made in opening an account which began with so big a check and so sound a reference."

"All this is very wonderful, Tom. But it does not prove the man's honesty."

"It does not, I confess. But so far, not a single check has been drawn at any of the banks. I have found that out, and it seems to me a very significant circumstance. Well, one more discovery I also made. The checks were paid in personally. The first was brought by an old man, infirm and crippled, who could scarcely walk—Paul; the second was brought by a middle-aged man with an immense light-brown beard and spectacles—Paul again; the third was brought by a man in Eastern costume, browned-skinned, with a thick black beard and black eyes. I have Paul's photograph painted and adorned with a turban and a black beard—here it is—the true portrait of Surabjee Kamsitjee—only, unfortunately, they do not remember at the bank."

Tom continued summing up the situation. "Well. The position is sufficiently alarming. How could we prove that Paul caused these checks to be drawn by false pretences?

Mesmeric influence is not recognized by the courts of law, though undue influence might be urged. You have to prove it. A man apparently in the full vigor of his intellect orders, in an autograph letter which cannot be disputed, the sale of certain shares. He then with his own hand draws these checks—the counterfoils being entered with care—and signs them. The signature cannot be disputed. He then writes three letters, in each of which he vouches for the respectability of a certain person. His only answer to these facts is that he forgets all about it—that he does not know these persons; but he cannot tell how he came to do it. Next, how are we to connect Paul with the money? How can it be proved that he was the infirm old man? I confess that it will be difficult."

"As for Mr. Rupert Zeigler, the beard is all one has to go by, although I am perfectly sure that the beard was on Paul's chin. And as for the gentleman from Bombay, they remember very little about him, though they own that my picture seems very like. So far, you see, I think the most acute detective would fail to connect Paul with the checks. It remains to find out, if we can, his method of working upon your father, and on that point I hope to be able to throw light before long."

"And meantime, I suppose," said Sibyl, "he will make my father sell his land and his house and everything."

"It is possible. In such hands anything is possible."

"And yet you are not alarmed."

"Not a bit. I have no fear. Paul is only working up for another miracle. He is arranging his effects, and getting together his little properties. It will be, he thinks, a truly beautiful miracle; only, this time, perhaps, we may have the satisfaction of knowing how he does it. And perhaps, Dodo"—he took her hand again—"perhaps the discovery, if we do make it, may act as an eye-opener to your father, and the Vestal virgin of the cause may be allowed to leave the temple of a fallen god."

CHAPTER XI.

ONLY A KISS.

THERE was one room in the house into which we have not yet penetrated—a small room on the first floor, which for beauty, comfort, and daintiness excelled all the other rooms in the house. It was so beautiful and so dainty because it had been the girls' room, formerly so called, but was now Cicely's room. When school came to an end, and the last of the governesses departed,

Sibyl left the room, but Cicely remained. Everything belonged to the blind girl: the books which Hetty read to her; the pictures, also read to her by Hetty; the pretty things which she could not see; yet it is undoubtedly good for a blind girl to be surrounded by things beautiful. The music was hers, which Hetty played to her; the piano was hers on which she herself played, letting her fingers wander over the keys, while to her sightless eyes there came visions. What visions? What do they see—the blind? How do they shape and color the world? What is form—what is color to the blind? How do they imagine the tender green of the young leaves in June—the fragility of the flowers—the thousand hues of nature—the charms of beauty—the magic of the eyes—the witchery of art—the slopes and shadows of the hills? What are they like—the visions and the fancies of the blind? I know not. Cicely's visions came to her, bringing happiness unspeakable, sometimes when she heard sweet music, sometimes when she heard great poetry, sometimes when she listened to the voice of a certain young man who spoke as she had never before heard any man speak.

He came often to this room, he came nearly every day; generally he came in the afternoon, between tea and the first dinner-bell; a quiet and lazy time when the lamp was lit, the curtains drawn, and the cold east wind shut out. There was no concealment about his visits; he went openly to the room; anybody who wanted him at this time would look for him in Cicely's room. The whole house was his. If you had asked him why he came here, he would have replied, with as much candor as you have any right to expect—it is not possible, unhappily, for any man to be wholly candid—that he loved above all things (except perhaps, distinction) material comfort, physical ease, warmth, and the contemplation of things beautiful. Like many other preachers and philosophers, while he despised riches, he ardently loved those things which only riches can procure. Indeed, it is too often forgotten, especially by parents, guardians, tutors, and teachers, how much more intense is the craving for these things in first manhood, when these things are the least attainable, than in age. In the early twenties a young man yearns and craves for physical ease and for love and for beauty; he grows sick for lack of these; life is worthless because he cannot get them. By the time he gets to fifty he has had much experience of little ease, hard work, and cold weather; and besides, has had some moderate share of happiness and of love, insomuch that the old yearning, like a fierce fire that has burned itself out, only smoulders. And as for things beautiful, they are intimately connected with persons beautiful; and therefore it is no use yearning after what belongs to the young. Now, alas!

> " Love will not lip him;
> Maid will not clip him;
> Maud and Marian pass him by."

If further pressed, Paul would have gone on to confess—but he had a most wholesome Protestant hatred of the confessional—that he could get warmth and easy-chairs in other parts of the house, even in his own room, by himself, or in Tom's room; but he could get nowhere else the undivided companionship of two beautiful girls, sweet, confiding, and believing. Every prophet, even a false prophet, loves to have disciples who never question.

Hither he came, and here he talked of things the contemplation of which lifts the soul which submits to be lifted and to be guided. Men are too stiff-necked to submit. I have never seen in any club smoking-room either a prophet who wanted to lift other men's souls, or men who submitted their souls to be lifted. A shove-up, as Baxter poetically put it, is the last thing which men ask of each other. But how many women are always looking for it! Paul spoke of life and death, of the barrier which lies between, of the eternal world of which this life is but a tiny episode as the soul marches upward or downward. Was it nonsense which he talked? I know not. His soft and musical voice, his dark and beautiful eyes, his presence and his comeliness, made it more than sense — divine wisdom — so that the hearts of the two girls glowed.

"There is not," his words flowed musically, "anything in this world that man can make, or desire, or aim at, which is really of the smallest importance. Love? He may wait for it, because beyond the barrier—as we say, but there is no barrier—love awaits him far deeper and more holy than any earthly love. Wealth? It can do nothing for the soul. Knowledge? They do not understand —they can never understand—that the secrets of nature, which they so painfully seek and so slowly acquire, are all revealed in the wisdom we call the Hidden Way. Long life? It is only to be desired while those we love are still unable to see and converse with the spirits. When all can see as I can see, and converse as I can converse, we shall die without a pang or a regret. Cicely—Hetty"—he lowered his voice—"there are some things which one cannot speak of before the world; in this room, with you, we may speak freely, for we believe. Oh, we are always, everywhere, surrounded by spirits. I see

them"—he looked around—"they are in this room now; they are speaking together of you. They pass and are gone, and others follow. Some stay with us always to whisper words which may warn and advise; they protect us from evils—real evils; they laugh when we complain of imaginary evils, and of wrongs which cannot harm the soul; they fill us with lofty thoughts; you might see them if you had my eyes. Yet a little while and you shall see them; yes, you shall see them, Cicely—you as clearly as Hetty. I cannot give you the power of seeing things earthly, but things spiritual you shall see clearly as I myself."

To read these things is foolishness; to hear them spoken in a soft and musical voice, in the accents of truth and conviction, by one who had shown that he could do things which to other men are impossible, in the seclusion of that room, was to these girls nothing short of a new gospel—all their own—all to themselves. Think of a new gospel all to yourself! And while the young man gave the girls these glimpses into the unknown, his eyes wandered from Cicely, listening, like some sweet cloistered saint, to Francis of Assisi, her blind eyes looking heavenward, with parted lips and glowing cheeks, to Hetty, who lifted her heavy, lustrous eyes not to heaven but to the prophet, moved less by the delights of eternal study—as some are moved less by those of eternal singing—than by the joys of companionship with those one loves.

Sometimes he read poetry to them — the poetry which fills the soul with vague yearnings; and he would leave the verses half finished, and in talk carry on the theme, playing on their emotions as a musician produces variations of the same air. Sometimes he would tell them stories taken from I know not where; but his memory was good and his imagination strong. They were stories such as are not written down; no editor would receive them; they had no plot, and they were not constructed with any art; they ran on, and their interest lay in the manner of telling; and sometimes, like an imaginative child, he would carry on the story from day to day. Generally the hero was a poor lad of obscure origin, who worked his way to great fame and distinction by courage and by genius.

Sometimes he would tell them of places which he had seen and people he had met. He knew New York and Boston; he knew Florence, Rome and Venice, Paris and St. Petersburg; he could tell them all kinds of strange and curious things. A young man who has travelled so far has seen many things, high and low. And remember, this young man told the girls nothing that was

6

low and common. He did not abuse his position. Always he raised their souls, and lifted them above themselves. Always, at his coming, Hetty put on, mentally, her Sunday frock, and Cicely attuned her mind to higher things.

A prudent young man, especially one who has been solemnly warned of the dangers which belong to the society of young ladies, and knows beforehand that love is fatal to the Higher Philosophy, would have kept out of this room, set with the only trap which Cupid ever lays—a lovely girl or two—and would have attended strictly to business. Every young man's future, but especially Paul's, depends upon his sticking to business. Yet it is difficult when one is young to be always thinking of the future. The present, you see, is ever with us; the future, child of the present, seems so far off. And then the present is forever changing, which prevents monotony, though it causes us to call it names, such as fugacious, illusory, a cheat, a false promiser, and the like. And even if the present be a Fool's Paradise, that kind of garden is very delightful, and wholly free from anxiety and forethought. Why, it is not everybody who can find out the flowery lane that leads to that garden gate; and when it is found there are very few who have a key that will open it.

One afternoon—a day or two after the failure of Brudenel & Co. — Hetty was sitting alone in their room reading a story. The book was all about the happiness which love brings to those girls who are so lucky as to win a lover, young, rich, handsome, well-born, and clever. I think the hero in this story was a Guardsman—nothing less, if you please — of noble family, of course; great wealth, naturally; and the poetic temperament for which the Guards' Club—and Skindle's—is so remarkable; he was two-and-twenty, and she was eighteen: it is an age too young for real and solid love; only most novelists and poets do not perceive this great truth—nor do the boys and girls who read novels. It was a most beautiful story, in short, ending, happily, with rice, but no wedding breakfast. Somehow Hetty did not much care for it. Her thoughts wandered.

Suddenly, and without any footstep being heard, the door opened, and Paul appeared. That was nothing unusual. But Hetty, for some reason, blushed a rosy red.

He came in softly—not secretly—shutting the door behind him. He went to the window and looked out. It was six o'clock, in the middle of April. A gray sky covered the garden, where the east wind ground together black branches of the trees; there was not yet a touch of spring upon the

boughs or on the flower-beds. Paul shivered, and half drew the curtain to keep out the sight of the cold. Then he took Cicely's chair beside the fire, and sat down and looked at Hetty. She laid down her book and waited.

"Where is Cicely?" he asked.

"She is lying down. She has a little headache."

"Bring her here, and I will send it away." This young man had a surprising power of sending away toothache, headache, earache, neuralgia, and all—or perhaps nearly all—the aches and pains which afflict humanity. He cured the servants and the servants' friends. His remedy was the application of his hand, which immediately caused the pain to vanish. In the same way I have seen a negro cause a sprain to disappear instantly. The human hand, accompanied by a certain amount of energy on the one side and faith on the other, does it. Perhaps the toothache came again after a while, and in the end they had to go to the dentist and have the horrid thing clawed out; but think of the relief for the time!

Hetty rose to obey.

"No, no," said Paul; "let her stay—lying down will do her good—and we will talk, Hetty."

She sat down again, and waited submissively.

He rose and stood over her.

"Look in my eyes," he said.

"Oh, Paul—no, no; spare me."

"I will do you no harm, child."

"You make me faint and dizzy. When I grow unconscious you will make me tell you what you please. You will do with me as you did with the butler when you made him tell us how he drinks the wine. Spare me, Paul."

He laughed, and sat down.

"We will talk, then. Are you happier, Hetty?"

"Yes."

"Are you happier because I am here?"

"You know I am, Paul. You make us all happier; you have brought such happiness into this house as was never known before. Even Sibyl says that you have brightened the place."

"Are you happier because you see a little more clearly than before?"

"I did not desire to see more clearly, yet it does make me happier to feel that things are not all a pretence. Oh, Paul, it is a dreadful thing to feel ashamed of your mother. I know the things that are done. I have had to keep my eyes closed. In this house I have had to preserve silence, even when I knew there was imposture, and I could have exposed the cheat; but then I should have had to tell how I knew the tricks. And at last to feel that there is really truth in it in spite of all—to know that my mother really does. converse with the spirits, even if they are only the lower kind. It has made me inexpressibly happy, Paul, to be certain of this."

"I am glad, Hetty," he replied. "It is no small thing to make you happy, Hetty."

"Besides, you have made Cicely happy. She has no knowledge of unworthy tricks; but you have made her happier and more cheerful. And you have made the whole house cheerful. Formerly it was as gloomy, especially after another disappointment, as a sepulchre."

"Hetty"—Paul abruptly changed the subject—"you are young; you will not always remain with Cicely; what will you do with your life?"

"I do not know. I have not had the disposing of my own life so far. I do not suppose that will ever be given into my hands."

"Do you look forward? Do you think what may be in the lap of Fortune for you?"

"Sometimes. But I dare not think too much upon the future."

"Look forward now, Hetty. Nay," he repeated, imperiously, "I command you. Look forward, and tell me truthfully what you see. Remember, it is not the real future that you will see, it is the future that you least desire and most dread."

The girl closed her eyes. Then she shuddered and trembled, and opened them again.

"I cannot, Paul."

"Tell me," he said. "You must."

She resisted no longer.

"I see a long life of poverty. I am always somebody's companion. There will never be any one so kind as Cicely. I get older and poorer, and I am always solitary. It is a dreadful life, Paul," she cried. "I see the end of it. I will not look any more."

"There is another picture," said Paul. "Look again, Hetty. See what I see."

"Oh, I see a girl—it is myself—and a man before her, and he leads her away by the hand; and oh, she is full of happiness!"

"Do you see the face of the man?"

"No, I cannot see it. But I know the shape of his head. It is—oh!" she covered her face with her hands, and said no more.

"Play to me, Hetty," said Paul, springing to his feet. "Play me music—quickly—play to me."

She obeyed, her cheek blushing, and her eyes down-dropped, and began to play such music as she played to Cicely when the blind girl wanted to dream and have the visions which music brought.

Paul walked restlessly about the room. So,

in far-off America, a certain lad named Ziphion walked to and fro while a certain girl named Bethiah played to him.

"Hetty!" he cried.

She stopped and turned her head.

"Your music does not soothe me; it maddens me. Oh, stand up and take my hands. Hetty, Hetty; look in my eyes again. Do they subdue you? Do they compel you? Do they make your brain reel and your eyes move? Do they, child, make you afraid, now?"

"Oh no, no!"

"Because they are subdued by yours, Hetty. Because they are conquered." He drew her gently, and his arms lay round her neck and waist, and he kissed her a dozen times. Then, without another word, he pushed her roughly from him and rushed out of the room, banging the door behind him.

CHAPTER XII.

SIR PERCIVAL.

"YES," said the clerk in the secretary's office. "The man is here. You will find him within. He arrived in the *Willing Bride*, of Quebec, three months out, and he's madder than ever. Three prayer-meetings he's held already, and he's at it again. I wonder how they stand it so well. You can go in if you wish."

The place was in the Sailors' Home, Dock Street. Paul passed through a short passage, and found himself in a large, low room, set with solid square timber pillars to shore up the roof; tables of a heavy and solid kind were set about, and benches stood beside them. It was the common room of the Sailors' Home, where they take their meals, and sit and converse. If you go through the common room you find yourself in a place which reminds you of a ship and of a monastery, and of those solitaries who lived in caves, high up in the sides of cliffs and precipices, and you turn dizzy and reel. For there are rows of little cells or cabins, in every one a sailor, piled one above the other, and in front of each row a gallery in light iron, with iron staircases, the sight of which makes you think of falling over or through.

The common room this morning was thinly attended. A lusty negro, coal-black, rolled about, and on one of the benches, pipe in mouth, two or three mild-faced Norwegians sat, with the newspaper of their native country in their hands; a dozen fellows lounged and leaned against the pillars with crossed legs, doing nothing, with the contentment only possible with sailors and fishermen; one or two men were writing, one or two smoking pipes; there was a smell as of 'tween decks; one thought of the fo'k'sle; tar was present, and one thought of ropes; if the men had lurched and pitched as they went, one would not have been surprised.

In the middle of this room, however, surrounded by a little group of sailors, chiefly young, was a young man sitting in a chair, talking and arguing. In reality he was preaching; but it seemed as if he was merely talking earnestly from his chair, while they gathered round and listened. But from time to time he sprang to his feet and raised his voice, and addressed them in impassioned tones which were surely those of the preacher; and he used a certain gesture which has of late become fashionable among orators of the fervid type. I think it is an American importation, made, like all American things, for the purpose of impressing Demos. For my own part I prefer the old English gestures used for impressing persons who possess the critical faculty, just as I prefer English cheeses, English bacon, English apples to the American importations. This gesture consists in throwing the right arm up and back, and then hurling the hand, so to speak, at the audience. It is easily learned, and may be acquired by half an hour's practice before a glass. When a man is really and truly in earnest, and possesses the gift of impassioned speech, it helps him to become effective; when a man only wishes to seem in earnest, and therefore shows the pretence in his words, the gesture is grotesque, and destroys what effect his oratory might otherwise produce. Demos is no fool; above all, he is ready to detect a man who is not really in earnest. That is the reason why so many leaders disappear early, and why so much vigorous speech is thrown away and wasted.

Paul drew near, and sat down to listen.

The speaker was dressed as a common sailor; his face was weather-beaten, but the features were regular; his hands were tarry, but they were small; his figure was tall and graceful; his short hair was dark; he spoke like a gentleman, and he looked above the rank of a common sailor. His eyes were remarkable for their bright and even fiery appearance; in the low dark room they glowed. They were the eyes of a fanatic or a madman. Once I saw crouching in a corner of a darkened cell a madman who had killed a warder. He was perfectly quiet, but his eyes were two balls of fire, and he was ready to spring upon the first man who should venture within the cell. Such were the eyes of this young sailor.

It was apparent immediately, from his words, that he belonged to the narrowest order of Christians. We who live in great towns and choose our own religion, and sometimes choose a broader form of Christianity, permit ourselves to deride the narrow brethren. We should not deride them. They belong to a very big school indeed. There are ten millions of them in England, four millions in Scotland, two millions in Ireland, three millions in Colonial Britain, and thirty millions in America who belong to this school. It is not, therefore, by any means extinct; nor will it ever become extinct so long as men who are unlearned claim to exercise the right of private interpretation. And it will always be a narrow school, although its disciples hold all kinds of conclusions, and divide themselves into as many sects as there are sauces in France. The arguments of this school are based upon premises which the wicked Rationalist will not allow; its followers know nothing of the science of religion, or of the development of the great central idea. The school is as cruel and pitiless as the letter of the law; it is self-sufficient and arrogant. We may say all kinds of harsh things as regards this school; but those who remember how terrible a tyranny is authority, how truly hateful a thing is ecclesiastical rule, and how monstrous a being is the priest in power, will take heart though a dozen new sects are invented every day, and will continue to praise the Lord that such thinkers are enabled to exist at all.

Paul had been brought up in this school himself. He knew all the tags and the phrases of the school; if he was ever to get religion, it would be this sort of religion. But it was a long time since he had concerned himself about the condition of his soul. For many reasons such an inquiry would have been undesirable and unsettling. Besides, was he not in the hands of friends who knew all about the next world?

As Paul sat and listened—the man who was speaking was a born orator—his mind went back to a certain plain building, whitewashed inside, where the people sat in narrow pews while a man in a black coat thundered and pleaded, threatened, coaxed, and promised, and threatened again. He remembered how that man looked, and how his voice resounded in the building. Some of the congregation had already experienced religion; these groaned, sighed, and murmured; others were looking for it with anxious hearts; others only looked on with apathetic faces, as if the thing did not concern them in the least. He remembered how they all looked, and how he, from his seat in the gallery, used to gaze into the faces below and read their thoughts. As this sailor went on, Paul's eyes closed; he was again a boy listening to an address for the unconverted; it was delivered so often, and it converted so few. The arguments were the same; his memory took him back to the child who believed, and wondered why religion was so long in coming to him, though Bethiah was already converted, and was a church member. Then an unexpected phrase brought him back to the Sailors' Home. Why, this man was a preacher indeed. Had the pulpit been occupied by him in the old days Paul must have been converted long ago. He would have become, in fact, a church member. He would then have stayed in his native town. He would have risen to the proud position of superintendent of the Sunday-school, and deacon. Or he might have gone to college and become a minister, and preached those same things himself. Then he would have married Bethiah! Where was Bethiah? And then he never would have seen Hetty! Now his conversion was impossible. It would interfere too much with his prospects. He had, in fact, other engagements. Paul sighed, and returned to business.

The speaker went on. He chained his audience. He forced them to listen. He told them that he had converted every hand aboard the *Willing Bride*, insomuch that when the men were paid off not one of them was found to go into a public-house, nor would a single one venture in Ratcliffe Highway, although we now call it by another name. And he said he was going to convert them too, and that right off and without any delay. At the prospect of immediate conversion some of those honest fellows looked blank, remembering what would follow—the renunciation, namely, of all those practices in which they had been accustomed to find their only joy. Not one or two, mind you, because the church of this gospeller is a very strict church indeed, and allows no indulgences at all. No more drink, neither beer nor rum; no more happy gatherings, with pipe and pewter in snug back rooms. No more jovial evenings, with grog and song, and Polly of Poplar and Rosy of Ratcliffe. Poor Polly and Rosy! Whither would they go? What would they do? No more fights, no more dances, no more anything. Oh, my countrymen, what a blank was left! Others, again, looked as if they were fit to sit upon the stool of repentance. And others, just as it used to be in the chapel, looked as if salvation belonged to the others, and had nothing to do with themselves. The preacher stopped at last, with such a picture of the next world as made one poor lad burst into a blubber, while another trembled and shook. Then he sang a hymn—his voice was strong as well as *musical*—and then he began to go *round and to talk to each* man in turn of

those who would listen. Most of them, however, broke away from the circle, which is always the way, and only what every preacher expects.

He knelt beside the boy who wept, and prayed for him; he knelt beside the boy who trembled, and prayed for him; he knelt in the middle of the room, and prayed aloud for all; and then, his service over, he stood and looked around him with anxious eyes, as if he was still an unprofitable laborer and had neglected much.

At this juncture Paul approached him.

"I have a message for you," he said.

"Have you finished your prayers and preaching?"

"Who are you?" the sailor replied. "If you come on what the world calls business you need not deliver that message. Do not speak to me about money; bestow the money where you please."

"You do not know me. It is no use telling you my name. I come from your sister, not from your lawyer."

"I have no sister."

"Don't talk nonsense. You have a sister who is blind and helpless. She wants to see her brother."

"I have neither father nor mother, brother or sister, or wife." I belong to Christ alone. My hand is to the plough, and I must not turn aside."

"Come to see your sister. You must. I know you, Sir Percival, though you do not know me."

"I am no longer Sir Percival. Titles and honors are vain things. I am John Percy, able seaman. I am called to preach the Gospel among the sailors."

"By all means. I do not ask you to abandon your vocation. I have just heard you preach. You have a very remarkable and persuasive power. You also believe in what you say. I should think that your efforts will be greatly successful. Some of your arguments are fresh, and your illustrations are apt."

"I want no man's praise and I heed no man's blame," said the sailor, roughly.

"Of course," said Paul, "there is nothing to praise. You have received the conviction of the truth of certain doctrines; you have the power of oratory; you have therefore a natural desire to persuade others; you have left your estate and the duties to which you were born for the sake of gratifying others; you have become a common sailor for their sake, and have learned how to speak to them. There is nothing to praise in this. I did not say there was. It is all quite common; anybody could do as much. It is nothing."

"Nothing at all," said the sailor, yet with a doubtful look. Could anybody do as much?"

"It would be impossible to persuade you to give up your life. I suppose you know that it will probably end in being cast away with some ill-found crazy craft."

"It will end as my Master pleases."

"Therefore, I do not ask you to give up your work for a single day," Paul continued. "I do not ask you to change your dress even. I ask nothing more than that you should pay a single visit—one—to your sister. It will make her profoundly uncomfortable, but she desires it."

"I cannot leave my people. I am ordered to preach to them day and night. I *must* be continually in the service of the Master. Oh"—he tossed his head impatiently—"I have no sister—I have no relations at all."

"Your Master does not order you to neglect your sister. It is not as if she was like other girls. She is blind, and dependent on others. Come to see her once, if for an hour only."

"Is my sister converted? Has she been yet convicted of sin?"

"I don't know," said Paul, "I never asked her."

"And yourself—are you converted?"

"No."

"What are you doing with her?"

"I am on a visit to Lady Augusta."

"Ah!" the sailor looked at him fixedly; "I remember now. It is a house filled with devils. They practise forbidden things; they conjure by means of tables and chairs. Are you one of those who delude and deceive them?"

"I am not a medium, if that is what you mean."

"There is no voice permitted from the dead to the living. There is no revelation except the one already made. Nothing can be added to what we know. After death we separate, each to his own place. Between the world and heaven on the one hand and hell on the other is a great gulf fixed, so that those in hell cannot hear the hymns of the saved, nor do those in heaven hear the cries of the lost. It is vain and impious to inquire. Is my sister saved?"

"I do not know."

"I will see her," said Sir Percival. "I may leave my work, provided that I cease not from the task of saving souls alive. Think not that my sister's soul is any more precious to me than any soul among those poor fellows. All are alike in the eyes of Him who made them. Yet I will see her, *and if it is permitted* I will move her to repentance. We have talked enough. Tell her I wish to see her."

"When will you see her?"

"I do not know. When I am commanded," he replied, with the light of fanaticism in his eyes. "I cannot promise."

"You might come, for instance, when she was not at home. It would be a pity to waste your time."

Sir Percival seemed struck with this objection. It did not seem to him that if he was commanded to go the order would not be issued for a time when Cicely was not at home.

"Will you come when I send you word?" Paul asked. "Not to-day or to-morrow, because it is obvious that you are very much occupied with your labors — I wish they may meet with every success — but a little later."

"Send me word, and I will come. Let me look at you. I know you now—I know you." His eyes shot fire, and he recoiled as one starts back at the sight of a deadly snake; and then he assumed the attitude of one who is going for that snake to make an unpleasant minute for the creature.

"I remember you now. I remember where I saw you. Oh, you are yourself one of those who go about to deceive. That house attracts everything that is of the devil. You are an emissary of the devil. The house has long been filled with devils invisible. Now it is a devil incarnate in you. Is my sister in your hands? Then I must hasten to take her away from you. Liar and deceiver—go!"

Contrary to reasonable expectation, Paul did not fly at his throat. He staggered, hesitated, and then obeyed, leaving the place with no dignity at all. Outside, he felt mean. His early teaching suddenly and vividly brought back to his mind, made the words—while he was still under the impression of that memory—fall upon his soul like a lash laid across his shoulders. They were ignominious and humiliating words; he ought to have hurled them back again. He didn't, because he couldn't. Emissary of the devil! Liar and deceiver! Alas! while the old chapel was still in his mind could he deny those words? Alas! again—in the old days when he attended that chapel, if any one had called him a liar and a deceiver he would certainly have gone for that accuser with any weapon that he could catch up.

He walked away, but the stiffening was out of his back; he was limp; he had meekly borne a most deadly insult. And what did the man mean when he said that he remembered him? What did he remember? The day of final triumph was rapidly approaching and he could not afford any awkward memories to come along. Paul not only felt mean and small; he felt uneasy.

CHAPTER XIII.

SLEDGE.

PAUL called the first cab he passed, and hastened to get away as fast as possible from a place where this disgusting plainness of speech was possible; but he arrived at Beaumont Street with looks still perturbed and a soul still agitated. To be called a liar and a deceiver and to have no words of reply—not even a kick or a cuff—naturally causes a hurricane of rage and shame.

"What is the matter, boy?" asked his friend.

"Nothing. Well — something incidental to the profession, I suppose."

"Yes. As for example—"

"The charge commonly made against those who deal with supernatural forces; and I had no reply."

"No reply, Paul?" The old man looked up sadly. "No reply? And after all these years!"

"None ready. Oh, I know what I ought to have said. I had no reply ready for my enemy, because I could think of none for myself."

"The old prejudices again, Paul? Strange! I thought they had been long since removed."

"Old prejudices never die. They seem to be dead, and then at a touch they awake again. I began listening to a sermon—I was thinking only of the present. What was it? A touch, a word, and the years rolled back. I was in the old village chapel listening to the old preacher. I fell back into the old grooves—about sin and wrong, and falsehood and truth, you know. Before I got back to the practical grooves the man who was preaching turned upon me and used words concerning the profession—they were like a stick upon my back. I could find no reply, and slunk away like a beaten man. That's all."

"Why, Paul, I thought you were harder. Have all these years—seven years of apprenticeship—done nothing for you? This it is to have an imagination as well as the magnetic gift. I should have thought that you had the reply always ready in your own mind. As for myself, I have that reply always ready, and it makes me perfectly easy. Why, let us confess it, my whole life has been spent in trading on men's credulity. My present competency has been acquired by the profession which, above all others, demands credulity. Your travels, your manners, your developed powers, are also the result of my success. You are my professional son. Without me and my success you would have had to return to the paternal store. Therefore, we ought both of us to be always ready with our reply—first to the enemy and next to ourselves, in order to keep a calm conscience and to be able to entertain the same gratitude to Providence for our success which men of other professions cultivate."

"Well?" said Paul, a smile lighting up his gloomy brow as a ray of sunshine across a black and surging sea.

"Paul," continued the veteran, "there is not among the whole tribe of mediums, clairvoyants, oracles, and prophets a single man who does not put the question to himself—What reply can I make to my own conscience? Not a man but seeks for an answer which shall justify himself. We must find that answer in self-defence, because we know very well the things that are said of us. I know not what answer other practitioners find, but the answer which I have found for myself satisfies me completely, and it ought to satisfy you. I have lived and grown rich by trading on men's credulity. Let us admit so much. Men think I control the spirits. For aught I know there are not any spirits to be controlled; yet I keep up the pretence. Am I, then, torn by remorse in my old age? Not a bit. And why? Because, Paul, in every trade and in every profession there must be deception. Without deception no trade, no profession, could be carried on. Does the shopkeeper sell what he pretends? Never. There is adulteration everywhere. Things of no value are blended with things valuable; the polished wood is veneer, the silver is plate, the sardines are sprats, the very rubies and emeralds are worthless stones polished up. Lies everywhere. Does the merchant content himself with a fair profit? Not if he can get an unfair profit. Does he pay the producer what he ought? Never. He sweats him whenever he can. Into my trade, which is that of prophet and oracle, and a very difficult trade it is, requiring the possession of the rarest faculties, which ought to be paid for at the highest rate, I brought a swift and keen intellect, kept polished and sharp by continual training and constant watching. I had to be learning and storing away in my memory every kind of fact which bears upon the conduct of life. I had to learn all the various ways which men live. More than that, I had to learn the hearts of women and what they most desire. Boy, until I taught you what I myself had learned, there was no anatomist who knew so much about the body as I knew about the soul, and I taught you, Paul. You are wise, but you are young.

"Yes—daddy, yes"— Paul took his hand with an almost feminine caress—"I owe everything to you."

"I had to keep in training. For this purpose I had to forego all the joys of life. For me there was no love, because love, more than anything else, destroys the powers which our work demands. He whose mind is filled with the thought of one woman cannot keep his power over all women. There was no feasting in joyful assemblies, where men forget their own thoughts and submit to the influence of the crowd. I had no holidays because I could never relax. But I had my reward. I could read the thoughts of those who came to see me, and I could reveal the future as soon as they had told me the past. You know, Paul—you know that there was no prophet, no oracle equal to myself."

"No! You were alone."

"My intellect so far outstripped the sluggish brain of the multitude that it seemed to them due to supernatural help. I accepted that explanation. I even advanced it. If I had told the foolish people that there were no spirits except in their fancy, they would have deserted me. I had the gift of understanding things in a tenth part of the time that they required. I called it — or they called it—we both called it—clairvoyance—advice of the spirits—anything. The people exaggerated my cleverness, and I traded on their stupidity. I made use of their stupidity. In order to do this it was necessary to dress up and set off with all kinds of little devices and pretences—what actors call business—which I employed mechanically, while my mind was acquiring and piecing together the real data of the problem. Why, even a shopkeeper sets off his wares to their best advantage, so that a paste diamond, set with sham gold, looks in its plush case the most precious jewel."

"Go on," said Paul, smiling. "I know it all by heart; but it is comfortable to hear it all again."

"Between ourselves we do not deny the machinery, Paul. We need not. Our answer to those who charge us with cheatery and trickery is to get behind our machinery. Among ourselves our answer is that there is nothing done by us which is not done by every other profession. Can the physician stave off disease? Certainly not ; yet he pretends. Does he know how his drugs act? No, but he pretends. Does he even know what is the disease which is killing his patient? No; he gives it a name and classifies it according to its symptoms, but he does not know it ; yet he pretends. Does the physicist understand that nature whose laws he is always discovering? Not a bit. He finds a law; he discovers a force. What then? We are no farther advanced. Who made the law? Who directs the force? He *does not know;* but he pretends. Is the

lawyer more competent than yourself to manage your affairs? Not a bit ; but he pretends. And to keep himself employed he makes business as complicated as he can. Does the clergyman know any more about the next world than we ourselves know? Not a bit ; but he pretends. In order to keep himself going he pretends to supernatural powers. If he were not to pretend, his congregation would leave him. Is the writer of the political articles in the papers any better informed than his neighbors? Not a bit; but he pretends. The world is carried on by the men of the professions, and the men of the professions live—they all live—upon the credulity of the people."

"Yes," said Paul. "It is quite true."

"The best of it is that we all know it, but we do not whisper it even among ourselves. The whole of education is meant to fit a clever man with the best means for discovering and trading upon the credulity of mankind. You and I, my dear boy, and our tribe, are only like the clergyman, the doctor, and the lawyer. We all have our pretences and our shams; on the other hand, we all have our natural gifts and the skill which comes from training. You, with your machinery of the Hidden and Ancient Way, conceal or set off a power which is real, though not so great as they believe. Is that a sufficient reply, Paul, to this old prejudice?"

Paul sighed.

"It is sufficient, I suppose. Let it pass, daddy. I was a fool to be vexed with the words of a fanatic. Let us talk of other things. The time is running short. Only a few days now before the grand *coup.*"

"You will carry your grand *coup*, Paul. In fact, it cannot fail."

"And after?"

"Yes, Paul—after; what will follow?"

"I am divided. I do not see my way so clearly as I ought. I cannot decide. It seems as if I have somehow lost nerve of late."

"At this point, Paul, the path becomes extremely perilous. You propose to burn your boats. It will be impossible for you to go back upon your steps. You can never, once having achieved results so magnificent and unheard of, become the adviser and the oracle. The fame of this achievement will spread far and wide. Too much will be expected. Already the papers are beginning to speak of the Indian paper mystery. There is a note on it in yesterday's *Pall Mall Gazette*, and another in *St. James's Gazette*. They are nasty ones, but that you might expect. One of them demands a repetition—says that if the thing could be done once it could be done again; the other asks for an authorized and attested account of what was really done. Nothing could advertise you better, and if I knew the London journalists as I used to know those of New York, I would keep the ball rolling with paragraph after paragraph. The time is come, if you are to reap any solid advantage out of these miracles, when the Press should take up the thing seriously. Paul, the more I think of it the more persuaded I am that the Press exists chiefly for the advancement of the adventurer. First he begins to be noticed in a short paragraph and in an obscure corner of the paper—a good many never get beyond that corner; if he is a good man he is able to push the advantage ; next he advances to the stage of being reported whenever he makes a public appearance; thirdly, not only do his utterances get printed, but his journeys and wanderings are published; he has become a man of the age. Moral, Paul: You have excited the public curiosity; keep it up."

"You are always wise, daddy," said Paul.

"Will you tell me, now, how you did the Indian paper mystery?"

"My friends—" he began, but burst out laughing. "Daddy, it was too simple. I almost feared that they would find it out on the spot. Even Tom, who came on purpose to detect me, was caught with the rest. Some day I will tell you all about it."

"Very well. I will wait. Remember, Paul, you cannot be always working such miracles as the appearance of this day's paper brought from Delhi."

"That is quite true," said Paul. "And it is the chief danger of the situation."

"People always expect more miracles and fresh miracles. They will want you to heal the sick—"

"I have done it. The servants bring all their friends who have got toothache or headache. I heal them by imposition of hands. I can go on doing that—unless—" He stopped short.

"To get them messages from the other world."

"That is always easy."

"To advise them as to their conduct in difficult junctures."

"That also is easy. You have taught me how to do that."

"To bring them to-day's *New York Herald*—"

"Yes," said Paul, rubbing his chin. "The Indian experiment cannot very well be repeated."

"You are going to save a family from the loss of a great sum of money. They will want you to save everybody from getting into trouble."

"Ye—yes. Perhaps that will be only part of the advice or oracle business."

"No; because you can never put the blame on the spirits. Your friends must be infallible. Paul, I see only two ways out of it."

"Namely?"

"The first is to imitate your predecessor, the illustrious Caghortio, and get as much money out of your disciples as you can. Form a new freemasonry as he did."

"The other way, daddy?"

"The other way would be to get your college established under a magnificent name, and become the director. Then you could declare the Age of Miracles closed, and so prevent anybody else from stepping into your shoes. You are clever, Paul. There is nobody that I ever heard of who has possessed your gifts of quickness, thought reading, and magnetic powers. You must own that I cultivated them."

"You did, daddy, you did."

"Yet a quicker man than you may any day come across the ocean. Do not nourish illusions."

"I will not. My powers may fail; there may be a better man coming along. Yet I see a third way."

"What is that?"

"It is that which I indicated a month ago. At the very height of greatness, and in the very glow and first excitement of the crowning miracles, to disappear."

"How will you live afterwards? whither will you go ? If to New York, your fame will follow you. Paul, be reasonable. Make hay while the sun shines. Make money while the disciples are flocking in. Use your musical voice and your dark eyes, my dear boy, for practical purposes. All the women will fall in love with you. Let them, if they wish, bring offerings, but keep your own heart cold if you wish to retain your powers. Mark that, Paul. A man of your temperament, if he dares to fall in love, will plunge head over ears and will be ruined hopelessly, Paul. I looked for such great things from you. I thought that after your European tour, and after learning all the newest jargon from the newest pretenders, you would go back to America the pride of the profession. Do not disappoint me, Paul. I did pretty well for many years. You know how large a circle of believers I had. · They would do nothing without consulting me. You remember I was the most respectable of practitioners in the city. But what was I compared with what you might be with youth and all your gifts? Paul—be persuaded. You may be, if you play the cards rightly, the king of the profession."

Paul hesitated.

"The whole charm of the thing," he said, "lies in going off suddenly. To disappear; to be no more heard of; to be a dream in the memory of those who have believed; to be written about as one who appeared, wrought great marvels, spoke of strange powers, and then vanished. Think of that! A figure in history for writers to discuss and to wrangle over. The mysterious Herr Paulus—whence came he? Is he a myth?"

"Yes, it is a grand conception; it is worthy of you, Paul. But be practical. Oh, my dear boy, don't give your career away for a dream. It's like killing yourself just at the moment when you are certain to have a grand funeral and a beautiful send-off notice in all the papers. It is grand—but don't do it, Paul."

"I will consider," said Paul.

"When is the next miracle coming off?"

"On the 23d—in four days. Nearly everything is ready. It will be a truly touching day. Even Sibyl will be reconciled to me, and Tom will be disarmed. I wish you would put in an appearance, my dear daddy, for one night only, as Izák Ibn Menelek."

"Could that be managed, Paul? I am so lame with this confounded rheumatism that I am afraid—no—no—it can't be. The idea must be abandoned."

"And on the day after—while their hearts are all aglow—to vanish! It will be magnificent! But, daddy, that man to-day. His voice brought back the old chapel and the old simplicity, and the old thoughts. A prejudice—a survival—think no more about it."

CHAPTER XIV.

ON ADVANTAGEOUS TERMS.

WHILE they talked there was heard a single knock—the single knock of a humble person at the door. One knock for the humble person, two for the postman, three for the person of social pretensions. Reader, let us be thankful that we can use the triple knock. The old house-keeper presently reported that a man wished to speak with the professor on business. Party of the name of Medlock, they heard the caller explain.

"Here is the man Medlock, Paul," the old man whispered. "I will talk with him alone. Best for him not to know that you are in England. Go into the back room and keep the door open. If I call, you can come in. If not, you can listen."

The caller was a man of fifty springs or thereabouts. He left his hat and great-coat in the hall, and appeared dressed in black with an open frock-coat, a waistcoat with a rolling collar, and a broad expanse of shirt, *clean and* spotless. But his clothes were ill-fitting and gave him the appearance of a very humble Baptist minister, one of those who have taken the first step only from the counter to the pulpit in the little country town. He was clean shaven, thin, and pale. His hair was gray, he was slight of figure, somewhat shorter than the average, and presented generally the air of complete insignificance. Nobody is really insignificant, because anybody can light a lucifer-match and burn down a palace. But some men look insignificant, especially men who are short and spare and have small features."

"I do not remember you, Mr. Medlock, but you have written to me."

"No, sir, you do not. Naturally, because you have never seen me before. I have admired you, sir, from the crowd. I am respectable, but I hail from the crowd." There was a perceptible American twang in his talk, but not fully developed. Probably it had been acquired late in life, and was grafted on that branch of the Essex dialect which we call cockney.

"You wrote to me about my late pupil. Before we speak of that matter tell me who you are and what credentials you possess. What you ask, Mr. Medlock, is perhaps a bigger thing than you suspect."

"I will tell you, sir, if you will grant me five minutes of your time. I will show you my credentials, and I will tell you why I wrote to you."

"Then take a chair and proceed."

"My name, sir, is Medlock—widely known as Haynes Medlock in the profession, just as they say Henry Irving and not Irving, or Charles Dickens and not Dickens."

"In what profession? Are you an actor?"

"No, sir. Not an actor. I have been engaged—largely engaged—in the show business for many years—for eighteen years, in fact."

"In the show business. Did you make much in that business?"

"I did not, sir. There is money in it, as nobody knows better than myself. But the money goes to the boss, not to the men who run the show for the boss. I've helped to run a good many shows, but it seldom amounted to more than grub and plank, and as for hours—a tram conductor is not in it."

"Well, sir?"

"Well, sir, I am coming to the point gradually. First, I want you to understand that I am a man of experience. Haynes Medlock is a well-known man in the States, though as yet he has never run a show on his own account. I've been most things that a man can be who has been connected with shows. I know the whole business from taking the money at the doors, which any one can do, to preparing the posters and writing the newspaper paragraphs, which wants genius. I have also been travelling lecturer; I have described a diorama between the music; I have lectured on lime-light views while the operator showed them; I have introduced to the audience the young lady without arms who played the harp with her toes; I have made talk on the stage while the conjurer managed his tricks; I've travelled with a giant and a drawf, and lectured on them in their presence; I have gone around with a camera obscura. I have been assistant to a craniologist. There is nothing, I believe, in the nature of a show that I haven't done, short of playing the cornet—not that I would be too proud to play the cornet, only I don't know how."

"Proceed, sir."

"Well, sir, I have acquired so much knowledge of the business—I may truly say that in posters I yield to none, and my advertisements are allowed to be works of genius of a high order—it occurred to me that I might rise to be a boss myself, and run a show of my own."

"How long did you say you have worked in this line?"

"Eighteen years."

"And a paid help all the time. Are you an American born?"

"No, sir; I am an Englishman."

"If you had been an American you would have made yourself boss a dozen years ago and more. Go on."

"The kind of show I thought of was a superior Spiritualist show. I would have everything in it, sir. The old-fashioned medium, though this is a little out of date, as one may say, always draws if the thing is carefully worked. I would have the raps and messages and all that, not forgetting the heavenly music. I play myself, very sweetly, on the concertina, so that the heavenly music may be safely advertised. I can also use the camera, so that spirit - photographs will always appear upon the posters. As for drawing on the ceiling, I have practised with the lazy tongs; and as for floating in the air, I've done it on the stage with the conjurer. Thought reading, of course, I understand, and finding things hidden away."

"Pray go on."

"I would also include palmistry, which I am told is now fashionable in this country, and reading characters from handwriting. This always fetches in the money. Craniology—they always like that if the patter is well done."

"You might add astrology and astronomy and alchemy while you are about it, to make the show complete."

"Thank you, sir, I will make a note of your suggestion. Anything from you—"

"And now, sir, what do you propose?"

"To run your pupil, sir, on advantageous terms, sir. I know what is due to that young gentleman. First, sir, allow me to continue. I had a wife in the old days before I went to the States. She became a medium and frightened me. I confess, sir, that she frightened me out of the house with her spirits. Fairly drove me out. I was a fool to go, because she afterwards became a great medium, and I could have run her on advantageous terms, of course; whereas she has only fooled herself away, and is now, I hear, in reduced circumstances. I ought to have known there was money in it. But I did not, and I ran away. Well, when first I thought of this, then of course I naturally remembered my wife."

"Naturally."

"And I came straight home to look for her. I thought she would be just the medium that I wanted."

"Well—and you have seen her and she won't go away with you?"

"No, sir, I wasn't fool enough to speak to her before making inquiries. I have seen her but she hasn't seen me. She's lost all her business and all her powers, as far as I can learn. Nobody goes to her and she's poor, and she's old, and, which is worse, she looks poor. Lavinia never was much in the way of looks, but when she was young she had her points. My show wants beauty and youth; at all events, youth. If I had youth and beauty I could do anything. Well, I was obliged to give up the idea. Then I heard that you were in London and I remembered hearing of your pupil, and I thought, sir, considering that he will probably be wanting a run through the States, and that he must have an agent, why should he not have me? Stop a moment, sir. Don't say no all at once. Consider. I know all the dodges—every one. I do indeed. I am up to everything within the show and out of it. Not that I actually do the things myself, but I am a skilled assistant to those who do—a confederate who can be trusted —a bonnet, if I may so speak, of fidelity and zeal. As such, sir, I should be invaluable. And as for terms, they would be advantageous—highly advantageous."

"What, sir?" The professor sat upright in his chair, and bent upon this unhappy man eyebrows so white and bushy, and shook in his face a crutch so thick and threatening that he trembled and gasped. "What, sir! You dare to ask me to engage you in the capacity of a successful confederate and a cheat? You dare to insult me by assuming that my life, my blameless and honorable career, has been stained by trickery? You dare, sir, I ask, to come here and do this? Go, sir, go. Remove yourself from my presence. If I were younger, if I had the use of my limbs, you would go through the window, not for the insult you offer to me, but for that you have offered to the sacred cause of Spiritualism."

An archbishop accused of cheating at euchre could not have exhibited a loftier indignation. The good old man fell back in his chair exhausted, but glaring with wrath and indignant virtue.

"I beg your pardon, sir. I—I—"

"It is such men as yourself, with your accordions and your speaking-tubes and your lazy tongs, by which you imitate the phenomena of manifestations, who bring discredit on our sacred calling."

"Sir!—professor! I beg your pardon. I do indeed. I didn't mean any insult. I won't say another word about the conjuring tricks. But if I could get an appointment I should give every satisfaction. I've excellent manners and a winning way"—he smiled engagingly, to show how winning that way was. "In the outer office, to receive visitors and to prepare their minds and raise their curiosity, I should be invaluable. Forgive me, sir. If you won't help me, sir, I must go back to my wife—to Lavinia." He shuddered. "To Lavinia, in order to borrow money to get back to the States, where I am honorably known."

"Your name is Medlock, you say. Is your wife Lavinia Medlock?"

"Yes, sir—Lavinia Medlock."

"She was formerly a medium of some note. You do not wish to go back to her; you would only be a burden to her. You had a daughter, I think. Yes, yes. For your wife's sake, only for her sake, mind, I might help you—yes"—the professor gazed steadfastly at the man as if he was reading him through and through. "What is your present address?"

"I have a bedroom in Hunter Street, Bloomsbury."

"What were you formerly?"

"I was a clerk, sir, on a hundred and twenty pounds a year—and we let lodgings —but Lavinia filled the house with ghosts to such a degree—"

"Yes—and you've been all the time in the States going about with shows. Well, you are not going to be my pupil's agent, but I may help you if you show me that you are worth help. Can you stay on at Hunter Street for another week?"

"As long as you like, sir, if it will lead to anything."

"You are not to go near your wife at present. You are not to write to her or to let her know that you have returned."

"I don't wan't to."

"Very good. Here is a sovereign. You will have a letter from me, perhaps, in a day or two. Take care to obey it. Now you can go."

The man retired, and Paul came forth from the bedroom, where he had overheard the conversation.

"Well, Paul, how does this coincidence help you? Coincidences are always happening, always. What brought that man here? Why, he is the father of that girl, Paul."

"Yes, he is Hetty's father. What will Hetty think of him? He is not exactly a father to be proud of, is he?"

"To restore to that girl her long-lost father would be, methinks, a miracle of the more wonderful, Paul. Pity he isn't rich, as he would be in a novel."

"He seems a most detestable little snob. But still, it would please Hetty. I will do it, daddy; I will do it. Hetty's father and Cicely's brother. Both in one day! Both in one day!"

CHAPTER XV.

TOM'S DISCOVERY.

ONLY one day before the 23d, and not a word or a sign from the mysterious three who held those checks. Paul, however, preserved an unabated cheerfulness. On this morning—the 22d—when the party broke up after breakfast, Tom and Sibyl, obedient to a sign from the former, lingered behind.

"I told you, Dodo," he said, as soon as they were alone, "that I should track him out."

"Well, Tom, and have you? And it is not too late?"

"Come up to my workshop. No one will look for you there; and I've got lots of things to tell you."

"Now, Dodo," he said, having gained the security and loneliness of that retreat, "I have really done it—I have found him out— and I am ready to spring the whole thing upon him."

"Does he know or suspect anything?"

"Not a word."

"Oh!" Sibyl smiled sweetly, as a woman can smile who sees her enemy humbled. "And he is after all, as I have always suspected, a mere impostor and swindler. Well, it is only one more. He will be followed by another, I dare say, quite as bad."

"Not quite, Dodo, dear. Your feminine way of putting things is perhaps too downright. Women love a clear outline."

"We love truth."

"Unfortunately," said the physicist, "nothing in nature has a clear outline. Well, my child, I am not prepared to call bad names. A swindler or an impostor is generally a person who obtains money under false pretences. I have no evidence at all, as yet, that our friend Paul has obtained money under false pretences. He may, for aught I know, propose to stick to all those very considerable sums now lying in the bank to the account of the illustrious Izák Ibn Menelek, descendant of King Solomon and Queen Sheba; Reuben P. Zeigler, of Philadelphia; and Surabjee Kamsetzee, of Bombay. I say that he may, but I do not believe that he does. If he does he will find himself in Queer Street, with a clear prospect of a healthy life under lonely conditions for a longish term of years. I say, Dodo, that if he does he will be astonished. Because I am ready to demonstrate in open court the method by which that money was extracted from your father."

Sibyl sighed. "Oh, I knew all along that he must have taken it."

"He hasn't stolen it, Dodo; that is to say, not as yet. But he was the means by which the shares were sold—of that I am certain. Remember, please, that had it not been for the sale of those shares everything would have been lost."

"Everything is lost, Tom," said Sibyl, with assurance.

"First of all, I told you that Lavinia put me on the scent. An old gentleman who had been in the service of the company, and had all his money invested there, came to her alarmed by a whisper from the office. She could get no counsel and asked Paul's advice. Paul understood the situation and saved the man's money. More than that, he saved ours—"

"So you say."

"It was not, you observe, his 'friends' who warned him, nor was it at the instigation of his friends that he acted. It was by an accident: he was consulted. I have seen the man whom he advised. He tells everybody how he asked the spirits and how, Lavinia's spirits being unequal to the task, he sent his case to Herr Paulus, who ordered him to sell instantly. Without his advice he would have gone to the workhouse. Without his action a like fate would have befallen us, sweet Dodo. If not quite the workhouse, our union would have been put off indefinitely."

"It is put off indefinitely as it is," said Sibyl. "Only yesterday my father called me into his study, and after reminding me of the vocation to which he had destined me from the cradle, told me that the time was now come when I must put my life seriously under the instruction of our prophet."

"And you replied?"

"I told him that my vocation was quite in the opposite direction, and then we had a scene. How can I change his resolution?"

"I shall try what I can do, presently," said Tom. "Meantime, we can at any time make it impossible for that resolution to be carried into effect."

Sibyl shook her head.

"No, Tom; not without his consent. But go on about Paul."

"I was greatly pleased at this little discovery, and I began to think. I kept on thinking and watching. One morning when he went out I followed him. It was not difficult, for he never looked round, and I kept on one side of the street while he walked on the other. When he came to St. Pancras Church, the great new church, he left the Marylebone Road and walked across the church-yard into the Marylebone High Street. He crossed the street and walked along a row of small houses which they call Beaumont Street, and at one of these he stopped, and opened the door with a latch-key, and walked in as if the place belonged to him. So, you see, our man, who came straight from St. Petersburg, and who, we thought, knew no one at all in England, had a friend living in Beaumont Street, Marylebone."

"It shows that he told us lies, but it does not show anything else, Tom, does it?"

"First, my dearest Dodo, to use the words of the Quaker, thou utterest an untruth, and then thou askest a question. As he never said that he had no friends here it does not show that he told lies. When I came to find out the name of his friend it seemed to prove a great deal. For his friend is no other than the great Professor Melchers himself, of New York."

"I never heard of him."

"Nor had I until I was told about him. Professor Melchers, until his health broke down, was the greatest oracle in New York. Hundreds of our fellow-creatures, presumed to be sane, would take no decisive step, however trivial, without consulting the professor, whose advice was followed blindly. There are heaps of stories told of his insight, and the wonderful results obtained by those who bought his opinion. Of course he was connected with the other world, presumably with the spirits of Dick Whittington, Jacques Cœur, Sir Thomas Gresham, Messrs. Astor, Vanderbilt, Stewart, and all the goodly company of those who have made money and no doubt still keep up their interest in the process. Well, Sibyl, here comes in the interesting part. The professor grew old; the professor took a pupil; the professor retired from business and went away on his travels; his pupil went with him. The pupil's name was Signor Paolo. Now do you begin to understand? None of the old business with raps and Emmanuel Chicks and Lavinia Medlocks; nothing of the kind—a fine old established City Oracle; a place of inquiry for those who deal in stocks and shares; magic and mystery brought to bear on finance; the spirits made useful; communications with the other world restricted to matters of business. No wonder the professor did well and made a little pile."

"Is this important?"

"Very important, indeed."

"What next?"

"Come on the roof with me."

There was a trap-door in one corner and a short ladder, which Tom raised, and, mounting it, opened the door. Sibyl followed. Outside there was a tolerably broad area, bounded by a low parapet.

"Look over the parapet, Dodo. You can see into your father's study."

The study, as has been related, was built out from the house. Tom's room was at the end of the house, and from the roof anybody standing near the end could look straight into the large side window of the study, and could see what was being done over that part of it covered by the table and the chair and the hearth-rug—in other words, over the habitable portion of the study.

"I have improved upon this side view," said Tom, "by a little arrangement of glasses and things. Step in here, Dodo."

He had erected on the leads a small, low chamber, not much higher than the parapet, with coarse tarpaulin sides. He pushed the tarpaulin apart and Sibyl entered. Within there was a round table painted white. Tom came after her and closed the hangings behind him. Then it was quite dark.

"Tom, what is the meaning of it?" she asked.

Tom did something—turned a handle, perhaps—and instantly on the table there showed a picture, bright, clear, and in the natural colors. It was the picture of the study. Sibyl saw the hearth-rug, the fireplace, the great table with the books and papers upon it, the wooden chair, and the long low chair beside the fire. It was a beautiful picture, much better than a photograph, on account of the colors. Presently out of the external blackness Sibyl saw her father glide into the picture and sit down at the table. Then he took a pen and began to make calculations.

"We are unlucky this morning," said Tom. "I could have shown you how he

goes off every day to Abyssinia. I could have shown you how Paul exercises that power of his by which he made Cicely and Hetty see what he pleased. You would have seen your father, apparently dead, suddenly sit up—turn round his chair and write at Paul's orders. Then you would have seen Paul fold up the letters and put them in his own pocket, take the keys and examine the safe, read your father's correspondence, look in his drawers; even search his pockets."

"Let me out, Tom," cried Sibyl. "I cannot watch my father. Oh, it is horrible that a man should have such power."

"It is strange, but there is no doubt of it. After a time you would have seen him awaken his patient. In these trances, Dodo, he has made your father carry on the business about the shares—"

"But, Tom, this is awfully, terribly dangerous. This is far worse than I feared."

"It is very dangerous; nothing could be more dangerous. A man possessed of this power could strip a man of everything, if he chose. Because, you see, your father does not know that this man has this power over him. All he can say is that he does not know why he wrote certain letters and signed certain checks—he cannot remember. If a man cannot remember the performance of these most important acts, he had better go and be locked up at once. Now, you see, I am ready as an eye-witness. I have seen things done which prove to me, as clearly as anything can be proved, how the business was effected. Paul is a mighty clever young man, but I have been one too many for him. I warned him that I should watch him."

"What—what are you going to do with the knowledge, Tom?"

"I am going to denounce him, of course. I shall take the opportunity to-morrow, while all the world is admiring the wonderful way in which our fortunes have been saved, lost, and restored to us, of explaining the process."

"You do not know that he will give back the money."

"I am certain he will. I have my own theory of his purpose—and it is not robbery."

"And about the Indian paper, Tom?"

"I do not understand the Indian paper trick. But then there are many tricks which I do not understand; for instance, the great manço trick. That is a capital trick, which has, so far, defied discovery. So with the Indian paper trick."

"I am glad he has been detected," said Sibyl. "I shall rejoice to see him exposed. But will my father ever believe in your explanation? Will he give up his new gospel?"

CHAPTER XVI.

I GIVE CONSENT.

It was a pity that Sibyl did not remain five minutes longer in the camera obscura, because she would have been rewarded by the sight of Paul with her father. He entered the study, in fact, just as she left that ingenious machine upon the roof.

Mr. Brudenel was horribly nervous. The calculations he had been making considered the possible loss of all the money, and were therefore perhaps a measure of his faith.

"Paul!" he cried. "Oh, how glad I am you are come! Bring me some comfort, my dear friend. Have you no message for me? None at all? Consider."

"None. Have you no faith?" Paul pointed sternly to the calculations.

"I have perfect faith, Paul, perfect." Yet his anxious eyes might make one incredulous as to the perfection. "I am assured as to their good intentions. My only fear is that, considering the insignificance of the business and the worthlessness of money— mere money—and their natural indifference whether we get it or not—"

"Yes," Paul replied, gravely, "there is that danger. But on the other hand, remember that the money stands in the name of three. They have been transported from Bombay, from Abyssinia, and from America on purpose to receive this money and place it in the bank after the modern fashion. The venerable Izâk, I suppose, never had any money before in the whole of his long life. I think that the mere fact of his receiving it will remind him that it is not an indifferent matter to you, not because you personally value money—"

"I do not, Paul. You—that is, your friends—have taught me better things." Nothing could be more humble than Mr. Brudenel's attitude of mind, or even of body. The very humility belied his words. His forehead was lined with care and his eyes were haggard. If he had been thinking all day and all night about the money he could not have looked more anxious, nor would he have valued it more.

"You do not care about the money," Paul repeated. "But your honor is engaged."

"Yes, yes. My honor is engaged; and all the poor children's money—all. And the company—my company bankrupt. My honor is engaged. If they do not get back their money I have resolved to sell my house and all that it contains. Lady Augusta has enough for us to live upon in humble style; and as for the land, it would be a thousand pities to sell it now. I will give the rent to the children in my lifetime, and divide it among them at my death. I acted for the best; but if I have lost their money I must pay it back. If I could only remember why I sold the shares, and why I signed those checks—"

"You forget every day what has passed between you and Izâk Ibn Menelek. You have forgotten daily for two months. And yet you wonder why you have forgotten this single circumstance. Lay it all—forgetfulness and everything—at the door of Izâk, and have faith."

Mr. Brudenel sighed heavily. By constantly repeating that he had faith, he had come to believe himself; yet, as has been already stated, he trembled and tossed at night, and he fidgeted by day, just for all the world as if he had none. Yet he had an example in his household. Lady Augusta and Cicely, and with them Hetty, had perfect faith, and looked for the day with joyful confidence. There would be, they were persuaded, another manifestation, and the exhibition of such power as had never yet been vouchsafed to the imperfect West.

But behold! Strange and unexpected are the ways of sages.

While they thus talked together, these two, the message so eagerly desired came to Paul. He suddenly stood up as if listening, with respect and awe upon his face.

"He has spoken," he said to Mr. Brudenel.

"What does he say?"

"There are conditions. On certain conditions — nay, one condition only — their inheritance will be saved for the children."

"What is the condition?"

"You have always desired that your daughter should remain single, devoted to the advance of true Spiritualism, which you have now learned to call the Ancient Way."

"That is true. You have yourself taught me that in the highest degrees there is no marriage. I have desired for Sibyl the condition of the greatest happiness, in which the mind is distracted by no passion and suffers from no anxiety."

"You have. But you forget one thing. One human being cannot thus dispose of another without her consent."

"There is nothing which Sibyl will not do to please me."

"Doubtless she will obey, but not in the spirit. What is the good of being a celibate if the heart is always yearning after the lower, but the common lot. What do you think of the man who cuts the tonsure and takes the vows, yet all his life dreams of the outer world and the joys he has missed?"

"But Sibyl has no desire to change. She is happy at the prospect before her."

"She would be, perhaps, but for one reason. You have forgotten that Sibyl's nature is antipathetic to all your pursuits and aims. Such a man as myself has no power over her. Cicely believes, and is rewarded by visions such as were never before vouchsafed to a blind girl. Hetty believes and is rewarded"—he blushed, remembering—"in other ways. Lady Augusta believes. But Sibyl cannot believe."

"She will believe when she learns more."

"She will never believe. You yourself have been able to distinguish between the tricks of the charlatans who surround the mystery and the mystery itself. Men like Chick, women like Lavinia Medlock, who have some humble share of power, and supplement their deficiencies by tricks and shams, have disgusted your daughter. My dear sir, if she will not believe ME, whom will she believe?" Paul raised his eyes, full of candor and pure sincerity, free from any boastfulness, though with any other man the words would have sounded boastful. "Whom will she ever believe?" he repeated.

"She *must* believe. The things you have done—"

"She will never believe, I assure you. Resign yourself to that fact. I have no power over her. She is personally antipathetic. She is actively hostile: I have endeavored, but in vain, to soften her. She belongs to that large part of humanity to whom this world's phenomena are everything. She is a materialist by birth. Give her up. Nay, you must, since Izák Ibn Menelek commands it."

"If I give her up—"

"You will give her to the keeping of another. You will never more be troubled by anxiety on account of her infidelity."

"Give her to another. To whom?"

"You will give her—to Tom Langston."

"Sibyl! To Tom Langston!"

"They command it."

"But Tom is an infidel of the deepest dye. He has always scoffed—secretly in this house—openly out of it. I do not know why I have allowed him to remain in it—except because I am his guardian. Give Sibyl to a man who will teach her to deride her father as well as the cause to which he has given his life? Never."

"You must."

"Besides, you have just reminded me that one human being cannot thus bestow of another. Would you have me offer my girl to this young man?"

"Have you eyes, Mr. Brudenel? Has no one in this house any eyes at all? Do you not see that your daughter is beautiful? Have you never seen Tom looking at her?"

"Never." In fact, nobody had. If a young man is always about the house from boyhood, nobody ever has any eyes.

"Love is betrayed by looks, Mr. Brudenel. Give your daughter to Tom, and they will both be happy. More than that, you will turn derision into respect and scoffing into silence—if not conversion."

"This is the condition imposed by your friends. Does Tom—does Sibyl—know anything about it?"

"Neither of them knows of it."

Mr. Brudenel heaved a sigh.

"I cannot," he said. "It is hard. It is the shattering of a great hope. I thought that my daughter would become the high priestess of the new religion—the Vestal—the oracle through whom the secrets of the other world, which you have fully opened to me, should be made known to others—"

"And now that can never happen. Courage, Mr. Brudenel, there will arise pillars of the Temple, who will sustain the edifice—your edifice—when you have passed across the narrow line to the life beyond. But you must write. Oh, you will not forget this time."

"To whom must I write—to Izák Ibn Menelek?"

"He needs no letter. He is here; he is with us; he is looking on while we speak. Write to Tom. Say, 'Dear Tom,—I have been informed of your attachment to Sibyl. I did not suspect this. I am informed that you were silent because your own views on things spiritual are antagonistic to my own. I am now assured that the future I had imagined for my daughter will be impossible. The wise men, living and dead, with whom I am now daily conversing, tell me that they are powerless against certain natures, to which you and Sibyl belong. I withdraw, therefore, my original plan of Sibyl's future. Address her when you please. The joys of love and marriage are poor and transitory compared with the joys for which I fondly destined her. Such joys as the world and the present life have, you will, I trust, be able to give my child. And in the other world, when you discover that the phenomenal is not the real, you will, with her, begin to climb to the higher planes, where you will find me with others who love her and will joyfully welcome her.'"

Paul dictated this letter, while Mr. Brudenel wrote obediently. When it was finished he folded it and placed it in an envelope, which he directed in the usual way.

I mention this trivial circumstance because after doing so Mr. Brudenel lifted his eyes to Paul, who stood beside him. The action occupied a moment—less than a moment. He dropped his eyes again. But the letter was gone.

" Where is it?" he asked.

" I don't know. I suppose that Izák himself has taken it. Perhaps he will send it to Tom. Courage! To - morrow evening will bring happiness to all."

" Paul," said Mr. Brudenel, " how can I thank you?" The tears stood in his eyes. "How can I ever thank you for all that you have done?"

" You must not try to thank me. I am but a servant. Now rest easy, only take care to say nothing about the letter—not a word, mind, either to Tom or to Sibyl. Leave the delivery of the letter to—those who have taken it. My dear friend "—he took Mr. Brudenel's hand and held it—" it is, believe me, an infinite happiness to feel that I have been instrumental in aiding and in saving you. Sit down, amuse yourself, read a novel—there is that book of Ouida's still in your drawer, unfinished. Come out and see the people in the streets, go and talk at your club." Mr. Brudenel belonged to one of the sepulchral clubs, where about a dozen members are acquainted, and the rest of the men glare solemnly at each other. " Go and look at pictures; take Sibyl to the theatre this evening and laugh at something funny." Mr. Brudenel had not been to the theatre for thirty years. Perhaps he might have laughed once or twice during that period, but no one remembered it. " Anyhow, be happy and free from care. And own, Mr. Brudenel, that you have been, above all other men, strangely and wonderfully dealt with."

Mr. Brudenel sank back into his chair and clasped his hands, as one who is overwhelmed by what his former friends would have called a cosmic wave of psychic force. The contemplation of an elderly bald-headed gentleman in such a condition has in it something comic. Paul, with a light in his eye which betokens appreciation, retired and softly closed the door.

CHAPTER XVII.

SAMSON AND DELILAH.

OUTSIDE, he smiled—nay, he laughed, but not aloud. Then he made as if he was going to put on his coat and hat. Then he stopped, half turned, and hesitated.

Every young person who hesitates, whether a male young person or a female young person, is lost; for, before every young person at every moment the ways divide, and the only chance of keeping in the straight and narrow way is to stride along, looking neither to the right nor to the left. As one gets older, these ways still strike out on either hand, but one

ceases to regard them. Habit fixes the eyes, or age has deprived those ways of their attractions.

Paul, therefore, hesitated. He knew that in the upper room—Cicely's room—Hetty sat alone. He had seen Lady Augusta with Sibyl and Cicely getting into the carriage ; they were going to Regent Street on business of personal adornment. Hetty was up - stairs alone. Hetty was up-stairs—alone.

It was a week since that first fatal yielding to the voice of passion, when he kissed the girl and fled. He fled with hot cheeks and trembling hands, wondering and ashamed, conscience-stricken and terrified, fearing Hetty's wrath and dreading what might follow.

Wherever it was that he had spent his early manhood—whether in an Abyssinian valley, like Rasselas—only that prince always enjoyed the best of female society that could be had in the place—and it was insipid ; or in the States; or in St. Petersburg, among the occult philosophers ; or in Thibet, among the Mahatmas—it was where girls were conspicuous by their absence. He had seen these fair creatures, no doubt, at a distance—though in a monastery of Thibet a child may grow to old age and never see a woman — and marked with wonder and admiration those sweet qualities of loveliness and grace and sweetness which youthful womanhood wears, on the outside at least. But he knew no girls while he was serving his apprenticeship until he came here. Is not this fact enough to account for the trembling which a single kiss was able to produce? A week—and he had not dared to see Hetty alone since that moment. When he looked at her, his pulse began to quicken and his hand began to tremble. When she looked, enough by itself to account for the beating of heart, the quickening of pulse, and the trembling of hand which seized him at the mere recollection of a single kiss.

Hetty was alone — up - stairs. That was why he hesitated, and why his cheek glowed and his eyes softened.

Nearly a week since his fall—since the first imperfect taste of the forbidden fruit. Do not suppose that the unhappy youth did not struggle with his fate. He dared not trust himself with Hetty even in Cicely's presence : he dreaded to meet those eyes of hers; yet if by chance he did meet them they were calm and composed as if there was nothing to be remembered. Heavens! He had kissed the girl—actually kissed her: and her eyes were as calm, as limpid as if there was no history. Had she forgotten, then ? Could she forget? Alas, he was ignorant of female eyes. Had he been able to read their language, they would have said to him, " I am waiting. Come to me. Why do you delay ?" He saw nothing but the outward calm, and he wondered because he was himself so troubled. In these days he slept badly; he anticipated dreadful things in dreams; his friends in Abyssinia and elsewhere would have been pained had they known how little he regarded them.

Now, then, was another chance—shall we call it another temptation? Hetty was alone.

He hesitated no longer; for an invisible rope—but oh! so strong and thick that no jack-knife could cut it through—was passed round his waist, and an invisible hand more irresistible than his own magnetic power dragged him, with burning cheeks and trembling limbs, up the stairs. Why, it was Hetty's magnetic force which dragged him; she was at the other end of the rope; she it was who drew to her feet this young man who had kissed her once and ran away from her. Common mesmerism, as Emmanuel Chick would say. Yet the mesmerizer was himself mesmerized. The operator was operated upon. The subduer was subdued; Samson, the strong man, was going to Delilah to have his curls lopped.

Hetty looked up and smiled. In these cases the woman does not tremble.

"You have come back, Paul ?" she said. "You have not been near me for a week. Was it my fault?"

"Forgive me, Hetty." He threw himself at her feet and caught her hand. "Forgive me, Hetty. Oh, Hetty!"

She did not reply at first. Then she whispered, softly,

"Oh, Paul! Why did you kiss me? You?"

He rose to his feet. Again he stood over her and they were alone. This time he did not, as before, kiss her forehead and run away. He threw his arms round her neck and kissed her lips and her cheeks, whispering, brokenly,

"Oh, Hetty! I love you, Hetty; I love you." That was all he had to say.

She heard him without any reply. She even made no kind of reply when he rose and kissed her on the lips, and on the brow, and on the cheeks.

"Hetty," he repeated, "I love you."

No music falls more sweetly on the ear of nymph; no poetry more moves the heart than these words from the shepherd whom she has already singled out for that admiration which should precede all true love. He was great and was possessed of wonderful powers which he bore modestly; he had lifted her soul a hundred times; he was her prophet; and now he said that he loved her. Was it possible?

"But, oh, Paul!" Hetty cried, presently, "we are foolish. You are pledged to a life of celibacy."

"Only the highest adepts are celibates, my dear. I renounce for your sake the highest degrees. I shall be suffered to remain on a lower plane—with you, Hetty."

"You would repent—the time would come when you would repent—and regret your choice. No, Paul, you must not be dragged back by a woman. You would never lift me to the higher level. I belong—I have always known it—to the lower. Cicely might rise, but I could not. Paul, leave me and—and—forget me."

But she uttered these last words with so much reluctance that all the more they fired the young and ardent lover. Indeed, there was no coquetry in Hetty. It was her heart that spoke in this reluctance to let him go.

"I will never leave you, Hetty. For your sake I would willingly abandon—yes, I would abandon"— he remembered the monition of his master—"even my powers."

"For my sake? Oh, Paul, for my sake? But you would never abandon your wisdom. You could always teach me, whether you could converse with your friends or not—even if you ceased to talk with the spirits of the dead."

"If I lost my powers," he said, "I should lose my—I should lose you, dear Hetty, because—" He meant to say, because he would have no means of subsistence at all. But he could not say this.

"Whatever you lost, Paul, you would not lose me—if you desire to keep me."

"Without my powers, I should be a beggar indeed. Other men have a profession—or ambitions. I should have none. Yet if I love you—now I understand—while I love you—for the last week my mind has been full of you—I could do little. My powers are failing."

"Paul, you don't understand," said Hetty. "I do not love you because you have this wonderful gift. Without it you would be always the same Paul to me. It is you—yourself—not you clothed with a magician's robe that I love."

"Hetty, how can you love me?"

"Nay, Paul, it is I who must ask that question. Who am I that you should love me? I am poor, and I am not clever. I am not a lady, even by birth. My mother is a medium—oh, how the world despises a medium! —and my father was once a clerk. What he is now I know not, or where he is."

"I love you because you are the most beautiful girl in the world, and the best. I love you because you are Hetty."

"Oh, can it be? I thought no one would ever love me. I thought it was impossible."

"Impossible? Oh, Hetty! Impossible for anybody to love you?"

Hetty sighed—a deep and happy sigh.

* * * * * *

"Tell me some day, when you please, Paul, about yourself. Tell me all that is in your mind—oh, if you love me, let me share your ambitions and learn your desires."

"I will tell you—everything, Hetty—everything—but not now. There are things which I must keep hidden while I am here. Afterwards — but what will happen afterwards? I know not what will happen."

"While you are here? But—Paul—you are not going away."

He turned his head and answered with evasion.

"I cannot stay here always. I am, to begin with, only a guest, though I have been allowed to feel myself a son of the house."

"But where will you go? Paul, will your friends take you away suddenly and mysteriously—so that we shall not know where you are?"

"It may be so, Hetty." But he did not raise his eyes. "I know not. To-morrow evening—I tell this to you alone, Hetty—I have to restore to Sibyl and Cicely and Tom the fortunes they so nearly lost. When that is done my work here is done. I have delivered my message. I have put Mr. Brudenel in the path that leads to the Ancient Wisdom. I have cleared the place of low and deceitful spirits. I must go if I am called."

"Without me, Paul?"

He laid his head upon her shoulder. It is a feminine thing to do, but this young man had these feminine ways. He laid his head upon her shoulder, and Hetty's heart glowed within her to think that her lover leaned upon her. It was an omen and a sign. He would tell her everything. She would be his confidante as well as his mistress and his wife.

"Hetty, how can I go without you? And yet—oh!" he sprang to his feet and threw out his arms. "Let it all go—I care nothing—Hetty, it will be hard to live without you. I know now what I have wanted all this time. It was a woman to confide in and give me sympathy. I have had no sympathy, Hetty. I have not known any girls since—since—it is some years since I saw her last. She used to listen to me."

"Were you in love with her, Paul?" Hetty did not ask who she was.

"No; we were like brother and sister. You will be to me more—far more—than she could be. Hetty, I understand now, better than I did, even my own teaching. I understand the love of the spirits for each other. They are never divided, and they

never weary of each other's company. And yet the things that I have told you seem to have been empty words."

"Oh no, Paul. They were beautiful words. They have opened our hearts, Paul, and filled our minds with great thoughts. But, Paul," she came back to the old question, "you will not go without me?"

"My dear—if I must."

"Where will you go? When will you come back? How shall I live without you?"

"I don't know, Hetty. Must I make you suffer? I am sorry that I told you—"

"No, Paul, I would rather suffer anything than lose the memory of this day. Tell me again. Let me have it once more from your lips. Do you love me, Paul? Is it true? Is it really true?"

"True? Oh, Hetty, if you only knew how true it was—and is—"

"Yet you will go?"

"I must, my dear; if one must—"

"I do not believe it. There is no must. Who is to make you go? Your friends? I do not believe that there is anything your friends can make you do unless you choose to do it. Are you not a free man? What is the good of your hidden knowledge if you are not free? Can you not make your own path for yourself? Then what is the good of your wisdom?"

"Sometimes, Hetty, I ask myself that very same question. Sometimes it seems to me as if it were better to be an ordinary man—just like the rest of mankind—with no more power and no more knowledge."

"Yet, before you loved me, Paul, I thought how wonderful it was. Since you have loved me I care nothing about it at all. What matters for all the Ancient Wisdom? It could not make you love me more. Then what do I care for it? If it is to take you away from me I shall hate it—I shall hate it."

"Hetty!"

"Oh, Paul, when you told me that you loved me you drew my heart out of myself. It is all yours. I have no other hope, no other life, but for you. If you go away, what have I left? What shall I do? Will your friends make you do this cruel thing? I am only a girl, and they are great philosophers who despise girls and love; but they cannot make you do so cruel a thing as to desert me, Paul, can they? If they can, rise up and desert them. What is wisdom compared with love? Oh, what can wisdom do for you compared with what love can do? My dear—my Paul—" She threw her arms round his neck.

"My Paul, if I can make you happy, stay. It is better to be happy than to be wise. Everybody longs for love. Oh, I know why I have been so discontented and so unhappy. It is because I had no one to love me. Since your lips touched my forehead I have been in happy heaven; I have said to myself all day long and every night, 'He loves me! Paul loves me; he loves me. Thank God! Now nothing can befall to make me unhappy any more. If he dies he will love me still; if he lives I shall only live, too, that he may be happy. But oh, Paul, I never thought—I never thought—you could be taken away."

"Hetty!"

"You *shall* not go, Paul!" She held him with all her strength of arm, and more—with the strength of her eyes. "I cannot bear it. I will not bear it; you must not go, though they drag you through the air. You shall not go without me."

"Hetty, I must tell you; I cannot help telling you." He who tells his secret to his sweetheart is not necessarily lost—he only binds another chain upon himself. "My great gift, which I have, I do believe, above all other men, is the power by which I made Cicely see her brother at sea, and by which I could subdue your will so that at a look or a gesture you became, without knowing it, my obedient servant. By the same power I rule Lady Augusta; Sibyl is outside my power, and so is Tom. It is by my gift that I am enabled to convey the messages of my friends, and to enforce respect for the teaching of the Hidden Wisdom."

"Yes, Paul, I know that power."

"I have been warned, Hetty, by one who knows. I have been warned, again and again, that if I suffered a woman to fill my thoughts I should lose that power. Those who have it must keep their hearts free from love, from enmity, from hatred and from every absorbing passion. But the most fatal of all is love. My dear, for weeks the thought of you has been gradually stealing over my heart and mastering me. I can think of nothing else. I fear I have lost my power."

"Why, then, Paul, you will be no more than an ordinary man, in love with an ordinary girl. The common lot will be ours."

"Yesterday," said Paul, apparently not much comforted by this assurance, "I tried, as usual, with Mr. Brudenel. He only stared at me and began to fuss about the money which he thinks he has lost. I could not move him. Then I tried with Cicely. She laughed and chattered. I could not move her. And then I tried with Lady Augusta and she did not even know that I was exerting all my will to move her. Hetty, let me try once more. Sit as you used to sit—so. Fold your hands, hold up your face—look me full in the eyes. Oh, Hetty"—he stooped

to kiss her—"no woman in the world has such beautiful eyes. So—now."

She obeyed him. After five minutes he stopped. "Oh," he cried, "I feel that it is useless."

"Paul, I cannot help it. Your eyes have lost their old look. They have a much sweeter look. The authority has gone out of them."

"Yes," he groaned, "the authority has gone. Perhaps when I go away it will return."

"I hope it will never return," said Hetty. "No, Paul, no. If you wish it, you shall have your power again. What are your friends worth if they cannot give it back to you?"

"My dear, you do not know what you are saying. If I have thrown away my power, I shall never get it again—never—never! Without it I can do nothing. Think of all the things that I have done, and remember that without the power I could have done none of these."

"My dear, you have done these things once. What need to do them again?"

"Hetty, can you not understand? What am I worth without this gift? It was mine—my own—and I have lost it."

"You have lost it through love—through me. Leave off loving me, Paul, and it will come back, and I shall have the recollection."

She burst into tears, and Paul, carried out of himself, soothed and caressed her.

"My dear," he said, "I will never leave you. Come what may, you are mine and I am yours. Oh, Hetty," he laughed aloud, "you do not know what you have done in making me love you. Everything is changed. All that Lady Augusta has at heart is destroyed. There will be no more progress in the Ancient Way; there will be no more instruction for Mr. Brudenel; there will be no more miracles after to-morrow. It is shattered—the most wonderful, the most perfect creation—and there is nothing left for us but to walk the earth like common folk, hand in hand, with no help at all from my mysterious friends, and no communications with the spirits. Will you be happy still, love?"

"Yes, Paul, I ask no better than the common lot."

"Then be happy, dear. I must tell you more—some day—but now be happy, Hetty, if this contents you."

"Paul," she whispered, "if this mysterious power has gone you can never be a medium. You can never pretend and invent and stoop to play tricks for money. Oh, I would work for you night and day, Paul—there is nothing that I would not do for you, to save you from becoming a medium. Oh, but you could not.

You are too wise and too high-minded. The loss of your power will not touch your wisdom. You have still your lofty mind. Paul, when it is gone you will be better than before."

Paul dropped his eyes and changed color. This remarkable young man received both praise and blame with equal signs of shame. Sir Percival called him hard names, which wounded and hurt him; Hetty called him wise and noble, and this seemed to hurt him even more.

"Hetty—you must not. Oh, my dear—you must not. I am not wise—or noble—or anything."

"Yes, Paul, to me you will always be wise and noble, and all the better for losing the power which separated you from the rest of the world. All the better, Paul."

Did the lady of Philistia comfort Samson, after the job was done, with the assurance that, though his strength was gone, he looked much neater and trimmer, and better suited for moving in general society, than in his previously dishevelled long-curled condition?

At luncheon that day Paul did not appear.

"Perhaps," said Lady Augusta, "he is away in the spirit."

"Perhaps," said Tom.

"No message has come to me in my study," said Mr. Brudenel. "My dear, therefore, I confess that I am — yes — I really am—uneasy." He looked uneasy. He was so nervous that he could hardly sit in his chair. He drummed with his fingers and he played with his knife and fork.

Sibyl glanced at Tom, but said nothing.

"My dear," said Lady Augusta, "take your lunch, all will be well."

"I cannot eat." Mr. Brudenel drank a glass of sherry, pushed back his chair, and rushed out of the room.

"As for me," said Tom, "I am extremely hungry. Mr. Brudenel will be all right to-morrow."

"Only let us have patience and faith," said Cicely. "Something has happened to Paul. He stood over me yesterday and I felt nothing. Something has gone out of him. One of the servants might have been standing over me. But it will all come right. Let us have faith in Paul."

Whatever had happened, Paul was seen no more that day. At eleven o'clock in the evening he returned, looking pale and troubled, and he went straight to his own room.

CHAPTER XVIII.

THE FORENOON.

And then the birthday came.

On this day, by the wills of their respec-

tive parents, both cousins—the one, Tom, being four-and-twenty, and the other, Cicely, twenty-one—arrived at their majority, and should inherit their fortunes—if, that is to say, Messrs. Izák Ibn Menelek, Rupert P. Zeigler, and Surabjee Kamsetjee should be good enough to meet the expectations of their young friend and disciple, and restore the money now in their keeping.

The first to come down-stairs that morning was Tom. Paul followed next. The former preserved his usual cheerfulness, despite the anxieties of the situation.

"I wish you many happy returns of the day," said Paul. "It is your birthday, is it not?"

"Thank you. Yes, it is my birthday. As nothing else has been thought of, or talked about, for the last three weeks, I am quite sure that it is my birthday. And it shows how wrapt you have been in meditation not to know that it is a very important birthday for me. How would it be if the philosophers, your friends, were able to abolish a man's birthday?"

Paul smiled, but mechanically.

"Yes," Tom continued; "it is my birthday, and Cicely's as well. And with your help, my philosopher, and a miracle or two, which I have no doubt will be accomplished by the sages, your friends, I hope to be put in the way of enjoying two or three birthdays more. Otherwise, indeed—"

"Otherwise?" There was a gleam of menace in Tom's eyes. "Otherwise, Tom?"

"Otherwise means," Tom answered, lightly, "that if these miracles do not come along in due course, the Ancient Wisdom will have to wake up in an astonishing way. But what's the matter, Paul? You look uncommon flabby."

Black care, anxiety, trouble sat visibly upon Paul's brow. Tom secretly connected the thing with the three checks, but he was wrong. Those checks had never caused Paul the least anxiety.

"Nothing is the matter except headache."

"A week or two ago you cured Sibyl's maid of a toothache. Physician, cure thyself."

"I can't, Tom. This is a headache which cannot be exorcised."

"I'm sorry—especially because I've got to say something devilish unpleasant."

"What is that? Say it. You will not make my head ache any worse."

"Do you remember, Paul, how I told you at the beginning—the very first night that you came, in my workshop, the night you rang the bells—that I was going to watch you?"

"Did you say so?" Paul replied, carelessly.

"Perhaps you did. Yes, I remember now. You did say something to that effect. We were to be on good terms, but you were going to keep your eyes on me. I remember. Well, Tom, your eyes have been on me, have they, all the time?"

"All the time."

"And what have you discovered?"

"I have been watching all the time," Tom repeated, gravely.

"Have you?" Paul looked up curiously. "Communicate your discoveries."

"They are somewhat important. For instance, there was the little business with Mr. James Berry. Do you remember Mr. James Berry?"

"The man whom Lavinia Medlock asked me to advise? Yes, what of him? I gave him advice. I remember that he asked me whether he was to retain certain shares in a certain company or sell them out. I advised him to sell them out. Did he do so?"

"What company was it?"

"He did not tell me the name of the company. It would have been no use to me if he had told me. I remember Lavinia Medlock told me that if certain things happened the old gentleman would have to go to the workhouse. Why not go to the workhouse? They get food and warmth in the workhouse, and can meditate. But this old gentleman somehow did not wish to go there, and I advised him to avoid that necessity."

"Did you see that old gentleman?"

"No. Does he say that he saw me?"

"Did you not learn from Lavinia the name of that company?"

"Lavinia told me she did not know it."

Tom was silenced. In fact, both Mr. Berry, whom he had seen, and Lavinia, whom he had questioned, declared that Herr Paulus knew no more than was conveyed in a certain question : "Shall the inquirer—name unknown—sell out certain shares—company unknown—or keep them?"

"Well," he said, feeling baffled, "it is odd that the company should be Brudenel & Co., and that Mr. Brudenel's shares should have been sold out at the same time. I say, Paul, that is an odd coincidence."

"Perhaps. I did not make the world, and I do not rule it. Why worry me with odd coincidences? Tell Mr. Brudenel about them if you like."

His words showed irritation. And I do not know what Tom would have replied, because at this moment Sibyl came in, with Cicely, followed by Lady Augusta. Last appeared Mr. Cyrus Brudenel himself; he was terribly anxious; his face was pale and his fingers kept catching at his watch - chain. *He was what young* men call jumpy.

"Tom," he cried, with a miserable attempt at heartiness, "I wish you many happy returns of the day, and joy, j—j—j—joy, of your inheritance—when you get it. Cicely, my dear" (he kissed the blind girl with tenderness), "you are now your own mistress—at least—I—I—I—can only say, my dear, that I have done my best for you, and that I hope all will turn out well. You have given me so much happiness, Cicely, by living with us, but we hope you will stay on with us. You are of age, both of you. You have now—that is—I hope that you are coming into your fortunes. Many strange things have happened in this house—none so strange as the temporary — I trust, only temporary—vanishing of your fortunes. But we have faith—we have complete faith."

His jerky manner scarcely conveyed an impression of complete faith. Everybody looked at Paul. On a former occasion when everybody looked at Paul, he carried himself with a perfect disregard of the general curiosity and was absorbed in his breakfast. On this occasion, perhaps because they had not yet sat down to that meal, he showed himself conscious of their eyes, and blushed and hung his head. What had happened to him?

"Paul!" cried Lady Augusta. "Speak, I implore you. Bring us hope and comfort."

"I do not know for certain," said Paul, slowly and with hesitation. Again, what had happened to change Paul's bearing of authority into this manner of hesitation? "I have said all along that I could not know for certain. How can I tell whether they will regard a mere money matter worthy of interference? Yet as they have already interfered, it seems reasonable to suppose that they had some motive which could not be otherwise than benevolent to this household. Let us wait in patience and faith."

"Let us have faith," said Cicely. But Mr. Brudenel groaned audibly.

* * * * * *

Tom and Sibyl, when the others separated after breakfast, remained in the breakfast-room.

"Let us have faith," said Tom, derisively. "Yes, perhaps that is all we shall hear, Dodo, dear. Let us consider—"

"You will expose him, Tom."

"I can certainly testify as to certain things that I have seen. The difficulty is how far my testimony will go. You see, your father wrote letters of introduction and recommendation for the three persons to whose order he made out the checks. Suppose he is asked why he wrote those letters; suppose he says he does not know. In that case, your father will look—shall we say?—simple. Suppose he is asked why he sold out the shares and replies that he does not remember—he will again present—shall we say?—a simple appearance. Suppose he is asked why he drew those checks—"

"But, Tom, you can always prove that this man worked upon him."

"I don't know. There is no precedent in law, I am afraid, of one man being 'worked upon' by another. What can I prove, Dodo?" he added, gloomily. "I begin to fear the worst. I don't like his looks. For the first time since he came here, he looks guilty. I don't like it."

"Are we to lose everything, Tom?"

"Not if I can help it. Perhaps we shall be able to show cause for an inquiry. We might get an injunction—but for what reason? Suppose these perfectly unknown persons each draw a check payable to 'Herr Paulus or bearer,' or to 'No. 191 or bearer' —how can we do anything? We cannot find these men."

"You thought you knew them."

"I believe I do. But how to prove it? Dodo, dear, it is possible that we shall lose our little all despite the fuss that our friend made over it. And yet it can't be. Until this morning I thought one had only to look in his face—"

"Tom, men always think that good looks must cover a good heart."

"With girls I am sure they do. That is, looks like yours, Dodo."

Mr. Brudenel sat in his studio expecting Paul. He had pictured to himself, in hopeful moments, a beautiful scene. His wards' fortunes would be given back to him, and he would convey them magnificently to their rightful owners with a speech about the advantages of securing friends able to interpose in times of danger and to avert wreck and ruin. He liked to make up little speeches beforehand, so as to be always equal to the occasion; but as things never came off as he expected, these little speeches were always thrown away. Thus is man mocked of Fate.

Paul came not. Then Mr. Brudenel began to think that the expected message might come to him directly, without the presence of Paul, and he composed himself, sitting upright in his wooden chair—not the low leather chair by the fire. Presently he should glide insensibly into that attitude of mind when the outer world becomes unseen, unheard, and unregarded, and the soul is independent of the body and can fly whither she please, and space and time no longer have any meaning. When Paul stood over him and looked in his face and commanded him to yield up his soul to the influence of those who called, he felt instantly as a tired man feels when he lays his head upon the pillow. His limbs

became motionless; he felt them no longer. A kind of sleep rose upward to his brain and set free his soul. Now, he thought, he would induce that semblance of sleep without the aid of Paul. Nothing would be easier.

Strange to say, after five minutes of intense exercise, with the will resolutely bent, he discovered that no progress at all had been made. Worse than that, he was becoming fidgety; his feet refused to stay still; his legs kicked involuntarily; his fingers twitched; he was awake all over.

He gave himself another five minutes. The result left no room at all for doubt. He was not permitted to release his soul—he could not, therefore, go in quest of any message; because you cannot, yet, lug a lump of bones and flesh all the way to Abyssinia and back in a morning.

Then he tried another method. He arose and solemnly called aloud,

"Izák Ibn Menelek!"

The quiet room echoed his words, but there came no answer.

"Izák Ibn Menelek! Master! Hear!"

The master may have heard, but he made no reply.

A third time Mr. Brudenel called,

"Izák Ibn Menelek! Come!"

He sat down and waited for an answer. Perhaps the master was asleep; perhaps he was walking.

Mr. Brudenel waited for a quarter of an hour, concentrating his mind, with all the force of which he was capable, upon the master. So the prophets of Baal in the slopes of Carmel called all day long and hacked their flesh with knives to please their god. But no answer came, and presently those prophets were taken to the side of the stream and done to death. But to the end, I am sure, they believed profoundly.

There came no answer, no voice faint and far-off such as called him when Paul was present.

Then Mr. Brudenel—always ready to fall away from faith—sat down in despair. He was deserted. His new friends had deserted him, and he had thrown away the old friends. Emmanuel Chick's spirits would not have failed him even though they might bring no comfort. Lavinia's spirits might have told him things irrelevant and trivial, but they would not have heard him call upon them in silence. The busts of his former friends—Albertus Magnus, Paracelsus, Roger Bacon, Dee, Lilly, Mesmer, Home, and the rest—frowned upon him from their places above the book-shelves. The books themselves, whose outside he had been wont to admire, the acquisition of which had cost him such mighty sums, frowned upon him and threatened him. He had deserted his old friends; he had turned out of the house the old spirits whom he had formerly entertained. He had gone over to a new party; and what had he got for it?

Then a devil—I think it may have been one of Lavinia's mocking spirits—whispered in his ear, "If they have done so much to you they may do more. You know that it was not you yourself who wrote those letters and signed those checks, though they are in your handwriting. The power which imitated your handwriting can do more. Nay, it may even personate you yourself. It can make you say, and write, and do anything it pleases. Already it has robbed you of thirty-five thousand pounds." How Mr. Brudenel wiped his brow and shivered! The mocking devil went on: "You have indeed brought your pigs to a pretty market. If you rebel they may punish you by taking away your land. Why, in either case you are done for, because, if you do not rebel, but go on in the course you have begun, they will certainly strip you of all your possessions. Is not the foundation of their philosophy the maxim that wealth is contemptible? Live like Epictetus, in a cottage on herbs and onions—live like Diogenes, in a tub—go about with a wallet, begging crusts, like a Buddhist saint or a Franciscan—go in rags, unwashed, unshaven, beaten by the wind, and rained upon, if you would please your new friends."

Mr. Brudenel heard these words plainly spoken in his ear—very strange things, I have many times stated, went on in that house. But it is not too much to say that they scared him. The contemplation of philosophy reduced to practice filled him with horror. Would Lady Augusta also be deprived of her property? Would they go about together, meditating on the higher planes, and begging for crusts to put in their wallets? He pictured himself, being a person of some imagination, as the sage after the heart of the Abyssinian wise man—he would wear a frock-coat once black, but now gone green, with ragged tails, with holes in the elbows and a shimmering sheen of grease or age upon the wrists—he would have a tall hat with a broken brim, for as a new Lincoln & Bennett is an outward sign of respectability, so a tall hat, ancient, shabby, and worn is a sure and certain proof of poverty—his boots would be broken down and gaping—he would have a red comforter round his neck, and no collar—his nose would be blue with the cold—his white beard would be as venerable as that of Belisarius in his most penurious condition. He tried to picture Lady Augusta meditating beside him on the same exalted plane. But here he broke down. Nobody could imagine Lady Augusta in rags, revelling in these heights of philosophy.

The longer he thought upon this dreadful possibility the more probable did it seem. Yes, Paul—but Paul was clad in fine raiment and fared sumptuously, and seemed to enjoy the good things of the world prodigiously, as all young men should—Paul preached perpetually the doctrine of the nothingness of wealth: he despised wealth; his friends despised wealth; the loss of wealth was an incident not worth mentioning: yet, Mr. Brudenel thought, how would Paul look in rags, and with a blue nose, carrying a basket to hold the broken meats of charity?

The thing was dreadful, yet it was possible; it was even likely. Had he not accepted with more than submission—with ardor —all these teachings. Had he not already gone a long way down the Ancient Way, only somehow he forgot what the scenery was like? How could he complain if he was taken at his word and deprived of that earthly dross which stands between vanity and wisdom, so that one may not pass from the glittering realms of the one to the fair fields of the other without dropping the burden and weight of wealth, even as the Pilgrim dropped the load which bound him down? He would be taken at his word. His new friends would strip him of the wealth which he could not bring himself to despise. When his wealth was gone he would be able to start fair upon the way of wisdom. Great and signal and generous as was the gift of poverty which his new friends could confer upon him, Mr. Brudenel was not happy at the prospect. On the contrary, he groaned; he paced the room anxiously, he tossed his arms, he sat down and got up again. He was in an agony of terror, and it lasted all the day.

CHAPTER XIX.

STILL THE FORENOON.

PAUL was otherwise engaged. At eleven o'clock, while Mr. Brudenel, having failed in his attempt to transport himself to Abyssinia, was yielding a willing ear to the whispers of that devil, he went to Cicely's room. Not this time with burning cheeks and glowing eyes, but with hanging head. He went heavily. All this day he went heavily.

All four ladies were sitting there.

"Is there any message, Paul?" cried Lady Augusta, springing to her feet.

"None," he replied. "But have patience."

"What is the matter, Paul?" she asked.

"You look frightfully ill."

Hetty looked as if she would have asked that question had she dared.

"I am not very well, I think. I have gone through a great struggle, dear Lady Augusta; but I am perfectly satisfied with the result." Hetty blushed, and bent back her head over the work in her hand. "But it has been a struggle. This is an anxious day for me on your account, and there is an anxious time before me." He looked at his watch. "I want a moment with you, Hetty," he said, quietly. "Oh, not alone. Do not let anybody move."

They sat envious of Hetty. That is to say, two of. them were envious of the distinction. Sibyl, for her part, affected indifference. But she was curious. Nothing that this enemy of hers did was indifferent to her.

"Hetty, it is eighteen years since your father left you. It is so long that you can scarcely remember him. I believe you have never heard anything of him since he went away."

"No. My mother has never had a line from him. She believes that he must be dead."

"He is not dead, Hetty."

"How do you know, Paul?"

Only a week ago he would have replied by a reference to his friends. Now he made answer truthfully,

"Chance has brought me that knowledge, Hetty."

"He calls it chance," Cicely murmured, "as if, with him, there could be such a thing as chance."

"I have not only found out that he is living; I have also arranged that he should call here this morning."

"Oh, Paul! My father?"

"Oh, Hetty!" cried Cicely, "your father."

"He does not know that he is to come and see his own daughter. He will bring a letter. Then—"

At that moment a letter was brought. On the envelope was the address only, and in the corner the words, "From the Professor."

"Hetty, your father is below." She sprang to her feet. "Will you see him?"

"Will I see him? Oh, Paul! You have done this for me. But—Paul—does my mother know?"

"Not yet."

"What is he like, Paul? Oh! what is my father like? What will he say to me? What shall I say to him?" She stood irresolute and pale; glad, yet terrified.

"Do not expect too much, Hetty. Remember that he has been separated from you since you were a child. Perhaps he hardly remembers your existence. You know noth-

ing about his past life—what he has done, or how he has lived. It may be a career of distinction, or it may be a very humble history. He may be rich, he may be poor; he may be in rags, or he may drive in his carriage. If he were a rich man he would probably have returned home before now. Would you like to see him?"

Paul looked at his watch again. "Decide at once, Hetty."

"I do not remember him at all. Of course I should like to see him. Oh, Paul," she repeated, "it is you—you—who have brought my father home!"

There was something in her voice which made Sibyl look at her with meaning eyes, but she said nothing. Did her own experience cause her to recognize the accent of love? King Cupid hath a very sweet and tender voice, which he lendeth to his worshippers.

"With your permission, Lady Augusta, Hetty will go down-stairs and find her father in the breakfast-room."

"Go, Hetty dear. I hope— Go, my dear." Lady Augusta was going to say that she hoped Hetty would find her father everything that a daughter would wish, or words to that effect, but she remembered in time that he had been no more than a small city clerk, and she refrained. The result is generally unhappy when a city clerk is so ill-advised as to emigrate to America—a country whose people are reported as jealous to keep the whole of the national clerkery in their own hands, with all the posts and offices whose duties can be discharged in a sitting position, and to make new-comers the hewers of wood and drawers of water for them, and carriers of burdens and diggers of the ground.

Hetty obeyed, and ran down the stairs, overpowered with wonder at this new miracle. But at the door of the breakfast-room she stopped and trembled, comprehending the vast importance of the moment.

* * * * * *

"Let us talk, Lady Augusta," said Paul. "It will be the last time that we shall talk together as we have been wont to talk."

"Why the last time, Paul?"

"I do not know. The future is dark before me. I am on the verge of some great change; what will happen next I cannot tell. Let us talk."

Sibyl was guilty, because as she knew about the camera obscura the future seemed light. She arose, therefore, and softly left the room.

Then Paul, with the two women who believed in him, had his last talk. He knew that would be the last discussion he would ever have with them on the things they loved to hear.

At first he hesitated, and seemed at a loss. His depression weighed him down. Presently, however, he recovered something of the old fire, and talked of the other world, and of this, and of the spirits of wise men and just men, and holy women; of their love one towards the other, and of the blessedness of walking with them on the higher planes, hand-in-hand, journeying upward forever and forever, rising into heights of understanding and knowledge of which we can have no conception, and for which there are no words, and as they rise, leaving behind them ever more and more of the earthly dross, until even the soul, which is a sacred body, becomes converted into pure spirit after long ages of happiness beyond the power of speech to tell, and love beyond the power of human heart to feel.

"Oh, dear ladies," he said, with glowing eyes and softening voice, "this is the vision that came to Paul the Apostle. Eye hath not seen, nor hath ear heard these things, nor can any tongue speak them. The vision came also to Swedenborg. It has been granted to a few women. And those who walk in the Ancient Way have glimpses as they prove themselves worthy of the soul upon her pilgrimage. Let us not speak of the soul's abode, it is here and everywhere; let us not think, when we go alone upon the journey which seems so dark, that it is a lonely journey; we are never separated from those we love; nothing can separate in life or death the souls of those who are united in love and friendship, but unworthiness. The lower nature may disgust the higher, when love will perish. The higher nature will seem cold to the lower, then love will decay. But those who love are always together. Shall we walk together on those planes?" He gave one hand to Cicely and the other to Lady Augusta. "This is our last conversation. My message has been delivered. I have done what I came to do. I have no more to say."

"Not the last conversation, Paul, not the last," said Lady Augusta. "My dear boy, my son, my friend and teacher, you will stay with us. We shall have many more such talks. We will found the college we have so often discussed, and you shall be its first director. Do not speak of last words, Paul."

"Yes. I am a messenger and a servant. When the message is delivered and the service done the servant is dismissed. He then joins the common herd and fights his way to the higher planes with the rest. I have had my vision. I have communicated it *to you. Oh, Lady Augusta*, you know now how small a thing and how useless is your old craft of mediumship. You have risen above it, you have left it far below. You have learned the true Spiritualism which can be reached in this life only by purity and meditation and separation from the joys of the world. But as for me, I have done my work and I sink back to the common herd."

As he spoke, the glow of his cheek faded, the burning light went out of his eyes, the look of authority vanished. He became to outward show only a youth of four or five and twenty, with a comely presence and a face which proclaimed possibilities.

*   *   *   *   * . *   *

In the breakfast-room father and daughter stood face to face.

She saw before her a spare, undersized man, with black hair and small black eyes too close together, and dressed with a shabby respectability almost grotesque, in black, which was baggy everywhere—distinctly and at first sight not a gentleman; not in the least resembling a gentleman; not a prosperous man, or a rich man, or a successful man either. That was apparent from the low and humble bow with which he honored Hetty's entrance. He saw before him a young lady—distinctly a lady—young and beautiful, who looked at him with curiosity and astonishment. How could such a man, so insignificant in manner and look, have such a daughter, so tall and well formed and so beautiful? Yet there was a resemblance. Every face is capable of glorification and the reverse. Hetty's face was also her father's, but in the case of her father the face, originally in a mean and small form, had by a long course of a wandering, uncertain, and shifty life, become smaller and meaner, till it was quite degraded. In Hetty's case the face began with a large and noble copy of the model, and her life among gentlefolk and books and science and lofty thoughts had grown larger and nobler. Yet the same face!

"I was told," he explained, "that I was to come to this house. I suppose that you will be able to tell me why I was to come. If it is for any job, I may explain that I am at present out of work and should be glad of any, however temporary, having been disappointed in finding it. I have had great experience in many kinds of work, and if neatness and despatch—"

"Are you my father?" she interrupted. "My name is Medlock,"

"Oh, Lord! Are you my daughter? Who'd have thought it? My daughter—you?"

"If you are the husband of Lavinia Medlock, I am certainly your daughter."

"I forgot—I clean forgot that I had a

daughter. Oh, Lord!" He became breathless. "What a daughter for the platform! That's why I was sent here, wasn't it? to find my daughter. Your name, my dear, if I may be allowed—as a father—to use the adjective, was Belinda."

"Certainly not."

"No, no. I remember now. Your mother was ordered by the spirits to call you Belinda, and I wouldn't have it. We had a row about it, and the spirits kept rapping all night long. Hetty you were christened. I remember now—oh, Lord—just as if it was yesterday."

"Yes, Hetty is my name."

"You are my gal, then. Hetty—my daughter. There's no mistake about that. Lord, what a gal! I wish I'd known before."

No rushing into arms, no joyful embrace, not a word of welcome. This father only put his hat on the floor, between his legs, and sat down with his thumbs in his waistcoat arm-holes. This attitude conveyed some assertion of parental authority, but not much.

"You've grown, my child, since I saw you last. To be sure, you've had time to grow, and you've made a creditable use of the time. Nobody can deny that. You are dressed like a lady. Has your mother made money, then? I heard she was poor."

"We are very poor. I am dressed like a lady because I am the companion of a lady."

"Oh, very poor. That's a pity, now, isn't it? Lavinia just threw away her chances. It's a great pity, isn't it? I haven't got any money myself either. If you want anything, I can't give it to you; so don't look to me."

"I will not," said Hetty, considerably discouraged.

"I've been knocking about the world," her father went on, "for eighteen years, living on jobs, but mostly in the show business. As a lecturer to a show there are not many to equal your father, and none to beat him."

Hetty showed no sign of admiration. Supposing you were in ignorance of your father's profession and you had to choose one for him, would you select that of lecturer to a show? I think not. The imagination would dwell upon the respective glories of bishop, judge, statesman, general, admiral, orator, singer, actor, author, poet—but it would not consider lecturer to a show at all.

"You were a clerk in the city at first, I believe," said Hetty. "To be sure, I ought not to expect too much. When will you go to see my mother?"

"Well, my dear, the fact is we've got on very well without each other so far, and now I'm here only on a flying visit—looking for talent, in fact. Does your mother practice still?"

"Yes, but she has very few clients. She is very poor."

"You can tell her," said Mr. Medlock, with deep feeling, "that I could not go back and be a burden upon her. When I am rich—I always intended that—I shall send her money. For the present it's low water, and I should be truly sorry for her to think that I came home only in order to sponge upon her. Have you got any talent yourself?"

"What for?"

"In your mother's line, for instance?"

"No—no—NO!" Hetty replied, with the greatest decision.

"It's a pity, because with such looks as yours there would be money in it—money—and I would run you, my dear, on advantageous terms. If you've no talent we might fake up a bit and look the part. I know all the machinery for spirit-rapping and music and all. Think it over."

"Oh!" cried Hetty. "Am I never to get out of the dreadful business? I see my father after eighteen years—and the first thing he does is to propose that I should become a cheat and an impostor. No—no—no! I will not."

"Well—well." The little man hastily took his thumbs out of his arm-holes and pushed back his chair a foot or two. "Your temper, my dear, reminds me of your mother, but she never had your looks—never. Well—if you won't, you won't. And talk of cheating! Why, the whole world pretends. What's any show but pretence? We dress up the giants to look taller than they are, and the dwarfs to look shorter. We put a little man by the side of the giant on the platform to show how big he is, and a big man by the side of the dwarf to show how little he is. It's all pretence and sham, my dear, and the people like it." The aged philosopher of Beaumont street could not have spoken more wisely. "Well, if you won't—of course. Who are the people of this house?"

"This house belongs to Mr. Cyrus Brudenel."

"Cyrus Brudenel—Cyrus Brudenel—what! the great Spiritualist?"

"Yes."

"Cyrus Brudenel! I've heard of him. Hetty"—he dropped his voice—"is there an opening?"

"What?"

"Is there an opening? He's always receiving American Spiritualists. Suppose I bring him one. Do you think you can make an opening?"

"No—no—NO!"

She was so fierce that he pushed his chair as far back as it would go.

"Well, don't fly in a man's face. I only asked."

"Have you anything more to say to me?" said his daughter. "Oh! to see your father after all these years!" She sat down and burst into tears. "It's shameful! It's horrible! And to find that all he thinks about is to make money by cheating! I don't want to see you again. I am sorry you came. You have made me sick and sorry. Oh! to think that while my mother—poor dear!—has to drag on her miserable spirit-rapping, my father should want to drag me into a worse business still, where it is all pretence and cheating! If you have no more to say" —she got up again and composed herself— "you will go, perhaps."

Her father picked up his hat and retired without giving her the paternal blessing, and without even a word of farewell. He looked very, very insignificant as he walked across the hall. The footman allowed him to open the door without assistance. He left behind him, when he had disappeared, a most evil feeling of shame and disappointment. Hetty had found her father, and he was a person without principles, without morality, without manners—a person to be ashamed of.

Presently Paul himself came and sat beside her, and comforted her. It is a truly blessed thing in moments of discouragement to have a lover to comfort one.

"My dear," he said, "I have seen your father. I knew what he was like. Do you forgive me for sending him here? It was I who caused it to be done. I thought that you would like to know what he is—and—has he been very terrible, dear Hetty?"

"It is not your fault, Paul, that he is— what he is. He wanted me—oh! he actually wanted me to go away and join him in cheating! Oh, Paul, he asked me to pretend to spiritualistic powers—me—and I am engaged to you, to you, Paul!"

Paul's cheek flamed for a moment, and his lips twitched nervously.

"Yes, dear, yes." He kissed her. "Oh, Hetty, what matter for your father, what matter for anything, so that you love me? And now I am stripped of everything, and am only a common man again."

"I do not understand you, Paul."

"Only a common man. We must forget all the past, Hetty—all—all—all—and begin again. I am eager to begin again."

CHAPTER XX.

THAT day again Paul failed to appear at dinner.

His absence completed the consternation with which Mr. Brudenel regarded the situation. Never, even in the old days, when another medium, after leading them to what seemed solid rock, had proved another disappointment, had there been a more gloomy meal. All alike, even Cicely, in despair at the breaking down of faith, were oppressed with fearful forebodings. As for Mr. Brudenel, that voice to which he listened in the morning was still whispering in his ears that the sages, his new friends, would take him at his word, and make him demonstrate to the world his contempt of riches. He looked round his well-appointed table; he thought of his house, his habits, his personal comfort, and wondered if he could bear the miseries of giving them up even for the higher planes. He looked at his wife—she was in crimson velvet, very gorgeous—and he wondered how she would feel at beginning the spiritual ascent in rags. He drank a glass of soft, light claret, and wondered if there was anything in the Ancient Philosophy which would replace claret. "The spirits," whispered the voice at his ear, "walk hand-in-hand upon these higher planes, but they have got no claret. Suppose you have been already made to order the sale of your lands and of your houses, then you will soon know how pleasant life may be without claret or anything. O Lord! without anything!"

Thus this voice—assuredly one of Emmanuel Chick's neglected spirits—whispered in Mr. Brudenel's ear. As for Lady Augusta, she only feared that her august friend would not condescend to so trivial a matter as the money in question. And Sibyl was firmly persuaded that Paul at that very moment was making off with all his might, a bag of gold under either arm, containing no less then seventeen thousand five hundred golden sovereigns each, weighing him down to such an extent that his four-leagued boots, with all his efforts, barely covered three and a half leagues. Tom was gloomily asking himself whether he had made a mistake in supposing the man incapable of the lower forms of meanness. Lastly, Hetty, pale and anxious, was maddening herself with the fear that perhaps, in spite of his promises, her lover had been called away, made to go away, and reduced once more to discipline, order, and the rule of celibacy. O Heaven! Think of a girl just engaged, whose lover has to take the vows of celibacy. There was once a play written on this subject by an Elizabethan or Jacobean dramatist—Peele perhaps, or Tourneur, or I know not who. He called his tragedy 'Love's Cherry Bob.'"

"Tom," said Mr. Brudenel, when they were left alone,—"I fear the very worst."

"Well, sir,'said Tom, "now you mention it, so do I."

"I can hardly sit still in my chair"—Mr. Brudenel bounded out of it—"for the thought of what may happen to us all. We are in their power—completely in their power. I hardly dare to talk of it, for fear of giving them offence."

"One thing," said Tom, "is certain. A man cannot take five-and-thirty thousand pounds away in gold. The bank would refuse to pay so large a sum in specie. Our friend may give us trouble, but he cannot very well bolt with the swag. Even if he drew it short—in notes—we could find it out and stop them, I suppose. Yet I don't know. What excuse should we put forward?"

"The land may follow the shares, Tom. What is to prevent that? Why shouldn't they make me sign letters of authority to sell the land?"

"And then," Tom continued, "it may be difficult to fix on him alone the three separate accounts in the three banks. And it is undoubtedly awkward that you did give a personal introduction and reference for each of those three gentlemen."

"What may be done with the land and the shares," said Mr. Brudenel, pursuing his own line, "may also be done with this very house—with everything—everything. Good heavens! we are powerless; we may be reduced in a moment to absolute indigence! Was there ever a man so powerless?"

"We might employ a detective."

"A detective! What good are all the detectives in the world when you come to such work as this? Can a detective watch a spirit which is invisible, yet has control over matter?"

"I think, sir," said Tom, "that we are talking of different things. I want to procure, if I can by any means, that money of Cicely's and of mine which is now lying to the credit of three gentlemen difficult of access."

"And I am thinking that if the money goes, the whole of my fortune—all I have, may go after it in the same way. How do I know what I have signed besides those checks? Have I given authority to sell my land? Have I already parted with my house and my library? What do I know? Because, Tom, this is the strangest thing of all, that I have never been able to remember when and for what motive I sold those shares; when or why I signed those checks; when or why I wrote those letters of recommendation for three persons—no doubt of exalted character"—Mr. Brudenel looked round the room so as to give these spirits, if they were listening, the assurance of his profound consideration —"seeing I have only met one of them in

the valleys of Abyssinia, and I have never heard of the other two. Oh, I know that the fact cannot be disputed. The letters and checks are all in my handwriting."

"It is a deuced awkward thing," said Tom, "because, as you say, you may have been trapped into writing or signing anything. Paul must have great powers."

"Paul? Paul had nothing to do with it. Paul is only a messenger. You might as well suppose that Paul found out the company was shaky. Poor Paul! with as much knowledge of business as the housemaid."

"Well, sir, it seems like advising you to lock the stable door when the horse is stolen; but would it not be worth while to sever the connection?"

"What!"

"Why not bid farewell to the Ancient Philosophy, even if you do have to go back to the modern medium?"

"Tom, do not scoff."

"I am not scoffing. I am quite serious when I say that if I were you I would postpone the higher plane till I got into the next world."

"I have, I confess," said Mr. Brudenel, "thought of this. I have thought of asking permission, through Paul, to resign. I would resign. My only fear is that I have gone too far, and, being saturated with their teaching, I may not be permitted to resign."

"I would try if I were you," said Tom, with the least possible ridicule visible in his eyes.

"I may be considered as committed to the school. If so, I confess that should the philosophers—as I hope and trust they will not do;" he raised his voice so that there might be no mistake in the mind of Maitre Izák, should that wise man be in the room— "should they, I say, choose to deprive me of my fortune, it will only be in accordance with their precepts. Perhaps it may be taken into account that I am independent of fortune—I want to make no more money; that I am an elderly man of fixed habits which it would be difficult to alter; I want, I really want, my little comforts; and in this cold climate a man cannot sit on a stile wrapped in a sheepskin, and meditate. The misery of the ascetic life would destroy the power of meditation, Tom. It would make the higher plane impossible. We are not in the East; I cannot go about with nothing on; I should look like a fool if I attempted it—and so would Lady Augusta. Tom, in the West a man may be a philosopher, but he must be respectable."

"Why, yes," said Tom, "the fakir business does not become a frock-coat. Fancy

St. Simon Stylites in a tall hat! But there is another way out of it. Consider; may not Paul himself be a colossal humbug?"

"No, Tom, no. Certainly not. That is impossible."

"Consider, sir, you have had many disappointments before. There have been many others in whom, at the time, you firmly believed, yet they turned out impostors, and cheated you of your money as well as your time. You have yourself often said that the ease with which trickery can be accomplished is the greatest drawback to spiritual research—"

"That is quite true. I have said it and experienced it, Heaven knows, often enough."

"Then, sir, if one, why not the other?"

"No," said Mr. Brudenel, firmly, "not Paul. Any other, but not Paul."

"Well, sir," Tom insisted, earnestly, "if I were to bring you proofs—proofs that could not be denied that Paul might be—like any other, would you listen?"

"Tom, Tom," said Mr. Brudenel, with the smile of superior knowledge. "You do not know; you speak out of ignorance. I could not waste time even in listening to your suspicions."

"In that case," Tom sighed in resignation, "let us go into the drawing-room."

It was then about a quarter-past nine. The four ladies, who generally presented the appearance of cheerfulness, if not always of animation, were sitting in silence; nobody played, nobody talked, nobody sung, nobody laughed. It was a gloomy continuation of the gloomy dinner; the melancholy close of an anxious day. And everybody listened for a footstep which still delayed. As for Sibyl, she was in that frame of mind which impels a person, especially a Cassandra, to spring up before the multitude and cry aloud, "There, I told you so! All along I told you so!" Cassandra was a melancholy person at all times—misunderstood, disbelieved, mocked, and extremely unpopular. But there were moments when she had her triumphs, as, for example, when she stood beside the burning palace while the Greeks were hurrying upon their prey, and called aloud to Hecuba and her sisters and the shrieking handmaidens, "There! I told you so! All along I told you so!"

Mr. Brudenel took a chair beside his wife and sighed profoundly. No one ventured a word of consolation or of hope. The situation was past both consolation and hope. Tom stood outside the ring and fidgeted. Something was on his mind—something beyond the cause of the general depression, and it was as if he was uncertain how to open the subject.

Sibyl perceived it, and kindly gave him the opening. "You had something to tell us, Tom," she said. "Something important about Herr Paulus."

She said this so softly and with such sweetness of manner that everybody perceived at once that something disagreeable was coming.

"Is this a time, Tom," said Lady Augusta, "for telling us that you do not believe in supernatural forces?"

"It is a question of perfectly natural forces," Tom replied. "Shall I tell you a little story of how a man who pretended to do miraculous things was watched, and how his pretensions were proved to be based on tricks? It is really an interesting story, and has a peculiar fitness on an evening like the present."

"If you mean Paul," said Cicely, "you had better tell your story, and then we can ask Paul himself to prove that it is not true."

"Very well," said Tom, "it is about Paul. But perhaps, sir, you object to hear the story."

"I said I would not waste time in sifting so-called proofs. But tell us what you please —tell us—ah!"—Mr. Brudenel sighed again— "tell us what you please."

"I am only going to give you the result of certain investigations and experiments I have been conducting. From the beginning I mistrusted Paul, as I should mistrust any man who starts with the pretence of having supernatural powers. Personally I liked him, as you know. I thought he was a pretender, but of an order quite superior to the common run. I warned him that I should watch, and he laughed. Well, I have watched, and I have been rewarded by the full discovery of how it has been done."

"That is very curious and interesting."

Everybody jumped, because no one had observed Paul's entrance. Yet there was no pretence at magical appearance. He simply opened the door and stepped into the room. To be sure he was always noiseless, and the carpets were thick.

"The discovery of how it was done," Paul continued, "cannot but be extremely interesting to me, especially because I myself have never been able to understand it. And in future," he said, glancing at Hetty, who had suddenly recovered and drooped no longer, but sat up with color in her cheeks and light in her eyes—"in future I shall wonder all my life, more and more, how it was done. I thank you very much for finding out the mystery."

"You are very welcome," said Tom. "I will proceed, then, in your presence."

"In your presence," echoed Sibyl the implacable.

"As the evening draws on, and there is something which must be done before we separate," said Paul, "may I ask for the postponement—only the postponement—for one hour of these revelations?"

"Certainly; an hour will make no difference."

Tom even felt relief at the postponement. It is a truly horrid thing to have to tell a man to his face that he is an impostor. Especially is it horrid when that man is believed in by the rest of the household as a prophet.

"I have a message." Paul looked round the circle, addressing all, but resting his eyes on Mr. Brudenel.

"Oh!"

This interjection has as many meanings as a word in an Arabic dictionary. Everybody said "Oh!" and everybody in the room meant a different thing.

"My message will not take long; yet it is important. First of all, Miss Brudenel, there is a letter for you. Not a letter from Abyssinia or Thibet, not a communication from the other world." Paul smiled. "You will not suffer those of the other world to communicate with you. It is a letter written by a human hand, and it concerns you. This is the letter."

There were no bells, there was no heavenly music, there was no stretching forth of the hand suddenly to catch the letter falling from the ceiling. Paul simply drew from his breast-pocket a letter, which he handed to Sibyl.

And now everybody sat up, roused and alert. Lady Augusta caught her husband's hand and held it. The action cried aloud, as plainly as words can speak, "Heart up, oh thou of little faith!"

"Hetty," whispered Cicely, "tell me everything he does. Make me see him."

"The letter is not for me," said Sibyl, coldly. "It is for Tom. But, oh! it is in your handwriting, papa."

"Mine? Yes, yes; I remember."

"Will you yourself give it to Tom?" said Paul.

Sibyl obeyed, wondering and blushing. What should her father write to Tom that concerned herself?

Tom tore the letter open. Then his cheeks blazed a rosy red, signifying astonishment first and joy next, and astonishment last.

"Sibyl!" he cried, "did you know of the letter? Read it, read it. Oh, sir"—he turned to Mr. Brudenel—"how can we thank you? Lady Augusta, is it to you that we owe this letter?"

"To me? Tom, I do not know the contents of the letter."

"Mr. Brudenel gives his consent—a thing which we did not dare ask of him—to our engagement." Here he very properly took Sibyl's hand and kissed her on the forehead.

"Your engagement, Sibyl?" cried Lady Augusta. "Why, I thought—we all thought —that the celibate life—and with Tom? This amazes me!"

"I have consented, dear," her husband explained. "It was shown to me that Sibyl was more fitted for the domestic than for the meditative life. I have consented, since they both desire it. But, Tom, if you are a couple of paupers—if the principles of the higher philosophy are to be carried out—"

"Oh, papa!" Sibyl threw herself upon his neck. "How shall we be paupers when we have love? And Tom will work, and become a great man. And—and—oh!"—she was seized with a sudden suspicion—"tell me. You did not write that letter without knowing it, did you?"

"No, child, no. I remember perfectly why I wrote that letter, and when. I wrote it in full knowledge. It was explained to me that everything was changed. The whole of my previous knowledge—so called—was vanity; my idea of approaching and commanding the spirits by the help of a vestal, as was practised by the ancients, had to be abandoned so far as you are concerned, my dear. I was made to understand that you had already formed an earthly attachment which would be an effectual bar. I consented, my dear, to your taking a place upon the lower planes."

"Yes," said Sibyl, meekly, "we shall be much happier on the lower planes."

Again Paul, who had retired "up the stage," stepped forward.

"You are afraid, Mr. Brudenel, that you will be stripped of your possessions. That is not so. Our friends are not cruel. If you had been young, like myself, you might have had to give up all. Fear nothing. You will not be called upon to embrace poverty. It is quite true that, under all circumstances, the pursuit of riches is contemptible and detestable; it corrupts the soul and destroys the development of spiritual insight; if you had been engaged in the pursuit of wealth you would have had to cease. But you have never sought for money; it has been conferred upon you; your possession of wealth has enabled you to devote your time to research. A man like you must not become poor."

"He must not, Paul, he must not."

"Your apprehensions were natural. Henceforth have no fear."

He paused and sighed.

"I am loath to part with my message," he said, "because to part with it is to surrender my past life. That you do not understand. However"—he sighed again—"I have to acquit myself of my charge. Miss Brudenel, here is another packet for you; it contains your fortune. And for you, Cicely, is another, containing yours. And for you, Tom, an envelope containing yours. Do not invest your money in commercial companies, and do not seek to make more money. You do not believe in my friends, Tom, yet they send you good counsel. Cease merely to question Science. Persecute her continually, and never, never try to make your knowledge the means of making money."

Tom tore open his envelope. There was in it a check for fifteen thousand pounds signed by Izák Ibn Menelek, payable to order, crossed and protected by the magic words "Not negotiable." Clearly, the Sage of Abyssinia understood the forms and customs practised in London banks.

"Lady Augusta," said Paul, "my friends, you see, have not deserted you."

"Oh, I said all along," murmured Cicely, "that we needed nothing but faith. I knew that we should not be deserted."

"Was it probable," Paul asked, "that those who were wise enough to foretell the fall of the company, and thoughtful enough not only to cause the shares to be sold out, but the proceeds to be lodged in a place of safety, so that they would not be invested in any other dangerous concerns—I say, was it probable that these people should not restore this money on the day that it should fall due to the rightful owners?"

At this point Mr. Brudenel arose and took Paul's hand, and held it while he pronounced over his head—being several inches taller—an encomium upon the Ancient Wisdom. You have seen how, on a previous occasion, he congratulated all the beholders of a certain miracle upon standing on the solid rock. This little occasion was to himself and to his household of much greater importance. He rose to the calls of the situation. In a short but most eloquent oration he thanked Paul solemnly for the blessings he had brought to that household, for his own deliverance from superstition, for the solid rock of certainty which he had substituted for doubt, for the preservation of his wards' and his daughter's fortunes in the wreck of the bankrupt company, and, lastly, for the assurance that he himself would not be required to carry out to their logical end the principles of the Ancient Way as regards the foolishness of riches.

Tom was behind, holding Sibyl by the hand. The pair stood with downcast eyes and glowing cheeks. Coals of fire heaped upon their heads caused the cheeks of these lovers to glow. The enemy had done this—the enemy, the man whom one of the two had persistently snubbed, insulted wrongly, and unjustly suspected. He had saved her fortune and Tom's fortune; he had caused her father to write with his own hand a letter of consent to their engagement before it had been demanded. Once she raised her eyes and looked inquiringly at Tom. He understood her and whispered—it was when Mr. Brudenel was grappling with the most difficult and the most grateful periods—

"Dodo, never! Not even if I find him making your father go on all fours." We may guess what he meant, but there can be no certainty. Perhaps he explained to her in these words his intention not to expose certain little facts connected with Paul which might lead themselves to unfavorable conclusions, and turn that solid rock once more—oh, how often had that change happened!—into yielding quicksands.

"Paul," said Lady Augusta, when her husband had finished, "my dear Paul, how can we thank you? how can we reward you?"

"I want no thanks," he replied, somewhat sadly. What was the matter with him? He ought to have replied proudly, "I want no reward, Lady Augusta; I have done what I came to do. I must go away now." He caught Hetty's eye. "I must soon go away. My work here is done. I will go while I leave a kindly memory behind me."

"But my teaching—Izák's teaching," said Mr. Brudenel. "I cannot read him except through you; and you know—Paul—as yet—"

"I know. Izák Ibn Menelek must work in his own way. My—my hope, Mr. Brudenel, is that your recollections of his teaching will come upon you with a rush. After that your progress will be easy and rapid."

"You cannot go, Paul. You must not go," said Lady Augusta. "We have much —very much—to learn before you go. Stay with us."

"I cannot teach you any more," said Paul. "I must not stay."

"Stay with us," said Cicely.

"Stay with us, Paul," said Sibyl, with a blush. It was the first time that she had called him by that name. "Stay with us." She gave him her hand with the gracious smile which a beautiful woman keeps for such occasions. There was repentance in it, and gratitude. "Stay with us, Paul."

The young man sighed heavily. He drew his hand across his forehead, and looked about as if in search of something.

"I will stay a little," he said, looking at

Hetty. "But my work here is finished. I will stay until—until I find out what is to be done next. My friends—Lady Augusta—you have been very kind to me. I never knew before how kind people can be. You received me—a stranger. Well," he laughed, "I have been of some little use to you. Emmanuel Chick and his spirits are packed off. The old rubbish is carted away."

"You have done much more, much more for us, my dear friend," said Mr. Brudenel. "You have demonstrated the solidity of our faith; you have annihilated time and space; you have introduced us to the wisdom of the great, the incomparable Izák Ibn Menelek. You have placed us firmly on the solid rock."

"Yes," Paul replied, in the dry tone which is affected by the incredulous. Did he mean to bring doubt and suspicion upon his own teaching?

Well, the play was played; as there was no curtain to drop, it remained for the players to get off the stage—always a difficult thing, and one which requires the utmost skill of the dramatist to accomplish successfully. They lingered. Flatness seemed impending. Merely to say good-night, after getting back all that money; after the solemn assurance that Mr. Brudenel was not to become a wandering dervish in a ragged black frock-coat; after his fervid and eloquent oration—I am really sorry that there is no room for that discourse; after the appeal that Paul should stay with them, would be a plunge, head over heels, into bathos. All felt this. Flatness is the bane of the domestic drama. There is no curtain; there is no getting off the stage with a flourish; there are no lines with which to conclude. In the real domestic drama there is no conclusion. The finest situation ends with flatness, and after the most moving act the parlor-maid lays the cloth for dinner. All felt this; what could have been done or said? I know not. But at this moment there were heard voices in the hall. Voices—and in this house where silence was as unbroken as the law of the Medes and Persians.

"I forgot," said Paul. "There was one thing that I had to do. Cicely, I have brought your brother back to you."

"My brother? My brother Percival? Oh!"

"He is outside now. I will call him." Paul opened the door. Sir Percival came in and stood before them.

You have seen him already in the common sailor dress—the man with the weather-beaten cheeks and hands bronzed with sun and wind; the man with the strange and gleaming eyes; the man with the quick gestures and the fiery tongue.

"Percival!" Cicely sprang to her feet, holding out her arms. "Percival, where are you?"

Her brother suffered her to fall upon his neck; he allowed her to kiss him; he endured her fond words and her endearments; but he made no response, except that he kissed her once upon the forehead.

"Percival," said Mr. Brudenel, "you are welcome home. I hope you have returned home to resume your proper place."

"I am about the Master's work," replied the enthusiast. "This house is a house of the devil. Here you inquire of the oracle and seek learning of the witches. I have nothing to do with any of this house. Leave me with my sister."

"Shake hands, Percy," said Tom.

"I shake hands with no one in this house. Leave me, while I inquire concerning the safety of my sister's soul."

"Do not frighten her, Percival," said Lady Augusta. "I will give you ten minutes with her—no more."

They left him alone with Cicely.

When, ten minutes later, Lady Augusta went back into the room, she found Sir Percival on his knees, pouring forth a wild prayer for his sister, while Cicely sat trembling and terrified, her head in her hands.

Paul walked home with Hetty. She laid her hand upon his arm, and they went through the quiet streets together.

"My heart is full of you, Hetty," said the young man. "I am possessed with you. I understand now what was meant when I was warned not to fall in love. My dear, you have ruined me; but I love you all the more."

"No, Paul, I have not ruined you. I, who would die for you? I have made you lose that power. I am glad—I am glad."

"Yes, dear, it is all lost. I can do no more the things that you have seen me do. I have become like other men — as powerless."

"Paul, forgive me." She laid the other hand upon his arm. "Oh, forgive me. I ought not to be glad—but I am. I do not mind—not a bit—that you have become like other men. Remember what you said to Tom when he thought he had lost his fortune. Work will bring out your genius as well as his. And besides—oh, Paul, I hate the dreadful life of a medium. I should be in constant terror lest you should trade upon your powers. Now they are gone. I thank God, Paul, with all my heart that they are gone. I pray that they may never come back again."

"They never will, Hetty. I am certain they never will."

8

" And my love will be just like other men —as weak, as blind. Just like other men, oh, my dear, and there will be no other women hanging upon his lips. I shall have him all to myself. And as for the other world, why "—she sighed with relief—" we shall see the other world with no eyes—oh, how happy shall I be!—except the eyes of faith!"

They were at the door. Within, in the front parlor, sat Lavinia and Mr. James Berry, inquiring, and getting a wonderful " mix " in the nature of reply.

Outside, Lavinia's daughter stood praying Heaven that communications with the other world were closed.

" Kiss me yourself, Hetty. Good-night, my dear. Good-night."

She went in-doors. Paul lingered a moment after the door closed, as a lover does, because the house which contains his girl is a sanctuary, and the very door-step is an altar. Then he, too, turned to go, and stood face to face with another girl.

" Bethiah!" he cried.

" Ziph, oh, Ziph! is it—really—is it—Ziphion Trinder?"

BOOK THE THIRD.

CHAPTER I.

NO SYMPATHY AT ALL.

" WELL, now, Ziph, I am just glad to see you. I expected you all yesterday and the day before. You ran away almost before I had time to give you my address. Why did you run away? and why did you not tell me what you were doing? I knew you would come to see me. Why did you run away?"

The place was Bethiah's studio, and the visitor was none other than Paul, or Herr Paulus, whom Bethiah addressed as Ziph. The reader's natural intelligence has, no doubt, long since identified Paul with Ziphion Trinder.

" Sit down, Ziph; take a chair and let us talk. Will you have anything—a cup of tea —no? This is like old times, is it not? You foolish old Ziph! Why did you run away from your oldest friend—as if you could keep away from me? Tell me all you have been doing—stay—let me tell you first about myself, then your mind will be quite at ease. I am working at art. This is my studio. My poor dear father is dead and I have enough to live upon. I don't like living in leading-strings, like the English girls, and so I go about alone and independent. I have travelled, and lived in Rome and Florence and Paris. Now I am living here, alone, as you see; and I am not engaged, or married, or in love, or anything. I am quite well and strong, and I am as happy as I can expect to be, and I have made many friends since we two parted; but I am more than glad to see my dear old Ziph once more."

" You are looking very well, Bethiah," he replied, with a little constraint quite obvious to her.

" I am always very well, my dear Ziph, and to see you makes me seventeen again. _I think_ we _were_ sweet seventeen when we parted, and we are past four-and-twenty, which is a great age. Stay, Ziph. Let me look at you before you begin to talk, because, you know, when you do begin you will not let me think of anything else. Why, Ziph, I declare you have grown very handsome, my dear boy. Your mustache becomes you mightily, sir, and you have let your hair grow picturesquely long. I must take your portrait. I do wish all young men would pay as much attention to the style of hair which suits them. You cannot be an artist. No, it is impossible. You could never draw even a pig beside a haystack with any real feeling for the lovely curve of a pig's neck."

" No, Bethiah," Paul replied, with rather a wan smile, " I am not an artist."

" Let me see. Are you a great poet? You look like one—and now I remember. " When you left home you had quite a bolster of poems. Oh, Ziph, are you really a great poet under another name? Nobody would look half so poetic. What great poet has arisen in the last seven years? You can't be Swinburne — or Browning—no—that is impossible."

" No," said Paul, sadly, " my ambitions in the poetic direction were very quickly dismissed. The bolster has long since gone into the waste-paper basket."

" Have you turned actor? You used to be able to imitate very well. Do you remember one evening in the garden imitating some Spiritualist cheat and humbug who brought along his show?" Paul showed certain signs of confusion at the reminiscence. " Oh, I am sure you are an actor. What is your theatrical name, Ziph? Let me see. I have been to all the London theatres. I have seen all the actors. Could I possibly have seen you without recognizing you? What young actors have lately— Are you Mr. Charles Brookfield, for example?"

"No, Bethiah, I am not an actor."

"Well, then, let me guess again. You are a novelist, Ziph. Yes—you must be a novelist, and a successful novelist. Nobody but a successful novelist could afford such a beautiful fur-lined coat. What is your assumed name? Are you Frederick Anstey? Did you write "Vice Versâ?" Are you Rider Haggard? Oh, did you write 'She?'"

"No, Bethiah, I am not a novelist."

"Well, then, you must have gone out West and found a silver-mine, or you may have gone partner in a Government contract; or you may have speculated in railway shares; or you may have formed a ring and a corner; or you may have married the daughter of an English duke, so that the old man pays the bills; or perhaps you have invented something which everybody must have; or you've caught on with a patent medicine. Come, Ziph, tell me quick. I am burning to know. First, though, your father and mother are well. Have you written to them lately?"

"No," Paul replied, shortly.

"You have not written to them since you left home. You will have to explain that, sir. Without explanation, it seems very wrong of you. My Aunt Martha—you remember my Aunt Martha—told me in her last letter that Deacon Trinder kept smart. By-the-way, I don't like being called Bethiah. So, sir, change my name to Kitty. Do you like it better? Kitty—Kitty. It sounds somehow more Christian and cultivated than Bethiah; doesn't it?"

"It is much better," said Paul. Then he looked up with the old familiar smile and said, "I don't like being called Ziphion, and I have changed my name to Paul. Does that sound better than Ziphion, Kitty?"

Kitty laughed merrily.

"Paul? Oh, much better! Paul, Paul, you look as if you must certainly have been christened Paul, and I think you must be the son of an Italian nobleman. Is the deacon a count in disguise? Yes, I shall easily learn to call you Paul. Paul, now I think of it, we must have been Paul and Kitty in the old time days, only somehow we called ourselves Bethiah and Ziphion for short. Paul—yes, it is a very good name for you. And now, Paul, tell me what it is that has made you so rich and prosperous. There is another Paul somewhere in London. Hetty told me about him—you don't know Hetty. This Paul is a most dreadful humbug and impostor. He pretends to do the spiritualistic rubbish. Hetty believes in him, and—why, Paul, what is the matter?"

For Paul's telltale face, impenetrable no longer since the departure of the powers,

flamed swiftly. And Kitty remembered Hetty's description of the great magician. Young, dark, handsome beyond other men, voice soft and musical, his head shaped like that in his own sketch.

"Ziph!" she cried, with a sudden change in her voice, "tell me quick, my dear old friend; you are not that Paul?"

"Yes, Bethiah," he replied, not daring to raise his eyes, "I am that Paul—no other. I am the man of whom Hetty has spoken."

The girl sat down amazed and confounded. For a space neither spoke.

"Oh," she cried, presently, "is it possible? You, Ziph? Oh, my poor boy, you to be sunk so low! Oh, that is why you ran away from me!"

"You call it low?" he replied, trying to assume the air of one who is well satisfied with himself; but he failed. "Well, I supposed you would take that line. I might have suspected it. Outside the New England country town they do not call it sinking low. I am respected — respected, Bethiah. I am already nearly at the head of the profession."

"Profession? What a profession!"

"Yes, a profession; and one that is perhaps as honorable—"

"No, Ziph, no; keep that kind of talk to yourself. In the old time we should have called it a wicked profession. Now I tell you that it is a contemptible and a disgraceful profession. Yes, I tell you so openly, because, Ziph, we cannot make pretences to each other of any kind, even pretences to salve the conscience of one of us. Now I understand — oh, now it is quite clear why you ran away from me—why you have never written to your mother or to me. You were ashamed to tell us what you were doing. That is why you have not been to see me for three whole days after you found that I was in London. Oh, Ziph, this is terrible! I thought you might be dead! I never thought to find you here." She stopped.

"Bethiah," said Paul, "don't begin that way; you don't know. Hear me first. When I met you a week ago my head was filled with many things. Nothing surprised me more than to meet you."

"You tried to run away from me. You were ashamed, Paul—you were ashamed."

"No; I was astonished. When I got home I remembered that it might have looked like trying to run away—"

"It did, Paul, it did."

"Then I was prevented the next day. And at last when I do come, instead of giving me a little sympathy, you condemn me unheard. And you are the only person in the world who can advise and help me. Bethiah, for old time's sake, let me tell you everything. Then you can despise me if you like—you can send me away—"

"Oh, Ziph! as if I could ever despise you; as if I could ever wish to send you away, whatever you have done. But to think that you, of all men in the world, should have stooped to such a profession, Ziph! Do you never remember the days when your heart was filled with the love of truth—oh, how you would have scorned such a life in those days!"

"Bethiah, for pity's sake, hear me."

*　*　*　*　*　*　*

"No," cried Bethiah, after half an hour of greatly involved personal narrative in the style adopted by those who wish to make a good case out of a bad one. "It is no use, Paul, to talk to me in this way. You are wrapping up the truth and trying to hide it."

"What am I to tell you, then?"

"You are hiding quantities of things. I know already what you have been doing in London, because Hetty and her mother have told me from time to time. I know very well that you have become a medium, a mesmerist, a thought reader, a prophet, an oracle —and heaven knows what besides. Yes, yes, it is no use parading the inestimable blessings which you have poured upon the people who have trusted you. I know all about the miracles of the blind girl being made to see, and the Indian newspaper, and I know that you saved somehow their fortunes. I know, besides, that you have been pretending to preach a kind of new gospel, and that you profess to annihilate space and to see spirits and talk with them, and that you carry people out of themselves. I want to know more than this. I want to know what you do it for."

Paul made no reply. He was thinking, in fact, how best to carry out his case, the current of his narrative being thus rudely interrupted. He had prepared a most beautiful story, with which he thought to convince his old friend—in the story he posed as the possessor of a mysterious power which he used for beneficent purposes only—he was getting on very nicely with it—and now Bethiah pulled him up short. Girls have no imagination.

"My dear old friend" (the girl took his unwilling hands), "can you look me in the face and tell me that you are proud of yourself and of your seven years' work?"

It appeared, by that experiment, that he could not.

"Go back to the beginning, Paul," she said. "Tell me, exactly, what happened to *you in New York?*"

"Nothing happened, except that my contributions were all refused, and that I got through all my money."

"And then?"

"Then, by accident, I fell into the hands of the man who taught me all I know. Bethiah," he broke out, earnestly, "it is not all cheating and lying. I declare that it is not. You do not understand. It is a way of life that requires the utmost skill with the quickest intellect and the widest knowledge. Consider what we did. The people came every day to consult us; they asked us about their business; about their private affairs; about their health; about their love matters; about everything. We had to give them replies that would help them. For this purpose it was necessary to learn how to read their thoughts—that is, from the least hint of word and look and gesture to connect their questions with what was in their minds. Then we had to know all kinds of business matters, to watch the stock-market, and all the markets; to know the real meanings of telegrams in the papers; to know the laws of physiology, and especially the action of the nerves. Anybody might do so much. There remained, however, the power without which all this knowledge would be useless—the power of magnetism or mesmerism. Bethiah— Kitty—it was the development of this power in myself which raised the profession and redeemed it from — from what you would call it. For it is a real gift, a special gift; there is not a man in America who had this gift in such force and so well developed as myself. There were few, indeed, of those who came to our office who could not be subjected to my influence ; and those who most readily yielded were those whom we could most really help. We did help them. We were so much more clever than ordinary folk; we knew so much more; and we were so much better able to consider a case without passion or prejudice that we could give good counsel to any one whose case we understood. Even the unbelievers acknowledged the success of those who came to consult us. It was all done by superior knowledge and acuteness—all. We were paid, like all other specialists, for our skill and knowledge."

"So you say."

"Consider again, Bethiah. The doctor pretends to understand and give advice upon every kind of disease, yet his knowledge is very limited. The lawyer pretends to know the whole body of the law, and undertakes every kind of case, yet his real knowledge is small. The clergyman pretends to know more about the next world than other people, yet his knowledge is arrived at by the same book which we all possess. In the same way we undertook to advise upon all cases, whatever might be brought to us connected with the conduct of life. We knew more than most men, because one of us was old and had studied all his life, while the other was an apt pupil, Kitty. Yet there must have been many aspects of life strange even to the elder man's experience. Do you not see that in our profession we were only acting exactly the same as the members of every other profession?"

"Nothing of the kind, Paul. That is a mere subterfuge. You placed a gulf not to be passed between yourself and the other professions, when you pretended that your advice was dictated by spirits. You pretended to have supernatural powers, and you traded on that pretence. Answer that, Paul."

"I say," he replied, doggedly, "that we did what others did."

"You did more, Paul, and worse; and you were conscious of your sin; else why did you not write to your mother and to me? We mourned for you as for one dead. How your mother will mourn when she learns how your time has been employed!"

Paul left this question unanswered.

"I have shown you," he said, "that the life was one which required natural gifts of the highest kind, and great study. More than that, it required the greatest temperance and self-control, the mastery of all the emotions and passions, and the most rigid self-denial. No monk could lead a life of greater mortification."

"All for purposes of deception—"

"And I do think, Bethiah, that I might have expected a little sympathy."

"Sympathy! Oh, Paul! how long did you continue in this occupation?"

"Until about eight months ago. Then my instructor, who is growing old, decided to retire, and advised me to leave New York for a while, so as to reappear with a greater appearance of mystery. It is the sense of mystery which helps us. As to this pretence, as you call it, of spiritual assistance, that is nothing. Anybody could pretend so much. But it is not everybody who could command the sense of mysterious presence and influence."

"He talks," said Bethiah, addressing her teapot, "as if he gloried in his deceptions. Go on, please."

"We left New York and came to Europe. We have been travelling about, seeing the principal capitals. My master is now partly paralyzed, and will never again do anything; and—"

"Stay a moment, Paul," said Bethiah, interrupting. "You say it is eight months since you left New York."

"Yes."

"Eight months ago. Are you telling me the truth now?"

"I always tell you the truth. Surely, Bethiah, you do not think that I would deceive you?"

"You told those people that you came from Abyssinia; that you knew nothing about your birthplace or your people. You pretended to speak any language on occasion. You pretended— Oh, Paul, how can you ask me for sympathy with this monstrous pile of falsehoods?"

"It was only the machinery. We must have machinery. It is only the same thing when an English clergyman puts on a surplice and a hood. He isn't, really, unlike other men; but he wants a little machinery."

"What did you do it for, Paul?" Bethiah repeated. "Tell me, if you can, what you have got by it?"

"By coming here, you mean? It is no use telling you in your present mood. You would not understand me."

"Tell me, however; I want to understand. Did you come here for the purpose of getting money out of the English?"

"No, I wanted to distinguish myself."

"To distinguish yourself? Distinction! in such a way as this?"

"Why not? I know myself to be the cleverest and most skilful mesmerist in America. I know the whole of the Spiritualist business from the lowest to the highest, from the common medium with his taps to the occult philosopher with his Mahatmas. I thought I would come to London, where my exploits would be witnessed by the whole world—London is somehow the real centre of the world. Then I would aim at the highest thing ever attempted. I would soar by myself, without any aid, far above the petty familiar tricks of the mediums. In the history of Spiritualism I would have a chapter to myself. I learned that there was an Englishman here, rich and credulous, who wanted to be considered the chief of the Spiritualists, and was always anxious and ready to cultivate the acquaintance of every new and promising arrival. All American Spiritualists knew the name of Brudenel. Then I thought I would introduce myself to him with a great preliminary flourish, and when I had contrived to win his full confidence, with that of as many of his friends as possible, I would execute a *coup*, the possibility of which could not be explained by any other supposition than the direct interference of supernatural agency. I knew I could do this because I had learned the developments of the magnetic force which I am sure have never been attempted before.

I had in my mind the general plan. I trusted to chance for the details. It was to be the achievement of a feat which Spiritualists have often been invited to do, but which they have always refused to do — of course, because they are unable to do it. This feat I resolved to accomplish. I would do it before a room full of people. I would announce beforehand what I was going to do. Other mediums would be jealous, but they should not be able to deny the fact, and they should not be able to repeat it. The believers would rejoice greatly, and be strengthened in their faith. Then everybody would want me to repeat the performance—and then—"

"And then—" said Bethiah.

"Nothing more. Because I intended at this point to vanish altogether. I should leave a message to the effect that I had returned to Abyssinia, and I should go back quietly to America, and under my own name carry on my prime business again. That, Bethiah, was the object with which I came here."

"Well, Ziph, one cannot praise your object, and yet it was not altogether ignoble. You did not mean to make pretences by which to get money for yourself. Go on with your story. You found this unfortunate and credulous person. You went to him with your story about Abyssinia and the rest of it."

"Yes; I found him far more credulous than I could have conceived possible. All the Abyssinian machinery proved quite useless. As for my story of Prince Menelek, it wasn't wanted, though the girls liked it. I now understand that I should have done better—I see it now—to have maintained a perfect simplicity. I ought to have been, myself, the sage. The machinery only encumbered me."

"And have you played off your great miracle?"

"I have succeeded far beyond my expectations. I have been enabled not only to perform the greatest miracle of modern times —the appearance of this day's paper from India—but I have actually saved their fortunes for these people, and now the whole world is ringing with my praises."

"Is it? I see the papers every day, but I have seen no account of your miracles."

"You don't go into society, Bethiah," said Paul, irritably. "I tell you that in the best circles they are talking about nothing else."

"Well, Paul, if that is so, your programme is complete so far; and it only remains to crown the deception with your disappearance."

"Yes, yes, unfortunately I cannot carry out that part of the programme."

"Why not? Are you obliged to plan another miracle? What a horrid thing it must be to be always arranging a new miracle!"

"No, no, there will be no more miracles. Bethiah, I told you I wanted your sympathy. Never mind what has been done. That is done, and cannot be helped. I want your advice about the future."

"I advise you to leave your present employment; buy a hammer and break stones in the road, Paul, if you can get nothing better to do."

"I will; I will. In fact I must. Bethiah—oh, my old friend, I have lost my power."

"What do you mean?"

"I mean that I have lost everything that gave me the power of doing that which I have done. I can no longer carry on my profession. I can no longer read thoughts, nor can I influence others. I cannot do the simplest thing except the conjuring and the mere mechanical part of the profession. I have lost my power?"

"Why can't you do these things? How have you lost the power?"

"Everything depends upon the magnetic power and the control that has gone from me."

"Why has it gone?"

"Because—how can I make you understand? Anybody, you see, can mesmerize if he finds a subject suitable to his powers. But the complete mastery over the mysterious magnetic force— Bethiah, upon my word I am not talking nonsense"—indeed, he looked earnest enough for the most sublime truths. "I say that complete mastery over magnetic force can only be developed by long and patient study and continual practice. And it can only be maintained by one who keeps a perfect control over his own passions and emotions. A man with this gift must never fall into a rage, never be moved by pity, love, hatred, revenge, ambition, or anxiety. He must be complete master of himself. Bethiah—Kitty—I declare that I am not deceiving you. It is, indeed, a most real force, which I was able to wield and control. It gave me the most wonderful power over all those whom I could subdue. I admit there were many who would not come under my influence. I could do nothing with them. But at this Englishman's house, from Lady Augusta and Mr. Cyrus Brudenel down to the boy in buttons, they were all—except two —my slaves, obedient to my will, ready at a moment to execute my orders, and to perform, unconscious to themselves, whatever services I required of them. I treated their ailments, I found out their wishes and wants, I learned all the secrets of their lives, I was more than a confessor to them, because they confessed without their knowledge, and they always confessed the truth."

"That seems a power which no man, not even the noblest, ought to have."

"Yet I possessed that power. It was mine—and I have lost it."

"That seems a good thing for the world. How did you lose it?"

"I have totally lost it. I can do nothing. Even Cicely, the most emotional, the most readily respondent, remains wholly unmoved. She believes still—nothing would shake her faith in me, I think; but I cannot move her."

"I begin to have hopes of you, Paul," said Bethiah the unsympathetic. "You cannot exercise this terrible magic any longer. So much the better. You have not told me how you came to lose the power. Did you fall into a rage?"

"Worse than that. The most fatal thing of all is to fall in love, Bethiah. I have fallen in love."

Bethiah laughed merrily. "Oh, Ziph! if you only knew how rueful you look. You have fallen in love! Are you very much in love?"

"Very much. I can think of nothing else."

"And that is how you lost your power. My poor, dear boy, you are so terribly to be pitied. Fancy throwing away all that splendid power for the sake of a poor, insignificant girl!"

"Now you laugh at me."

"There was once a boy named Ziphion Trinder, and he called himself Paul for improvement sake—in all mutual improvement societies they begin by improving their names—and he had a gift from the fairies. He was empowered to subdue men and women, and to learn their secrets, and to make them do what he liked—you will observe, Paul, that the gift was not of the slightest use to him except for vanity and display—or to his fellow-creatures, because he could do nothing for them even when they were his most abject slaves. But there was one most disagreeable condition attached to the gift—it is really a very pretty fairy story. The young man was never to feel any emotion; he was not to let his heart be moved at all; he was never to be carried out of himself; he was never to be like other men at all; he was to be perfectly cold, passionless, and selfish. Is that a true statement of the case, Paul?"

"It is near the truth."

"On this condition he could exercise the useless gift. Well, the young man did exercise it for some years. He found that combined with a system of falsehood and pretence it could be made useful for making

money. By-the-way, did you make money, Paul?"

"Yes; we made a great deal. My partner, who was my instructor, keeps the money. Oh, I have a great pile of money laid by in his hands."

"So he made money, and if he had gone on he would have made a great deal more. And then he would have grown old in pretence and deception, and he would have become every day more selfish and colder-hearted. The end of that young man is dreadful to think of. But kind Heaven willed otherwise, for he was made to fall in love. And as soon as he began to have his heart filled with the thought of another creature besides himself, and when the longings and yearnings of love seized him, his magic power fell from him, and he became exactly like his fellows. Paul, is that well said?"

"Perhaps. But I have lost my livelihood—my profession is gone."

"I hope, at any rate, you have fallen in love with a girl who appreciates your profession at its true value, Paul."

"She does not know anything about it. I have not told her."

"But you will have to tell her. What is her name, Paul? How did you come to know her? Is she an English girl?"

"She lives in this house. Her name is Hetty Medlock."

Kitty sprang from her seat and clapped her hands.

"Hetty! Hetty herself! Oh, this is delightful. Why, Paul, there is not in the whole world any one who hates Spiritualism quite so much as poor Hetty."

"I know."

"And does she know that you love her?"

"Yes."

"And does she—has she accepted your attentions, Paul?"

"Yes, Kitty—Bethiah—I must call you by the old name when I am most in earnest! She is the dearest girl and the most beautiful in the world. I am madly in love with her. Oh, you know her, you understand how I could not choose but fall in love with her."

"I think I can understand, my dear Ziph. She is a beautiful girl, and she is sweet and good. Yes; you have done well to fall in love with her."

"I do not know what my partner will say when I tell him that I must leave the firm. What am I to do?"

"I don't know. Hetty will not mind waiting, will she?"

"I have said nothing yet about waiting. She trusts me in everything."

"How much does she know about yourself?"

"Nothing—or very little. I *could* not tell her all. It is enough for me to have to tell you. I have gained your contempt, Bethiah. I could not bear her contempt as well."

"Not my contempt, dear Ziph." She gave him her hand. "I am sorry for you. It was a great temptation. You were tempted by the appeal to your own cleverness as much as by necessity. I am very sorry for you. But not my contempt. And if Hetty loves you as she should, it would be her forgiveness as well as her pity—but never her contempt—that you would earn by telling her."

"I cannot tell her."

"But not to tell her is to continue the deception. Does she believe that you really possessed supernatural powers at all?"

"Yes; she believes that the things that I have done were effected by powers which we call supernatural, though she knows that I am now no more than any other man. It makes her happier to believe. Remember her history. If she believes in my powers she is also able to believe in her mother's—any way, in some part of her mother's pretensions. That makes her happy. She has long been ashamed of her mother, and now she must be ashamed of her no longer. I cannot tell Hetty yet. Do not betray me to her, Bethiah."

"No, Ziph, I will not. You may depend upon my honesty. But let me think a little. I am carried away by all that you have told me. I must think for Hetty as well as for you."

She threw herself upon the sofa, and buried her face in her hands.

"I have thought about it a little more clearly, Ziph. Sit down and let me tell you what I have thought. Give me your hand. Do you remember, Ziph, how we used to walk hand-in-hand to church on Sunday—the old-fashioned church built two hundred years ago and more? We talked as we went along about things too high for children's comprehension, but of one thing we were quite sure: it was impossible that our own lives could be other than true and honest. We were foolish children, and we have learned better now. But think, Paul; suppose we knew that our fathers were making their livelihood by false professions and pretence. Think what misery and shame we should have endured."

"I have broken from it. I have left it, Bethiah. I can never return to it."

"Thank God; you cannot, dear Ziph. But there is another thing. You will marry Hetty. You will not tell her the secret of the past. Some time or other she will discover it. A roll of forgotten papers, an old letter, a chance recognition; anything may break the secret to her, and with its discovery all her happiness, and her respect and love for you, will vanish. You must tell her, and that at once."

Paul hung his head guiltily.

"I cannot yet; I will tell her some time. Oh, Bethiah, I shall have to confess to many—pretences. She can never love me if I tell her the truth."

"She will never love you if she finds it out. You must tell her, Paul. You must. There is no way out of the difficulty except to tell her. Nay, you must confess to all these people."

"No, no, no! Bethiah, I could not. To Hetty, perhaps. To Lady Augusta—to Cicely? Never."

"You must, Ziph; you must confess to all, even to Mr. Cyrus Brudenel, before you can stand at the altar, and give your bride the hand of an honest man."

CHAPTER II.

HUSBAND AND WIFE.

IT is pleasing to turn from the winding ways and specious talk of one who wishes to change himself, to his natural, simple, straightforward ways when he is making love. Paul, with Bethiah, was shifty and self-conscious. Paul, with Hetty, was brave and candid of soul.

They met where they could, and exchanged a hurried word just to keep up their hearts, but three or four days passed before Paul found an opportunity for a serious talk. Love is very serious. Young people may laugh and joke with each other before they fall in love. After, there are no more quips and jests. When lovers are together they laugh little; smiles are plenty; it rains smiles and happiness and kisses, but of laughter there is little, and it is soft and low, as when the girl laughs if her lover calls her a goddess and an angel. She likes it, but she knows that the language is a little—just a little—exaggerated.

This day—the very afternoon of the day when his old playfellow had brought him back to the cold earth and reality again—he found Hetty alone in Cicely's room, and entered it with the transport of a man who has nothing at all on his mind but love. In fact, he had nothing. The plain truths he had just heard fell from him and were forgotten for the moment, because he was so fully possessed with love, and because to him the present was all, and the past and the future did not exist. What mattered it if Bethiah disapproved of certain things? They were old things. And here was his girl looking up to greet him with the light of welcome in her limpid eyes, and a blush upon her cheek. Yet she dropped her eyes again, because his were so full of longing that they terrified her.

He closed the door behind him, and ran with out-stretched arms and fell upon his knees, not to worship her, but to look up in her face.

"Hetty, we have hardly spoken since that day—"

"No," she murmured. "Oh, Paul"—for he was kissing her hands—"you must not. Oh, you must not."

"Must not love you, my dear?"

"You are so far above me, Paul. You know what I am—not even clever. Who am I that you should love me?"

"No, dear; who am I that you should love me?"

"You are so wise and noble, Paul, and you have such wonderful powers."

"As for my powers, they have deserted me, Hetty. You have destroyed them. My dear, they gradually vanished as the thought of you began to fill my heart. It is strange. I was warned of what would happen. Yet I could not resist."

"Oh, Paul, have I really and truly destroyed your powers?"

"Really and truly, Hetty. My mind can think of nothing but of you, and all my power depended on the clearness and freedom of my mind."

"It is strange. Paul, were you — were you never in love with any other girl?"

"No, Hetty, never. For seven years I lived apart from women. My teacher and I had no women in the house. I saw them only when they came to consult him. I never thought of woman's love except as a danger to be avoided. It has proved a rock, indeed. Yet oh, Hetty, if I have your love I shall be the richest man in all the world."

"Oh, Paul!"

She conferred this boundless wealth upon him. It needed no more words. Why, he knew that she had already conferred this great gift. He kissed her a thousand times, and called her as many sweet and tender names.

"Oh!" he replied. "To think that so much happiness was possible! And to think that all these years I have been running after a thing not worth the having, when there was love waiting for me."

"But it might have been love for some other girl, Paul."

"No, no, Hetty; we cannot escape our fate. I was reserved for you. And will you have me? I am but a commonplace man after all; an American, without a profession even. As

for my wisdom, that has gone too; the fine things which you used to admire will never be said again. As for my nobility, perhaps"—with a touch of bitterness, thinking of the morning—"perhaps that has yet to come."

"But you are Paul, always Paul—whether you are doing wonderful things or whether you have ceased to do them. It is Paul that I shall love, whatever you say or do."

"My dear, I have met an old friend of my boyhood. She knows you. She lives in your house. Go to her and ask her to tell you all about me in the old days. She will tell you"—he was sure that Bethiah would tread delicately on the dangerous places—"better than I can. She will save me the necessity of explaining quantities of things. Dear Bethiah! She looks no older than she did some years ago."

"Do you know her? Did you really know Bethiah before you knew me? Paul, is it possible that you did not fall in love with her?"

"Why, I always loved her, I suppose. She was a kind of sister to me. I always told her everything. But as to falling in love—you don't fall in love with your own sister, do you? And I had to wait for my fate—Hetty, my fate; oh, my fate!"

That Fate which gives a damsel, sweet and lovely, to such a young man, even though his conduct has not been wholly straight, is a kind and generous and forgiving Fate; no relation at all to the lady who carries the scissors and snips the thread.

In the arms of his mistress, Paul forgot everything unpleasant, even the plain truths that Bethiah had presented to him. These truths at the moment caused him pangs unutterable. Now he found the pangs needless; he would not bear them any longer. Pangs of this character can be put away by a resolute and imaginative man. Why should he bear them? There was no reason for confessing anything to anybody. His power was gone; he could no longer magnetize anybody. Perhaps he was fatigued, and suffered only temporary loss of will. Perhaps he was right in attributing the thing to the depth and strength of this passion of love. Very well, let the power go. This innocent Delilah had lopped his lovely locks. Samson's were doubtless of coarser texture. Very well, no occasion at all to speak of the loss. Even Bethiah's clumsy way of putting the thing—as if he had been a common cheat, as if he had never possessed any power—could not destroy the wonderful halo which his late achievements had caused to spread around his head, so that he looked and felt like the sun in splendor. He felt that halo pressing lightly on his brows. Hetty, he was sure, saw it. So did Lady Augusta and Cicely—poor, blind girl!—and perhaps Sibyl and Tom, though of them he was uncertain. He was perfectly satisfied with himself. He had come out of his important embassy from the Sage of Abyssinia with *éclat*. He had perfect reason for the cessation of the powers which had been his credentials. And besides, the whole world — of this he was persuaded — was ringing with the story of his achievements. To the end of time the story of the things he had done would form the brightest page in the chronicles of Spiritualism.

As a matter of fact, the whole world knew nothing at all of his achievements. The Indian paper story was old, and had never found any real credence, and the recent business was going to be kept in the family, because the very remarkable manner in which Mr. Brudenel sold his shares and forgot all about it would not bear relating to an unsympathetic and sniggering public. But this Paul did not know; and therefore he was perfectly well satisfied with himself, and naturally went about with stuck-up chin.

"Hetty," he cried, buoyantly, "let us talk of the future."

"Yes, Paul, the future."

"What would you like best, Hetty?"

"To go away—quite away—where there are no spirits and no manifestations."

"We will go away, dear. I think"—he spoke as if he had only to choose his retreat anywhere out of the whole world—"I think," he said, considering carefully, "that we will go to America; we will winter in Florida—I do not like the hard winters of the North—and spend our summers on the New Hampshire coast. Or perhaps you would like winter in Sicily, and summer—say on the English coast. We will go somewhere; we will find a place where the air is balmy and the sun is always warm. We will have a house with large rooms—I love large rooms—and a library full of books, and a deep veranda, where in the hottest day we shall be able to sit in the shade behind lovely creepers and flowers. There will be a garden full of fruits and flowers; we will live upon grapes and peaches; in the evening you will play to me, and I will walk about. Oh, I remember, years ago, in the old days, how Bethiah played while I dreamed. I wonder if the dreams will come back to me. I used to turn them into poems —pretty bad they were, I expect—but they seemed beautiful and pathetic to me. I have never had those dreams since. Hetty, let me look in your eyes. Oh, I see deep depths in them. What gives those depths to your eyes? You will fill me with those dreams again. *Oh, we shall be so happy—so happy, Hetty.*"

She was only half carried away by this vision of happiness, because her imagination could not suddenly rise to the same heights; but still she was half carried away, and she repressed the desire, natural to one who still has her own foot resting on the earth, to ask where the money was to come from.

He divined her thoughts.

"I have got plenty of money, Hetty," he said. "Do not let any thought of money trouble you. I have got a great pile of money; it is being kept for me. Besides, I dare say I shall do some work as soon as I find out what I can do. I think I should like to paint; it must be delightful to spread the rich colors on the canvas, and watch them growing into flowers and lovely women's faces. I have often dreamed of being a painter. But I cannot, unfortunately, draw at all. Bethiah used to draw very well; she made many portraits of me. Sometimes I have thought that it must be splendid to be a great orator, and to move the people. But then—Bethiah used to say—orators have to tell lies, and exaggerate and misrepresent, otherwise they cannot move the people."

"Don't be an orator, Paul; don't try to move the people."

"I will not, Hetty," he replied, virtuously and firmly. "Sometimes I think I should like to be a preacher, but without conviction"—he went back to the old phraseology of his youth—"that is impossible. As for being a lawyer, that is impossible too, because I should have to study law, and I can never study anything again; I have had enough of study." His mind went off in an unexpected line. "I have had seven years of study such as never any man had before, I believe. Some day, perhaps, Hetty, I may tell you all about it. Seven years, during which I had to think all day long of nothing else. Other young men had friends and fun, I suppose; at least, I have heard of such things. I had no friends and no fun. I seem now to have wasted my youth. It is gone, and all that I took so much trouble to learn and to cultivate has gone too."

"Never mind it, Paul."

"It made me so different from other young men. Why, Hetty, when first I came here I could not understand how Tom could be always laughing and joking. I came to imitate him afterwards, but at first—what a solemn, conceited ass I must have seemed to you."

"No, Paul. Those were your gifts."

"Yes, yes—my gifts. Well, Hetty, I had led a very serious kind of life for a long time —seven years, and the atmosphere of youth and beauty intoxicated me; and so I fell in love. And about the future, dear. There is plenty of money. I don't know how much, but there must be a great deal—very likely enough to keep us all our lives. Not that I don't want to work. Oh, Hetty, to work for you, I could clear a forest for your sake!"

"I wonder," he went on, "how I could have lived so long without you, Hetty. It seems to me now as if life would not have been worth living. Why, if I were to die tomorrow I should feel that I had not lived in vain because I have loved. The dreams that I told you of—the dreams that came to me when Bethiah played—I understand them now—they were the first yearnings of a young man after love. Oh, my dear, there is nothing in the world worth thinking of besides love. My heart is full of love and of thankfulness and joy for love."

He looked so completely happy; he spoke with such a perfect contentment; in fact, he looked and spoke as he felt, that no one would have guessed the pangs of shame he had endured only that morning in the attempt to put things in a pleasant and comfortable manner to his old playmate.

"Paul," Hetty cried, suddenly, breaking up the paradise, "what shall you say to my mother?"

"I shall tell her that we are engaged, and that I am going to take you away."

"Then we must leave her—all alone?"

He made no reply.

"Yes," she said. "Yes, I know we must. Poor mother! She has something to live upon, and we have never been companions. Oh, we could not endure to bring into our own lives, Paul, the dreadful rappings and the spirits."

"No, we will have none of the spirits with us. That is certain, Hetty."

"Yet, Paul, it is to you that I have told the awful suspicion which has always rested like a black veil between my mother and myself. They are, after all, real spirits who rap for her. My mother may be deceived by them, but she is not a deceiver of others."

"Lady Augusta will take care of her, Hetty—and Sibyl, and Cicely, for your sake."

"And there is my father, Paul; it was you who brought me to him. Sometimes I wish you had not. He is—he is—not altogether what I could wish him, is he? And he has been here two or three times since; and he keeps throwing out hints that if I will go with him to America he will be able to do great things for me. And oh, he says he is in the show line. Can I ever"—she sprang to her feet and threw out her arms—"can I ever rid myself from the show and the medium—the sham and the pretence? Paul, you will take me away from them, won't you? Where we go, I don't care where it is, we will never

hear of this other world except as others hear of it, will we? We will consult no spirits; we will have no powers and no gifts; we will go through life seeing no more than others see. Oh yes, I know—to you, Paul, to you —your gifts have been precious and glorious. But to me my mother's gifts have brought shame unutterable!"

"Why, Hetty!" His eyes were soft and suffused, and his cheeks were glowing, his lips were trembling with the sympathy which welled up in him at the touch of pity. "My Hetty! Henceforth, then, there is no other world but that which you can see with your eyes, and that which you can feel with your heart—my dear, the other world which each of us will see and feel all day long. It will be the other world of each other's hearts."

CHAPTER III.

SATISFIED WITH HIMSELF.

THERE was not, happily, any occasion for anxiety as to Mrs. Medlock, for even while Hetty spoke of her she was reunited to her husband. Yes. Mr. Haynes Medlock, either stricken by conscience, or led by the reawakening of affection, or guided by self-interest, had returned to his wife after eighteen years of separation. The reunion of souls once parted, the return of heart to heart, is indeed a sweet subject for contemplation.

* * * * * *

"Lor-a-mercy!" cried the wife. "It's Haynes!"

"Yes, Lavinia, I've come back," said the husband.

That was all. The words are simple. The poetry lies beneath.

* * * * *

It was the evening. Haynes Medlock, seated once more at his own fireside, was enjoying domestic happiness.

It steamed in a tumbler at his side, fragrant, hot, and strong. The lemon lay beside it, and the whiskey-bottle, only just begun, promised more domestic happiness to follow.

"This, Lavinia," he said, "is comfort."

In his fingers he held a church-warden. This kind of pipe is a symbol of domestic happiness. It is leisurely to smoke, indicating tranquillity; it is fragile, indicating mutual forbearance—confusion and violence destroy it; therefore it indicates domestic peace, and cannot be removed from the lips for any length of time without going out. It, therefore, teaches the necessity of few words. Its length requires elbow-room; therefore the children have gone to bed.

"Yes, Lavinia," said Mr. Medlock, slowly, "I was wrong to go. You ought to have warned me that there was money in it. If

I'd stayed I could have made that money for you. Well, there is still money in it, I've a notion now."

"It's no use, Haynes. The profession's wasted away for want of customers. People no longer want to consult the spirits. Why, there's even palmistry cutting into it—palmistry that the gypsies used to practise. Now that's all the fashion. The spirit-rapping trade's gone: now I'm too old to learn any other. Lucky I was able to buy the house when I did."

"I've a notion, Lavinia. I came back with that notion, and it's stuck. First I thought it wouldn't do; then I thought it would; then I thought it wouldn't. I came home, Lavinia, because I was tired of being assistant and I wanted to be boss. I knew the whole bag o' tricks, and I said to myself, 'If Lavinia will only join me, there's a fortune in it.'"

"What is it, Haynes?" ·

"It's Spiritualism and palmistry and fortune-telling and advice and craniology and telling character from handwriting and casting nativities all in one. You shall do the Spiritualism. I can do the palmistry and the craniology—and I know a man who can cast nativities. We can't dress you up to look young, Lavinia."

"No, you can't," she replied, with a pathetic sniff. "That's too late."

"But we can dress you up to look old, my dear. In crimson velvet, with a snow-white wig, and rings upon your hand, and a little paint under your eyes, you would look truly venerable. An old woman isn't so attractive as a young woman; but then she looks venerable. She commands respect. People believe in her."

"You'll want some capital to start with. Where's your furniture and rent and advertising to come from?"

"I'll manage that. If only we could get a young woman, Lavinia"—he jerked the pipe over his left shoulder and looked cunning—"there's Hetty."

"Haynes! If she would! If she only would! If you could get Hetty to come with us, you would have the best clairvoyant in the world. I've seen her under Paul's hands. She went off like a lamb the moment his eyes were upon her. She said what he wanted her to say; she stood up when he told her; she sat down again when he told her; and she remembered nothing afterwards. It's easy to find a mesmerizer, but a really good clairvoyant—"

"Lavinia, say no more — our fortune's made. Of course she'll come. When first I set eyes on that girl—that is to say, not the *first time, which was* one-and-twenty years

ago—time flies—one-and-twenty years ago. She's a fine girl, Lavinia—a very fine girl—with such eyes and such a figure! She'll drag in all the men in the place for love, and all the women for jealousy. When first I set eyes on her, I say—but a week ago—I said to myself, says I,' Young woman, if you were only in my hands'—meaning what I could make of her. But a parent without money—it's like making a law when you've got no policeman." He heaved a deep sigh. "Now if you'll give in, Lavinia, listen. We'll sell this house; that will put us in funds; and we'll go across the water. Lord! what a show we'll have! With that beautiful girl dressed— How shall she be dressed? In tights?"

"Not in tights, Haynes. It isn't delicate."

"In Syrian costume, then; we'll call her the—the Syrian siren. Can she sing?"

"Hetty plays and sings very well."

"She shall sing. That shall be part of the entertainment. Mesmerizer! what do we want with a mesmerizer? I'll mesmerize her."

"You can't."

"Well, we can pretend. It is all the same thing."

"No, Haynes, it isn't the same thing. You can't pretend clairvoyance — not to take in anybody who knows. You might as well pretend to spirit-rapping."

"Well, so you can. Everybody knows that."

At that moment there were heard from behind the stove three loud and distinct raps. Haynes Medlock jumped from his chair and upset his tumbler. "Good Lord, Lavinia, what's that?"

"Why," continued his wife, "if it is just the same thing, do a lot of people go round pretending to be mediums? No, Haynes, you take a low view of the profession. I don't say but what we have to make up a good deal. Even Paul does that, I know, with his Abyssinian business, which I wonder he can have the face to put before people who've got heads. To be sure, in that house nobody, except Sibyl, has got anything of a head. They all believe anything."

"Who's Paul?"

"That is Herr Paulus, the most wonderful medium that ever came over. Haynes, I was beginning to disbelieve in the whole concern until I saw what he did. Chick says it's all mesmerism. Well, mesmerism does a good deal of it; but there's more than mesmerism in it. If we could get Paul there would be something in your show."

"Paul? There was a fellow called Paolo who used to help the old professor. What's he like?"

"Like an Italian. Dark hair, lovely black eyes—there—handsome."

"It's the same man! Yes, if we could get him. Why not? We must have somebody, and the professor's about come to the end of his rope. Why not, Lavinia? Bring me within speech of him. I did speak to the professor, but he got on stilts at once."

"There's some talk of his losing his power. But that's what he says himself. Therefore it must be part of his make-up. They say he is going away. It's the talk of the servants. I always talk to the servants, Haynes, wherever I go, because there's many a little secret comes out that way, and very useful I've found it."

"As for Hetty, now—"

"You won't find it easy to persuade Hetty. She's an unnatural daughter, Haynes. She isn't proud of her mother's distinguished position. She won't help me any way. Sometimes she says disrespectful things about the profession. Very cruel things she has said when I've wanted her to do any little thing for me—just to pass me a roll of paper at the right moment, when it would have made all the difference between a successful séance and a failure. No, not even the crook of her little finger will that girl give me. Spirits must be helped and encouraged, and she knows it; but she won't help a bit—says it's cheating."

"That's bad. Because we shall want the crook of all her fingers," said her husband.

"And something's come over her. She never says anything at all now; has her breakfast and goes off to her work; comes home and goes to bed. But now she isn't grumpy any more, and her eyes are soft. She looks happy. Perhaps it's our American lodger that she's so fond of."

"Well, Lavinia, she's got to come with us, and do what we please. Exercise your authority, Lavinia, as a mother."

"That's all very well. But you are her father. It's your authority, not mine, that's wanted. Let me mix you another tumbler, and don't spill it again."

"My authority shall be exercised," said Haynes, firmly. "I shall command that girl. She shall obey her father. I've never commanded anybody yet, but now the time's come, I shall go through with it. I will be stern, Lavinia."

At this moment Hetty arrived.

"You here?" she said, with more surprise than welcome. "I thought my mother was not to know that you had come back."

"I concluded to come home," said her father, simply. "Take your bonnet off and sit down, Hetty. Your mother has got something to say to you."

"That is to say, my dear, your father—"

Hetty turned from one to the other. They were afraid. They looked mean and small beside this beautiful daughter of theirs, to whom they were about to propose a life of lies.

"Well," she said to her father, "say what you want to say."

"We are going to America together—your mother and me—on business. You will come with us, Hetty, also on business. On advantageous terms, of course," he added.

"I shall do nothing of the kind."

"I am your father, Hetty. And your mother is—your mother. And we mean to be obeyed."

The words were strong, but their effect was greatly marred by the manner of utterance; also, the handling of the church-warden did not add to the authority of the words.

"I am not going to obey you. But what do you want me to go to America for?"

"Your mother and I, Hetty, are going to run a show—I mean—conduct a high-class Spiritualist variety entertainment of an instructive character. Your mother's world-wide fame as a medium—in crimson velvet and white hair—has preceded her across the wide waves of the Atlantic Ocean. American citizens have long been asking why they, the bigger and more important half of the Anglo-Saxon-speaking race, dwelling under the flag of liberty, should not have the opportunity of beholding the manifestations which this renowned medium has lavished upon her own countrymen. That opportunity will soon be granted to them. Lavinia Medlock, whose agent is the well-known Haynes Medlock, for many years largely engaged in the conduct of similar enterprises, will shortly land upon the sacred soil of freedom, and be greeted by the citizens of that great and glorious republic. She will be accompanied by her daughter, Miss Henrietta Medlock, a clairvoyant whose feats have been hitherto designedly kept a secret in order that she might burst with full lustre upon the enraptured gaze of the American eagle. Henrietta is now in the bloom of her seventeenth year." Mr. Medlock at this point, carried away by his own eloquence, rose, and assumed a position on the hearth-rug, where he stood, his left thumb in his waistcoat arm-hole, and the left hand spread out. In his right he gracefully brandished the church-warden. The effect of this attitude, combined with his spare figure, open frock-coat, and small insignificant features, was imposing. "Her seventeenth year," he repeated. "In her sweet seventeenth. Heaven never made a fairer creature than this favorite of the spirits. She is dark, with large and limpid eyes, charged with magnetism. Young men have been known to fall down beneath the gaze of those eyes. Constant meditation and communion with the other world have given her youthful face the lofty and abstracted air of the aged philosopher. She is nobly formed. She possesses a voice at once soft, musical, and powerful. She plays and sings only music taught her by the spirits. In the hands of her father, the only operator whom she will admit, she performs the most extraordinary feats—things never before attempted—of clairvoyance. There is nothing that she cannot do. She reads letters in envelopes, she tells the numbers of bank-notes, she prophesies the future, brings news of the absent, conveys messages to the dead—"

"Stop!" said Hetty. "Enough of this nonsense. I will have nothing — nothing to do with your shameful and disgraceful cheats. Oh, it has been misery enough to see what is done day after day, and to hear what is said and thought of mediums; but to join—to pass my life in it—oh!"

"Hetty, my dear," said her mother, in imploring tones, "don't be hard on us. Think —oh think, we are so poor, and there is a great fortune to be made. And indeed it isn't trickery. It is only dressing up the thing artfully so as to catch the people. It must be dressed up. You are a beautiful clairvoyant, Hetty. I have seen you under Paul's hands—the first night he came. Oh, I could have sung for joy when I saw you. Oh, we have no right to throw away this splendid gift. It was given to you, Hetty, so that you might make a great fortune out of it for yourself and your parents. Do you think, Hetty, your own father would ask you to do what is wrong?"

Her own father endeavored to dissemble with the aid of his tumbler. But it was a feeble attempt. The involuntary smile with which he received his wife's last question broadened to a grin.

"It is no use," said Hetty, declining to answer that question. "Nothing — not the blackest destitution — would induce me to lead such a life. Besides," she added, softly, "the matter is taken out of my hands. I am engaged."

"Engaged! Engaged! Oh, Hetty—Hetty. To whom?"

"I will tell you as soon as he allows me. Yes, I am engaged. I will not insult my love, even by listening to such proposals, any longer. Oh, how can you — how can you—both of you—how can you in your old age"—fifty seems so old to one-and-twenty; and, indeed, one is no longer quite in the *first blush* of early manhood at fifty—"how

can you?" she repeated, because the conclusion of the sentence was contrary to the spirit of the fifth commandment.

Then she walked straight out of the room and sought the studio, where Bethiah was reading a novel, with no other companion than her lay figure.

"Engaged! She is engaged!" said her mother. "Oh, she's an artful creature not to tell me. Who can it be? There's not a young man in the world that I know of that she knows. There's Tom Langston, to be sure. But he's engaged to Sibyl; and—and —O Lord! Haynes, what if it were Paul himself? It must be. There's no one else. Oh, Haynes!"

"Paul? Signor Paolo as was? If it's him," said her husband, moved beyond the reach of grammar—"if it's him, don't say another word about the show. Don't let her set him against us. If it's him, I say, our fortune's made, because there isn't a cleverer or a more promising man in the profession. She's a lovely girl, Lavinia. In greatness and loftiness of mind she takes after her father's family; in spiritual gifts, no doubt, after you, my dear. Humor her. If it's him, give in to her. He'll make her a clairvoyant fast enough. And oh, with such a son-in-law and such a daughter, my dear Lavinia, our declining years will slide as easy as a drawing-room car, replete, as the advertisements say, with every comfort. Give in to her; humor her; buy little things and give them to her—new gloves, for instance; make her feel that we look up to her. And oh, Lavinia, be judicious. Say nothing more about the show. Leave that to her lover. My dear, this is a joyful evening indeed."

CHAPTER IV.
THE FIRST BLOW.

IT is now my cruel duty to record the succession of cruel blows which one after the other shattered Paul's self-satisfaction. They began the very day after that blissful talk with Hetty, part of which has been preserved from oblivion. Each one was unexpected; each was more severe than its predecessor. They were blows dealt by Nemesis, who is always unexpected, always silent in her approach, and who always chooses the moment when her victim is at his happiest and his proudest, prancing gayly along the way, believing himself to be admired by everybody, exulting in his imaginary triumph.

Nothing, for instance, could exceed the respect, admiration, gratitude, and affection with which Paul was at this moment regarded in this house. No one could have been more conscious of this admiration than himself. Yet all was taken from him in three days, as you shall hear.

It began in the study. Mr. Brudenel was going through his correspondence. Paul sat in an arm-chair, with a cigarette and the paper. Peace and serenity lay upon their brows.

"Here is a letter from Anna Petrovna. You remember her, Paul?"

"Anna Petrovna? Of course. She gave me a letter to you. I have never quite understood whether Anna is more dupe than knave—or the opposite. You see, the two characters very often overlap. There is Lavinia Medlock, for example. She believes in everybody but herself; she envies all other mediums, and she despises herself. Anna is like Lavinia, with less conscience."

Any one who took any interest in this young man would have observed that a great change had fallen upon him in a single week. Things external do not alter the shape of a man's features unless he engages in a prize-fight, or goes welshing to a race-course. Formerly Paul's face was thoughtful, reticent, and authoritative. There was always a watchful look upon it. This watchfulness made some, like Sibyl, suspicious. To others, as to Hetty, it conveyed assurance of reserved power. Now the watchfulness and the reticence had gone out of his face. His expression was frank and candid. He told everybody freely that he had lost his power. That explained the change completely.

"Anna Petrovna writes to me that they have a wonderful medium in St. Petersburg—one Olga something by name. She wishes to send her over here." Mr. Brudenel looked dubiously at Paul, as if uncertain how he would take it.

"I thought you were not going to have anything more to do with mediums."

"Not with the common sort. But there are mediums of the higher class. As for the common kind, you yourself cleared the house of the lying spirits, Paul."

"Yes."

"And, of course, you would not wish us to become perfect unbelievers. After all you have yourself done here, that would be impossible."

"I wish nothing, Mr. Brudenel. As you know, I am no longer qualified to give an opinion or to advise anybody. I know very little, but I should say that it will be time to treat the subject seriously when you get a message worth having — which tells us, by means of the rappings, something we could not find out for ourselves. As for me and my message, you saw—what you saw."

"You found me in uncertainty, Paul, and floundering among quicksands; you placed me on the solid rock."

"On the solid rock," Paul repeated, but without enthusiasm.

"We have learned," Mr. Brudenel went on, "that there are wise men to whom space is nothing. I have been myself transported daily in the spirit thousands of miles in a moment. We know that life is continuous, and that some have acquired the power of seeing and conversing with the spirits—you yourself could do so."

"Perhaps. But I have lost my power."

"We have learned that the incidents of unearthly life have no significance unless they affect the march of the soul. All this we have learned from you and from your friends. If the Russian medium, Olga, is able to continue this teaching, I would keep her here as long as she would consent to stay."

Paul made no reply.

"Paul," Mr. Brudenel went on, "put me in communication once more with Izák Ibn Menelek. Try. Stand over me as you used to do. Look me in the eyes as you used to do. Try, Paul."

Paul threw away his cigarette.

"I will try, but it is useless. I know it beforehand."

It was useless. After ten minutes Paul desisted.

"You have lost the compelling look in your eye," said Mr. Brudenel. "I thought once that I was going off, but it was only my right foot gone asleep. Do you think he will ever resume his teaching, Paul? Do you think I shall ever remember what he taught?"

"I do not know. My power has left me. If I call on Izák Ibn Menelek he will not reply. I am forgetting who he is. I want you to understand that if he has used me he has now cast me aside. I have been an instrument. I cannot advise, help, or promise you anything in the matter. I know not what is going to happen. Probably nothing. You have learned what it was intended that you should learn. Perhaps you will be left entirely to yourself; perhaps not."

After all, to have learned so much as Paul had taught was a considerable boon on the part of a person of whom Mr. Brudenel had never heard. If all of us felt our feet as firmly planted on the solid rock, what an age of faith would be again commenced! Mr. Brudenel would have replied, but he was interrupted by a servant who brought in a card.

"It is our friend Athelstan Kilburn. Show Mr. Kilburn here. You remember Athelstan Kilburn, Paul? He was present at two of your evenings."

Paul nodded.

Mr. Athelstan Kilburn was, in general, a person extremely well satisfied with himself.

Men who are well satisfied with themselves frequently have loud voices. Mr. Athelstan Kilburn had a loud voice. Men who are well satisfied with themselves are frequently of a portly presence. Mr. Athelstan Kilburn was portly; but to-day he was perceptibly smaller, and his volume of voice was shrunken.

"I am not interrupting, I hope," he said. "I know that you are always in your study at this time, Brudenel, and—and—in fact—"

"I will return presently," said Paul, springing to his feet. "You have business with Mr. Brudenel. I will leave you."

"No, no," said Mr. Brudenel. "Why should you leave us? Paul knows all my secrets—if I ever had any. Shall he stay, Kilburn? Is it very private business?"

"Private business of your own—your own, Brudenel."

"Then stay, Paul. Now, Kilburn, take a chair and go on. What is the matter, my dear friend? You look ill. What is it?"

"I am ill. Who would not be ill? Brudenel, I am come for an explanation."

"Certainly. What am I to explain?"

"It is now five weeks ago since I sought your counsel on some investments. You wrote me a letter. Have you forgotten that letter?"

Mr. Brudenel jumped in his chair.

"Good heavens!" he cried; "I had clean forgotten that letter."

"I will read it. Then you will remember. Then Herr Paulus will know. Then you will be able to give me an explanation." Mr. Kilburn pulled out his pocket-book and turned over the papers. He found the letter he wanted, and opened it and read it slowly.

"'Dear Kilburn,' this," he explained to Paul, "has been our style and title between each other for forty years. It is more than forty years since we became united by the bonds of a common pursuit. During the whole of that time we have been the closest friends. I will now go on. You shall draw your own inference, Herr Paulus, and Brudenel will perhaps be able to give me an explanation. 'Dear Kilburn, since parting with you I have considered the question of your investments. It is true that gas keeps up, and that water is a thing which everybody must use. At the same time, the interest you get for your money is not much. It occurs to me that you would do better by purchasing as many shares as you can get—they do not often come into the market—of my old company, Brudenel & Co. At present prices they bring in about five and a quarter per cent. The shares have gone slightly up every year since the company was formed. I myself hold shares to the extent of many

thousand pounds. Think this over. Yours ever, Cyrus Brudenel.' Think this over," repeated Mr. Kilburn, "'I did think it over."

"Good heavens!" Mr. Brudenel cried a second time, "I had completely forgotten that letter."

"I did think it over," Mr. Kilburn repeated, hammering at his point. "And I bought those shares. I am not a rich man, Herr Paulus, but for a bachelor I have been comfortable. Now I am a poor man, and for the rest of my life I shall be uncomfortable. I took that advice, Herr Paulus, and I invested the half of my fortune in that company. It is bankrupt, and the share-holders will not get one penny."

"I had altogether forgotten that letter," said Mr. Brudenel a third time. "How could I have forgotten it?"

"He might have made a mistake"—Mr. Kilburn continued to address Paul. "Anybody may make mistakes. But on the very day—the very day—that he wrote that letter he wrote also to his banker to sell out his own shares, if possible, and immediately. Well, sir"—he turned sharply on Mr. Brudenel—"your explanation if you please. As I take it—as it seems to me—you deliberately put an old friend, one who you knew would act on your advice, to buy shares in a company that you no longer trusted. You knew that demand would keep up the price. You sacrificed your old friend for the sake of keeping up the price. That is what it looks like. I say no more. It looks like that sort of thing; men do these things constantly. Oh, I know that very well. We must expect them to be done. But I did not think that such things would have been done by Cyrus Brudenel, by whose side I have sat for forty years, and received the communications of the other world."

"This is dreadful," said the unfortunate Cyrus. "Paul, help me—advise me. How can I explain it? I did write that letter, Kilburn—I did write that letter. I remember writing it very well. I gave you, as I thought, the best advice."

"Yet you wrote the other letter on the same day."

"Did I? Was it on the same day? You are sure it was the same day? Kilburn, I declare to you that I—I have no explanation." He remembered in time that no Spiritualist would accept the only explanation he had to offer. Paul offered to explain. "Mr. Brudenel," he said, "was made to sell out those shares against his own knowledge, by unseen protectors."

Mr. Kilburn groaned and shook his head. "Not by the spirits," he said. "You may think yourself happy if you get a plain answer to a plain question from the spirits. I've been questioning for forty years, and I would not trust them an inch. As for Brudenel being made to write a letter by the spirits, that—you'll excuse me, Herr Paulus—is rubbish."

"But there is no other way of explaining the circumstance."

"Spirits have very little power at the best," said this experienced person. "I have known one lift a pencil and write with it, but that is the most I have seen. As for taking a man and making him write against his will, that is rubbish. I have been directed by an old and trusted friend to invest money in a concern which he knew to be rotten. Oh, Brudenel, to think that you, of all men, could have done such a thing."

Mr. Kilburn rushed out of the room.

"Paul, can't you explain this?"

Paul changed color and looked confused. He understood, for the first time, the great law of political economy, that if one person is saved, another is lost. He had saved one man and ruined another. He had thought himself so clever; but he had forgotten this simple thing, and he had involved his unfortunate friend in a situation out of which there was no way except one, and that way no Spiritualist would accept.

"Paul, can't you help me?"

"No; there is no help. It is most unfortunate."

Yet he had thought himself so clever—so wonderfully clever. And now all Mr. Brudenel's most intimate friends would have to believe that their leader had entrapped one of themselves — a friend of forty years — to his destruction, in order to save himself from loss.

CHAPTER V.

THE SECOND BLOW.

WHEN the tardy Avenger at length arrives within reach of the sinner and warms to his work, his blows generally fall in an increasing scale of weight and rapidity. The first blow, for instance, caused a certain dismay and mental confusion. It was a nasty one, from an unexpected quarter. It left an uneasiness behind it—as used often to happen to school-boys in the old days. The second was heavier and much more painful, and came more unexpectedly.

In the afternoon there was merriment—merriment, if you please, in the House of Silence and of communicating spirits. It came from the girls' room. No more talk there of Menelek, and Izák the Falasha, and the Ancient Way; no more solemn uplifting of the heart to the contemplation of the things behind the veil. The veil was hanging down

as low as it could go. Nobody tried to lift it, or to peep behind it. Nobody regarded it. Here was a change.

There were three girls and two young men. One of them was learning to dance, and he was so stupid that he made them laugh.

"Oh," cried Sibyl, springing up from the piano, "take my place, Hetty, and I will try. Now, watch Tom and Cicely." They were illustrating the art of waltzing for an example. To dance at any time with one who could dance well was the greatest pleasure in the world for the blind girl. "See how they turn; watch their feet. You see, he doesn't catch his heels, and he keeps time."

"But I can't get round without catching mine. I can beat time, but when I turn round to time I am lost."

"Nonsense; now—one—two—three; one —two—three. Well, that is better. Now— ah! your heels again!"

Paul sat down and laughed.

"I am too stupid. Give me up, Sibyl."

"No; try again. You must learn to waltz before the dance next week."

They were going to have a dance. The House of Silence, sacred to all the spirits, actually going to have a dance! One might as well dance in a chapter-house, or in the solemn cloisters of a cathedral, or in the awful halls of a bishop's palace.

In the old times—now a week old—when the house, purged of the evil and mocking spirits brought by Chick, was still haunted with solemn whispers and sacred messages, a dance would have been impossible. How could sages come from Abyssinia to teach wisdom, save fortunes, sign checks, transfer shares in the most supernatural manner, while the young people danced? With what heart could the Vestal of the Cause, while she was still a Vestal, spin round to the tinkling of a piano? But the message had been delivered, the book was closed, there would be no more miracles; the spirits and the sages had gone; the house was cleared, and ready, if need be, for secular purpose. And there was going to be a dance!

"I must give up trying," said Paul. "I am too old to learn. Do you know, I have never been to a dance and have never even seen one."

"Never seen a dance?" said Sibyl.

"Well, I have seen the Germans dance on Sunday evenings, and I have seen dancing on the tight-rope at a circus, but I have never been present at a dancing-party of society."

"Is it possible?" Sibyl's voice conveyed another question which it was not manners to ask. The question was, "Where in the world were you brought up?" Paul perceived that question.

9

"Since," he said, "I have lost my powers, I have recovered the memory of the past. I now remember the whole of my own history, and I find myself forgetting the later periods. What is the use of remembering things which have left no trace behind?"

"And now," said Tom, "you have got so far as to remember never to have been to a dance."

"Would you like to hear something about myself? Perhaps it would be more amusing than trying to make me waltz."

"Tell us all that you please," said Cicely, "about yourself."

They all gathered round him as attentive as if he were about to narrate the exploits of Prince Menelek.

"I was born," he began, "in a little New England town not far from Boston. It would be no use telling you the name. It was a very little place. The principal people were the minister, the doctor, the lawyer, the school-teachers, the general store-keeper, and the hotel-keeper. We were taught religion at the Sunday-school, and it was hoped that we should get conviction and become church members. The creed of the New England ministry town is narrow, you know. As for dancing, it is considered impossible for those young people who take any thought of their future state. You do not know, perhaps—I am sure you do not understand—how narrow my people were."

"What were your amusements, then?"

"There was sleighing in the winter, and there were gatherings connected with the chapel. Sometimes a lecturer, or a circus, or a show of some kind came along. As for myself, I read all the books I could get, and I tried to write. Yes, I wrote—I dreamed all day long that I should become great and famous." Here Tom and Sibyl's eyes met. "What did I tell you?" was conveyed in Tom's glance. "I thought I would be a great poet. Oh, no one knows the yearning that was in my heart for distinction. It was not that I longed to do great work so much as to obtain distinction."

"And now," said Sibyl, softly, "is that yearning gone?"

"Yes," he replied, frankly, "it is wholly gone. I want nothing now beyond the common lot, with a corner in the village churchyard when I have had my life and the joys of life." Hetty blushed. Was she not going to be the chief joy of his life?

"It has quite left me. But, then— Oh, it was a madness. I took my manuscripts to New York when I was seventeen, and set up business as a distinguished poet in a cheap boarding-house."

"Well?"

"Well, the same idea had occurred to many hundreds of young fellows at the same moment. I believe I came at an unlucky time. Perhaps the editors and publishers are not always pelted with so many poems written by the distinguished poets of the future. No one would have my poems. I got rejection from everybody, sometimes with the intimation that I might have my manuscript if I chose to call for it, and sometimes without even so much grace."

"And what did you do then?" asked Sibyl.

"I stayed at my boarding-house till all my money was gone. Even the rejection of my poems gave me less humiliation than the thought that I should have to creep home and acknowledge my failure, and try something prosaic and undistinguished. Then an accident happened. I fell in with a certain learned gentleman acquainted with — with much knowledge of the kind not studied by most people—"

"The Ancient Way," Tom suggested.

"He made me his pupil. It was he who introduced me to the friends — you know who I mean." Only a week ago Paul would have referred to these sages with a confident air, instead of the hesitation with which he now spoke of them.

"Yes, we know, Paul," said Sibyl. "But they have thrown you aside now, you know. They belong to the part of the past which is to be forgotten, do they not?"

"Yes," said Paul, quickly; "let them be forgotten."

"But why did they throw you aside?" asked Cicely. "They were so wise and so great, why did they throw you aside?"

"Because I disobeyed them. They warned me against one thing — to keep the powers with which I was intrusted. It was, above all, necessary that I should keep my mind clear and calm. Therefore, when I allowed my mind to be entirely absorbed with a certain thought, I lost those powers."

"Could you," asked Cicely, the only one who could not observe Hetty's self-conscious blush—she knew what that thought was, you see—"could you not regain your powers?"

"Yes, perhaps—I do not know. I might again after many days, and when I had torn the thought out of my heart."

"Don't do that," said Cicely, quickly, "I love to think of the old Paul. But I could not have him back again at such a sacrifice. Do not make a girl unhappy by ceasing to love her."

"You knew, then, Cicely, what I meant?"

"Your words could have but one meaning. You will tell me some day more about her."

"Yes, some day, soon, Cicely," said Paul.

"And, Paul," said Sibyl, "we are all so much interested in you, and so grateful for all you have done, and oh, so unfeignedly thankful for the loss of those powers of yours, and so anxious that you should never regain them, that we want to know what you are going to do next."

"I am enjoying my holiday — the first I have had for seven years—and I hardly like to think what I shall do next. Frankly, I cannot tell you. I must go back to America and find out what I can do, and if it is possible for me, even now, to learn a trade of some kind. America is a hard country for a man without a profession; it is a far harder country than England. Yet I shall get on somehow. That is all I have to tell you, good people."

Presently, after a little silence, Cicely said, "We shall miss you, Paul. Often in the night I lie awake and listen to the voice—of the former Paul, I mean—telling us great and noble things and lifting up our souls. He is gone, but the memory of his words remains. Do you remember them, you new Paul?"

"I remember something. Do not dwell too much upon these things."

"I must. They have sunk into my soul. Oh, it is a beautiful thing to be very sure and certain of the world which lies around us. I cannot see the world you see, but I can feel the other — the spirit-world. When I am alone I seem to hear their voices, and to feel the rustling of their robes against me as they pass. Your words opened the other world for me. You say that you have lost your powers because you have fallen in love. I do not understand that. It seems to me as if, when people are in love, they should feel all the more in harmony with the whole creation. How could love make you lose your powers, Paul? You have told us, over and over again, how all the world, the other world, is full of love. Could love destroy powers that made you see and know these things?"

"Perhaps it was disobedience," said Sibyl, seeing Paul hesitate. "Come, Cicely, we must not question too closely. Let us remember what was pure and noble in his teaching. The rest may go."

It was a new thing that Sibyl should become Paul's defender. But since the great day of restoration, with that unexpected letter to Tom, she felt bound by no common ties of gratitude. Besides, the supernatural pretensions were abandoned, and she had penetrated Hetty's secret. This made her more than grateful. She was interested in a love story enacted before her own eyes.

"Since," said Paul, presently, "there is nothing else worth having except love, sure-ly those powers of mine were well lost even in bringing love to one girl."

"They were, Paul," said Sibyl. "All the fine phrases in the world are nothing, compared with one good deed. In the finest phrases I have ever heard in this house—which is the home of phrases—it has always seemed to me that I detected insincerity. The men who talk are not the men who act. It is better to act than to exhort. Your splendid talk about the Ancient Wisdom, Paul, with which you set Cicely's heart aglow, is it worth the truthful plain life of a simple man who works and does his duty?"

Paul made no reply. Only a week before he would have been ready with an answer based upon the wisdom learned of his unknown friends. Now he said nothing ; but he knew very well what Sibyl meant.

While they sat there, quiet and grave, the door was suddenly opened, and Cicely's brother, the terrible Sir Percival, stood before them in his rough sailor's dress. His eyes gleamed with the light of fanaticism. He stalked through the circle, and laid his hand upon his sister's arm.

"Cicely," he said, "I am sent once more to warn you. Fly from this house of witchcraft. Fly from those who converse with evil spirits and make inquiry of the devil."

Cicely shrank from him in terror.

"Percy," said Tom, "you are quite mistaken. There are no more witches, and we have left off making inquiries."

"I know the house of old. Cicely, come away from it. Leave the service of the devil."

"We have left that service, Percy," Tom answered for her again. "Exchanged, you know—sold out."

"You are a scoffer. Cicely, it is to you I speak. Listen!"

He delivered his soul. If he had been addressing an impenitent Magdalen, a person steeped in crime from his youth up, he could not have used language stronger and more fervid. Its violence terrified Cicely, but left her otherwise unmoved. You may call a young lady a sinner, and remembrance of certain little sins may fall upon her soul and convict her, and make her feel small and ashamed — which is a wholesome form of penitence. But to speak to a girl as if she had pranced gayly through the whole of the decalogue is an over-statement of the case, and therefore weakens it.

Paul presently interrupted him.

"Have you not spoken quite long enough?" he said. "That kind of talk may do for your sailors, but what is the good of it for young ladies? You may terrify your sister, but you will not persuade her with your bluster."

"I remember you. I know you now," said Sir Percival, with quite a new light in his eyes.

"Why do you come here?" Paul went on, not observing that change. "You told me you had neither brother nor sister. Why do you seek out your sister, then? She is happy; she is innocent; she is full of the religion of love. As for your religion of terror, she does not want it. Leave her in peace. I am very sorry that I asked you to see her."

"I thought I remembered you. Cicely, one word more. If you will not listen to the voice of religion, will you listen to the voice of prudence?"

"I will listen to anything, Percival, if you will desist from your terrible language."

"This house is the abode of liars, impostors, and common rogues. Come out of it. Come with me and I will find you somewhere a home among Christian people. Come, Cicely, this is no house for a girl who—"

"Don't go too far, Percival," said Sibyl. "There are limits to our patience, even with you. As for Cicely, she will choose whether she will stay with her old friends, or whether she will go with you."

"I shall stay here with my friends," said Cicely.

"Tom"—Sir Percival was no longer a fanatic preacher, nor was he a sailor, though in a sailor's dress; he was now an English gentleman, calm, self-contained, and speaking with due carefulness. He looked down at Paul with a scorn and contempt which even his blind sister might have felt—"Tom," he repeated, "do you know this fellow? May I ask if he is a friend of yours?"

Tom hesitated. Could he, in fact, truthfully aver that he knew Paul, or that he regarded him as a friend?

"Herr Paulus," he replied, "has been a guest of Lady Augusta for six weeks or so. We are deeply indebted to him for a great and signal service."

"You do not, then, know who and what he is. I was in New York three years ago; I was persuaded to see one of the medium fellows. This medium was an old man who told lies as fast as he could utter them. With him—the medium's cad—was this fellow, dressed in black velvet. They called him Signor Paolo. While the old man talked, this fellow played pranks. And this is the kind of man who sits day by day with my sister. A rascally medium's cad!"

Paul sprang to his feet, with burning cheeks and flaming eyes. But Tom stepped between.

"Enough, enough. Percy, you have your answer. Go!"

"A medium's cad!" Sir Percival repeated.

"He and his master pretended to consult the spirits. They sold their answers; people went to ask them questions; they lived by their cheats. Is this, Tom, a man who should be invited to companionship with my sister?"

"Percival," said Sibyl, "you are under the greatest obligations to this gentleman. Had it not been for him, Cicely would be now a pauper. Whatever be his past history, in this house, where there is no more inquiry of any oracle, there can be nothing but gratitude for him."

"A medium's cad!" said Sir Percival for the fourth time. "I have told you who he was, and where I saw him, and what he was doing. Make him your friend, then, if you please; I have no more to say."

He left the room as a gentleman, not as a fanatic preacher.

Paul sank into a chair, pale and trembling. He could not even make an effort to conceal his agitation and his confusion. "It is true," he gasped. "What he told you was true. I was pupil to the man I told you of. He had great powers; he had great knowledge; he taught me. It is true, also, that he made money by his powers. Have I made money here? I ask you, all of you, what use have I made of my powers? Was it for money that I came here? Have I asked any of you for money? Have I taken money?"

"No, Paul, no," said Sibyl, "calm yourself. It was not for money that you came here. Oh, the past is over and done with. It is dead; forget it, Paul. Let us all forget the words that have been used. Your past is dead, Paul; our gratitude remains."

Paul rose from his chair. He staggered as he stood; he seemed like one about to reel and fall. Hetty sprang up and caught him in her arms. "Paul!" she cried, "you are my Paul; your life is mine—your future life. Oh, the past—the past; Paul, forget it!"

Tom left the room, followed by Sibyl. They left him there with the two women who loved him; one because for a brief space he had been a prophet, and the other because she was a woman and he was a man, and because he loved her.

CHAPTER VI.

THE THIRD BLOW.

IN the silent watches of the night the words of Sir Percival came back to the unfortunate Paul. They were shouted into his ear. "A medium's cad!" To be called a cad of any kind, even in the Eton boys' sense—that all persons who are not old or present members of that seminary are cads—is humiliating. It seems as if no one who is really a cad — say a "gym" cad, or a racket - court cad, or an omnibus cad, or a touting cad—could ever be able to hold up his head. But to be a medium's cad! Is it possible to descend much lower? When one actually is a medium, it is certainly best to magnify the office and be Medium the Magnificent. Paul had been such a medium—he had retired; the post had already lost its imaginary splendor; and to be called a medium's cad!

All his own doing—his own officious desire to prove his power—it was none other than himself who had brought this blow. Why had he ever assisted in the restoration of this man to his sister? Why, when he found and proved the manner of the man, had he not left him alone? He cursed his own short-sighted meddling; he rolled about in his bed a prey to the most poignant reproaches and the vainest regrets. Because, whatever had been said by Sibyl in her newly born kindness, everybody knew now that he had been a medium's cad. He might, of course, dress up the situation, but there was the plain statement, and they all knew it to be true.

When a man stalks about solemnly, wrapped in a cloak of authority, puts forward claims to supernatural power, and to wisdom derived from other sources than those accessible to the ordinary student, he is raised above their gibes, even those of such a fanatic as Sir Percival. These things may be said behind his back; they generally are said of every person who has risen above his fellows. But Paul was now no more than an ordinary man; worse off than most, because his past history was a load upon his shoulders which made him stumble and stagger—every stumble a fresh disgrace, and every fall a new humiliation.

More humiliations were to follow.

Next morning, for instance, he was confronted by a house-maid, her face tied up with a handkerchief. Beside her and behind her were other maids, anxious to witness a miracle of healing.

"Oh, sir," she cried, "I've got the toothache dreadful!"

He turned pale. Twice already he had cured this damsel, in both cases assuaging the pain so that minutes afterwards she tripped it merrily, and would have sung as she tripped it but for fear of Lady Augusta. Now he could do nothing.

"You've cured me twice, sir," she said. "Oh, please, sir, it's worse than either of the times before!"

"I—I can't cure you any more, my good girl," Paul replied, looking foolish. "I'm very sorry, but I'm really unable to cure you."

"Oh, sir, it won't take a minute for you.

It's nothing for to do. Last time you only looked at me and it was gone."

"I can't—I have forgotten the way, I mean. I can't do it. Go to the dentist and have it out. I shall never be able to cure anybody again."

He fled, leaving the afflicted one overwhelmed with disappointment. What had she done that he would not heal her as before? What did he mean by saying that he could not cure anybody any more?

But Paul was humiliated. It was a small thing, but up to this day the servants had regarded him with the awe and wonder which belongs to him who works miracles. Now he would work no more miracles; he was no better than an ordinary visitor. It is sad indeed to take the lower place.

This was before breakfast. After that meal was it fancy, or was Lady Augusta distinctly colder in her manner? He proposed to go out and spend the day somewhere. At the door he encountered Emmanuel Chick. The worthy creature was in a rage; he was in one of those rages which are called blind. Now, in a blind rage a man does not heed his speech. He says what comes uppermost.

"Oh!"—Emmanuel Chick roared this interjection—"oh, it's you, is it? And it is all your doing! You made up your mind from the beginning that I was to be shoved out of the way. Oh yes, the old friends were to be shoved out of the way to make room for you. And if need be, we were to be ruined. Now, Mr. Paul, or Herr Paulus, whatever you wish to call yourself, I'm going to see Mr. Brudenel, and you will come along with me, or I'll drag you along."

"Mr. Brudenel, I dare say, is in his study. You will find him there. I will go along, Mr. Chick, without any compulsion."

He was curious to learn what Mr. Chick wanted to say, and followed him into the study. He observed, as the medium went before, that he walked with head down, swinging his shoulders and squaring his elbows, as one who is resolved on something desperate.

Mr. Brudenel was not alone. Sibyl and Tom were with him, and they were conversing cheerfully about dances, weddings, festivities, and such things long forgotten in the House of Silence.

"What is it, Chick?" asked Mr. Brudenel, impatiently. The study was not a place where he was accustomed to interruption. "What do you want? What does he want, Paul?"

"I'll tell you, sir, in one moment. Give me a minute. I've run all the way. I've been out of town—on business, and most beautiful manifestations were the result. And on my return I learned the dreadful news."

"What is it, then?"

"I am ruined, Mr. Brudenel. That's all. Ruined is the word. And through you. Oh, nothing but that. Ruin and wreck. And through you. Through you. No doubt to oblige this young smooth-spoken villain who came from America or somewhere to delude and cheat you out of your money—smooth-spoken as he is. Yah!"

"You ruined! Through me!"

"I had two thousand pounds saved. After a hard life—nobody knows better than you—I'd managed to scrape together two thousand pounds. I was going to retire from business. Think, sir, what it was to me when every young bantam cock who could play a set of new-fangled tricks was preferred to the steady honest old medium—and now I've lost it all."

"Good Heavens!" said Mr. Brudenel, "you don't mean to tell me that you had shares in the company, too?"

"Why—didn't you advise me? Didn't I act on your advice only five weeks ago? I have your very letter! I've got it in my pocket."

Like Mr. Athelstan Kilburn, Chick produced a letter.

"Here is your letter, sir. I've kept it, fortunately. Now, sir, I don't think you will deny that this is your own handwriting. And the very day after you wrote it—I heard from a young gentleman in the city—the very day after you wrote this letter your own shares, all your own shares were sold. Oh, he knows it for a fact! So that while you were actually writing the letter you knew that the company was going to bust up, and you were going to save yourself. Oh, Mr. Brudenel, to think of the many, many times that we've sat around the table in a circle while the blessed spirruts sent us their messages and the spirrut music played and our hearts were warmed! After all these manifestations, that you—you—above all men, a gentleman and all, should play us such a turn!"

Mr. Brudenel said nothing.

"I will read your letter," the man went on. "Perhaps the hearing of it will refresh your memory as to the writing of it:

"'DEAR CHICK—DEAR CHICK'—(In the friendliness of it, who would have suspected?)—'If, as you say, you are dissatisfied with the safety of your mortgage and have called up your money, I am sure you cannot do better than buy shares, if you can get them, in my old company—Brudenel & Company. The shares have been going up steadily ever since the company was started, and even at the present prices I believe you can get a trifle over five per cent. Any stockbroker will find out for you if there are shares in the market.

"'Yours faithfully,

"'CYRUS BRUDENEL.'"

"This is truly terrible," Mr. Brudenel cried, looking at the letter and the date. "Yes, it is quite unaccountable—quite. I wrote this letter—I remember it now—and the letter to Athelstan Kilburn in the afternoon before dinner. And on the same day, the very same day, I wrote the letter which I do not remember, for the selling out of the shares. It is truly wonderful. No, Chick; I've no explanation to offer. I have nothing to say."

He sat down and rapped his knuckles with his eye-glasses.

"That is, I have an explanation," he added, "but you would not accept it."

It was by some inscrutable working of instinct that Mr. Brudenel arrived at this knowledge. Mr. Emanuel Chick would certainly not accept the explanation offered to Mr. Kilburn. No one, in fact, is more stubbornly incredulous concerning supernatural forces, other than his own, than the ordinary medium of commerce. You might as well look for belief in magic from a conjurer. He believes nothing; he has no kind of feeling, for instance, as regards ghosts; he would set up his tent calmly in the most ancient and lonely church-yard; he would wrap himself in a blanket, and go to sleep in a charnel-house, with a lighted candle stuck in a skull, and hundreds of skulls grinning at him, miles away from any other human creature, without the slightest tremor of his nerves. To tell Emmanuel Chick that his old patron had been made to write that, or any other letter, by the spirits, would have been an insult to his understanding.

"Well, sir," said the man, roughly, "what are you going to do for me? You have ruined me. That you can't deny. You sold out your own shares while you recommended me to put in my money. That you can't deny. And me, grown old in your service, though you've left off employing me now, what are you going to do for me?"

"I don't know." The justice of the claim was not to be disputed, nor the accuracy of the statements. "I don't know, Chick. I can't say. I will think. Go away now."

The man made no sign of going away.

"I haven't got the money," he said, sullenly, "for the quarter's rent, which is seven pounds five. I owe for a ton and a half of coal, which is thirty-five shillings. I've got no engagements; business is terribly slack. And you've ruined me."

Mr. Brudenel sighed and took a check-book from his drawer.

"Here," he said, "take this check. It will serve you for the present."

"Two thousand pounds, at four per cent.," Mr. Chick replied, looking at the check, "is eighty pounds a year. This is the first quarter. I will call again, Mr. Brudenel. You and me have been very friendly, and a lawyer between us would break friendship, as one may say. Good-morning, sir."

On this occasion no one looked at Paul. When the message of the bank-book revealed the sequestration of the money, everybody looked at him. Now every one looked away from him. It was as if a look would have been construed into a reproach.

"If one man saves his money, another man must lose it," said Tom. "We have saved thirty-five thousand pounds, therefore other people have lost exactly that same amount. Mr. Athelstan Kilburn has lost, it appears, eight thousand, and Chick two, by our action and our advice. It seems to me, sir, that reparation will have to be made to Chick, at any rate."

Mr. Brudenel shook his head sorrowfully. Why, when the spirits made him sell those shares, did they not also prevent his writing those letters? It was true that his feet stood at last upon the solid rock, but still ... there was a sense of incompleteness. Paul offered no explanation, but he looked unhappy.

At this moment a card was brought to Mr. Brudenel.

"Gentleman says he won't take a minute, sir. Wants to see you and Herr Paulus together."

It was Mr. James Berry, who followed on the heels of the man and stood at the open door, hat in hand, bowing pleasantly.

"Berry!" cried Mr. Brudenel. "Here is another of them! Are you here to say that you are ruined, too?"

"No, sir, no. It is only this morning that I learned, to my great joy, that you had been advised to sell out of the company in time. No doubt it was this same adviser—my benefactor—who saved me from ruin"—he waved his hat gracefully in the direction of Paul— "Herr Paulus. And I came round, sir, to thank him—in your presence, Mr. Brudenel, sir."

"I don't quite understand, Berry."

"I'd been in your service, sir, your father's service and yours, and in the service of the company, for fifty years. If anybody except the spirits had told me that the company would fail I should have laughed in his face. But I've always been accustomed to ask the spirits, through Mrs. Medlock, and when I was warned day after day by a man who ought to have known, being in the general manager's own office, and when I could get

no satisfaction at all from the spirits, but entire silence or silliness—as nobody knows better than you, sir, will happen at times—I grew fidgety first, and frightened next. And Lavinia, who is truthfulness itself, confessed that she could do no more, but offered to give my case to Herr Paulus."

"How long ago?"

"Some weeks ago." This was two weeks before Mr. Brudenel's sale was effected. "And I wrote my case, and gave it to Lavinia. And next day I got my orders. I was commanded to sell at once."

"Did you," asked Tom, "tell Herr Paulus the name of the company?"

"I did not, sir. It would have seemed black treachery in me to hint in a letter that I had suspicions of this company, which has been my livelihood. No, sir, I put the case and I got my answer. Herr Paulus did not know the name of the company, and I understand that he is a complete stranger to London. The advice was given by the spirits, his friends, without his knowing anything of the company."

Paul coughed gently. It was not in human nature to avoid calling attention, however gently, to the triumph of the moment. He had not known anything of the company.

"It was my little all that was saved," Mr. Berry went on with emotion. "As for my pension, of course that stopped with the company. It is only three per cent. I get on my money now, and it's a sad blow; but I can live on what I've got, and I'm saved from the workhouse—saved, sir, by Herr Paulus, whom I desire to thank in your presence, sir, and in the belief that he has saved you too."

"Indeed he has, Berry," Mr. Brudenel replied. "We owe everything to Herr Paulus."

"Sir"—Mr. Berry addressed the blushing Paul—"may I venture—so far—sir—may I presume to touch your hand? Ah, sir, you are young yet, and have a great career of usefulness before you, with the help of the spirits—a great career. Go on, sir; scatter blessings; do good all around; bring their help to bear upon sufferers; ward off dangers. Oh, what would one give for a day — only a day—of such powers as you possess!"

"I am glad—truly glad," said Paul, "to have been able to do something for you at least."

"Something, indeed! And not to know the name of the company! Next day, to be sure, talking it over with Lavinia, she found out that you had put two and two together." Paul withdrew his hand and suddenly betrayed every sign of confusion. "To be sure," this foolish old man went on, "when you'd been told that I was in the service of a shipping company, formerly the property of one

man and then of his two sons and then turned into a company, it was easy to guess."
"Yes," said Paul. "You think so, I dare
say. Good-morning, Mr. Berry."

And again nobody looked at Paul when
Mr. Berry had gone, and Mr. Brudenel in his
chair rapped his knuckles with his eye-glasses
—as one who is mentally wrestling with the
giant Doubt. And nobody looked at Paul.

CHAPTER VII.

THE FOURTH BLOW.

I DO not quite know how Paul got off the
stage after that situation. He did not know
himself. He only remembered that he looked up and met Sibyl's eyes, and they were
full of pity, and that the others were not looking at him. Then he murmured something
and went out of the room with Mr. James
Berry, whom he left at the door.

It is not enough for a man to say that the
past is gone, done, finished, over. Every
man's past—his boyhood, his manhood, his
old thoughts, his old deeds, his words—lives
in his memory and clings to him like the
fabled shirt which could not be torn off.
Sometimes that shirt burns and tortures and
eats into the quivering flesh; but it cannot
be taken off. Sometimes it is a soft, warm,
and comfortable cloak with which to encounter cold December blasts; and it cannot
be blown off or taken away. When the man
dies, what becomes of the living past?

Everywhere he saw detection, exposure,
and contempt, and always from some unseen
and unsuspected hand. It was known that
he had been connected with a New York
Spiritualist—a medium's cad—oh, ye gods,
to have been called a medium's cad! It was
known that he had learned before the sale
of the shares the shaky condition of the company, and all along he had posed as the most
ignorant man in the world concerning companies! The very servants looked at him
with eyes of contempt; from every quarter
he felt the cold nipping wind of contempt.

Men have proved themselves capable of
bearing any kind of misfortune except one.
They cannot bear contempt at any age. Contempt maddens. To escape contempt, Spar-
tacus and his friends braved the might of the
Roman republic. To escape contempt men
will march to the cannon's mouth. But when
contempt is served out as a ration or a help-
ing of Fate, man bows his head and dies, or
he slinks into a corner and hides.

And no one, certainly, is an object of greater or more universal contempt than the pretended trafficker in things supernatural when
he is found out. Many things may be forgiven. The author of a play that is damned

is presently allowed to walk with head erect.
A man may steal a pig and yet redeem the
respect of his fellow-creatures. A statesman
may eat all his words and yet contrive to find
a faithful following. But a man who has
been found out in spiritualistic trickery remains an object of contempt. And Paul saw
in himself an object of this contempt. Once
outside the pretences with which he had
clothed himself, as a starving player struts
the stage and believes himself to be king, etc.,
Paul had believed in those pretences—he was
as quick as any others to see the past in all
its true ugliness. The contempt did not exist
in two hearts at least. As one pretence after
another was laid bare, one woman's heart
was filled with pity and another's with love,
but there was no contempt.

Since he felt that way it was natural for
him to turn his steps in the direction of
Beaumont Street. That tie should be broken
at once and forever.

*   *   *   *   *   *   *

"Yes," he concluded, "I will not hear a
single word. I have left the horrible, detestable, contemptible profession."

"So?" The old man had listened without
a word of interruption, though his face grew
darker and darker. "So? You have left
the profession, Paul?"

"I have left it. I wish to Heaven that I
had never entered it! Better have gone before the mast—or weighed out sugar; better
—anything—anything."

"Ungrateful Paul!"

"It is over at last. I have done with it.
Oh, what a relief—what a relief to feel that
I have done with it at last!"

"You have found some other profession,
Paul?"

"Not yet. There is plenty of time. I can
look about me."

"You have found a patron with money,
then, as well as a wife without?"

"No. What need of a patron? I am come
to draw my money. Give me my money; I
will take it away with me. Let me regulate
my accounts."

"Your money? Your money?" The old
man looked him steadfastly in the face from
his white shaggy eyebrows. "What money?
What accounts?"

"My money—my share."

"Oh, your money? This is interesting.
Wait a little; we will come to that question
afterwards. Now, Paul, do you think—I ask
you seriously and without any anger on account of your hot words—do you think you
are using me well in this matter? In your
new-fangled notions about truth and honesty
I think you have forgotten my claims."

"What are your claims?"

"Let us examine the position. Seven years ago you came to me quite poor and quite ignorant. During that long time you have been my pupil. I have kept you and clothed you. I have taught you all you know—nay, I have taught you things that you could never have learned except from me. Is this true, Paul?"

He spoke gravely and earnestly.

"It is quite true. I do not deny it."

"I found in you the germ—only the germ —of that power which you have developed, by my assistance, into the highest kind of magnetic influence. I made you what you are."

"What I was, what I am no longer."

"You do not deny, then, that you owe everything to me?"

"In all the arts which you profess and I have practised, I acknowledge my debt to you."

"Do you suppose that I have taken all this trouble for nothing? Do you think that it consists of pure love that I gave you my time and imparted to you my knowledge?"

"I never did suppose that."

"On the contrary, I looked to making my profit in the future. I thought that common gratitude would attach you to me, and that when, as has now happened, I should be laid on the shelf, you would carry on the business still, the business which I made, and which I taught you, as my partner instead of my assistant."

"Your assistant? I have been your partner—"

"I thought that the time would come when I should say, 'Paul, here are deeds of partnership. Let us sign them and henceforth share.'"

Paul jumped and turned pale.

"Henceforth share? What do you mean? Why, we have shared all these years, we have been partners."

"Partners? Oh no. Certainly not. Partners? Indeed, my gifted young friend, you are carried away by your imagination. Never partners. You entered the house as my pupil. You remained as my assistant. You were my hired help. It remains with you to determine whether you will, in good time, become my partner."

"Oh! This is monstrous. Why, I have done the lion's share of the work for six years and more. You have spoken of the business a thousand times as one joint concern."

"So I have. So I have. The joint concern of master and servant, as we say in England."

"I was your partner," Paul cried, angrily. "As your partner, I demand my share of the money. I never had any money. You kept it all for me. Where are the books? Give me my money, I say, and let me go."

"Reach me my desk. Thank you, Paul, thank you." The old man sat up in his chair and opened the desk. "Now, here, my paid and hired assistant, is a paper in which I have jotted down, as near as I could make it out, a statement of our position as regards each other."

Paul, otherwise Paulus, otherwise Paolo,
In account with
Professor Melchers, Spiritualist.

Creditor.		Debtor.	
Six years' salary as Assistant Spiritualist at $1,000.........	$6,000	Board and lodging in the best style, at $1,500 a year, seven years.........	$10,500
		Tuition fees for seven years at $1,000 a year..	$7,000
		Dress, chiefly in black velvet and lace, in the best style, at $1,000 a year	$7,000
		Moneys advanced for seven years, etc., exact account in cash-book	$2,100
Balance due to Prof. Melchers	$23,600	European tour for nearly eight months.........	$3,000
Total.......$29,600		Total.......$29,600	

"Here is the account, Paul." He handed the document, which was very neatly written on a piece of note-paper. "I think that no one can find fault with any of the items unless, perhaps, the charge for maintenance. But that is balanced by the enormous salary which you have received—and consider the luxury in which you lived. The tuition fee is moderate indeed."

"Oh," cried Paul, "this is monstrous!"

"Not at all, not at all. Quite regular and moderate. Should you accept the partnership which I now offer you, the little debt would soon be wiped off. I might even make a reduction."

"I deny everything—everything," cried Paul. "You have called me your partner a thousand times. You have always spoken of one business. As for tuition, what had you to teach me after the first few months?" He tore up the paper and threw the fragments on the table. "Give me my money," he said, hoarsely. "Give me my own and let me go."

"If," said the old man, blandly, "if I said words of encouragement it was in order to make you zealous, and I will say that you became very zealous. There is not a trick of the trade, not a knot in the great web of deception which we weave, but was familiar to you. I took pride in my assistant. My old friends congratulated me upon you, Paul. You had your little weaknesses, such as inordinate vanity and a foolish desire to become a great man, which you could never be, and a constant craving for flattery. But I did take pride in you, and for the three years that you worked for me I did very well, very well indeed. The dollars rolled in. That is not to be denied. I had need of them in order to pay myself back something of that awful load of debt."

"Oh, debt! debt! I will not hear of it. Come, are you going to give me my share?"

"I am not, Paul. Once for all, I am not. If you persist in giving up a glorious business, and sacrificing my future as well as your own, not one solitary dollar do you get. That is my last word, Paul. Think it over. Think what it means."

Paul sunk into a chair. He had not looked for this. The old professor was his banker. If he wanted any money he asked him for it. He had always considered himself a partner, and he knew that the income of the firm was very large during the three years when he worked for it. And now to be told that he was only an assistant! To be shown a sheet of paper by which it was made to appear that he owed his instructor three-and-twenty thousand dollars!

"It is my last word, Paul," the old man repeated, looking at him steadily with his keen eyes under his white eyebrows. "I shall proceed to consult a lawyer on the recovery of this debt."

Paul made no reply.

"Consider, my dear boy," his partner went on. "You have lost your power because you have neglected my warning, and suffered your mind to become wholly occupied with a woman. Well, I have no objection to your marrying. I will even see that you start handsomely. When you have been married a month your mind will begin to recover its balance again, and your old power will gradually come back. Then we will all three go back to New York. I will have a deed of partnership properly drawn up; you shall conduct the active part of the business. I will sit by and advise. You will keep your wife in style and luxury; you will be always learning more and more, and you will be always becoming a greater power in the land. Listen now. Come down from your stilts and be reasonable. I have matured a scheme for getting at the private affairs of every man of standing in the City of New York; it is a scheme absolutely safe, which shall never by any accident be connected with you and me. And you shall work the scheme. Come, Paul, *I offer you the most* enviable, the most de-

lightful, the most honored way of living possible, and you think of throwing it over for a mere scruple."

Paul made no reply.

"I confess, Paul, that I am loath to let you go, if by any persuasion or offers I can make you stay. I like you, boy. I have always liked you. And I admire you. I could never find, anywhere, another boy who would quite so well answer all my requirements. Indeed, I am too old now to look for another. You will be a very great, an irreparable loss to me."

Still Paul made no reply.

"As for the money I have saved"—the old man kept his eyes on Paul, watching the effect of his words—"that will be no more than enough for my own very simple wants. If I wished to be generous and to give you money, I could not afford it."

Paul's face refused to show the least sign of being tempted.

"And all for a wretched little scruple! Paul, it makes me sorry for you. I have told you over and over again that in our profession we do no more harm than in other professions. They want our advice; we sell it. They want counsel on all kinds of subjects; we profess to give it. Very well. Sometimes it is good advice; sometimes it is bad. We do our best. Meantime we learn, and watch, and keep eyes and ears wide open. A laborious profession, Paul, but not without honor."

Then Paul arose and spoke with dignity and sadness.

"Yes, it is hard upon you, after all your expectations. I will not work with you or for you any longer. I am sick and ashamed of the whole business. Whatever happens to me I will no longer be a cheat and a rogue by profession."

"Words, Paul, words; empty words."

"People did not come to consult us; they came to consult the spirits with whom we professed to communicate. I will have no more to do with it."

"Then, Paul, let us waste no more words. Go from me as you came to me—a pauper."

CHAPTER VIII

ONE MORE ENGAGEMENT.

"I sent for you, Paul," said Lady Augusta, coldly, "because I wished to have a little conversation with you."

"I am always at your command, Lady Augusta." He was returning from Beaumont Street and thought to go straight to his own room, there to consider this unexpected blow. He was so ignorant of affairs that this parade of an account, with its preposterous list of charges, deceived him. He had been so careless of affairs that he never asked his partner—of course they had been partners—for any statement, but he blindly believed himself entitled to a vast sum — a thousand dollars seems a vast sum to a young man who has never had any money to spend, and does not thoroughly understand arithmetic. And now he was in debt, and in England, where they have, he knew, the Fleet Prison and the Marshalsea and the Queen's Bench Prison, and Correction Houses for debtors. How was he to pay that debt? and what would happen to him when he had no money? The young man would fain have sat down to consider these things in his own room, but on his way he was met by Lady Augusta's message.

"Thank you, Paul."

She hesitated and appeared to have some difficulty in formulating her questions. Then, moved by some recollection or thought, she put on the gracious smile of a *grande dame de par le monde*.

"You have been very different from the ordinary medium, my dear Paul. You did not come here for money; you came a gentleman on a visit, you have made us all love you—especially Hetty. Let me talk to you as a woman old enough to be your mother, and very much interested in you."

"You have always been too kind to me, Lady Augusta. I have not deserved your kindness."

"First, my dear boy, is it quite true that you have lost your powers?"

"It is quite true."

"Consider. Men, I know, sometimes pretend things for ambitious purposes. Tell me frankly, are you hiding something? Take me into your confidence, Paul."

"I assure you, Lady Augusta, upon my hon—" He checked himself, remembering that he had never owned any of that precious possession, all of which had yet to be won. "I assure you that I have entirely lost such powers as I ever had."

"And shall you never recover them?"

"I have resolved to make no attempt to recover them. I have entirely closed that chapter of my life."

"Really? But why, Paul?"

"I cannot tell you exactly why. But I have no other choice."

"Oh, Paul, *must* it be?"

"It must."

"When we are only standing on the threshold of the Temple—when you have done little more than open the door for us to peep in? Frankly, Paul, I am disappointed."

"I am sorry."

"You came to us with credentials far be-

yond anything we had ever received before. My correspondent, Anna Petrovna, promised us achievements the like of which we had never before heard."

"I did some things for you. Were you disappointed in them?"

"No, we were not. We were both surprised and delighted. But, Paul, the things you did were as nothing compared with the things you taught. I for one can never forget your teaching. You raised us, Paul. You lifted our souls—and yet you abandon us—you give up your work. Oh, it is as if an ancient prophet had resolved to listen no more to the Word of the Lord, and had gone back to his plough and his vineyard. How can you abandon your calling, Paul?"

"I have no choice," he replied.

"There was never any man," Lady Augusta went on, "who was able to move me so deeply as you could and did, Paul. No preacher, no teacher, no singer, no novelist, no poet, no actor. I longed daily for your voice, and now it is silent, or it utters only common things. Why is it, Paul—why is it?"

"I cannot tell you."

"I looked for greater things, Paul. I looked for more teaching, more elevation of soul, a deeper communion with the other world."

"You would always look for greater things; you would always expect more." Paul recovered a little of his lost authority. "Those who first converse with spirits through a medium, and witness manifestations, are always asking for more. You, to whom a glimpse of this other world has been permitted, are impatient and dissatisfied, because you cannot have at once full sight and full communion. Have patience, Lady Augusta. Perhaps this will come in time—perhaps not."

"Yes. But acknowledge, Paul, that the message wants completeness."

"It may be so. Some allowance should be made for the imperfections of the messenger."

"There are always imperfections in the medium, to be sure—even in the best—in such as yourself. For instance, you promised that before you went away I myself should be endowed with your power of seeing and conversing with the spirits."

"Do you think that you would like that power? Think, Lady Augusta."

"You have it yourself. Do you like it?"

"I have it no longer. Think, however, what it might mean. There are countless myriads of human souls—all immortal and imperishable—the souls of all the generations which have passed away: try to think of the air filled with them. They are the souls of the ancient barbarians and savages—wild men and women of the woods—the souls of prehistoric man, as well as man of these recent times. The common medium offers to call the spirit of Julius Cæsar or Homer. How can he, amid all these myriads, call for one? Think of being always conscious of their vast multitude. You would see them wherever you opened your eyes: darkness would not hide them—walls would not protect you from seeing them. Unless you had, as well, the power of conversing with them, they would pass you in a never-ending silent procession. If you could speak with them, how many would you care to address? Think of the thousands of savage faces, brutal and ignorant still—of the bad faces, many more bad than good. They would come and glare upon you in the night. You would never sleep for thinking of their dreadful faces. There would be no kindness for you in their faces; there would be no sympathy for you. Could you endure this revelation?"

"No, no; I could not. It would be too awful. But we shall die. Shall we join this dreadful procession of savage souls?"

"I say not that. You will be enabled to find and join your own friends, to walk upon your own level."

Lady Augusta shook her head. She had never before realized how small a band her own friends constituted. To look for them in this vast crowd might be a hopeless task.

"And consider, if my message has been delivered, that something survives. Mr. Brudenel says that he stands upon the solid rock. The fortunes which were in such shipwreck have been saved. And there are those conversations which we have had together. If what is true in them survives I shall be content to remember them with gratitude."

"But is your power really—hopelessly—gone?"

"It is hopelessly gone."

"What a pity—what a pity!"

"Perhaps."

"Well—it cannot be helped, then. I have enjoyed your visit very much, Paul. I am very, very sorry that it is all over. And—and—oh, my dear boy"—the tears came to her eyes and she wrung her hands passionately—"to think that it is all over when I hoped for so much! You do not know the dreadful disappointment I have had to endure year after year, when one man came after another and all—all—were found out. If it were not that we know—as the outside world cannot know—the grand truth which underlies the pretences of these creatures, and that they actually have something of the power which we crave, I should have gone out of my senses long ago. And then you came, and everything seemed opening up for

us at last. You wanted no money. You came bringing wisdom and power with you. Oh, my heart leaped up. At last, I thought, we have the prophet we have longed for."

"Oh, stop—stop," Paul murmured.

"And then I discerned that what I had longed for and prayed for all my life had come to me at last; and the other world was to be no more an article of faith but a thing proved like a mathematical theorem. I thought that the immortality of the soul was going to be demonstrated so that every man in the world should know that this life is but an episode in which we may advance ourselves spiritually or degrade ourselves; make friendships and alliances to last forever. Oh, think of the change which would happen to the world. Did you ever try to think what would happen if we all knew for an actual fact that we are immortal, and that we are always forever going upward or downward? Then those who are on the upward slopes would encourage those lower down, and then would arise a universal longing for better things. Then vice and selfishness and all the sins of the world would vanish away, and we should understand the beauty of holiness. Think of the great hymn of praise which would go up from all alike if this were once proved and the living and the dead could commune with one another."

"If that could be done!" said Paul, meekly.

"I thought that you would do it—you, Paul. And I thought that we would build a great College for Spiritual Research, and that you should be its director, and that we should attract all the highest minds among the young people to make them students, and then our advance would be so rapid. Oh, I thought I saw world after world unfolding, planet speaking with planet, star to star. Paul—Paul"—her voice rose higher and higher—"all these things were in your power. You would have done all this and more—and more—and you have basely abandoned everything, and are now no more than an ordinary young man, one of the world—blind, and deaf and dumb, though the spirits call aloud and order you to speak."

"They do not, Lady Augusta. I hear nothing. I see nothing."

"Oh, it is dreadful—dreadful—to have this last hope, the best grounded of all, wrecked and ruined. Well, Paul, you could not help it, I suppose."

He was silent. For a while neither spoke. Then Lady Augusta went on in a changed voice: "There were two other things I had to say. What were they? Oh! First, Have you heard about our Conference?"

"What Conference?"

"I thought my husband had spoken to you about the Conference of Spiritualists. It is the first reunion of Spiritualists ever attempted to be held in this country. Mr. Brudenel has been asked to preside. They will come from all parts, from America, from Russia, from India—"

"A conference of Spiritualists? Will Mr. Chick and people like him be asked to speak?"

"All will be invited to attend, from the most serious seeker to the commonest spirit-rappers! We shall present to the world an imposing array as regards numbers and names; we shall encourage and stimulate ourselves by the communion of speech and the exchange of experience. You will speak, Paul?"

"I do not know. I think you had better not ask me," he replied, with lowered eyes.

"I must ask you. Why, Paul, there has been no experience at all to compare with your own in the history of Spiritualism. The sudden loss of your powers is in itself a most striking corroboration of their genuineness. You must speak! We shall have papers of the commonplace kind from men like Mr. Athelstan Kilburn and Mr. Amelius Horton. There will be, I am afraid, papers full of exaggerations, which we Spiritualists always expect. There will be, I dare say, papers containing downright untruths and inventions. There always are."

"What subject do you wish me to speak on?"

"You may, of course, take any that you please. In fact, the word Spiritualism covers an enormous field of research. But, Paul, the subject which I should like you to take up is the History of your own Embassy."

"The History of my own Embassy? Yes, Lady Augusta"— he looked up with a strange light in his eyes—"I will give the Conference the history of my own embassy."

"Very well, that is settled. And now, Paul, let us return to yourself. You have lost your powers, and you have at the same time fallen in love with Hetty. I questioned her about it, and she confessed the whole; and you are going back to America. What are you going to do when you get there?"

"I cannot say yet."

"Have you any money?"

"None at all. I have no profession, no private means, and no influential friends."

"But you cannot marry, Paul, unless you have an income."

"That is true. I ought not to have spoken to Hetty."

"You have rendered the greatest services to this house, Paul. You must not go away empty-handed. It must not be said that we suffered you to go away without solid proofs of gratitude."

"No, no," Paul made haste to reply, "it is impossible for me to take money of you or of any one else in your household. Lady Augusta, you said that I came a gentleman on a visit. Let me go as I came, a gentleman who ends his visit."

CHAPTER IX.

YET ANOTHER BLOW.

IT was the day of the dance, and an unwonted stir and restlessness, with the running about of the servants, and the voices—actually the voices—of strange men filled the house. The preparations of festivity, the gayety and happiness of the girls, mocked the melancholy which filled Paul's breast. How can people be heartlessly happy in the presence of other people who go in sadness? Everything conspired to make him sad. He was only a young American, a medium, a mesmerizer who had somehow lost his magnetic power, and a pauper. The only thing that distinguished him was his great achievement in saving the family fortunes, and that feat was damaged by the discovery that, whoever caused those letters to be written, he himself knew beforehand of the danger that threatened the company. The only consolation to his soul was the importance which the mysterious flat conferred upon him.

"Come up-stairs, old man," said Tom. "We'll have tobacco and talk. I've got nothing to do this afternoon, and you never have anything to do."

Paul followed him with a sinking heart, and the certainty—less sensitive men would have felt a little uneasiness only, but Paul knew for certain—that something unpleasant was going to happen. Every day brought fresh disgraces and humiliations. There was going to be another.

Tom had no intention of making unpleasantness. He construed all the fine talk about the loss of power, and the recovery of memory as to the past, and the rest of it, as the machinery prepared beforehand to cover a graceful withdrawal, with perhaps a final little miracle to mark the departure of the magician. "Thank the Lord," he observed to Sibyl, "there will be no more Abyssinian Philosophy. That's done with and decently buried. The fellow's ashamed of his rubbish. He has the grace to be ashamed, Dodo, wherefore I like him the better. Strange that you and I should like a fellow who came here with a mass of lies, and has made a fool of everybody in the house except you and me. He's ashamed, Dodo. He won't ever do it again."

Tom had no desire to be unpleasant, yet he became horribly unpleasant; for he knocked away the last prop which kept up Paul's self-respect, and plunged him into the lowest depths of abasement. But he only meant to straighten up things a bit before Paul left them, so that there should be no misunderstanding afterwards. It surprised him to think how unpleasant he had made himself.

"Well," he said, cheerfully, "it's all over, isn't it? Prodigies came out unexpectedly strong. Miracles undoubted. Manifestations not to be explained on any other reasonable hypothesis than the direct interferences of supernatural agency. I haven't had an opportunity of talking to you privately about the thing—but I hope you are satisfied."

"Quite. I had a message to deliver—"

"I thought you were forgetting that. Well, let us put it so, to save explanation."

"My message once delivered, of course everything was done."

"And now, I take it," Tom went on, "we may consider that the whole business may be frankly discussed, just as if you had not been the principal actor in it."

"Ye-yes. I suppose so. Why not?"

"Well, if you come to that, why not, indeed?" Tom sat down and lit his cigarette. He smoked it straight through without saying another word. Then he threw the stump away and took another.

"Paul, old man," he said, "I took to you from the first; you know I did. It wasn't so much your cleverness, because clever men are often beasts. And it wasn't because I saw at the first go off that you were a long way ahead of Chick and his lot. Of course I admired your wonderful cheek, and some of the stories you told were first class. But I liked your manner, and I've always liked your manner ever since."

"Thank you."

"Yes. It was your manner. You cast yourself upon us. You made everybody your friend from the very beginning, except Sibyl. You've got a most surprising manner. It's irresistible. No wonder you mesmerized the girls and cured the house-maid's toothaches. It was your manner that caught on to me. It's admirable, Paul; admirable. Now that you remember where you hail from, you might perhaps remember how you got it. Was it from some Italian marchese, your grandfather?"

"No. We are plain New England people, who came over for conscience' sake two hundred years ago."

"For conscience' sake, just as you came back to the old country—the Puritan blood still showing itself."

Paul blushed.

"Your manner is most certainly inherited. I expect you came in reality from some great English house. What was your name before you were christened Herr Paulus?"

"My name is Trinder."

"Trinder—Lord Trinder—Earl Trinder—Sir Paul Trinder, baronet. Tough old Sir Tom Trinder who fought at Agincourt. No, I can't remember any Trinder in history, but it's the fault of the historians. There must have been some Trinder, brave and handsome, clever and courteous. He was the comrade in arms of Bayard, his grandson was the friend of Philip Sidney, his great-grandson the sworn brother of Crichton."

"I know nothing about my English ancestors," said Paul, gravely.

"Well, old man, before you go away let us have a little explanation. You've given up the business entirely, I hear. I am not sorry, because though the miracles are exciting at the time, the machinery must give a great deal of trouble, and the—the—acting, you know, has got to be kept up all the time after."

"I have lost my power and I shall never get it back again. That is what you mean, isn't it?"

"That's near enough. Well, old man, I told you the very first night you came that I should watch you all the time. I told you that, didn't I?"

"You certainly did. I hope you have been watching me."

"That's just it—I have—and I've arrived at some rather curious and interesting results. First of all, before I tell you what they are, tell me what you propose to do; that is, if it is not an impertinent question."

"I have not decided."

"Look here," Tom laid his hand on Paul's, "let us make no mistakes about things. You saved all that money. Nothing could have made my dear old hump of a guardian believe that the company—his company—could be in a bad way. You saved all that. Very good. Then we are grateful. And you made him write that letter to me. Nobody else could have done it, because he'd got an idea in his blessed chump that the cause wants a Vestal and that it was his duty to provide the Vestal, and so he had determined to carry it through like another Jephthah. Nobody but you, I say, could have made him write that letter. As for the three checks and the letter of introduction, and all—they were just part of the machinery. You can't throw off a miracle to advantage without the preliminary patter, and the scenery, and properties. Therefore, don't think I am crowing over any little discovery that I have made. Well, then, the long and short of it is, Paul, that we are deeply indebted to you—so deeply that nothing can ever pay that debt of gratitude."

"It is paid already. There is no need for gratitude."

"We are so deeply indebted to you that I venture to talk to you about your present affairs. You will not, I know, stay here much longer. Indeed, since you have ceased to—to manifest — you know — Lady Augusta, who is nothing if not a Spiritualist, has ceased to desire your stay to be prolonged. I dare say she will tell you so herself very soon. So you will go away. I have no right to ask where you are going; but you have given me the right to ask whether we can in any way make your path easier for you—whether we can find some of the funds necessary for comfort—whether in fact you are rich?"

"Yesterday morning," said Paul, "I should have replied that I was possessed of ample funds. This afternoon I can tell you that I have but a single sovereign in the world besides a lot of useless and expensive things which I can sell, or pawn, in order to get back to the States."

"And then?"

"I do not know. I must get back. I must get away from this. And I must take Hetty away, too."

"My dear Paul, you must take something from me. You have saved everything that Sibyl, Cicely, and I possessed in the world. You *must* let us provide for you."

"No, Tom. If there were nothing but splitting rails for the rest of my life I would not take your money, nor the money of anybody in this house. I *could* not. Oh, you must understand why!"

"I think I can, old man. I am sure, on the whole, that I can. Then let us lend you money. Borrow, if you will not accept."

"No, I would rather die than borrow your money." He sprang to his feet and rushed to the window. Tom thought he heard something like a choke ; he therefore preserved silence.

"I have noticed," he went on presently, "for some days that you've been looking unhappy. Is it the trouble about money?"

"Perhaps. Never mind the money. Talk of something else. It drives me mad to talk about money."

"Well—if I must not—yet it is a very important subject of conversation at all times— let us talk of something else. Let us return to that watch I have been keeping up, you know. Would you like to know what I have learned?"

Paul turned pale to the very lips. "Yes," he faltered, "I should like to hear."

"First when I came to think over the very wonderful manifestations, you know, of the first night, which, I must say, were far away the best things of the kind I ever witnessed, I connected them, as our friend Emmanuel Chick did, with mesmeric force or magnetism. Then I began to read up the subject. I read many books which contained many lies. I even began to practise at the Laboratory. And I succeeded in putting two or three of the students into a mesmeric trance, and I made them do things. You see, I was on the right track."

Paul made no reply.

"I then made another discovery. I found that legerdemain, added to mesmeric powers, would enable a man to do all kinds of things. The two things together explained how the girls were made to see and to say exactly what you pleased, and how the paper came fluttering from the ceiling, and why the photographs represented the girls' thoughts."

"Go on!"

"I also found it abundantly proved that a person may be cured of many disorders by being subjected to mesmeric influence, and that mesmerism is an anæsthetic which deserves to be considered scientifically; and that a man who has developed this power, which I suppose to be latent in every one, may get another into his power completely, and make him do all kinds of things of which he will afterwards remember nothing."

"All this is perfectly true."

"Then, Paul, come with me, and I will show you something more."

He led the way up a stair to the roof. On the roof stood a little kind of tent.

"Come in here."

Paul followed him. The canvas fell over the entrance and they were in darkness.

"This," said Tom, "is not a photographer's tent, though it looks like it. The tent is in fact a camera-obscura, and it is so arranged as to command a view of a place with which you are familiar. See!"

The little table which stood within the tent became suddenly lit up with a picture in colors. It was a picture representing Mr. Cyrus Brudenel in his study. That gentleman sat in his wooden chair before his table, papers and letters were lying before him, but he sat tapping his knuckles with his double glasses.

"Do you recognize that look in his face?" Tom whispered. "I have seen it a dozen times. It means doubt and discouragement. It is the old story. One after the other they have come here, bearing in their hands the keys which set open the gates of the other world. Mr. Brudenel has been permitted to look through the gates. He never sees anything, but he is always going to have a full view next day. He pays large sums of money for the privilege. Sometimes the spirits on the other side converse with him; they have even appeared to him ; he has seen them; he has been permitted to grasp their hands, to feel their breath upon his cheek, and to be kissed by them. But they have never told him one single thing which conveyed the least instruction. Just as he had seen nothing, so he learned nothing. All his life has been spent in accumulating testimonies to the existence of the other world, and the possibility of communicating with its inhabitants. It seems to me a waste of a good life, does it not?"

Paul made no reply.

"Each claimant as he came brought him at first complete assurance and firm conviction. In fact, he never doubted for one moment the truth of Spiritualism. But every successive operator has left behind him a doubt, to say the least, as to his truth and honesty. Something unpleasant has come out before they went away or after. As for poor old Chick, he has been discredited a hundred times; yet he still turns up again with a new message which means nothing. He, however, is quite used to be treated as a humbug. Look—he is very uneasy." Mr. Brudenel at this point rose from his chair and began to walk about the room. "He is thinking of what that old boy said about your power of putting two and two together. His mind is filled with the suspicion that it was you who found out the state of the company, and not his Excellency the Right Reverend the Lord Bishop Izák Ibn Menelek, the Falasha, who interfered. The suspicion keeps him stretched upon the rack. It is turning the solid rock into a quagmire. Paul, my dear boy, it was awfully clever, but it won't hold water after Mr. James Berry's innocent observation this morning. Paul, if I were you I would pack up and go very soon. He will recover a little when you are gone."

Paul uttered some inarticulate kind of groan.

"I have occupied myself," Tom went on, "in a very interesting series of observations, the nature of which you can guess. I have seen our dear old friend there morning after morning reduced to insensibility. I have then seen you, Paul, take his keys out of his pocket, unlock and ransack his safe, open and read his letters, and examine his papers. I have seen you—not heard you—put questions to him and receive answers from him. I have seen you order him to write letters which you dictated. By the help of a magnifying glass I was enabled to read those letters. In this way I acquired information which was very useful to me. In fact, *Paul, I knew all along* what you were doing,

though I confess there were some things which I did not quite understand—for instance, the appearance of the day's paper. That of the month old paper was a very feeble performance. Anybody could do that with the help of the mesmeric power. But—"

Paul groaned heavily and fell across the table over the image of Mr. Cyrus Brudenel, who was just then sitting down again. He had fainted.

"Why," said Tom, when he had got him down-stairs, and made him sit down on a sofa, "who on earth would have thought that you were going to take it like this?"

"Oh, you knew—all along—"

"Yes—I knew."

"And Sibyl knew?"

"Yes — certainly. Sibyl knew. But no one else."

"And every time I spoke you were laughing at me?"

"Not exactly laughing at you. We were wondering, perhaps, what was coming next."

"I will pack up and go at once," Paul cried, springing to his feet.

"Not yet, Paul. Sit down again. After a fainting-fit you must rest a little. Tell me, Paul, you did not think that we took you seriously—you never insulted my intellect so far as that—did you?"

"The others did, and I hoped—I thought —that after those letters you would. Oh, I am only a detected impostor. Let me go."

"Not just yet." Tom gently forced him to lie down. "Such a fainting - fit as that shows that you were knocked over by more than my little story. Rest awhile."

"I am a detected impostor," said Paul. "I can never look any one in the face again."

"Tut—tut—nonsense, man. I know all about it, now. I know about the old man in Beaumont Street. I know all about Bethiah. I know all about Hetty. And I've known all along—who could help knowing?—that you were playing your own game. There are people who believe in the clumsy jimmy about the Mahatmas and the occult philosophers and Karma and all that stuff—and so you were quite justified in thinking that there would be people ready to believe in your own little fake about the Falasha and Prince Menelek—only I never thought that you reckoned me among the possible believers. That's all. You came to England in order to distinguish yourself. You thought you would perform your miracles and get the world ringing with your name. Well," he continued, "the miracles came off. No doubt about the miracles at all. Well, where's the honor? Where is the ringing voice of fame? The miracles have fallen flat. The papers never took them up. Just now the papers will not take up Spiritualism, except to relate how another medium has been detected. The thing is in bad odor, you see. One or two people have asked me about the Indian paper trick, but no one really believed it. Flatness, Paul, dead flatness—a frost—has fallen upon the miracles. Devil a bit of distinction after all your trouble. The old man in Beaumont Street is the New York medium who taught you—"

Paul groaned, and buried his face in the sofa cushions.

"I know everything, you see."

"Does—does anybody else know?"

"Sibyl knows. She has known all along."

"Oh!" Paul groaned again.

"Hetty does not know. It is left for you to tell her—what you please. If I were you I would tell her all."

"I cannot."

"As for me—there is one thing more that I have to learn."

"I will tell you nothing more. Oh! have you not tortured me enough?"

"Sit up, Paul—so." Paul obeyed. "Look me in the face—so. Keep your eyes fixed on mine—so—so—"

"A strange giddiness fell upon Paul. Then he stiffened in all his limbs and sat upright. He who had mesmerized so many others was now himself mesmerized.

* * * * * * *

"You have told me everything, Paul. I am much obliged to you. You have been in a mesmeric trance, and you have told me how you did the Indian paper miracle and the musical bells and everything. You are a prestidigitateur, a ventriloquist and a mesmerist all in one. Thank you very much."

Paul rose, pale and confused.

"Is it true?" he asked.

"It is quite true. But have no fear. I will not do it again. And now, old man, it's all over; your cleverness will go off into some other line, won't it? The last is a very striking and attractive line, but it is liable to misconstruction if people take it seriously. Better have done with it. The magician will soon be forgotten, and Hetty will make you happy. She has every virtue except one—she cannot be persuaded to honor her parents. She is full of prejudices about truth and tricks. All the more reason why she should be able to honor her husband, isn't it?"

Tom said no more. He felt ashamed, so to speak, of the shame he had brought upon the other man. He held out his hand.

"I cannot take your hand," said Paul.

"You can—you shall, Paul. Take it at once; else, by the Lord, I'll mesmerize you

10

again, and make you sit down and write a letter and give up Hetty!"

CHAPTER X.

THE DANCE, AND AFTER.

SOME of the young people who were present at Lady Augusta's dance found it, I believe, a most delightful evening. They danced, they talked and laughed, they danced again. They had supper; again they danced, and they went home early in the morning or very late at night, just as you choose to put it, and just as they always do on these occasions. The elderly people who came with the girls took perhaps a less keen delight in the entertainment. Towards daybreak they grew silent; their smiles were set, their eyelids were heavy; and they all with one consent began to fidget in their seats. Everybody knows that stage of the evening when the elderly people begin to fidget. The sensation commences in the backbone and works upward to the head and to the arms and fingers, and downward to the knees and feet, until the whole frame is fidgeting. That means that the poor old frame should have been lying sound asleep between the sheets long ago. In a more civilized state of society middle-aged and elderly people will be "fetched," like children, at an early hour. The comfort of the thing will remove the apparent ignominy.

Did you ever ask a man who has gone to a theatre with toothache how he enjoyed the play? Or another, who was deaf, how he liked the concert? Or a man with gout if the sermon did him any good? Or a man going to be hanged how he enjoyed the scenery on the way? The accounts given by these gentlemen of the entertainment provided for them would probably vary considerably from those given by others free from bodily and mental pain. Sibyl, for instance, found the evening much—very much—too short; to Paul, on the other hand, it was insufferably long.

He was horribly miserable; he was at the lowest depth of shame; he felt mean beyond any power of expression. He had endured being called a medium's cad, but with difficulty. He had endured the suspicion—call it the proof—that he knew, beforehand, about the tottering company; he had learned that he had no money at all. Yet there was one consolation—the fortunes of the family had been saved, and that by his mysterious friends. No way out of that mystery was possible. On that achievement he would rest his claims to be remembered when he was gone. That one thing enabled him to retire with dignity, as one who abdicates. And now, good heavens!

he had been all the time in the company of a man who had found him out — more, had watched him and seen him at work every morning — opening letters, searching safes, making his patient write to dictation. Yet that man, with that knowledge, had treated him with a friendliness which in his abasement seemed contemptuous toleration. Paul —Paul—who had scorned the clumsy medium who is caught stalking about the room wrapped in a newspaper, who derided the poor wretch convicted of producing the spirit message on the ceiling with a pair of lazy tongs—how was he a whit better than any of the petty cheats and liars who haunt the outer fringe of Spiritualism?

This was an extremely unpleasant mood to bring to the dance. Not many of the young men who were preparing for that festival were quite so gloomy, though debts and duns, disappointments and defeats, and unsatisfied desires do surround the path of early manhood, and too often spoil and corrupt what should be the most delightful time of life.

Paul thought that it would be best for him to creep into the room when it was quite full, and when all the guests had arrived. Then he would be least noticed, and would go and stand in a corner all the evening out of the way. To stand in a corner all night while other people dance and look happy— it does not, at first sight, seem as if it would be a pleasing mode of passing the nocturnal hours. Yet many deliberately choose thus to spend their nights.

Unfortunately he was little versed in the ways of dancing, and concluded that by appearing a quarter of an hour after the time named he would find the rooms full.

No one was in the rooms except Sibyl herself.

"Paul," she said, "you are looking horribly ill. You have been ill and miserable for several days. What does it mean? Nothing new has happened?"

"No; nothing new. It is only that I have been told a great many things that are old. Oh, Sibyl, how can you speak to me? Why do you not order me out of the house? Tom has told me everything. I am a wretch, and you have known it all along. And now Hetty must know it too."

"Hetty will know nothing, Paul, except what you please to tell her. All that is past and gone. Cheer up, Paul, and look happy for Hetty's sake. Come, you used to be so good an actor."

"I cannot act any longer. I can do nothing now. Sibyl, I ought not to be here— I have no business to be among these people."

"*All that is over*, Paul. Cheer up, for

Hetty's sake. Do your best to smile. See, here she comes, beautiful and happy."

It was Hetty, dressed in white. Cicely gave her the dress. Paul's face cleared up a little at the sight of her. She came prepared for a happy evening. What girl, who knows she is looking her best and has her lover waiting for her and is going to dance, but would feel happy?

And when the people began to arrive, which they did in a full stream and all with one consent at the same time, and the dancing began, Hetty and Paul stood aside and talked. She gave him as many dances as he chose to take, and agreed to sit out for them, because he had proved unable to manage the revolution of the right heel.

"You are looking ill, Paul," she said. "Are you unhappy about something?"

"No, Hetty. How can I be unhappy when I am with you? But there is nothing," he added, mendaciously. "We will go presently to Cicely's room—no one will be able to follow us there, and we shall be able to have a long talk. But you will want to dance."

"There will be plenty of time for both, Paul. You shall take me to Cicely's room about supper-time, if you like. Now don't look at me like that or people will notice it. Remember, Paul, please, that your eyes are a little—well—more expressive than most. When we are alone—yes, Paul—when we are alone—as much as you please. Now forget everything except that you are at a dance. What do you think of it? You have never been to a dance before, have you?"

"No. Of course I like the animation and gayety of the scene, though some of the men look solemn over their steps. Perhaps, Hetty, they are thinking of the right heels. It seems as if there was no trouble or care or necessity for work. Do you know what they would have said about dancing in my town?"

"What?"

"They would have asked how waltzing can be consistent with care for your immortal welfare, and they would have groaned over the wickedness of laying your arm round a girl's waist."

"Oh!"

"The best thing about society is the way in which everything like care and trouble must be left behind. Those who form society, Hetty, ought to be the most delightful people in the world."

"Why? Because they must all be well bred?"

"No. Because the whole object of society is to make life happy, and in order to do that everybody must do all he can to make everybody else happy. It is the very essence of society, I suppose, that everybody must be always trying to make everybody else happy —so that everybody must be always giving way." Here an awkward couple collided heavily with Paul. "You see, Hetty," he explained, "I had to give way. Outside society everybody grabs all he can for himself. We will belong to the very highest society, Hetty."

"We will, Paul—even if our circle only consists of two."

"I suppose that most of the young men here have got their own private troubles, but they don't show them any more than I do. We are all actors, Hetty, and we make each other happy by pretending to be happy ourselves."

"To me, Paul," Hetty whispered, "it has always seemed as if the worst trouble, next to being ashamed of things which you could not help, was the trouble of money. That was because we were so horribly poor."

"Many of the young men here, I know, must be horribly troubled about money. But they hide the trouble. Yes—money—yes—money must be had, somehow. Without money there is nothing—not even elementary society. I never thought much about money until—well, I will tell you about it another time. You have never looked so beautiful as to-night, Hetty."

"Oh, Paul!"

"It makes me happy again only to look at you. Hetty, I shall have to look at you a great deal, because there is more to forget than I thought there would be."

Then they heard voices close to them. A young fellow and a girl, resting for a moment, are talking as they rest.

He was a young fellow of the truly British type—big-limbed and strong, capable of saying very downright things, and with no nerves to speak of; and the girl was a London girl — one of those who know everything, and go everywhere, and say what they please.

"This is the home of mystery and magic," said the girl. "Here the spirits do congregate."

"Don't you think they must be driven away to-night?"

"Why?"

"By rage and envy, because they can't waltz with you."

"Waltzing with a spirit would be quite a novel sensation. I will ask the next medium I come across if he can raise a spirit who can dance."

"Have you ever seen any of the spirits?"

"Oh, I've been to lots of séances, and we have had most wonderful messages. I've seen pale lights and shadowy-sheeted figures."

"Where do they buy their sheets?"

"At Whiteley's, I suppose. Well, you know, it's delightful while it lasts, but one is always trembling lest something dreadful should be said or done, because the mediums do not pretend to have the spirits under control; and you go away in a kind of glow, and it is not until the next morning that you begin to understand that the messages amount to nothing, and that the raps and things might have been imitated, and that the whole thing was probably all a sham."

"Probably, I should say."

"After the lights were turned up Mr. Brudenel always made a little speech. He used to say that after this night there could no longer be any doubt in the minds of the most incredulous. That sent us away happy. As for the mediums, I've seen them of all kinds—young and old, American and English—and they are always truly dreadful persons!"

"Well," said this delightful young man, "a fellow would have to climb down pretty low before he took up with that trade."

"Come away, Paul," Hetty whispered.

"No; I will hear it all," he replied, with flaming cheek.

"The last one who came here," the girl went on, "I did not see. I believe he is gone now. But I heard about him from Mrs. Tracy Hanley, who saw him do some wonderful things. She said he made up very well, like an Italian count, and told stories about Abyssinia, and pretended not to know where he was born; and he showed them one day an Indian daily paper of that same morning."

"It's wonderful to think how people will believe everything," said the young man.

"In this house they do, anyhow. If you were to come here and pretend anything you please they would believe you, if only you said the spirits did it for you."

"Let us try and see what will happen. You make up something and I will swear I saw you do it. I suppose when a man is not good enough to make a conjurer they turn him into a medium?"

"I dare say. How can people be so foolish?" This young lady had spent the afternoon with an amateur professor of palmistry, who had sketched out for her the whole of her life, with the assurance of marriage and the tale of her years and the number of her babies, all written down prophetically. "How can they be so foolish?"

"Are you rested?" said the young man.

"Paul, don't show your feelings so much in your face." He was looking as if a Malay muck running would do him good, or a leap off Waterloo Bridge. "What does it matter? It is as bad for me as it is for you

—and worse; because I feel for both, Paul. Now you understand what I have suffered all my life. That is over and done with. You will take me away from it. And oh, Paul, it is a bond between us."

He sighed heavily.

"I declare, Hetty," he said, "that until the other day I had quite forgotten that such things were said and thought about Spiritualists and such men as myself. I thought that I would win favor and honor, and draw all hearts to myself. Oh, what a fool—what a fool!"

"Will one heart satisfy you instead of all? Hush! Here is my partner. Oh, Paul, why could you not learn to dance?"

Left alone, Paul began to spend a very enjoyable evening. He could not dance, and he knew nobody. He did not want to be introduced to anybody, being miserably conscious that he was only the last medium imported and the latest medium found out.

And it seemed, as the night slowly passed, as if everybody in this room was talking about nothing but the spirits and the medium and the humbug of the whole thing, with contempt only veiled when their hostess or Sybil might overhear. In fact, to avoid speaking of Spiritualism in the temple of that cult was impossible; and it gave such an excellent opening for conversation; the newest beginner understood how to make use of such an opening ; it was better than the weather. And nobody seemed to regard him or to recognize him, or to understand that here was the very man about whom some whispered and some jested — Spiritualism lends itself with fatal readiness to the most elementary jester. Not a youngster fresh from school who had not some contemptuous little joke about the medium.

He felt presently as if he were invisible, and condemned to walk about in places where he should hear the truth about himself. The whole truth, you see. None of the quarter or half truths with which some of us try to put things in a better light. The whole truth. He was condemned to hear what was said and thought about himself by old and young, by the elderly ladies who came with the girls, and by the girls themselves, ingenuous and frank, most of all by the young men of his own age — from all alike he heard contempt—no pity, or sympathy, or attempt to excuse—contempt simply. A dreadful punishment for all of us, but most dreadful to such a young man as Paul. To all of us, no doubt, it would be a salutary punishment, though so severe that we should none of us ever dare to do any work again, especially literary work. *Then the publishers* would be ruined, and

authors and publishers would sit side by side in the casual wards, their quarrels forgotten, and the general public would fall back upon the old masters. To Paul this was the last of the many scourgings with which Fate had afflicted him within the last few days. It finished him, as you will see. He could bear no more.

I suppose his imagination was growing morbid, because presently this fancy passed away and was succeeded by another. He thought he was there in person, but that the others were ghosts—shadows—figures moving about to mock him and to let him understand what the world said of him. Only he himself of all the crowd was real. It was his punishment, he thought, for all his pretences and disguises, that he should be isolated. The rest of the world was apart from himself—he stood alone. That feeling of isolation comes to many men at times of grievous depression. We come into the world alone, we go out of the world alone; we walk through life alone, save for the love of women and children. Those who have not that support are indeed alone.

Presently one of the ghosts stepped out of the crowd and spoke to him.

"Herr Paulus," she said, "I am going to scold you." He knew her now—it was the lady who wanted him to go to her Sunday Evenings. "You have never once come to see me, and after all your promises."

"I am very sorry," he began.

"Will you come next Sunday?"

"I may be called away. I will come with the greatest pleasure if I am in London."

"Then I shall rely upon you, and I will have the brightest and most delightful and most appreciative circle to meet you. We shall not expect you to do anything, but if you should be in the mood it would be pleasant on a Sunday evening, when one is surrounded by friends—not mere acquaintances —but people whom one can love and trust, and when the atmosphere has been charged with a certain seriousness, you know, and all that, a communication from the other world would be particularly suitable."

"I will try," said Paul, "if I am still here."

"I was present when you produced those two papers. Do you know, Herr Paulus— *may* I call you Paul? Thank you. Do you know, Paul, that I have always wondered why more has not been made of that miracle. I met the professor the other day and asked him what he made of it. He replied that if you would do it again before a committee formed of half a dozen prestidigitateurs and half a dozen men of science, and would leave the paper, not take it away, he was quite ready to give the matter serious consideration. Will you do this for him?"

"I think not."

"And they say everywhere that Mr. Brudenel was made to sell out his shares in the company without knowing it, so that he saved an immense sum of money. If that is true it must have been done by you, Paul."

"Yes," said Paul, smiling, "that is true, and it was done by me. I believe that Mr. Brudenel does not desire the transaction to be a secret."

"Oh! It is wonderful—wonderful! May I tell everybody you are coming, Paul? It will be so great an attraction. Photographs falling from the ceiling, or even the bells of heaven, would be better than nothing."

"Yes," said Paul, "even to hear the bells of heaven would be— Yes, Mrs. Tracy Hanley, I will come, if I am still here, on Sunday next."

"Come and talk to me again presently, Paul. There are some delightful people here. But you have no eyes for more than one delightful person."

She laughed in the light way of her kind, and sailed away, and Hetty joined Paul again.

"There are two dances remaining for you, Paul," she said. "Come, we will go to Cicely's room. I think nobody knows of it, and we shall be alone."

No one was there. The lamp was lit; the door was shut; nobody knew anything about this room.

Paul sank into a chair.

"Hetty," he said, "you must give me up."

"Why, Paul?"

"Because I must give you up. I cannot drag you down to my level."

"Oh, Paul, you are thinking of what those wretched people said. I know now that you were with a medium in New York. Bethiah told me all about your youth and your failure to make a name in literature."

"A medium's cad, Hetty. That is how Sir Percival put it."

"Nonsense, Paul. You might as well call Tom a professor's cad, because he is demonstrator in the physical laboratory."

"No, to have been a medium at all is infamy. It brands a man for life. He can never recover his self-respect. Hetty, bid me go and give you up."

"Paul! If you meant what you say—but you do not."

"I am disgraced forever." He threw out his hands and began to walk up and down the room. "Hetty, go away—leave me. I am lost. I am utterly miserable. I have nothing in the world except you, and I have

no right—no, not the smallest right—to love such a girl as you."

She looked at him with wonder.

"We two, Paul," she said, "have both had the same enemy. No one can hate the very name of Spiritualism more than I do. I have had to look on and know that the professional medium is full of cheats and tricks and lies. And my mother is one! Oh, had it not been that you showed us beyond a doubt that there is a way open to the other world, I could have run away and drowned myself for very shame. Now I know that it is not all trickery. But we will have nothing more to do with the other world. The present shall be enough for us. Why, Paul, you are young and quite clever—all the world is open to the man who is young and clever. And I can wait in patience if only I know that you are working like other men. Now you are apart from other men. But in the future—oh, Paul, in the future—when we are together, and far away from this place, we shall look back upon the past like a bad dream. And of the other world we shall be satisfied to know that some men have found a way to speak with those beyond; but as for us, we will cling to the old paths, and go to church and have faith, just like the rest of the world."

"I *cannot* tell her," said Paul. Then he lifted her hand and kissed it humbly.

Hetty laid her head upon his shoulder.

Then Paul put his arm about her waist and kissed her lips.

"Yes," he said. "The past is gone. I have but one thing more to tell you, Hetty. When I have told you that, and not until then, our new world will begin. But I cannot tell you that to-night. Kiss me. Oh, my love, if it is the last time, kiss me! Kiss me, Hetty."

The tears were in his eyes and in his breaking voice. Why? Hetty partly knew and partly guessed. But as yet she did not know the whole truth.

"I shall not go back with you," he said. "I cannot go back and see them dancing. I shall go to my own room, and stay there locked up like a convict. I am not fit to stand among them. Is there anywhere another story of how such a wretch as myself—such an object of contempt and derision—once dared to love a true woman? And was it ever told that the woman could ever love him in return?"

"You must not think such things, Paul, my dear," said Hetty. "I love a man who is strong and brave and clever. He has made mistakes, but they are past and forgotten. He will yet do great things in the world, and I shall be proud of him. Or if he does not do great things he will do good things, and I shall still be proud of him."

Hetty took both his hands in hers and laughed gently—the woman's laugh which drives away the evil spirits: it is always the woman of whom the devil is afraid, because she is clear-sighted and direct and cannot be humbugged. When she laughed and pressed his hand Paul felt a little stronger, as a fainting man after a teaspoonful of brandy. His mistress knew already that the guidance of this man's life would be her own. He was so ignorant—but ignorance may be cured; so sensitive—a thing which can never be cured; so unaccustomed to men and the ways of the world that he must lean on some one, and upon whom better than his wife? Some women despise the man who is not masterful —I think most women love to be "directed" either by their husbands or their parson-persons; some of whom—Hetty was one—love a man all the more for his weakness and his unfitness to fight the battle of life.

"You shall not go back to the ball-room, Paul," she said. "You are ill to-night, you are not fit for the noise and excitement. Little things—like the talk of those two people —vex and worry you. Go to your own room and try to sleep. In the morning you will have forgotten these dreadful thoughts. If they trouble you any more, dear, remember that everybody in this house knows as much about you as I know myself. And they all love you just the same as if you had been the son of some Italian marchese and had been brought up in Florence or Venice—or even in Abyssinia itself, for that matter. Lady Augusta loves you as if you were her son, Sibyl loves you, Cicely loves you. It is no great credit, then, for me to go on loving you when you love me above all the others. Oh, Paul, if you suffer, I suffer. If you reproach yourself, you reproach me. We have had the same memory. Good-night, Paul, good-night, my dear."

She kissed him and clung to him for a moment, and then let him go.

Paul left her with bowed head and went straight to his own room. Then Hetty went back to the dancers.

But she left the door open, and other couples discovered this temple of incipient love, and came here and were perfectly happy. Thus doth the same room witness many emotions. It is not, you see, after all, monotonous to be a room.

Paul reached his own room. Struck with some indecision, he stood at the door, his hand upon the lock, and listened.

Below the music was playing a waltz. He seemed to hear the voices of the dancers as *they went round* or as they stopped to rest.

"Full of ghosts it is. . . . Mediums all humbugs. . . . Every kind of credulity here. . . . Fellow said he came from Abyssinia. . . . Are we finding them out? . . . Came for what he could get, of course. . . . Told that he's in the room somewhere. . . . Hope he won't hear what is said. . . . Do him good if he does. . . . Some cad pretending to be a gentleman. . . . Ought to be kicked down-stairs. . . ." He heard these words and voices quite plainly and distinctly above the fiddles and the harp and the cornet; though several stairs and walks interposed between himself and the speakers, he heard them quite clearly. It was his punishment to bear them. And then he heard the voice of Mrs. Tracy Hanley. "Even to hear the bells of heaven would be better than nothing." His early teaching it was, I suppose, which caused him a dreadful pang. "Even to hear those bells—afar off —how should he get within hearing of those bells?"

Lastly he seemed to hear the voice of Hetty. "Go to your own room, Paul." It was a voice of authority, and Paul obeyed, and shut his door.

So while the young men and the maidens, who were really not thinking about Paul a bit, and had only used the subject for an opening, were making merry, and some of the young men were trying to say clever things, and some were trying to look used up, and some were trying to look handsome, and some were trying to look distinguished, and some were trying to seem as if they were behind the scenes in everything, and all were trying to look twice as interesting and attractive to their partners as nature had made them—this young man, who had also tried to make himself a good deal more interesting and capable than nature intended, was creeping, miserable and guilty, between the sheets. The music went on and the champagne corks popped, and the young men laughed, and the girls smiled, and many seeds were sown that night which are now growing into fine trees, covered with *pommes d'amour*. In the ball-room they were all so happy, and in the bedroom there was one so miserable.

"Where is Paul, Hetty?" asked Sibyl.

"He has got a dreadful headache. I have told him to go to bed. He is making himself miserable about having been a medium, Sibyl. Say something kind to him, will you, to-morrow?"

"Yes, I will. You must console him, Hetty dear."

"I will, if I can. But he thinks so much of what you say, Sibyl."

"He will be all right to-morrow, Hetty. Don't be uneasy about him."

It was about half-past five in the morning

when Paul woke up. He woke with a start, expecting to hear the music below and the voices of the dancers. There was no music —the house was quite silent. He sprang from the bed, and pulled the curtains aside. The sun had been up already an hour and more. He threw open the window. The cold air and the sunshine dispelled the ghosts of the night. He was able to think. First, he thought he must leave the house at once. After all that had happened he could not possibly remain another day. He must leave the house before breakfast—before they came down-stairs.

He considered, next, the subject of money. He had a few pounds in his purse; he had a box full of rings, studs, chains, and pins—he would sell or pawn all these. He had a splendid dressing-case, with everything of silver; he had a quantity of gorgeous apparel, some of which he would also sell. He could, in fact, raise enough in this way to get back to America. Hetty would have to wait.

He dressed and packed his things. Then he opened the door, and went softly down-stairs, carrying his portmanteau upon his shoulder, and his dressing-case in his hand. The house was quite silent, with the feeling that belongs to a house where everybody is asleep. Arrived in the hall, Paul set down his portmanteau and went into the study.

He sat down at the table, and took pen and paper. How familiar it seemed to him—this study with the long rows of invaluable books of magic and mystery; this great solid table, the safe in the corner, the busts of departed humbugs. Now he would never see it any more. He was going out of the house where he had been so tenderly and kindly entertained.

"DEAR LADY AUGUSTA," he wrote,—"After our conversation of yesterday you will not be surprised at receiving this note. I am going away in the early morning — before any of you are down-stairs. I do this to avoid further explanations and farewells. But I cannot possibly go away without expressing my most sincere and heartfelt thanks for the kindness you have extended to me since I became your guest. I never knew before what the gracious hospitality of an English lady meant. Now I understand, and I shall remember all the rest of my life. I may be allowed, I hope, to write these few words of thanks, though I have to add the expression of my sincere remorse for the manner in which I have repaid your kindness. I intended to tell you in full what I mean by this; but I find I cannot—now. And yesterday I could not. Lady Augusta, your kindness was misplaced, but I do not think

that it will ever be forgotten by your most humble servant,   PAUL."

He folded this letter, placed it in an envelope, and left it on the table, addressed to Lady Augusta.

Then he went back to the hall, put on his splendid fur coat—it was an easterly wind, the breeze of soft, delicious May—took his umbrella and hat, and shouldered his portmanteau; and then he left the house.

There are not many cabs about at six o'clock in the mornings of May. Paul walked as far as the Marylebone Road, staggering under the weight of his portmanteau and his dressing-case and his fur-lined coat. The poetry of the flight was completely destroyed.

"Where to, sir?" asked the cabman who at last came along the road.

"I don't know," said Paul.

"Don't know, sir?"

"No," said Paul, irritably. "How the devil should I know?"

"Well, sir, if you don't know, who should? Want an hotel, sir?"

"Yes, to be sure—of course I do. You are an intelligent man. I must have a hotel. Drive me to a hotel. Drive me to the Langham. I'll double your fare. Of course," said Paul, "I wanted a hotel all along."

CHAPTER XI.

A COUNCIL.

THE day after the dance there was a committee of three in Bethiah's studio. It consisted of Bethiah herself, Tom, and Sibyl.

The business before that committee was the actual condition and the future prospects of Paul, or Herr Paulus, by baptism Ziphion, and by patronymic Trinder.

"He went away," said Tom, "before anybody was out of bed this morning. It is alleged by a house-maid that she was up at six, and that his bedroom door was then open; but this evidence is not considered trustworthy."

"I hope and trust that he has not resolved to vanish," said Bethiah. "I know that he did think of vanishing when his last miracle was accomplished."

"I should not think so," said Tom. "He packed up and took away all his things. The illustrious pretender who jumped into Etna took away nothing but his brazen slippers, which the volcano refused to keep, as useless. What does a volcano want with slippers? Paul took away a beautiful new portmanteau, large, and stuffed with things; and a lovely dressing-case crammed with silver things; and seal-skin coats and fur-lined coats, and gold-headed umbrellas. Oh, he hasn't vanished."

"Did he leave any letter?"

"Yes. He left a note for Lady Augusta, thanking her briefly for her great kindness to him during his stay."

"And what does Lady Augusta say?"

"She has come to the conclusion that his friends in Abyssinia have called him away, and that he is now sitting in a white linen robe, exchanging maxims with the Sage Izák Ibn Menelek. Mr. Brudenel is of the same opinion, and Lady Augusta talks of getting together the fragments of philosophic teaching which the young prophet has left behind—"

"Oh, Paul must see her," cried Bethiah, in distress. "He must tell her the truth. He *must*. Mr. Langston"—Bethiah turned to Tom with pleading eyes—"please try not to despise my poor boy too much. He was always imaginative and sensitive. I never saw anywhere a boy of quicker perceptions. He was like a girl for jumping straight at a conclusion. He was like a girl in many other ways. He hated rough work and rough talk. He was perfectly unfit to struggle with other men. As for money, there was not another American in the world who cared less about it and was less qualified to make money."

"Well—but—still—" said Tom.

"Wait a little, Mr. Langston. He left his native town—oh, why did we let him go?—at seventeen. He went to New York resolved to become a poet—all at once. He failed, of course. He spent his money and then fell into the hands of a man who called him his pupil, humored and encouraged him, and kept him ignorant of the world. Never was any boy so ignorant of the world as Paul. He knew nothing. This man, who must be a most dangerous, unscrupulous person, persuaded him that his power of magnetic influence could be made a lever by which he could conquer the world. Then he gradually encouraged him to set off the plain and simple mesmerism with all kinds of artifices and pretences. It was setting his own cleverness against the cleverness of the world, it was doing what all other men did, to pretend all kinds of knowledge in order to make use of the one kind they knew. For seven years this man used Paul; he kept him all the time apart from society, from papers, and from other young men; he exaggerated his importance and his reputation; he made the lad believe that he was an object of general admiration, and that the grandest thing in the world was to gain distinction as the possessor of supernatural powers. With this object everything was permissible. The man had an apt pupil. Paul has told me much, and I have *learned more from some* New York friends

now in London. It was the young Italian—he was called Signor Paolo—who attracted the people to the house where this pretender offered supernatural guidance to all who were willing to pay for it. They flocked to ask his advice, or to witness his marvellous quickness and readiness. The money flowed in; the old man has got it all, and will not give Paul any. Eight months ago they left New York for a tour in Europe, meaning, I suppose, to return with bigger pretences still. You know the rest."

"He certainly did pretend—tremendous," said Tom, persistently.

"If he pretends no more, Mr. Langston, will you forgive him?"

"Oh, forgive him? certainly, with the greatest pleasure," Tom replied, readily. "There is no question of forgiveness. I knew all along that he was humbugging us, and I set myself to find out. I liked the fellow, I confess, and we got chummy in the evenings, and I supposed he knew all the time what I thought of him. As for forgiving—why, I declare that nothing in the world ever astonished me so much as to see the way he took it when I showed him how it was done. The man actually fainted! Yet he must have known that I never took him seriously."

"He thought," said Bethiah, "that he had compelled you to take him seriously ; and I suppose—oh, I know the poor boy—I am certain that he concluded that you intended to expose him publicly and immediately, and he suddenly realized the shamefulness of the position and his own degradation."

"Again, touching forgiveness," Tom went on, "we are, on the other hand, deeply, very deeply indebted to him for saving a vast sum of money—all we had, some of us. To be sure, he made a miracle of it. What did that matter? In that house a miracle is neither here nor there. Sibyl has seen so many that she expects the order of things to be reversed rather than to follow in their usual sequence, whenever a new medium comes along. Of course, we despise the medium; but in his case we will separate the medium from the man beneath."

"We shall always be grateful to him," said Sibyl. "Whatever he does cannot destroy our indebtedness. If he marries our Hetty and gives up his old pretensions, he may be our friend if he likes."

"Not," said Tom, "that one would commonly choose for a friend a chap who has been convicted of tricks. Yet—hang it—Miss Ruysdael, we did get to like the fellow. And he really was more like a girl than a man, with his soft voice and his big eyes and his smooth cheek. One generally wants to take such a man by the coat-collar and shake him up. But he did not inspire that desire. I wonder where he is."

Things like this — simple things — are always being said at the right moment, so as to produce more of those coincidences for which this world is famous. We may have many failures—some of our brothers, for instance, are less beautiful than others—and the history of man is not a thing of which we can be altogether boastful; but we may be proud of our coincidences. These are served out abundantly, one a day, on an average, to every human creature."

At this moment a telegram was brought in, addressed to Miss Ruysdael:

"I am at the Langham Hotel. When can I see you?—Paul."

"There," said Bethiah, with a sigh of relief. "He has not vanished, then, or run away to hide himself. It is just like Paul to send for me. He used to do the same thing, long years ago, when he was a boy and in any trouble. I shall find him in a state of profound misery, full of self-accusation. Well, I know what to do with him."

"What will you do with him?"

"First, I must bring him here, and leave him alone to have it out with Hetty. He must tell her everything. If she forgives him, which I expect, I will arrange for us all three to go away at once. We will go back to America; but he must marry Hetty first, in order that he may have somebody always with him to have the care of him."

"Do you think he may refuse?" asked Tom.

"No, he can never go back to the old life. That is impossible. If I feared that, I would not suffer him to marry Hetty. But he must have some one always with him, if it is only to make him get up and go to bed at proper times, and see that he works in a healthy manner."

"What will he do, then?"

"For such a man as Paul there is only one kind of work possible. He must become a journalist and get on presently to become an author, perhaps, or a poet. It will not take Paul long to learn the trade, and he will get employment. Oh, Hetty and I have sketched it all out."

"But before he gets employment," said Sibyl, "he will want money. You must suffer us—in common gratitude—"

"No, Sibyl, no. He cannot take any of your money. Do not deprive him of the one consolation which remains. No one can say that he did which he did for money."

"But—through Hetty, for instance?"

"No. Not even through Hetty. There must be no question of money at all. He can never recover self-respect if he takes your money."

"You are right, I suppose. Only it seems cruel to let him go away in poverty."

"I am his sister. I have enough for all. Besides, there is his father."

"Then he has still a father?" said Tom.

"Deacon Trinder has the principal store in the town. He has put by dollars, I believe. How he will receive his son after seven years of silence I do not know."

"Trinder. Yes, he told me, the other day, that his patronymic was Trinder. Deacon Trinder—and a store— I suppose a village store, where tea and golden syrup and candles can be bought, and cotton stuffs and currants and ginger and flour and ham and cheese and ribbons and gloves?"

"Yes, and everything else," said Bethiah, laughing.

"It seems a drop from an unknown parentage and an education from the sages, doesn't it? Well, Miss Ruysdael, won't you let us help at all?"

"No. You must leave him to me, please. If you will see him, Mr. Langston, and shake hands with him before he goes, it would be kind. I don't know whether the recollection of the fact that you have treated him as a friend will help him out of his Slough of Despond or not; but it will be kind."

"In that case," said Tom, affably, "he is welcome to two shakes. Seriously, Miss Ruysdael, I shall always remember the Herr Paulus with admiration and gratitude. The happiness and joy I experienced when I found out how he sent my poor guardian off to Abyssinia, and stole away his senses, and yet made him do just exactly what he pleased, can never be forgotten. At the same time it is best for him to go away. Further acquaintance, after what has passed, would not be desirable, would it?"

"I fear not. There is another reason why Hetty must go. Most unfortunately, Paul found out her father, and took her to see him. Well, it is a great pity that he did it, because it seems that the fellow, who is quite a low kind of creature, wants Hetty to take up the spiritualistic business and run it with her mother in the States. He blusters and threatens all kinds of things, but, of course, that means nothing, except that we had better marry her at once, and then he can say no more."

"May I be allowed, good people," said Tom, unexpectedly, "to interrupt this conversation for the purpose of drawing a moral? Remark, if you please, that all the miracles performed by this great prophet have brought misfortune to some one. He miraculously shows Cicely her brother at sea, and unsettles her mind, which was beginning to be accustomed to his absence; then he brings my amiable cousin to see her. What happens? Percival bullies and frightens his sister, and rounds on Paul, calling him a liar and a deceiver and a medium's cad. There is a rich reward for a benevolent worker of miracles. Then he restores Hetty to her long-lost father's arms, and the father turns out to be a most undesirable person, who regards his daughter as the means of making large profits if she will lend herself to his untruthful ways. Then he introduces his host to his Eminence Cardinal or Archbishop Izák Ibn Menelek, the Falasha, commonly called Izák the Sage, who gives him gratuitous instructions every morning, and imparts wonders of the most astonishing depth. Unfortunately, the poor man, when the lesson is over, forgets it all immediately, and goes about as melancholy as King Nebuchadnezzar after his dream. He makes Mr. Brudenel, unknown to himself, write a letter ordering the sale of all his shares in a certain company; unluckily, the poor man has written two other letters on the same day, recommending two friends to buy shares in the same company, which bursts a fortnight later. Mr. Brudenel is saved, and his friends are ruined. Naturally, they ask the reasons why he sold out everything on the same day that he advised them to buy in; and when we say that the spirits wrote that letter for him they sniff. This miracle, of which I desire to speak with gratitude, was the most unlucky that poor Paul ever worked, because everybody knows now that he had been told, before Mr. Brudenel wrote that letter, what was the condition of the company; and besides, it afterwards covered him with confusion, because he now knows that I had found out how he did the trick. And there is no glory out of it at all, partly because we have not published any report of that miracle, which is a private and family miracle, and partly because, as I have said, we know how it was done. Then he brings the paper of the day all the way from India. Does he get any glory from it? Not a bit. They say, 'Do it again. If it is a genuine thing you can do it when you please. Produce your paper. Don't flourish a dated rag in our faces and snatch it away. Bring this day's paper from Delhi and let it lie on the table.' And he has not responded. Lastly, which puts on the coping-stone, the only natural and truthful and honest thing which he has done—his falling in love like a man—has destroyed the only power which he really possessed. He could influence some people —not all. He could magnetize them or mesmerize them, whatever you please to call it, *and now he cannot do that.* Never was a

prophet so *défroque.* I would advise you, my sisters, to take this lesson to your chamber and to meditate upon it, and when you wish—you, Sibyl, or you, Miss Ruysdael—to become a prophet, remember Paul, the son of Deacon Trinder."

To think that such a truly beautiful discourse should be delivered before an audience of two!

CHAPTER XII.

A PLENARY CONFESSION.

MANY sins shall be forgiven a man before he marries, provided there is a reasonable prospect of reformation. Hetty was about to hear a confession and to pronounce an absolution. The former brought as much shame to herself as to her lover, but the latter cost her little.

Bethiah brought Paul to the studio and went away, shutting the door upon Paul and Hetty. To be sure, she had prepared Hetty beforehand with such excuses and ways of putting things as might soften the blow. You have heard how she put the case to Tom.

"But," said Tom, "he did pretend—tremendous."

That was so. You may explain as elaborately as you please the process by which the wicked man arriveth at his wickedness; you may show how he was led by a tempter and driven by a fiend and enticed by a siren; you may show him poor, starving, and hopeless; you may explain how his conscience has been soothed and deadened, and how he has come to live in an enchanted castle. The fact remains that he has arrived at his wickedness. It is always an ugly fact; it cannot be righted; all we can do is to forgive it.

"And Hetty," Bethiah concluded, "whatever Paul has to say, remember that it is all finished and done with. No kind of temptation could ever make him repeat the past. My dear, no one hates Spiritualism more than you, except Paul. No one is more ashamed of it than you, except Paul. When you have told me about the shame and the sin of it, the pretences by which silly people are beguiled, and the preparation for the spontaneous manifestations, I have felt as if of all people in the world you were the most to be pitied; because there seemed no escape for you, anyhow, except to run clean away from all of it. I could not imagine a more horrible lot for any girl than to live half the day in the house where manifestations were prepared, and the other half where they were exhibited and believed. Paul's lot, however, is worse. You have not to reproach yourself. He knows how deeply he has impressed himself on the minds of his friends, and how the whole structure rests upon a colossal falsehood."

"Not the whole."

"Yes, the whole. Paul will tell you. He has promised me that he will hide nothing from you. The whole structure, my dear, and not a part only, as you think."

* * * * * *

The most terrible sight in the world—a thing which somehow covers one with shame only to witness—is that of a man confessing a shameful thing, feeling himself the whole shame and guilt of it. If there be really, as many still believe, a day in which the secrets of all hearts shall be laid open, it will be also, I am sure, a day in which the baseness of those secrets will be fully manifest to every man. We shrink from letting even our dearest friends know our own secret thoughts. But to think of the secrets of all hearts — all hearts — being laid open! Then the hero and the statesman and the philanthropist and the preacher and the sage will be on the level now occupied by the convict in prison and the convict out; and where the convict will be, Heaven knoweth, and we shall all be ashamed for one another as well as for ourselves; and poor Humanity shall hide her guilty head and cover her face and call upon the rocks to fall upon her. It is not enough, you see, to be forgiven. One has also to forgive one's self.

* * * * * *

"Yes, Paul; yes, oh, stop! I cannot bear it," cried Hetty, the tears flowing down her cheeks. "I cannot bear any more. Oh, to think that it is all deception—all! Oh, my poor mother! All is deception."

"I speak only of myself," he said. She was lying on the sofa—her face in her hands.

He stood over her, stooping, his hands clinched, his eyes stern and hard, his arms bent. It was as if he was accusing and vehemently reproaching her; but he was not. He was accusing himself, though every word fell upon the girl like a blow from a heavy stick.

"You must hear all," he repeated.

* * * * * *

Well, it was done. He had no more to say. He had confessed everything.

"Tell me to go, Hetty," he said, at last. She gave him her hand.

"You must go, Paul; but I must go with you."

"I loathe myself, Hetty. I could kill myself but for you, and for the thought that even by killing myself I should not escape."

"Oh, how dreadful—how terrible it is!" said the girl. "All my life I have had the horrible pretence about me, and I could never escape it. And to think that even the man who loves me — oh, who loves me — should have been dragged into it! Well! Oh, my poor Paul, shall we carry the sham spirits and the mock messages about with us? If we go away together, far away, where nobody will know my maiden name or your story, do you think that they will follow too, and will go on rapping messages and playing concertinas?"

"No, Hetty, no. We shall leave them behind us, and all the inventions and lies of the craft. We will go and live among the woods out of the reach of them. Only love me, Hetty, if you can, and forgive me."

"Oh, Paul, if I can love you!"

"And forgive me?" he repeated.

"If I can forgive you!" She laughed and cried together. "You do not understand, Paul. There is nothing that I could not forgive you, even if you went back to the old life. I could forgive everything, even if it broke my heart."

"My dear, what should I deserve if I went back to the old life?" He had been bending humbly over her. Now he suddenly sprang upright and threw out his arms. "Oh," he cried, "it is all gone. I feel like Christian when he threw off his bundle. I am breathing a purer air already. I broke the last chain that bound me when I told you the whole. Help to make me forgive myself— and forget, Hetty. Lift up your head, dear. These shall be the last tears you shall shed for me. Kiss me. Let us talk of this new life. Bethiah says that you will take care of me. She says that I know nothing. You will teach me, then? I am not afraid of work, though I do not know what work you will set me to do. Only find me work, even if it is only rail-splitting, and I will do it for you, Hetty. What a fool I was! And all seemed so grand that nothing but supernatural assistance could account for it. I was in a Fool's Paradise, and the way out of Fool's Paradise is through briers and brambles, and across the Great Dismal Swamp."

* * * * * *

Well, he had said all he had to say, and Hetty loved him still. She loved him, I think, all the more, because of the courage of this self-inflicted humiliation. Many sins, I said, will be forgiven before marriage. After marriage they are condoned — which is not quite the same thing — or passively endured, or even accepted as part of life. Even suburban builders, I believe, have wives.

It happened while this pair of lovers sat hand-in-hand, with tearful eyes and softened hearts, whispering to each other words of consolation and hope, that Mr. Medlock, returning home, learned that his daughter was sitting alone with her fiancé in Miss Ruysdael's room. At ordinary times this information would have caused him to respect the sanctity of the room with the greatest carefulness, because, you see, he was afraid of his daughter. But this afternoon he felt bold. Perhaps he had acquired courage after the manner erroneously attributed to the Hollander, though a single glass of hot rum-and-water with a slice of lemon and one lump of sugar is nothing but an old-fashioned stomachic after an early dinner, like your worship's glass of port, and, I doubt not, affects the head no more. Perhaps, however, the chance of introducing the subject emboldened him.

Hetty indeed showed in her outward carriage little or no respect for her father. She knew what he wanted her to do—how could she respect him? And he was so mean of aspect and of manner; and he had lived such an ignoble life. To travel around with a show; to lecture at a panorama; to lead about a giant or a dwarf; to companionize a two-headed nightingale—it is not immoral, but it is not ennobling. And to ask your daughter to go on a platform as a clairvoyant is to deprive yourself of all the privileges conferred by the Fifth Commandment.

Mr. Medlock, as we know, had been arranging a little scheme for the future; the programme, in fact, of a show which for talent and completeness would eclipse every Spiritualist caravan ever wheeled before the public. Lavinia, as the Sibyl in extreme age, in crimson velvet; Hetty the world-renowned clairvoyant; the Signor Paolo, already famous from the Pacific to the Atlantic shores, in direct communication with spirits who cannot lie, with himself as the illustrious craniologist, professor of palmistry, or graphiologists, as the case might be. The prospect was splendid. And now the most important member of the company was engaged to his daughter, and was at that moment under his own roof, courting his own gal, and no doubt in an amiable and yielding mood. Mr. Medlock thereupon tapped at the door and coughed. To cough when you rap at a door is—I don't know why—the surest sign of the suppliant. The man who would like something on account, something in advance, a temporary loan, an interview for an explanation, always coughs when he knocks at the door. As no one replied, Mr. Medlock turned the handle and opened the door.

Hetty drew her hand from her lover's and rose from the sofa where they were sitting.

"Do you want anything?" she asked, with *severity.* "This is Miss Ruysdael's room."

"I wish, my dear," he replied—a girl ought not be taller than her own father. "I came"—nor ought she to look at a parent in such a terrifying manner. "I am sorry to interrupt. I was wishful of a few words with your—my intended son-in-law, Hetty. A few words only." He coughed again, behind his hand, in an exasperating way. There was really very little to be proud of in his personal appearance.

Hetty turned to Paul.

"This is my father," she said, with the least possible emphasis of the pronoun, as if to convey that in the matter of fathers she was not richly endowed, "and he has something to communicate to you, Paul—a proposition of some kind to make. In fact, I know what it is, but I think you may as well hear it." One must not condemn any proposition unheard; but there was something about the young lady's tone which did convey unqualified condemnation of that proposition beforehand.

"Well, sir?" Paul rose and offered his hand; it was perhaps remarkable that in returning to the world of the phenomenal—the every-day world—he had also returned to a strongly marked American manner of speech. "Well, sir, what can I do for you—or you for me?"

"We can do, sir, a great deal for each other. We can make ourselves indispensable to each other. That I shall be able to prove to you in a very few words."

"Very well, sir. You remember, when you called upon my old master, the professor, a fortnight or so since, you had a talk with him and you made him a proposition."

"I did. It is quite true. He knows everything, Hetty—everything. That's what they used to say of him in New York. No question but he had an answer to it, and always right." Hetty looked anxious, but only for a moment.

"I am right now," Paul said, quietly, "because I was in the other room and the door was open,and I heard what you said." Hetty's face indicated relief. "Therefore, I know beforehand what you have been doing in the States, and what you would like to do when you go back—so far as I myself am concerned."

"And will do, sir; and will do," said the little man, kindling with enthusiasm at what looked like a good beginning. "You have no idea—you can't have any idea—of the splendid success that I will make of you."

"Pray go on, Mr. Medlock."

"I take it, sir, that in your last show—I mean in the salon where you received the cream of the New York aristocracy—pretty much all the money went to the boss."

"You have no right to say that," Hetty interrupted.

"Well, I've been assistant, and I ought to know, and so far as I do know, nearly all the money does go to the boss. It did wherever I was assistant."

"Go on," said Paul.

"What I say is this, then—leave the old man. Run your own show. Leave the old man. Get a man who knows his way about to run it for you."

"Meaning yourself."

"I do mean myself. I couldn't mean a better man for the work. I know pretty well every town in America, if you conclude to travel, and I know my way about New York, or Philadelphia either, if you conclude to stay there. You are going to marry my daughter, sir, I believe?"

"I am," said Paul, "since your daughter consents."

"She ought to consent with pride and alacrity. I should, if I were my daughter."

"If you were, I should not ask you," said Paul.

"Well, sir, well! I won't insist on my rights as a father. I've been too long separated from my child to exercise those rights. I know that very well. But I ask you, sir —I put it to you as a reasonable man—here are you—A 1, tip-top of the profession, the cleverest and the most envied man of all, on the highest rung. I grant all that. The connection, I admit, brings honor to us all." Paul looked at Hetty with a smile of the sadder kind. "But there's another side. What is talent unless it's stage-managed and business-managed? Wasted, lost, thrown away. That's where I come in. Signor Paolo's agent is his father-in-law, experienced and tried and zealous. What is talent run by itself? Soon worn out; worn to death. That's where your mother-in-law steps in. See at a circus. Between the really creditable bits the clown runs round—anybody can run round—and the young lady jumps through the hoops—any girl can jump through hoops —and they're just as well pleased. Lavinia, with a white wig and crimson velvet, will hold one of her celebrated séances while you are resting. I assure you, sir, that got up in a white wig—and plenty of it—and in crimson velvet, with heavy gold chains and plenty of them, your mother-in-law would rake 'em in. She would, indeed. There's very little new to be had, in reality; but your manager will always be putting up old things in new dresses. And then there's Hetty. You are aware, sir, that my daughter has the making in her of a really first-class clairvoyant. In your hands she would develop into the best clairvoyant in the world. A good clairvoy-

ant is scarce. I don't quite know where to lay my hand on one that I could confidently put forward. But Hetty! Look at her, sir. Look at her figure and her face. Look at her eyes—"

"Paul!"

"You have said quite enough, Mr. Medlock," said Paul. "It is useless to go on, because our minds are made up. Nothing would induce your daughter to play the part you propose—nothing in the world. That is fixed and decisive, and nothing would induce her to allow me to continue in the—profession—you called it. Therefore—"

"Leave the profession? You to leave the profession? The great Signor Paolo to leave the profession? Why, you must—but perhaps you have made your fortune?"

"No, I have not."

"Then why—why?"

"Because it is—the profession. That is why. I do not think you would understand any other reason."

"Leave the profession! And haven't made your fortune! Then, sir, I'm hanged if you shall marry my daughter!"

Hetty laughed. It is wrong to laugh at your own father, but she did laugh.

"I think there is no good in talking about it any more," said Paul, quietly. "Your daughter is of age. Will you leave us now, Mr. Medlock?"

"Hetty," he said, "I could laugh at the poor man; I could laugh at the whole business. Now, alas! we can never laugh at it, either of us, even in the future, however far back in our lives it has receded. Kiss me, Hetty. Oh, let us get away quickly; let us begin our new life as soon as ever we can."

CHAPTER XIII.

THE CONFERENCE.

THINGS have got to such a pass with conferences that the papers refuse any longer to report them. This is sad, because in former days many a small man thought to become great, and many a weak man thought himself strong, merely by dint of reading at a conference papers which the wicked favoritism of editors would not allow to be published. Also, the conference gave all who were present and whose names were reported, the consciousness to themselves, and the appearance to others, of belonging to the van of science and progress. Conferences, as a natural consequence, are falling into discredit. One conference, formerly famous, has been abandoned in disgust, after it became a bore, not only to the general public, but even to its own friends.

The Conference of Spiritualists, held last

May, although a most important and truly representative gathering, was not reported by the morning papers. That is the reason why a certain remarkable incident, which shall be faithfully recorded here, made no impression on the public mind. One or two of the evening papers, to be sure, accorded some slight notice to the meeting. The *St. James's*, in a nasty, sneering one, made the noses of all those who took part in the Conference to swell and burn. The *Pall Mall*, in a short article, gibed at the President, and asked the usual stale old questions as to the practical outcome of so many years' messages. It is, however, better to be derided than neglected. Ridicule calls attention; misrepresentation allows an answer. It is silence which is deadly. Reporters were not sent to this Conference. And yet the subjects prepared for discussion — there was not time for all of them—covered nearly the whole field once contemplated by the student who proposed to write the History of Human Error. Had the programme been carried out in its entirety, the Conference would be sitting to this day. Among the subjects, men, and peoples set down for discussion were the Chaldeans, the Sabeans, the Cabeiri, the Eleusinian Mysteries, the Cabalists, the Magi, the Essenes, the Esoteric Buddhists, the Zendavesta, Confucius, Zoroaster, Pythagoras, apparitions, telepathy, incarnated spirits, spirit pictures, spirit writing, Madame Blavatzky — but not Madame Colomb—dreams, clairvoyance, the Brotherhood of the Rosy Cross, the Secret of the Rose, Theosophy, Cornelius Agrippa, Lilith and the Larvæ, Akaz, Yogi, Koot Houm, Karma, Hermes, Mithra, the Rod of Jacob, Invocation, Evocation, the Pentagram, the Book of Thoth, Mesmerism, Astrology, Second Sight, Palmistry, Healing by Will, the Works of Eliphaz, the Teraphim, Abracadabra, and the Astral Light; not to speak of Nostradamus, Mother Shipton, and Old Moore—and without mentioning those who came on the chance of being heard as to the Israelitish origin of the British people.

The Conference lasted a week, during which these and many kindred subjects were discussed. When the meeting broke up, the members, wearied, but not satiated, agreed that on the score of unanimity the Conference had been a most wonderful success. No nasty scientific man or philosopher (foolishly so called) had got up to question and contradict; the carping and critical spirit was conspicuously absent; none—which was most remarkable—came to mock; none stayed to deride; and, but for one single hitch, the progress of business was throughout uninterrupted and smooth. Nay, the only thing *that was wanting*, those who were present

agreed, was more discussion. If any fault could be found with the Conference it was that the leaders, those who had been invited to read papers, showed undisguised impatience with the papers which preceded theirs, and did not pretend any interest in any subject outside their own. This gave an air of haste and breathlessness to the meetings; a lack of personal dignity was observed; the more sober among the audience lamented that time was not given for discussion and comparison of arguments. Papers concerning the unseen world ought not to be read and then pushed aside as if they were merely papers in the *Contemporary* and the *Nineteenth Century* dealing with the things of this world.

The papers read at the Conference will, however, be published before long, when men from the ends of the earth will no doubt read them. It is a favorite delusion with people that if they once get a thing printed all the world will read it. I know a man who once wrote a book, proving conclusively, beyond every possibility of doubt, that what the world wants in order to be completely happy, and to get the full flavor out of every hour as it hurries past, is to—but on this point I refer you to his book. It was published at his own expense by a very eminent firm of publishers fifteen years ago. Strange to say, the world has never made the least move in the direction indicated by that book. "And," he says, reproachfully, "my book has been in their hands all these years!" So it has, in a way of speaking. "In their hands!" Oh, those careless hands! In fifteen years fifteen thousand books have been placed in those hands; and the hands go on just as if they had not had more than half a dozen given to them.

One cannot report the whole, or even a sixth part of this Conference. I have only to narrate the exact circumstances relating to the single hitch which occurred at the first morning's meeting.

The hall, a room of some size, was what reporters call well filled; that is to say, there was plenty of sitting-room for every one, and the galleries were half occupied. A well-filled room. And all of them, apparently, ladies and gentlemen; that is to say, they were well dressed and well behaved. Any one not *en rapport* with the meeting would have observed a fidgety manner, as if everybody had, more or less, got the jumps. Some there were who closed their eyes in silent meditation; others there were whose eyes glowed with a strange brightness; these were restless, and got up and down and changed their seats; others, again, sat waiting in impatience for the expected rapture that would seize their souls at the right moment. For a meeting can be magnetized even more easily than a single person, and presently, when the right man speaks with the right voice, and the right gaze which meets and holds every eye, you shall see this multitude awed and subdued into calm, the bright, unsteady eyes fixed, the lips parted, the heart glowing, the soul in a brief ecstasy. Such things sober men have recorded; mankind is emotional; it is with all of us even as with the dervises or with the Hallelujah lasses when the contagion of emotion spreads from bench to bench. The platform was occupied by the leaders, among them our friends Mr. Athelstan Kilburn, the Rev. Amelius Horton—he was going to read a paper on his own miraculous gift of healing—the Rev. Benjamin Rudge, and Mr. Emmanuel Chick. In the body of the hall were to be observed Lavinia Medlock, her husband, and Mr. James Berry. Hetty was not there, but Sibyl, the infidel, had brought Cicely. Mrs. Tracy Hanley was also present. At the stroke of ten the President, Mr. Cyrus Brudenel, accompanied by his wife, Lady Augusta, and followed by the Honorary Secretary, appeared upon the platform, and with some applause from the audience took the chair.

Then, after the preliminary look around—which no president ever neglects—it is a reminiscence of the school-master's habit of looking round to see that every boy is in his place—Mr. Brudenel rose and delivered the opening address. In every address there are interesting parts and flat parts. Let us confine our report to one or two of the most interesting parts.

"Friends and fellow-students," he began, pleased at the number of his audience and warned by the visible proof of so large a sympathy. "Friends and fellow-students, let us congratulate ourselves upon the magnitude and importance of this meeting, as proved by numbers only. For the first time in history, we, who devote our lives to spiritual research and endeavor, after deeper and closer and readier communication with the other world, meet openly in public without fear of repression or derision. Four hundred years ago they would have burned us as sorcerers and witches; two hundred years ago we should have been a small, obscure body, unable to meet, because unconscious of one another's existence; one hundred years ago, those who still kept alive the sacred Lamp were reduced almost to the point of extinction—only here and there one who prevented the spark from vanishing and fed the feeble light which to the outer world seemed extinguished forever. One hundred years ago? Why, no one believed that we were still surviving. Our cause was a byword. Even fifty years ago, when some of us were boys, what was the condition of the Spiritualists? They were absolutely unknown. Literature had ceased to speak of them. Ridicule no longer clung to them, because they were not believed to exist. They were considered to belong to the Dark Ages. Godwin's "Lives of the Necromancers" sufficiently attests the low estimation—the contempt—in which they were held. Suppose this congress had been summoned fifty years ago, how many would have attended? Who would have been invited to speak? In some obscure college room at Oxford or Cambridge there would have been found, sitting among his old books, one here or there who knew something of the Mysteries, and knew what was meant by Initiation and what by communication with the spirits—but he would not dare to speak of these things in the hall or the combination room. He would have been locked up as a madman. Yet, fellow-students, look at us to-day."

The President then proceeded to sketch briefly the history of modern Spiritualism from its revival in 1847, when the famous rappings were first heard in America, to the present time, dwelling upon the wonderful development of communications and the vast strides made in so short a period, so that if the same rate of progress be maintained, we may hope, he said, within a hundred years, to combine with the spirits as freely as with one another, in which case all our books may be burned, because all the learning that we want will be derived at will and just for the trouble of asking from those unearthly teachers. He also took the opportunity of naming, with the highest praise, those immortal pioneers who have one after another taken up the cause and labored to reduce a mere series of experiments to an exact science. Among these he did not omit the illustrious Sludge (commemorated in Browning's deathless verse), the devoted Home, Slade the spotless, Emmanuel Chick, and Lavinia Medlock. "These men and women," he acknowledged, "have had, it is true, during their professional career, to contend with much misrepresentation; they have met with ridicule; their motives have been distorted and derided; the facts of the manifestations have been doubted; their good faith has been denied; their antecedents have been inquired into and misstated. In short, they have encountered enemies and detractors. All great men do. What then? Truth will prevail. We can afford to wait, even to wait long after this life."

He then dwelt upon the great advance made during the last few years, speaking from his own knowledge of the power possessed by Emmanuel Chick and by Lavinia Medlock among the mediums of the day. This was kind of him, because everybody knew that he had now deserted the old paths and begun to consult other oracles.

"But now, fellow-students, I have to speak of events which have happened, not only to my own knowledge and under my own eyes, but actually to myself and to those of my own household. What follows is a history.

"Many of you have heard part of this history. Things have been whispered about. Nay, the papers have given garbled and imperfect notes of what has been done in my house. But it has been left for this Conference to hear the truth concerning the most wonderful, the most startling, the most extraordinary manifestations of modern times.

"We heard from St. Petersburg from our friend, Anna Petrovna, that we were to receive a visit from a young Spiritualist of whose powers she spoke in terms which excited our highest expectations. He spoke, she said, all languages equally well, but only that of the country where he happened to be for the time. With her he would speak Russian; with us he would speak English. He was coming to England charged with a message to me and to my household. There would be no question at all of money. I was not to offer him fees or payment of any kind; his wants were amply provided for, and she begged us to receive him as a person of the highest distinction, whose stay would confer great honor upon us.

"We expected our guest with impatience; we received him with delight. We were not disappointed in him. We found a young man, apparently not five-and-twenty, possessed of manners which were charming, good-breeding, the self-possession which comes of belonging by birth to the best society, and of a beauty which I can only describe as supernatural. I have seen nothing in earthly faces which I can compare with the face of our visitor. His voice was soft and musical, and the sight of his eyes, soft and lustrous, yet full of power and authority, commanded respect and awe. For six weeks or so we were ravished out of ourselves by a continued series of manifestations, the like of which we had never before experienced. Paul—he allowed us to Anglicize the German form of his name, Herr Paulus—first proved his powers by reading a girl's thoughts, and then showing them actually photographed: we have seen thought-reading and recognized it as a branch, and no mean branch, of communion between soul and soul, but we had never before seen such *a thing as spirit* photography applied to

thought-reading. Again, he made a blind girl see her brother, then at sea; and he photographed the picture of what she saw. On another occasion he annihilated space and time, and actually placed in our astonished hands the daily paper—that very morning's issue—published at Delhi. There were many persons present at this miracle, among them scientific professors of the highest repute. I have not heard that any attempt has been made to explain the method of accomplishing this marvel, though I have heard a demand to have it repeated. It is always the way. When we tell the world of some new and startling manifestation, we are desired to do it again. I dare say it will be done again, but we Spiritualists prefer to move in our own way. We shall not be bullied or driven into experiments which our friends on the other side do not appreciate.

"Again, Paul healed the sick. Not those who had diseases for which the surgeon is wanted, but those who suffered from disorders of a nervous nature, such as Spiritualists are able to relieve. Those who had neuralgia, toothache, headache, and ailments of like nature, Paul restored to health by the simple exercise of will.

"Again—and this I declare solemnly to you as my own personal experience—Paul brought me an invitation from one of the friends resident in Abyssinia that I would visit him every morning to converse upon the divine philosophy of which we hear so much and know so little. Fellow-students, I rejoice to be able to affirm that I have spent morning after morning in a certain valley in that far-off country, beside a stream with the venerable Izák Ibn Menelek, in such discussion as lifts up the soul and enlarges the mind. It will be my privilege and my happiness to write down for the benefit of the whole world the teaching of that sage as soon —as soon "—here the President's eyes grew troubled, and he tapped his knuckles with his eye-glasses—"as soon as my mind can free itself from the splendor and the intoxication of that wisdom, and settle down calmly to write. There is one thing more. Finally, my new friends, finding out the actual financial position of a certain company— perhaps you know the company—in which I had invested the whole fortunes of my two wards and my daughter, caused me, without my knowledge, to write letters commanding the sale of those investments. My fellow-students, on the day on which, unconsciously, I wrote—if I did write—those letters, I also, consciously and in good faith, wrote two others recommending the purchase of shares in that very company, so strong was my belief in its stability. My friends took my advice, I deeply regret to say, and suffered. The orders to sell were obeyed, and my wards were saved.

"Ladies and gentlemen, most of us here present have long felt convinced of the reality of spirit communications. Many among us, I say, have long been standing with their feet planted upon the solid rock. Others there are, perhaps, of—of—lesser faith, who require a succession of manifestations in order to make them constantly realize the presence of the spirits about us, around us, over us. There are, again, others, of whom I am one, consistent and complete believers, whose minds are filled with those evidences of sight, touch, and hearing which nothing can overcome, who yet are always delighted to hail every new brother in the craft and to recognize every new manifestation, however crude and simple, provided that it be only genuine.

"I ask you," he continued, waxing eloquent, "if anything short of supernatural force—energy—will—call it what you please, so long as you admit that it was something supernatural, over and beyond the powers and perceptions of ordinary man—I ask you, I say, if anything short of supernatural force can account for these miracles? Has any thought-reader before this made a girl tell what was in her mind and then show those present her thoughts photographed? Has any Spiritualist before this ever made a blind girl see, and shown a photograph of her vision? Has any occult philosopher—of whose miracles we hear much—ever produced in India the London *Times* of that very day? Never; they have been challenged to do so, and they cannot. Their powers do not extend so far—as yet. This proves that the wisdom of the Abyssinian is greater than the wisdom of the Thibetan, as we might expect. There are, it is true, some who have the gift of healing—our friend, Mr. Amelius Horton, is one of those rarely gifted men; but I have never seen the exercise of that gift so spontaneous, so free, so ready, as by my young philosopher, Herr Paulus. As for the other thing — the interposition of his friends, without his knowledge, to save my children's fortune—it speaks for itself. That these things have been done; that they have been attested by witnesses hostile as well as friendly; that they are not to be challenged by the most determined enemy of our cause, marks, I declare, a step upward, which lands us all upon a higher plane." He spread his arms and threw back his head as if to breathe the purer and rarer air upon that elevation.

"Upon this plane—nay, I know and feel—we shall commence with a nobler kind of spirit and more easily and more freely than before. We all know that we have been frequently misled and betrayed by mocking and mendacious spirits. It is reasonable to hope that on this higher plane they will not be permitted to dwell—unless that vision of Swedenborg's is true which showed the spirits choosing the planes on which they would dwell, and being compelled by their nature to dwell only on those which fitted their stage of development. Think, my friends, oh, think of the time when we shall all converse freely and uninterruptedly with the spirits of the wise, of the just and righteous, of those whom we have loved. We shall be face to face with them. We shall see them, I am well assured, as well as talk with them. When death lays us low our spirits will join them, and the living and the dead shall not be separated even for an instant. Then all will seek the higher life, because it will be a shame in the eyes of those who see all that we do, and know all that we think, to lead the lower life. There will be nothing but emulation of all the virtues, with meditative study, and striving after truth. The old will not regret their youth, because before their death they see and feel the joys of the other world.

"All this, we knew, was to come some time or other. It has already come. The man who brought this power to us is Herr Paulus. Let us, before we proceed to the business of the meeting of which this story is, I am sure, a welcome witness, pass our best thanks to Herr Paulus."

The motion was carried by acclamation.

"I may, therefore," said the President, smiling sweetly, "convey to Herr Paulus the fact that it is your pleasure to thank him for what he has done, and done so well. I must, however, tell you one very singular circumstance connected with this business. To my mind this circumstance corroborates and confirms all that went before. Herr Paulus assured us when he came that he was a messenger only; he brought a message; he showed his credentials in the powers which he possessed. Very well. During the time that he was delivering this message he had lost his memory as to himself and his antecedents; he knew nothing; he could not tell how he had been taken to Abyssinia or by whom, or from which country; he had no parents and no relations; he spoke and wrote all languages equally well as the occasion demanded. In Russia he spoke Russian; in Germany, German; in France, French; in England, English; and in each country he could speak only the language of that country. Observe: The moment the message was delivered, and what he had been sent to do had been accomplished, he lost all his powers; he could do nothing; he became like any ordinary young man; he is no longer now a medium.

"More than this. He began to lose the memory of what he had done, and why it had been done, and everything; and he began to remember about himself and his early life—interesting, but not remarkable or unusual. He was, in fact, a messenger caught in Russia, I believe, carried away in the spirit to Abyssinia, charged with powers and with knowledge, and conveyed to my house for the execution and delivery of the message. The wise men might have chosen any other mode of conveying that message. It is no business of ours to ask why they chose that particular way. I take it that a message delivered through a young man, handsome and well-mannered, attractive in himself, would commend itself to us more readily than the same message delivered, say, by means of the ordinary medium. However, I state the plain fact. Your vote of thanks shall be conveyed by me to Herr Paulus. We will now, ladies and gentlemen, proceed to the regular order of the day. The programme before us is a very heavy one. Those who have prepared papers are invited to read only essential parts, and if we have time for discussion I beg that speakers will be brief, and confine themselves strictly to the points in question. I now call upon the Rev. Amelius Horton to read a paper on 'Healing by Will.'"

The senior fellow of King Henry's rose and stepped to the front with a sweet smile and a roll of paper, which he began to unfold. No practised speaker unfolds his papers until it is time to begin. In all public performances there are certain little ceremonies which the actor calls "business." The popular statesman, for instance, likes to arrive a little late, so as to come on after the minor stars are seated. Therefore Mr. Horton, while standing before the expectant audience, began by unrolling and smoothing out his papers. That would make them expect a little longer, and enjoy all the more whatever might follow.

He had, however, to postpone that paper for a few minutes; for while he stood there a young man, whom no one had noticed sitting just below, rose and leaped upon the platform.

"Mr. President," he said, "I beg permission to say a few words in this room before the proceedings go on. Ladies and gentlemen, I *am* Herr Paulus."

The President turned very red and then pale.

"*Paul,*" he whispered hoarsely, not loud *enough for the people* in the front part of the

hall to hear, "Paul, sit down or go away. Do not speak, I implore you."

"I must speak."

"Ladies and gentlemen"—the President rose with some dignity—"Herr Paulus cannot be refused a hearing after what has been said about him. You will, however, remember what I told you. He has unfortunately lost those powers which were lent to him for a time and for a purpose."

"I have a confession to make," said Paul, lifting his head quickly.

The appearance of the young man startled everybody, and there was a dead silence, and the young girls murmured "Oh!" softly, and without looking at one another, because he was so beautiful a young man. No young man in a picture—not even in the old steel-engraving days, when they could put so dazzling a gleam into the eyes, and so soft a light over the brow, and such a romantic dimple in the chin, and such a careless wave in the hair, and such genius in the necktie tied in a sailor's knot—ever looked so romantic and so beautiful as Herr Paulus, the messenger of the wise men, standing on that platform. Sibyl only, by the red spot in his cheeks, knew what it cost him to stand there—in a pillory of his own making, where the bad eggs and the dead cats, and the putrid fowls and the rotten apples would be represented by eyes—the eyes of the assembled two thousand—full of contempt and loathing.

"My confession," he said, "is this: Two months ago I came to England in the hope and with the design of making a great *coup* —not of money, but of what could afterwards be turned into money. I resolved to achieve something that could not in any possible hypothesis be explained except by the admission of supernatural force. Science was not to be able to suggest anything. It was to be something outside the ordinary phenomena of Spiritualists. When it was done, I thought, I would vanish suddenly and be no more seen; or I would go away and return to New York, flushed with a triumph which would raise me head and shoulders above my brother Spiritualists. You have heard what I did."

"I think it right," said the President, "to remind the audience again of what I have already twice told them. I mean that this young gentleman has clean forgotten the powers which once he exercised, and now cannot understand or believe the things that he achieved."

"I do not wish to take up the time of the meeting," Paul went on, as if the President had not spoken. "I have only to explain that the things I accomplished were such as everybody could do with the aid of an accomplishment which most people can have if they set themselves to work. I was a mesmerist—I understood, in practice, what you call the art of mesmerism. I had worked for seven years on the subject, making experiments of all kinds. I succeeded in being able to make those persons who became subject to me think and do exactly as I pleased. I also succeeded in making them remember what I had made them think. You now understand that I had in my hands an instrument of tremendous power, provided I could subject a sufficient number of persons. In this English household, to which I introduced myself, I subjected every person except two. Had I succeeded with those two, you would have heard tales of mystery compared with which your President's history would have appeared commonplace. But these two persons defied me. I never acquired the least control over them; and one of them was always on the watch to find me out. He did find out, in fact, how I accomplished the great feat of saving the fortunes of himself and the two young ladies. Remember, I could mesmerize. That was the foundation of everything. That explains everything. I made the blind girl see her brother. I knew where the man was, and I had prepared the photograph beforehand. I mesmerized Mr. Brudenel, and made him write at my dictation; and before I brought him back I·filled his mind with the rigmarole about Abyssinia. He thinks he went there every morning. He never went anywhere; he sat in his chair, magnetized, in a mesmeric sleep every day. As for the Indian paper, it was a mere trick. The paper had the imprint, and the appearance of the day and the place, but inside there was nothing. I took care that it should not be opened, and while they talked I put it back in my pocket. All that was done by me in that house was sheer pretence and trickery. You ask me how I dare to stand before you and make this confession? I dare it because I have left the ranks of the charlatans. I am no longer a medium. As for your Spiritualism, I neither believe it, nor do I disbelieve it. But one thing I know well. In America, where there are many mediums, there is not one who has not been charged, some time or other, with fraud and falsehood. There is not one who can boast a clear record. And another thing I know full well. There is not a single message purporting to come from the spirits which has advanced human knowledge one single inch, or that has been above the intellect of the man or woman whose mediumship was employed. You may argue that Spiritualism places the immortality of the soul beyond possible doubt or question. Why so? Because you believe in your

mediums. How much safer are you than the Christians who believe in Christ and his apostles?"

"I will say little more. In your presence I declare that this confession of mine is literally and exactly true. In your presence I humbly ask pardon of Lady Augusta first, of Mr. Cyrus Brudenel next, and of all those who constitute his household, for intruding my unworthy presence into their house, and for the long series of deceptions and falsehoods which I carried on. I am going away, and I shall never return to a city which would always remind me of a shameful past. Before I depart I make submission and confession."

He bowed low—first to the audience, and then to Lady Augusta, and then to the President.

"Paul!" cried Lady Augusta.

He bowed a second time, but made no reply. Then he slowly descended the steps, and walked with bowed head through the wondering assemblage.

Then Lady Augusta sprang to her feet.

"I *must* speak," she cried. "Never before have I spoken in public, and never again shall I speak. You have heard that unhappy boy. He has lost his powers, and he tries to account for what he did by a theory of magnetic influence. Do not his very words—the part of his confession which was wrung from him—the acknowledgment of the facts—prove his supernatural possession? That possession has left him. He has a confused memory of what happened. He knows that in New York he practised Spiritualism and used magnetic influence—whether for purposes of fraud, I do not know; and the rest he cannot understand. Oh, I knew all along that this man was not himself. No young man could speak as he spoke; no mere youth could make our hearts glow as Paul made the hearts of those who heard him. Never, I think, did any man rise to such lofty heights of wisdom and fill his hearers with visions of the glories and splendors of the other world. Our Paul has gone—you have seen his shell. It is now a shell filled with a commonplace soul, no whit above his fellows, and perhaps below them. But while he stayed with us—a time never to be forgotten—we were rapt into heaven. It was not the manifestation of power which enthralled us—it was the voice of this man. You have heard but the faintest echo of the music of that voice—it was the beauty of the man's face. You will never see the splendor of that beauty—it was the depth, the love, the holiness of his eyes, wherein lay all wisdom. You will never see those eyes. He has gone—our Paul has gone. Sad—sad to think that this shell has not gone too. I pray you, oh, my friends and fellow-seekers, let not the words of that young American who has just left this room trouble you. We who have heard—have seen—who can testify—we only know how false are those words—how utterly meaningless they are to explain the wonder and the mystery, the heights and the depths of the Heavenly Wisdom which Paul was sent to teach us. My husband and I are now endeavoring to commit to paper such of those utterances which we can remember. Alas! would that we had known how short a time he would be with us! One thing comforts us. He promised, before his powers left him, that his friends would give us the Book of the Ancient Wisdom, the same which was written by King Solomon himself and given by the first priest Isaac to Menelek, Prince of Abyssinia. We await that gift."

Lady Augusta resumed her seat. She had spoken with such vehemence, with such earnestness of words and gestures and looks that she carried her audience completely away. The young American who had just left them was an impostor and a charlatan—he was only the shell of Paul, and the real Paul had gone to join his friends, the sages of the Ancient Way. They breathed again; confidence was restored. They were no longer a flock of silly sheep following any leader who led the way. The dismay and doubt which had been caused by that confession vanished, and they were again ready for more.

The President rose and replaced the glasses with which he had been tapping his knuckles.

"My friends," he said, "you have heard my wife. I am quite certain that there is now no doubt in any of our hearts. The true Paul has gone from us—for a time only, we hope; let the shell, the shell"—they all felt an infinite contempt for the shell—"depart in peace. But as the result of the teachings and the manifestations of our Paul, we stand—we stand, I say—upon the solid rock.

"We will now proceed to the order of the day. Once more I call upon the Rev. Amelius Horton to read us his paper on 'Healing by Will.'"

"Take me out, Sibyl," Cicely whispered. "If I stay here I shall suffocate. Take me out quickly."

Sibyl led her out and they drove home. In the carriage Cicely said nothing, but sat with clasped hands and trembling lips.

Hetty was in her room. She had been crying, and the tears were still in her eyes.

"Oh, Cicely!" she said, "Poor Cicely!"

"I have heard him," said Cicely. "Hetty, will you take a message to him from me?"

"Yes," said Hetty, humbly.

"Tell him that I loved him, Hetty. Not as you do, dear, because you love the man—I loved the teacher. Tell him that at the fall of his foot and the sound of his voice my pulse quickened, and my cheeks glowed, and my heart rose higher within me. Tell him that he has given me new thoughts and nobler thoughts. Tell him that many things which before had no meaning to me are now plain and clear."

"Yes," said Hetty, "I will tell him all you say, dear."

"Tell him that I can never forget the things he taught me. For the sake of them I shall go on loving his memory. And as for the things he told us to-day—if they are true—"

"They are true," said Hetty. "Alas! they are all quite, quite true."

"Then I pity and forgive him. I could not see him again—it would be too much to hear his voice and to think that he was ever playing a part; but no—he was not—he was speaking from his heart. Oh, Hetty, tell him that I forgive him."

"I will tell him, Cicely. There is something that I should like to tell you—something which he said last night—if you will hear it."

"Tell it, dear."

"I was asking him how it was that he was able to carry us out of ourselves while he told us those things which we both remember, Cicely. He said that we were not carried out of ourselves at all; it was the elevation of the soul caused by the contemplation of things spiritual and divine. Upon this elevation of soul wicked men work and deceive people, so that the noblest and best part of us is wickedly converted into a channel for carrying out their base frauds and cheats. It is only since the events of the last week or two that he has been able to understand the unutterable baseness of the whole pretence of Spiritualism. Oh, Cicely, you do well to pity him, and to forgive him. If only I can hope to succeed in making him forgive himself!"

"You will never cease to try, dear"—Cicely held out her hands. "Oh, the better nature will subdue the baser. You will be happy, Hetty. Let him never for a moment regret the vanished past. Take him where no one knows what he has been. You will be happy, dear."

"I escape, Cicely," said Hetty—"that ought to be enough for me—and I escape with the man I love. That is more than enough for me."

"Sibyl, dear," said Cicely, "when you go to your new home with Tom, take me with you. Promise, Sibyl. I will give you very little trouble. I will sit in my own room. But I could not stay in this house when you are gone—and Hetty gone. It is a haunted house. I hear all day long the voice of Paul —who speaks of death and of the soul and of the other world. Promise, Sibyl; let me go before that voice becomes the voice of a mocking and a lying spirit."

CHAPTER XIV.

A WEDDING-DAY.

THERE are weddings which must be festive occasions. They are those where the course of true-love has run quite smoothly past level lawns where the lads and lasses play lawn-tennis between trim hedges, past flowering banks, past lovely town gardens and stately houses. They are those in which the parents on both sides are convinced that the young people were made for each other. They are also those in which the marriage settlements are everything that can be desired. Other weddings there are in which the bride and bridegroom are married under some kind of cloud. There are many and varying clouds which darken poor humanity: the cloud penitential, the cloud pecuniary, the cloud of disobedience, or the cloud of elopement. When a couple marry under the shadow of such a cloud, their union must be strictly private.

Paul walked alone to the church on his wedding-day. He had no friends: no young man in the whole world was more friendless; the medium, to begin with, is always a solitary being; he who has resigned that profession is more solitary still, because he has lost such companions as he had among the scanty and jealous members of this calling. But he had recovered something of his gallant bearing, and walked with head erect, as a bridegroom should. He was now at peace with all the world, because he was no longer going to prey upon it; more than that, he was at peace with himself; at five-and-twenty the temperament is elastic and sanguine. And he was going to be married—and he was going away—and he was going to be advised and directed for the rest of his life by his wife—a prospect which filled this remarkable young man with infinite satisfaction.

In Harley Street—he was making his way to Marylebone Church—he was stopped by none other than Mr. Emmanuel Chick.

"I beg your pardon, Mr. Paulus," said the general practitioner of Spiritualism. "I beg your pardon, sir. I was in the hall the other day, and I had the pleasure of hearing your remarks."

"Oh! Then I hope you were edified, Mr. Chick."

"I was. I was both edified and pleased. What Lady Augusta said afterwards—but you didn't hear that—was all bally rot. We know—Herr Paulus—we know;" he chuckled and rubbed his hands. "Now, I ask you, sir—that night when you first sprung it on 'em, didn't I say that it was nothing but mesmerism?"

"You did, Chick, you certainly did."

"Well, you were down upon me after that, and you've been down upon me ever since. No more séances for Emmanuel Chick. Oh no! He's played out, he is! Dawg bite dawg! That's always the way with Spiritualists. Spoil the trade, they do, instead of stickin' together."

"Well, Mr. Chick?"

"Yes; and now you hold your head up high, just as if you hadn't gone and told everybody openly that you've been a humbug all along."

"That is so, Chick. You can't hold your head high, you see, because you haven't told anybody."

"I always thought it was your doing—Mr. Brudenel writing that letter when he told me to buy shares in his company."

"No, I knew nothing about that letter. There you wrong me, Chick."

"I don't half believe you," said the man, with a cunning look. "Well, whether you did or whether you didn't, p'haps you'll be sorry to hear that Mr. Brudenel has behaved like a gentleman."

"Not at all sorry. I always thought he was a gentleman."

"And he's repaid the 'ole of that money, the 'ole of it, sir, in water shares—two thousand pounds' worth; because it was his fault that I took the money. Two thousand pounds' worth. I thought you'd like to know, that's all."

"Thank you, Chick, thank you. I'm very glad to know it."

"We sha'n't see you much more over there, I take it?" he jerked his thumb in the direction of St. John's Wood.

"No, Chick, no," he replied, cheerfully. "Good-day to you—good-day."

Chick looked after him as he walked away. "He's got what I never had," he murmured. "And he looks a swell. It's written in his face and it's spoken by his eyes. He is a swell, and he'll always be a swell. Wonder what he did it for. Wonder why he got up on the platform and told 'em. Wonder what his game is. You can't make much by being a converted medium, or I'd try it. I wonder, now, what he did it for."

Every professional medium in the world, when the story of this great renunciation reached his ears, wondered why Paul did it. Virtue, in cases where there is no reward visibly sticking out of a hand-bag, is difficult of comprehension by the professional medium.

Hetty's wedding was, therefore, private and quiet, as was suitable to the occasion. Mr. Medlock refused to give away his daughter, but was observed at the doors of the church looking on with a gloomy brow at the flight of all his hopes. When the service was concluded he walked away in the direction of Beaumont Street, doubtless to condole with the other victim of Paul's contumacy and Hetty's disobedience.

Lavinia was present in her customary dress of black stuff, looking like a pew-opener. She wept copiously during the service. Did she weep because her daughter was going away from the house of tricks and shams? or did she weep at the failure of her husband's scheme? or did she weep because she herself was left behind to carry on the old, the stale old game? Contrary to reasonable expectation, no rappings attested the satisfaction, or the contrary, felt by the spirits at the auspicious event. And they might have made the occasion so important in the annals of Spiritualism. This is how the best opportunities get fooled away. Not a single rap, not a note or a bar of celestial music, not the quiver of a single concertina. Nor, again, did the Sage of Abyssinia make a sign of friendship towards his old pupil and messenger. Think of the splendid effect of a letter straight from Izák the Falasha fluttering down from the roof of Marylebone Church upon the head of the bridegroom! Think of the splendid effect of the philosopher's apparition! Sibyl and Bethiah were the only other witnesses of the marriage, and the bride was given away by the verger.

It was a gloomy ceremony. The only actor in it who was perfectly happy was the bride. Hetty was going "out of it" at last. Farewell forever to manifestations, séances, rappings, messages, and the music of heaven! No more guilty consciousness of tricks which she could not reveal because the performer was her own mother; no more inquiry of any oracle—all that was done with. Paul was coming with her "out of it" too. How could she disguise her happiness and her joy?

When the service was over, and the book signed and witnessed, the bride and bridegroom took leave of their friends in the vestry.

"My daughter," said Lavinia, "when shall I ever see you again? Oh, Hetty, Hetty!"

"I will write to you, mother," said Hetty. "I will write through Sibyl. You are not to know, on account of father, where we are living. I do not wish to see him again ever, *I think*. But *you* I shall see again when— *you know*—I told you last night, mother."

"I can't; it's no use; Haynes won't hear of it. I can't give it up. How are we to live? Your father won't hear of it. We are going to America on a tour. It's my livelihood, child; and now he's going to live on it as well."

"Good-by, mother. When you are tired of it send me word through Sibyl. Good-by. Oh, mother!" she whispered once more, "give it up!"

They drove away to Victoria station in a four-wheeled cab which had their luggage on the top, and the rest of the forlorn bridal party remained standing outside the church, under the great porch. Lavinia was weeping still. A very quiet wedding, without a single wedding present, except certain "things" which Hetty had on; Bethiah gave her those. She would take nothing from any one in the house where Paul had played his adventurous game. Not a single present, even from Cicely, who loved her, or from Lady Augusta, who was grateful for her services, or from Sibyl. Her husband must not profit by so much as a single pair of gloves from that house.

"It isn't for the marriage that I am crying, Miss Brudenel," said Lavinia; "Paul will make her a good husband, I'm sure. The like of him—clever and soft and easy led—mostly make good husbands when they don't take to drink. But it's the awful throwing away of the most splendid chances that were ever offered to any young couple. That's what I feel. He was offered only yesterday—for a last chance—a half partnership, and to take the money himself, and two thousand pounds down, and he threw it up. And why? All for a silly scruple. All because he would have to work by his cleverness and not by the spirits at all. Why, I knew from the beginning that he couldn't be a medium. You can tell a medium at first sight. There's a look in a medium's eyes, even in such a medium as Emmanuel Chick, though he does make the whole room smell of rum; Paul's eyes never had that look."

"Oh, but Mrs. Medlock, Paul and Hetty felt that it would not be honest," said Sibyl.

"It's as honest a trade as any. There's pretence everywhere. And isn't it throwing in her own mother's teeth a reflection on her own mother, that she won't let him carry on that trade? How are they to live, I should like to know? And they are going away, and I shall lose my daughter; because she says that she will never, never, never let that good old gentleman who offered Paul the partnership know where her husband is living. I've lost my girl. She wasn't altogether what she might have been; she would never help her mother in the way of her profession.

And she has thrown away the most beautiful and heavenly gifts of clairvoyance. Oh, what a sin and a shame it is!"

Then the two girls left her, and walked slowly away.

"It is all over now," said Bethiah. "There is nothing left to do but to take him back to America. Sibyl, don't publish any story about him."

"My dear, I never intended to."

"Don't let Lady Augusta publish anything. She said she was going to, you know, at the hall the other day. It might follow Paul and find him out and make him unhappy. His only chance is to forget everything."

"Can he ever forget?"

"You don't know my boy," said Bethiah. "If he wants to forget it he will put it behind him and forget it in a week. He forgot to write to me, or to his parents, for some years. Why? Because of the incongruity between the bare, ugly truth, and his pretensions. I suppose it would have made him uncomfortable. So while he was in New York he was the Signor Paolo; he learned the language of a wandering Italian ; the native village, the general store, and the village shop were forgotten — and so were his father and his mother, and all his old friends. They had to be forgotten, else he would have felt uncomfortable."

"He could make believe, in fact."

"Oh yes. Nobody in the world could make believe better. I am quite sure that he felt himself an Italian when he was Signor Paolo, and he felt himself a teacher of the Ancient Philosophy, and believed, in a kind of a way, in his Abyssinian sage. Why, you heard what Lady Augusta said of him. If he had not believed himself in what he was teaching them, how could he have impressed her so profoundly?"

"Where did he get his wisdom from?"

"Well, Sibyl, I come of a Puritan stock, and so I think he got it out of a certain Book in which he used to read a great deal when he was a boy. I have seen him in our old garden declaiming aloud the splendid passages of Isaiah and Ezekiel. He drew upon his memory. I am sure of it, because Cicely once tried to reproduce some of his discourse, and I remembered the ideas and the language."

"Has he communicated with his mother?"

"Yes, I made him write. He expressed his penitence for his long silence, and said that if he had been doing any good for himself he should have written before; but that he was ashamed to tell the story of ill-spent time. I have dissuaded him from telling all the story or any of it. His mother would be too truly horrified if she knew it. He told

her, however, that he was bringing a wife home with him."

"But," said Sibyl, "how will Hetty like living with the old people?"

"She will not live with them. Paul can never go back to the little town. I think he must live in the country, but near a great town—perhaps near Boston. It is not likely that people will remember Signor Paolo, even in New York, and in Boston they have probably never even heard of him. It was only among Spiritualists that he was known."

"Do you think that Paul will ever be able to do the rough work of a journalist? Have they not to attend meetings, and be up all night, and run about perpetually?"

"I do not expect that he will do that. But our journals want all kinds of work; they are the literature of the people; they present reading of every kind. Paul will quickly learn to provide the kind of thing which will take and sell. He is quick to see, and I know that he can write."

"Poor Paul! Poor Hetty!"

"She is not to be pitied at all. She loves her husband; that is everything."

"Bethiah"—Sibyl touched her hand; it is a woman's sign of affection and consideration —"why is it—why did not Paul fall in love with you?"

"Well, Sibyl, I don't quite know. It is just as well as it is. For my part I have always loved the boy; and if he had reminded me that he was not, after all, my brother, I might—but this is rubbish, he is my sister, and I love him just as much as ever. And so, you see, Sibyl, as I am his sister, I can never let him want, can I?"

*   *   *   *   *   *

A week later Tom and Sibyl stood upon the platform at St. Pancras. They were come to say good-by to the man who had saved their fortunes and persuaded a consent to their marriage out of Mr. Brudenel.

"For such services," said Tom, "I would even shake hands with a dynamitard."

It was not an ordinary leave-taking. They could not say "Come again soon," or "We expect you over again next year," or "We shall not be happy till you repeat your visit." Nothing of that sort could even be hinted at, because Paul must never return to England, not until every one of the multitude who filled that hall and heard that confession had passed away.

"You will write, Hetty," said Sibyl. "Write to Cicely first, and to me sometimes. Tell me what you are doing and how you are getting on. My poor Hetty!"

"I am very happy. I am going to be as happy as the day is long," she said, bravely, taking her husband's hand.

"Now," said Bethiah, "the guard is looking at the tickets. Good-by, Sibyl. I will write to you as well, if you will let me. Here is a little present for you. Lay it at the bottom of your desk, and look at it now and then. Good-by."

"Paul," said Tom, holding his hand with the firm grasp of friendship, "we are your debtors. We can never pay that debt. Some day, perhaps, you will remember that fact. Promise me that, if occasion arises, you will remember it."

Paul shook his head.

"It is good of you both," he said, "to see us off. I shall not readily forget that, anyhow."

Then the train rolled away and they were gone.

Sibyl opened the parting present when she reached home.

It was a pencil sketch of Paul's face drawn by Bethiah. The face was idealized. It was Paul as he might be. Paul filled with noble thoughts. Paul purified. Every face may be thus idealized and purified. My dear young lady, you think yourself beautiful as things are. You would be astonished at your own beauty could you see your face when it has passed through this process.

"Yes," said Sibyl, "I shall look at it sometimes. It is with this expression on his face that I shall remember Paul."

EPILOGUE.

Six weeks after their wedding Tom and Sibyl came home again. The period of profound meditation and philosophic calm which we call the honey-moon had not saddened them, or made them discontented with their lot, or diminished their hopefulness for the future. Quite the contrary. They were profoundly satisfied with themselves and with their lot and with the world in general. As for Paul and the late events, which we have rescued from oblivion, they had nearly forgotten them. Paul was only one more of the many impostors and pretenders who had fastened for a space upon Sibyl's father, different from the rest in the fact that, oddly enough, he had not endeavored to get any money for himself, and that he was a comely and well-mannered youth, and that he had repented in sackcloth and covered his head with ashes, and rent his garments and wailed aloud and done penance, and confessed his sins before the assembled multitude. These incidents in his career would naturally keep his memory green for a space. But he was passing out of Sibyl's mind in her new wedded life, and his portrait lies at the bottom of *a drawer full of letters*, and she never takes

it out to look at it. Tom is enough, you see, to fill all her thoughts.

As for Paul's teaching—that wonderful philosophy which so moved the heart of Lady Augusta—nothing of it has yet been written down, and now I do not think any will be written down. Nobody talks about it, and the promised present of the Book of Wisdom, written by King Solomon and taken to Abyssinia by Prince Menelek, has not yet arrived.

"I do hope, Tom," said Sibyl—it was before her marriage—"that the house is going to be kept clear of the old spirit business. If Paul did nothing else, he cleared the house of all that rubbish. My father ceased for a while, at least, to believe in his old mediums. I do hope that the effect will be lasting. But I fear, Tom, I fear. They have both been engaged too long in their research to abandon it altogether, even after such a blow as this."

"But they will not acknowledge it to be a blow," said Tom.

"No"—Sibyl sighed—"they never will acknowledge any blow, however hard, though they feel it all the time. One medium after another arrives and shows off his little tricks, and gets applause and money. Then he is discredited. It is set down to the mocking spirit and the lying spirit. But he is discredited all the same, and has to go away. As for Paul, you heard what Lady Augusta said at the Conference about his wonderful and apostolical teaching. Well, it is already nearly forgotten. He is discredited, and he is gone. He will soon be remembered only as one among many, though he was the brightest and the cleverest of them all. But the cause is never abandoned—never even considered in any danger. Why, Tom, though I hate the whole thing, I find myself actually believing it sometimes, just because, I suppose, I have been in the habit of hearing it spoken of as a true thing of which there can be no doubt."

"You can make people believe anything," said Tom, "if you keep speaking of it as if it was established beyond any doubt."

Naturally, on their return home, Lady Augusta gave a dinner-party.

Sibyl saw without astonishment, yet with sorrow, that there had been already a return to the gods of the old school—the pre-Pauline period, so to speak. The Rev. Benjamin Rudge was a guest; Mr. Emmanuel Chick was present; Mr. Amelius Horton, Mr. Athelstan Kilburn, Mrs. Tracy Hanley and her husband, with others of the persuasion. It was a large dinner-party, and during the period of waiting Sibyl became aware that there was another guest of honor beside herself.

"We are to have another intellectual feast this evening," she heard the Rev. Benjamin

Rudge's loud voice proclaim. "So much is certain. It is a lady—they say from Russia —but we have not heard her name. She has arrived and is in the house already." That well-known and uncomfortable sensation of having seen the thing already, crept over Sibyl, and her heart sank because she found that this dinner was to be followed by another manifestation of peculiar interest.

"Yes, my dear," said her father, tapping his knuckles with his glasses, and speaking with the fidgety nervousness which she knew so well. "We have a visitor whose social position alone guarantees her good faith. She is not by any means an unknown adventuress, such as we have sometimes entertained. She is a Russian princess of the highest family—even connected with the imperial house. Her manifestations prove a very advanced stage of spiritualistic effort. But you shall see, my child, and judge for yourself. We always prefer to be judged by those who are hostile to us. Tom shall himself pronounce an opinion."

"It is not," Emmanuel Chick was saying, "it is not by making experiments and showing off fireworks in magnetism that we can accomplish results. We have got to feel our way step by step—little by little. We have got to encounter lying spirits and mocking spirits. But think of the results we have already achieved. It is a science, sir, and it must be conducted on scientific methods. The medium must feel his way. He ought to be endowed by the State, and the results ought to be published in full, so as to remain on record."

Here the Russian phenomenon—the Princess Olga Alexandrovna — appeared at the door.

She was young and remarkable in appearance, if not beautiful. She was dressed in black velvet and lace, very rich, simple, and striking. She stood for a moment in the door-way, where the light fell full upon her, just as an actress when she appears upon the stage stands for a moment in order to let the audience take in the beauty of her face, her figure, and her raiment. This young lady's features were regular; the outlines were sharp—her friends said they were of extreme delicacy; her voice was harsh and rather rasping; her hair was dark, nearly black; and her eyes matched her hair. In other circles and in former times they would have been called "bold." Her mouth was firm—even hard; her smile was ready—her friends called it winning; those who did not like her so much said that it was icy and void of merriment. Her name was Olga Alexandrovna, and she was a native of St. Petersburg, but she had the look of the Tartar. She said sharp

things, sometimes very rude things, but her friends said they were epigrams, and she had written a book—it was in French, but had been translated into English—which old-fashioned people would not suffer to enter their houses, or to be upon their tables. Her friends said it was a book in which for the first time a woman had dared to speak the truth.

The dinner was like one of the old functions which Sibyl remembered so well, and those which the natural liveliness of Paul had banished. It was as dull, as stupid, and as solemn. A whole bench of beadles could not have dined together more solemnly; the whole body of cathedral vergers could not have been more solemn. Everybody wanted to hear what the new prophetess would say; and her remarks were sometimes inaudible.

Sibyl thought of the first evening when Herr Paulus came; and how the people craned their necks and strained their ears to catch his words. But Herr Paulus—Sibyl thought, being a woman, and therefore perhaps prejudiced—was a great deal more interesting than Princess Olga Alexandrovna, and much better looking.

The princess, it presently appeared, belonged not to Paul's school of the Ancient Way—which was peculiar to himself—but to that of the modern occult philosophy, whose prophet is, or was, none other than Madame Blavatzky. A good many people know by this time the language of the school, which has followers and puts forward pretensions. The princess talked glibly of Thibet, Mahatmas, astral bodies, Karma, Yogees, and the Esoteric Buddhism.

The guests, especially Lady Augusta, listened, and fancied that knowledge of the most valuable kind was being imbibed at every pore. But Mr. Emmanuel Chick paid no attention to the beautiful talk, making the best of his time over the truly excellent dinner and the wine, which he could not get anywhere else. It is the unhappy lot of mediums to acquire a taste for good old port and fine claret, which cannot be gratified except on those rare occasions when they are invited to such a hospitable board as Lady Augusta's. Mr. Chick was quite happy, and did not care twopence what the Russian medium was saying. His enemy, Paul, was gone, after such a disgrace as would have snuffed out any medium—even himself—forever. Mr. Brudenel had given him back the money that he had lost. He had also called him in, just as before, to carry on research on the old lines. Raps were again heard in the study when Emmanuel Chick was present, and messages of a most mysteri-

esting character were once more received and communicated.

Princess Olga Alexandrovna, therefore, talked after her kind, and the company listened. Just now there is a good deal of talk after her kind; one hears—but perhaps even as I write the thing is going out of fashion—of strictly private and select circles where the disciples gather together and whisper about coming marvels and great achievements, and the great and wonderful disclosures which are to be made the day after to - morrow. They have not seen these achievements, but they have been heard of. The coming marvels are on their way, but they have not arrived. The day after tomorrow is the only day which never comes. To-morrow is certain—not the day after to-morrow, which never arrives. No doubt the wheels of the chariots which bear the new prophets can even now be heard, by those who have ears, rumbling across the world from far-off Lassa. But up to the present moment Madame Blavatzky stands alone, and is as yet unsurpassed. Fortunately for the sacred cause of occult philosophy she is her own prophet, and does not use any of her bushels for the hiding of her light. She has also retained the services of another and more accomplished prophet, who is always proclaiming the truth divine. Between the two that truth is certain to prevail.

*   *   *   *   *   *   *

The manifestations were over.

"Lady Augusta," said the Rev. Benjamin Rudge, with note - book in hand, "we have had a glorious—a glorious evening. Never before, in man's memory, has there been such a generous, such a noble outpouring of spirit influence upon any circle. It must be recorded in public, and that without delay. And oh, Lady Augusta, when we get our college at last, what an opportunity, *what* a chance for the honor of the country if we could secure Princess Olga Alexandrovna for one of our professors! That college. How gladly would I act as its secretary, Lady Augusta! What zeal, what energy, would I throw into the cause!"

"We shall see, Mr. Rudge," said Lady Augusta. "The evening has been a remarkable one, indeed."

"What do you say, Chick?" asked Tom, *sotto voce*.

"Fireworks, Mr. Langston, fireworks!" His voice was just a little thick. The soundest port will produce this effect upon some constitutions. "Same as Herr Paulus. Fireworks and mesmerism and conjuring. Just the same. Give 'em rope for a bit, and then they will all come back to me and the old methods, same as they did with him. Nothing like science, Mr. Langston, after all. Why, I could give you results—"

"Princess — oh, Princess Olga Alexandrovna," murmured Mrs. Tracy Hanley, "I must, I feel I must, implore you to come to my Sunday Evenings. Not to do anything, unless you like; not to teach us, but to rest —to rest—among friends. We are all friends at my Sunday Evenings. May I have your promise to come? You are so great and so highly gifted that you will have many invitations from those who would merely like to show a Russian princess in their rooms and get you to exhibit your wonderful powers for the admiration and envy of their friends. But with us you will have repose and the quiet talk which refreshes the soul. You will come—only say that you will come. Oh, princess, there has never been such an evening!"

"My friends." It was the voice of Mr. Cyrus Brudenel. He had now assumed his pince-nez, and his face was radiant and his voice triumphant. "My dear friends, we have never been associated at an Evening marked throughout by such splendid manifestation of power. This night will ever be remembered as one of distinct advance; we are indeed nearer to the spirits. We have taken a step within the unknown land, and had such a glimpse as has never been vouchsafed before. Princess Olga Alexandrovna, I do not say that we thank you. Such a word is too feeble to express the joy of our hearts. We congratulate ourselves upon your arrival. We feel too deeply for expression the help that you will give us, the English seekers in Spiritualism." (Sibyl again experienced that uncomfortable sensation of having seen the thing before, perhaps because she recognized a certain look in her father's eyes, which told her what was coming.) "My friends," he said, with firm voice and becoming gesture of hand and foot, "we stand — we stand at last, I say — upon the SOLID ROCK!"

THE END.

CPSIA information can be obtained at www.ICGtesting.com
Printed in the USA
LVOW12s2323050515

437317LV00023B/446/P